DICKENS STUDIES ANNUAL

VOLUME
7

Edited by

ROBERT B. PARTLOW, JR.

SOUTHERN ILLINOIS UNIVERSITY PRESS

Carbondale and Edwardsville

FEFFER & SIMONS, INC.

London and Amsterdam

The Library of Congress Cataloged The First Issue Of This
Serial As Follows:

Dickens studies annual. v. 1–   1970–
   Carbondale, Southern Illinois University Press.
   /v. illus., ports. 25 cm.
   Editor: 1970–   R. B. Partlow.

   1. Dickens, Charles, 1812–1870—Societies, periodicals, etc.
I. Partlow, Robert B., ed.
PR4579.D49   823.8   78-123048
ISBN 0-8093-0867-3 (v.7)

Contents

Preface

THIS VOLUME, the seventh to be issued since 1970, marks the end of the series. Refreshingly, in these days of financial cutbacks, the print-shop is closing its doors *not* because Southern Illinois University will no longer provide support for the venture or even because there are increasingly fewer persons willing to keep up their subscriptions. Quite the reverse—orders are holding up very nicely, thank you, and the senior administrators at Southern Illinois University have reiterated their willingness to maintain a scholarly press and scholarly publications. The dean of the College of Liberal Arts and the vice-president for Academic Affairs have explored every possible means of continuance, even to considering the possibility of bringing in another editor from outside. But it has become clear that there is no feasible manner of continuance at this university. On the retirement of the senior editor, the *Dickens Studies Annual* ceases.

But perhaps not utterly. As long ago as Christmas of 1976 the question of the future of the *Annual* was considered during the annual meeting of The Dickens Society. Since there was general agreement that both the *Annual* and the *Dickens Studies Newsletter* have been useful and even reasonably exciting to Victorian scholars, and since the *Newsletter* was successfully transferred from Southern Illinois University to another university, the members of the society instructed the appropriate people to enter into a study of the possibility of continuing the *Annual* under a new editor at another university. Months of negotiation followed, unfortunately not yet concluded, but, by the time that you read this Preface, notices and advertisements may have alerted you to change the name of the press from which you order your copy of the only major outlet for longer studies of Charles Dickens.

I am firmly convinced that the *Annual* serves a need both for the established scholar who needs a lot of room for a special study and for the younger scholar who wants to speak to his peers on severely restricted topics. I am also convinced that the series has stimulated new thought: I note that articles in the *Annual* have been cropping up in footnotes in other articles and books, that some articles have been reprinted in other articles and books, and that some authors admit that their new work begins with an idea or an *aperçu* or an angle of approach found in an essay published in the *Annual;* most telling of all, though horrifying, pages have been taken out of our library copies of the run. These are the external, verifiable signs of at least modest success. Less verifiable are the telephone calls and letters from people expressing their pleasure in a given volume or study, asking permission to use material for some purpose, or just indicating their gratitude for the service to the profession that we are providing. I must admit that such expressions of support are pleasurable: anyone who writes or produces a volume has the awful experience of seeing the work disappear into an enormous void. He knows that a thousand, two thousand, ten thousand copies are out there some place; he knows that someone must have at least browsed through his deathless prose; but nothing happens, nothing, nothing, nothing at all. Maybe, a year or two later, there is a review or part of a review, maybe even a series of reviews, pointing out, typically, the errors in the book that the reviewers certainly would not have made. Hence the value of the personal, direct response. Now the editor's mind is partially satisfied: he only has to worry about the other 1,999 readers.

What, then, can the editors point out as the accomplishment of some eight years of effort? There is of course the solid bulk of seven hefty volumes, nicely printed on good stock, with nary an error in the footnotes, and seventy-seven illustrations. There is a total of 1,554 pages of scholarship, criticism, analysis, and speculation, organized into seventy-four essays of varying lengths, in all an impressive amount of intelligence and energy devoted to the great Victorian novelist. If only 20 percent of those essays are major, that is, deserving of more than passing attention, then we can still point to fifteen or sixteen important contributions to our knowledge of Dickens, his age, and his creations— and that alone would make well spent the time and effort that the editor and sub-editors have devoted to the *Annual* over the years. There is nothing to be gained by making a comparison of the number of articles devoted to Dickens as compared to those devoted to Milton or Joyce or Faulkner, but I doubt that more than a few major authors have received the same kind of intensive attention that the *Annual* and the *Newsletter* have fostered.

But sheer bulk is meaningless in the scholarly world: drivel and nonsense remain drivel and nonsense no matter how protracted. At least we hope so, though all the evidence is not yet in. So we do not base our modest pride in the run of the *Annual* merely on the massiveness of publication but rather on the caliber of the authors and the excitement of the work they have produced. The roster of contributors is virtually a roster of the major Dickensians now practicing their craft: Harry Stone, John Reed, Duane DeVries, Louis James, Jane Rabb Cohen, Angus Easson, Jerome Meckier, Michael Steig, Trevor Blount, Leonard Manheim, David Paroissien, Joseph Gold, Robert Patten, Warrington Winters, Milton Millhauser, William Axton, Edgar Rosenburg, Phillip Collins, Alan Burke, Stanley Tick, Deborah Thomas, John Greaves, Ian Watt, John Robson, Sylvère Monod, Margaret Ganz, Harvey Peter Sucksmith, Nina Auerbach, Robert Lougy, William Burgan. And we are also proud that we have been able to publish the earlier efforts of some promising younger scholars, a few of them still in graduate school when their essays were submitted and accepted.

My personal favorites out of all the long run—without in the least intending to comment even glancingly at those not cited—the studies which I found most impressive and useful, have been of quite a mixed character. Margaret Ganz's spirited analysis of the decline of Dickens' humor in the later novels ("The Vulnerable Ego," vol. 1) is a useful antidote to the "doom is dark and delightful" critical readings of the later novels and might be paired with Robert Lougy's ingenious reading of *Hard Times* ("The Romance as Radical Literature," vol. 2) as a proletarian novel in a world dominated by death. "The Pale Usher Dusts his Lexicons: A Preface to *Great Expectations*" (vol. 2), Edgar Rosenburg's brilliant and witty discussion of the difficulties facing an editor of a Dickens novel, is at once an exemplification of painstaking scholarly accuracy and of Dickensian verbal humor, in its way a proof that the work of one's maturity need, as Professor Ganz suggests, not be grittily dark. So too is Sylvère Monod's delightful tribute to G. K. Chesteron ("Confessions of an Unrepentant Chestertonian," vol. 3), a suave, sophisticated tribute to the earlier critic and wit, written with a delight in the possibilities of English prose that must attract all who admire the dexterity and rightness of Dickens' own prose. The only rival I see in the six volumes of the *Annual* to these last two essays is Robert Patten's "Dickens Time and Again" (vol. 2); this does not attempt the wit and humor that make Monod's and Rosenberg's work so charming, but Professor Patten does write such a powerful, supple, precise prose, marshals his arguments so clearly and persuasively, with such breadth of erudition and insight, that I am persuaded into accepting his reading of *A Christmas Carol* as essentially as a study of religious conversion, in fact the definitive reading.

For somewhat different reasons I refer to a series of essays which concentrate on technical details. For example, Jerome Meckier's study of the serial and posterity pattern in *Nicholas Nickleby* ("The Faint Image of Eden," vol. 1) is most useful in a Dickens seminar, not merely

as the basis for an understanding of the organization of this novel, but
as a paradigm of other novels as well. For a model of scholarly analysis
of Dickens manuscript material I turn to William Burgan's "The Refinement of Contrast: Manuscript Revision in *Edwin Drood*" (vol. 6),
perhaps less for the exact information contained than as a model of a
tightly controlled, sensitive piece of research. "Pickwick in America!"
(vol. 1) is Louis James' amusing, but precise, description of a matter peripheral to the study of Dickens' novels, one of the many plagiarisms of
the immensely popular *The Pickwick Papers;* Richard Vogler also analyzes what at first appears to be a peripheral matter—"Cruikshank's
Pictorial Prototypes" for *Oliver Twist* (vol. 2)—but suggests, and provides a plausible argument, that Cruikshank's claim that he influenced
both the characters and plot of *Oliver* has some validity, or at least that
the problem must be reexamined with an open mind.

Another grouping of essays in the *Annual* over the years has been
the biographical. Among those which I have found persuasive are
David Paroissien's piece on "Charles Dickens and the Weller Family"
(vol. 2), a charming, even classic, example of the proper way to turn
into scholarly prose one's original research into family documents, in
this instance the Sowerby family, still in possession of the journals of
Viola Meynell and the diaries and other papers of Christiana Weller.
Another biographical study of great interest is Albert Hutter's "Recon-
structive Autobiography" (vol. 6), a new analysis of Dickens' experience
at Warren's Blacking Factory which picks holes in the argument of Edmund Wilson, the argument which has been so influential in recent
Dickens criticism.

Two essays in volume 4 concentrate on the historical and sociological context of Dickens' work: Anne Humpherys' "Dickens and Mayhew
on the London Poor" and Harvey Peter Sucksmith's "Sir Leicester Dedlock, Wat Tyler, and the Chartists." Both argue for the establishment
of the novels in the proper historical background and so remind us that
a given novel is not a *Ding an sich,* a pattern of words to be interpreted
as structures or interlocking images. Having said that, I must immediately confess to a liking for close analysis of image and symbol patterns
in Dickens' novels, essentially a technique adapted from critical analysis
of poems. The pair I refer to most often are in volume 3: Alan Burke's
"The House of Chuzzlewit and the Architectural City" and R. Rupert
Roopnaraine's "Time and the Circle in Little Dorrit"; each is a well-
organized, intensive demonstration of the ways in which an informing
image or metaphor dominates a novelistic structure, binds it together,
and enriches the total meaning.

And finally, although having reservations about all psychological
criticism, I admire not only the Hutter piece already mentioned but
one by the dean of psychoanalytical criticism, Leonard Manheim, on

"Dickens' Fools and Madmen" (vol. 2), Ian Watts' brilliant comments on eating and drinking in the novels, and Nina Auerbach's persuasive reading of *Dombey and Son* from a feminist point of view.

All the remarks on the preceding few pages illustrate what has been the announced policy of the editors of the *Dickens Studies Annual* since its inception: to publish studies of the life, times, and works of Charles Dickens without imposing on any author any limitations of form, type of critical approach, or critical assumptions. Thus we have published essays of the most diverse kinds, essays which span almost the whole spectrum of modern critical theory and practice: psychological, psychoanalytical, biographical, historical, sociological, structural, phenomenological, New Critical, religious, radical—humor, illustrations, characters, plot, symbols, images, diction, sources, influences, and manuscripts. And this, I am sure, is not merely a hodgepodge, a mélange, a miscellany, but is rather the result of a deliberate attempt to provide an outlet for the best that is being said and done in contemporary Dickens criticism in a spirit of the utmost freedom. What the author and his readers want to talk about is the important consideration, not an editor's prejudices or predilections; author and essay then stand on their own merits—if they broaden, deepen, extend, or make more clear any aspect of Dickens or a theory of fiction, then they will receive the accolade of quotation. In effect, as previous prefaces have emphasized, the *Annual* subscribes to what has been called "pluralism," that is, to the concept that no single approach to literature, to a writer, or to a given work, is ever complete, definitive, or final, that eventually only many different approaches and techniques can hope to come to grips with the complexity of a major literary work. Norman Friedman's chapter on "Pluralistic Criticism" in his *Form and Meaning in Fiction* (Athens: University of Georgia Press, 1975) comes close to summing up the principles that have been operative as the editorial practice of the *Annual*.

This, our final volume in the series, includes the same variety and spread of interest already noted; the collection of essays exhibits a full range of interests and techniques.

The biographical study by Andrew Kappel and Robert Patten, "Dickens' Second American Tour and his 'Utterly Worthless and Profitless' American 'Rights,'" is a model, a classic, of scholarly research and precise writing. It is the only major revision of that part of Edgar Johnson's monumental study dealing with the battle over copyright, the payments Dickens received from his American publishers, Dickens' relations with those publishers, and the American reception of Dickens in 1867–68.

James A. Davies' reassessment of John Forster and the *Life of Charles Dickens,* entitled "Striving for Honesty: An Approach to For-

ster's *Life,"* is most interesting in that it quite properly reminds us that
Forster was an accomplished biographer long before he took on the immense task of trying to get his friend down on paper. Davies argues
that the *Life* can be better understood by reference to Forster's habits,
practices, and values as exemplified in his earlier work. Such an approach helps us to understand, if not condone, some of the deficiencies
critics have seen in his last book.

Earle Davis' "Dickens and Significant Tradition" is, rather oddly,
the only overview not only in this volume but in the series, the only
essay which meditates on the whole career of Dickens and the entire
canon. As such it may perhaps be considered a necessary corrective to
the limited, intensive analyses not merely of single novels, but even of
single characters, single images, single words. An occasional Chestertonian essay reminds us that the long overview has merits that the mi-
croscope cannot provide.

David Paroissien's "Dickens and the Cinema" utilizes an approach
to critical analysis increasingly popular: considering why Dickens
transfers to narrative film so magnificently. In the course of his discussion, Professor Paroissien properly concentrates on those qualities of
Dickens' genius (his visual imagination primarily) which film makers
can capture, but in so doing reminds us forcefully of those aspects of
the novels which help to create the brilliance, integrity, and allusiveness
so attractive to literary critics and readers as well.

Thomas J. Rice's *"Barnaby Rudge:* A Vade Mecum for the Theme
of Domestic Government in Dickens" is a neatly constructed piece in
which the author offers a new reading of the novel, not in the more
usual terms of individuals and families caught in the turmoil of civil
riots, but the reverse: "an impressive variety of family situations"
against the background of the Gordon troubles—with rather surprising
conclusions. Rice insists on seeing Dickens not as a political and social
radical, at odds with his society, but as conventional for his times, even
as a conservative. Such a revisionist article should provoke counterar-
ticles.

Arlene Jackson's "Reward, Punishment, and the Conclusion of
Dombey and Son" is exactly what the title implies: a reconsideration of
the ending of that novel, an ending which many readers and critics
have found unconvincing, mawkish, improperly prepared for, psychologically unsound, morally suspect. Professor Jackson defends the novel
against such claims and demonstrates the psychological and moral
rightness of its conclusion.

Stanley Friedman's "Dickens' Mid-Victorian Theodicy: *David Copperfield"* can be regarded as an attempt to determine if that novel examines "whether effort or providence or chance is the decisive factor in
this world, whether suffering can be redeemed, whether belief in di-

vine justice can be reaffirmed." The article assumes that Dickens intended the book as a theodicy, an essentially Christian text rather than a moral tract, and proceeds to offer a sophisticated defense of that assumption, in many ways a more complete defense than those offered earlier by Hillis Miller and Alexander Welsh.

Bert G. Hornback's "The Hero Self," also on *David Copperfield,* is quite different in tone and intention from the preceding study. It is a subtle, penetrating, personal meditation on the question, "Can the imagination—abstracted, noumenal, looking at the phenomenal world—become substantial and heroic?"

The third essay in fortuitous grouping is Richard Barickman's "The Spiritual Journey of Amy Dorrit and Arthur Clennam," which, like Friedman's, considers the novel *Little Dorrit* as fundamentally a Christian document, a part of the great literature of spiritual journeys stretching from *The Divine Comedy* through *The Faerie Queen* down to *The Four Quartets,* with the crucial difference that Amy Dorrit and Arthur Clennam cannot escape the limits of the blighted secular world in their achieving transcendence.

E. Pearlman's "Inversion in *Great Expectations*" is, in the best sense of the word, a useful piece of work. All teachers and critics of Dickens know that Dickens himself announced that this novel would cover much the same territory as the earlier *David Copperfield* but that he planned to use an autobiographical mode of narration and to avoid unconscious repetitions. So the question inevitably follows and must be answered: how are the two novels alike, and how are they different? Professor Pearlman provides, if not a definitive answer, a closely reasoned analysis which can act as a basis for further discussion.

Melanie Young's "Distorted Expectations" extends Pearlman's thesis by beginning with the same Dickens' quotation but then assumes that the major difference between *David Copperfield* and *Great Expectations* is, more precisely, Dickens' new attitude toward language. In her explanation, "before his perceptions adequately reflect reality, Pip must overcome three linguistic difficulties: the dissociation of sensibility, linguistic distortion, and problems in semantics."

The final essay in this volume 7 and the final essay in the whole series is, appropriately enough, by the secretary of The Dickens Society, Professor Richard J. Dunn. Entitled "Far, Far Better Things," it considers in detail the ending patterns of Dickens' later novels as being further evidence of the Inimitable's increasing artistry.

Thus the editors of the *Annual* have continued to the end their policy of offering the best that is being written about Dickens and his fictions as a service to the community of Victorian students and scholars. Whether or not they have been successful is a moot point: the veiled allusion to Matthew Arnold hints at some of my reservations, not about Dickens scholarship per se, but about the whole set of modern criticism. Certain though we are about the immense development and improvement of criticism since about 1935, particularly of the Victorian period, we should recognize that there has been and will be a price to pay. And that cost is the virtual loss of an audience: modern criticism has become so specialized, in some instances so scientized, that "the common reader" does not wish or is unable to use it to enlarge his life or his perceptions.

Consider the *Annual* as an example. For whom is it written? To whom does it appeal? Certainly not "the common reader." Out of a run of about two thousand copies per volume, some five hundred are purchased by individuals, almost all devout Dickens students and scholars, themselves practicing or would-be critics of Dickens. The remaining copies go on the shelves of libraries all over the world, for use by professors preparing lectures or articles and students who need material for term papers. The audience is a small, highly specialized group with narrow interests. The authors who publish in the *Annual* and similar journals, yearbooks, newsletters, and so on, thus speak only to other people exactly like themselves, to the little band of brothers. At its best their work is the point or leading edge of the advance of a certain body of knowledge, of necessity a position for the leader and hence cut off from the main body. Eventually, if the leaders do their job well, the main body will pass through and absorb the territory explored and cleared by the point. The parallel is, of course, to the sciences where all the discoveries and advances are made by a few researchers and theorists whose discoveries are eventually built into the total fabric of their science; as the field becomes more subtle, more particularized on the one hand or more general on the other, fewer and fewer untrained or little-trained amateurs are able to follow, to take part in, or even to comprehend, what is going on—modern physics, for example, becomes a Dostoyevskian mystery whose priests are half-admired, half-feared little men in white coats who smoke pipes, make silly statements about Vitamin C, forget where they parked their cars, and regularly produce such miracles as lead-free gasoline and neutron bombs. But these scientists have one major advantage over literary scholars: even if their research is not understood, the products which others make from that research is useful, as in modern medicine. Scientific research and publication, even that which seems most remote and absurd, may result in profit for someone or an improved life for everyone.

This seems increasingly less true of literary research and publication. To whom do we speak?—each other. Why do we write books and articles?—to get promoted, to impress each other, to advance knowledge in our own field, to get rid of an irritable itch to know, to set right the idiot who wrote that silly article in *NCF*. These are all legitimate

and defensible, but, in the estimation of the general public, quite useless, even if the book or article is readable. But only too often the prose
of such scholarly books and articles, which one might expect such pro-
fessionals to use with grace and delicacy and accuracy, is opaque,
clotted, full of odd words used with special or private meanings, complex structures striving to make original something that is a cliché or a
commonplace, pedantic niggling about matters of little or no human
consequence—and all this in the service of literature, probably the
most humane of all human endeavors. Dickens speaks to all people of
their own problems in words that all people can understand; his critics
speak to each other in language that almost no one is willing to try to
unravel. It makes one wonder.

Perhaps we might reconsider the function of criticism, perhaps
redefine it in older, classical terms, instead of continuing to try to make
criticism one of the sciences. If, as Matthew Arnold has said, the critical
effort is "to see the object as in itself it really is," then we are so far on
the right track: certainly the effort of our leading scholars and critics
over the last forty years has been exactly the attempt to remove accretions, to secure accurate texts, to understand works of literature with
greater and greater clarity. But, when we proceed to Arnold's extension of his definition of criticism as "a disinterested endeavour to learn
and propagate the best that is known and thought in the world," we run
into a heap of difficulties: propagate how? for whom? for what end?
"There is a view in which all the love of our neighbour, the impulses
towards action, help, and beneficence, the desire for removing human
error, clearing human confusion, and diminishing human misery, the
noble aspiration to leave the world better and happier than we found
it,—motives eminently such as are called social,—come in as part of the
grounds of culture, and the main and preeminent part. . . . The moment, I say, culture is considered not merely as the endeavour to *see*
and learn . . . but as the endeavour, also, to make it *prevail,* the moral,
social, and beneficent character of culture becomes manifest." If we
consider, then, that criticism is a social activity rather than a solitary,
scientific search for truth and clarity; if we assume that the critic or
commentator is a mediator between the work of art and the reader; if
we decide that writing about Dickens or Shakespeare or any other author is a form of education *not* for others of the saving remnant but for
the general expansion of the reading public's culture—then we shall
abandon the increasingly isolated position of the critic of literature in
our society and return to the position of a Matthew Arnold. If not, we
may go the way of the teachers of Greek and Latin: when they failed to
convince students and others generally educated that their work had
relevance in the modern world, they were pushed aside, ignored, replaced by more useful professors. The drift of students to departments

or colleges of "Communication," the increased demand for "practical" courses in writing, and even such new phenomena as the vast popularity of film and television versions of the classics—these and many other signals should warn us that although the greatest works of literature still exercise their magnetic pull, still provide modern readers and viewers with food for the imagination, still offer answers to human problems, still tickle the word-sense, we teachers of literature and scholar-critics are ceasing to be relevant. What we purvey may attract a handful of the aliens, outsiders, potential teachers and critics—an absolute necessity for the future of the profession—but one may express some doubt that our proper task is self-survival by inbreeding. If our proper task is vastly increasing the number of aliens through teaching and writing, as was the task of the old-fashioned teacher of Greek and Latin, then we seem to be in trouble.

And the trouble may be largely of our own making. Our own interests have pushed us so far beyond the knowledge and attention of the reading public that we no longer speak meaningfully to most of them. And where the scientists can afford this luxury, because of the usefulness of their by-products, we cannot: we have no by-products, we only perform a service, that of mediating between a difficult work of literature and the common reader. If we do not perform that service at all, or if we offer a service that very few accept as useful, then we shall be forced into bankruptcy. Hence a large proportion of the articles which have been appearing in literary and scholarly journals may be viewed as a form of self-indulgence, pleasant for the in-group, occasionally pushing back the boundaries of real knowledge, occasionally providing splendid insights into literature, once in a great while even a worthy addition to the fund of English prose, but still essentially ivory tower palaces of art. Tennyson knew better; so did Ruskin and Arnold; so did Dickens and Tolstoy and George Eliot; so did all the great writers. So did great critics of the recent past: Shaw, Chesterton, Samuel Johnson, Goethe, T. S. Eliot, Arnold. As may be said of so many other parts of modern life, the further we fare along our present road the more lost we may become.

Carbondale, Illinois   *Robert B. Partlow, Jr.*
November 1977

Notes on Contributors

RICHARD BARICKMAN, Assistant Professor of English at Hunter College, presented two papers at the MLA Convention in 1977, one on Sairey Gamp and the other on self-parody in Victorian novels. He is also engaged in completing a book on images of women in the novels of Dickens, Thackeray, and Trollope.

JAMES A. DAVIES, Lecturer at University College of Swansea, University of Wales, has published on John Forster in *The Dickensian* and the *Review of English Studies;* he has also published on Dickens in *The Dickensian* and the *Durham University Journal.* His present project is a book on Forster and articles on Dickens' characterization.

EARLE DAVIS, longtime Chairman of the Department of English at Kansas State University, is best known to Dickens scholars for his *The Flint and the Flame* and articles on Dickens in various journals, but he has also written on Ezra Pound and Thomas Hart Benton, published three volumes of poetry, textbooks, and a satire. Now he is at work on studies of Jane Austen, Dickens, George Eliot, Pound, and T. S. Eliot's *The Waste Land.*

RICHARD J. DUNN, Associate Professor and Associate Chairman at the University of Washington, is the Secretary of The Dickens Society. He has previously published articles on Smollett, Dickens, Mary Shelley, Emily Bronte, and Carlyle, and has edited the *Norton Critical Edition of Jane Eyre* and *The English Novel: Twentieth-Century Criticism: Defoe through Hardy.* His chief project at present is a study of the problems of narrative authority in Victorian literature.

STANLEY FRIEDMAN, Assistant Professor at Queens College, has published on Dickens in *Nineteenth-Century Fiction,* the *Dickens Studies Newsletter,* and the *Victorian Newsletter.* Now he is at work on a long analysis of Dickens' themes and techniques.

BERT G. HORNBACK, Professor of English at the University of Michigan, has written many articles but is better known for his two major books: *The Metaphor of Chance: Vision and Technique in the Works of Thomas Hardy* and *Noah's Arkitecture: A Study of Dickens' Mythology.* A book on *David Copperfield* is now under way.

[xvii

ARLENE M. JACKSON, Assistant Professor at St. Joseph's College, has published on *Daniel Deronda,* Melville's *Encantadas,* and Thomas Hardy. She has just completed a book-length analysis of the illustrated novels of Hardy.

ANDREW D. KAPPEL, was a graduate student at Rice University when he wrote this, his first published article. An essay on Keats' "Nightingale" is forthcoming in *ELH,* and he is working on a book about Ezra Pound's ethics of individualism.

DAVID PAROISSIEN, Associate Professor at the University of Massachusetts at Amherst, wrote on Dickens and the Weller family in an earlier volume of the *Annual* and has also edited Dickens' *Pictures from Italy.*

ROBERT L. PATTEN, Professor of English at Rice University, has published many articles in many different journals but is perhaps most known for his edition of *The Pickwick Papers* and his *George Cruikshank: A Revaluation.* Forthcoming is his *Charles Dickens and his Publishers.*

ELIHU PEARLMAN, Associate Professor at the University of Colorado at Denver, has published on Robert Wilks, *David Copperfield,* Shakespeare, *Robinson Crusoe,* Chaucer, and Gosse. He is working now on Pepys and Ben Jonson.

THOMAS J. RICE, Associate Professor of English at the University of South Carolina, has written on Dickens, Poe, and Conrad in several journals. He is now completing the second volume of an annotated research guide for the study of British fiction between 1900 and 1950.

MELANIE YOUNG, a graduate student at Rice University when she wrote the article for this volume, is completing her dissertation of the postmodern American novel.

Dickens Studies Annual

Andrew J. Kappel and Robert L. Patten

DICKENS' SECOND AMERICAN TOUR AND HIS "UTTERLY WORTHLESS AND PROFITLESS" AMERICAN "RIGHTS"

> I believe there are hopes of throttling the continental Brigands. I have no hope, whatever, of stopping American Piracy in this Generation. But we may just as well serve the next, and assert our wrongs; and I *know* it galls them, and they wince.—That should be a comfort to us. It is a very great one to me.—Dickens to [Horatio] Smith, 19 July 1842[1]

DICKENS' SECOND American tour is seldom accorded the attention given to his first. There are several reasons for this comparative neglect. To begin with, his official biographer, John Forster, skips over the American readings perfunctorily, because he adamantly opposed them and the tour in general, and because he was in the later years somewhat estranged from Dickens. When Dolby, Dickens' manager, laid before Forster the "case in a nutshell" for Dickens' going to America, he found him unreasonable, inhospitable, and unyielding in his opposition: "A red rag could not have made a mad bull more ferocious than the discussion of the clauses in the moderate and business-like 'case in a nutshell' made the biographer of the novelist. He had made up *his* mind, and there was an end of the matter."[2] Forster objected that Dickens, ever since the Staplehurst accident, had been in poor health; he believed that the Forrest-Macready riots would be replayed because of Dickens' intimacy with the latter; "he was certain there was no money in America, and, even if there were, Mr. Dickens would not get any of it; and if he *did*, the Irish (by some means I could not quite understand), and the booksellers, between them, would break into the hotel and rob him of it. Even if the money were deposited in a bank, the bank would fail on purpose."[3] The basis for Forster's objection, as is well known, was his unalterable feeling that the readings were "degrading," coupled with his conviction that the Americans, having pirated Dickens' texts, would find means of enjoying his public performances for free too.

Forster was not alone in believing that Dickens' readings were infra dig. Until the appearance of Philip Collins' definitive edition of the *Readings* texts, and his articles describing the techniques of performance and their relationship to Dickens' imagination, most critics of the writer had but glanced at the occupation of the actor.[4] Since the first American visit supplied material for two books, *American Notes* and *Martin Chuzzlewit,* it was an important source (particularly through speeches, letters, and newspaper articles) for Dickens' subsequent publications (and political views), and has therefore been studied at length. But because the second one contained very little material later transmogrified into essays or books, it has been virtually ignored by Dickens' critics.

As a result of this benign neglect, the second American tour has been distorted by the prejudices of the few authorities who have commented on it. Compared to the wealth of marvelous letters to him which Forster patched together for his chapters on 1842, the 1867–68 period is represented by meager, predominantly business letters about hotel accommodations, box office receipts, Dickens' "American catarrh," and his general discomfort. The thirty pages devoted to these experiences, admittedly composed in a hurry as Forster struggled with ill health, begin baldly, "It is the intention of this and the following chapter to narrate the incidents of the visit to America in Dickens's own language, and in that only."[5] Imposing restraint on his indignation, Forster produces an account much shorter and much less colorful than the earlier chapters.

J. W. T. Ley's notes to Forster repeatedly refer the reader to George Dolby's book "for fuller details of this tour."[6] *Charles Dickens as I Knew Him,* covering both the American excursion and the farewell readings throughout the United Kingdom, occupies 466 pages, within which we learn much about the practical arrangements and the day-to-day routine of touring. Dolby's perspective, on the scene rather than at a distance like Forster's, is oriented to his legitimate professional pride in working out satisfactory plans. His veneration for Dickens colors, though it does not cloud, his perceptions. Of Dickens' arrival at Boston, fraught with misadventure, Dolby wrote: "Here was really my old Chief. . . . At last all was right, and I had the unspeakable delight of being once more face to face, after a hearty greeting, with the best and dearest friend man ever had."[7] From Dolby we get an intimate account of the triumph and tragedy of an aged, badgered, brilliant Englishman, of his devoted, clever, resourceful assistant, of unprincipled and ingenious speculators, and of an American audience that received Dickens with affection, respect, wild enthusiasm, and—for the most part—good manners. We also learn, night by night and pound by pound, how lucrative the venture was.

But when we turn to other writers whose topic would seem to be Dickens in America, like William Glyde Wilkins, we find skimpy treatment of the reading tour, or none at all. And when we look into Edgar Johnson's biography for the standard contemporary version, we find this tour assimilated to a pattern of self-destruction whose seeds were sown in an unhappy childhood and whose deadly fruit ripened throughout the sixties. The reading tour becomes significant as the most dramatic manifestation, prior to 1869, of that fatal "want of something": "So severe was Dickens's agony by the end of [his farewell] speech that he was forced to beg to be excused. Hobbling painfully on [Horace] Greeley's arm, he could not conceal his sufferings. The mechanism of the body, indeed, was disastrously weakened, but the steel-coiled will that dominated it would not surrender. . . . Though in some miraculous way the vessel had not been dashed to pieces against the Loadstone Rock and sunk, all its fabric was twisted and broken with the dreadful strain."[8]

The editors of the Pilgrim *Letters* have supplied us with new documents and gratifyingly full annotation concerning the 1842 visit, but it will be many years before the second tour is equally documented. Until then, our perspective on 1867–68 will incorporate the prejudices of the authorities we consult: Forster's stubborn disapproval, Dolby's affectionate management, Johnson's dramatic pathology. Each writer assimilates Dickens' excursion to his own patterning of those last years: Forster to the unworthy decline into performing mountebank, Dolby to the unprecedented popular success of the readings, Johnson to the feverish depression and growing disillusion of the writer in dissolution. Carlyle, who thought Forster's biography equal to Boswell's in penetration, sensed the same murderous strain in Dickens' pursuit of the dollar in "Yankee-doodle-dom": "So long as Dickens is interesting to his fellow-men, here will be seen, face to face, what Dickens's manner of existing was; his steady practicality, withal; the singularly solid business talent he continually had; and deeper than all, if one had the eye to see deep enough, dark, fateful silent elements, tragical to look upon, and hiding amid dazzling radiances as of the sun, the elements of death itself. Those two American Journies [*sic*] especially transcend in tragic interest to a thinking reader most things one has seen in writing."[9]

— 2 —

The second advent of Dickens in the United States promises a fine harvest, not only to himself, but to the whole fraternity of readers and lecturers, Dickens, Dolby and the dollars.—*New York Herald,* 11 December 1867 [10]

Surprisingly little has been made of the connection between the two American journeys. During the second, Dickens approved the changes he observed: "there is undoubtedly improvement in every direction," he wrote of New York, and in his farewell address he praised the "politeness, delicacy, sweet temper, hospitality, and consideration in all ways" paid him by his hosts, and thanked the public for the "respect shown, during all his visits, to the privacy enforced upon him by the nature of his work and the condition of his health."[11] Because Dickens had such a favorable reception, and testified so movingly at the end of his visit to his altered perception of America's altered condition, and because scholars have not scrutinized the prelude to the second tour and its aftermath with the same care they have given to the first, we tend to assume that the mutual good-feeling that reached its apogee at Delmonico's under the chairmanship of the eminent journalist Horace Greeley was inevitable.

For complicated, interlocking reasons which we will try to outline, the opposite is closer to the truth. Dickens' second journey nearly foundered on the same rock as his first. Storm warnings flew from every publisher's masthead in the months preceding his departure from England; the cry for International Copyright rallied partisans to several sides; and a long imbroglio between Dickens and his American publishers ventilated to the public the whole confused, sometimes acrimonious, history of Dickens' copyrights, income, and authorized editions.

Pressure on the United States to enter into some kind of reciprocal copyright agreement built throughout the forties and fifties. In England an 1844 act led to the signing of a bilateral convention with Prussia, and a second act some years later was succeeded by a whole series of treaties: with France, 1852; Belgium, 1855; Spain, 1857; Sardinia, 1861. Not all British authors were quick to cash in on this new source of revenue,[12] but Dickens began carrying a notice in *Household Words* in December 1855 that *"the right of Translating Articles . . . is reserved by the Authors."* The next year he ceded to Hachette "the sole and exclusive right of making a translation authorised by [him], of [all his] books, into the French language" in return for eleven monthly installments of one thousand francs each.[13] During the Civil War, Americans had little energy or interest to spare for the copyright issue, but, as commerce between the Northern states and Europe resumed after Appomattox, authors and publishers perceived that revenues lost to foreign publishers from the absence of agreements might exceed the profits derived from gratis American printings of foreign works. Between 1842 and 1890 twelve bills were introduced in Congress to establish reciprocal conventions, but none passed. Even when most European countries adopted the Berne convention in 1887, America held out, finally succumbing in part four years later with the Chase Copyright Act of 1891.

While agitation for international copyright continued, American publishers also continued to sell hundreds of thousands of copies of books by foreign authors, Dickens preeminent among them. The appetite for his writings, and the interest in his life, increased almost annually; the "violated letter" setting forth his reasons for separating from Catherine attained wide circulation and aroused much comment. Friends and strangers, motivated by affection, avarice, or both, tried to persuade Dickens to return. One of his most assiduous correspondents was the Boston publisher James Fields, who first broached the idea of another American expedition in 1858 and harped on it often thereafter. Fields had heard of Dickens' success with his readings and proposed that Dickens duplicate the feat throughout the States. It was tempting. "I should very much like to read in America," Dickens replied in June 1859. "But the idea is a mere dream as yet. Several strong reasons would make the journey difficult to me, and—even were they overcome—I would never make it, unless I had great general reason to believe that the American people really wanted to hear me."[14] Deeply scarred by the aftermath of his earlier voyage, Dickens tested the waters cautiously, but was convinced by Fields' summer visit to Gad's Hill that the time was propitious: "with the strongest intensity [he] urges that there is no drawback, no commercial excitement or crisis, no political agitation; and that so favourable an opportunity, in all respects, might not occur again for years and years."[15] Thomas Coke Evans was authorized to investigate further in New York, but he was both dilatory and unsuccessful; the time for striking had passed, and by the beginning of August, Dickens had concluded that he would not go just then. Confiding his decision to Fields, Dickens held out the hope that "a year hence I may revive the matter, and your presence in America will then be a great encouragement and assistance to me."[16] Incorrectly anticipating a favorable response then, Fields bought from Chapman and Hall fifty-seven hundred copies of the Library edition bound with special American titles and vignettes, which he obviously intended to work off during the tour.[17]

But in 1860 the time was clearly *not* propitious. During the war all hope of a visit was suspended, though Dickens referred to the plan in 1862.[18] But "every time [Fields] had occasion to write to him after the war, [he] stirred up the subject of the readings,"[19] until Dickens, believing that the booming economy would support an extensive trip, began to think it might be possible. Characteristically, however, he expressed his willingness to entertain a proposal by couching it in the most forbidding negatives:

> I really do not know that any sum of money that could be laid down would induce me to cross the Atlantic to read. . . . I am now just finishing a series of thirty readings. The crowds attending them have been so astounding, and the relish for them has so far outgone all previous experience, that if I were to set

myself the task, "I will make such or such a sum of money by
devoting myself to readings for a certain time," I should have
to go no further than Bond Street or Regent Street, to have it
secured to me in a day. Therefore, if a specific offer, and a
very large one indeed were made to me from America, I
should naturally ask myself, "Why go through this wear and
tear, merely to pluck fruit that grows on every bough at
home?"[20]

Was ever denial phrased in such transparently "come-hither" fashion?
Dickens sets forth his overwhelming popularity, dwells on the largeness
of his receipts, and stresses that even a "specific offer" and "a very large
one indeed" might not repay his "wear and tear." Were it to be advanced as a counterargument that new scenes and characters might
refresh him, he would reply: "It is a delightful sensation to move a new
people; but I have but to go to Paris, and I find the brightest people in
the world quite ready for me." So much for his American (provincial)
cousins. Yet, having baited the hook, Dickens sinks it remorselessly by a
repetition of the theme of money that would have made Beethoven
blush:

> I can put no price upon fifty readings in America, because I
> do not know that any possible price could pay me for them.
> And I really cannot say to any one disposed towards the en-
> terprise, "Tempt me," because I have too strong a misgiving
> that he cannot in the nature of things do it.
>   This is the plain truth. If any distinct proposal be submitted
> to me, I will give it a distinct answer. But the chances are a
> round thousand to one that the answer will be no, and there-
> fore I feel bound to make the declaration beforehand.[21]

The situation clarified during the succeeding twelve months. In
August 1866 Dickens finalized plans for a second series of readings
under Chappell's management, to run between January and May 1867.
Instead of the contracted forty-two, public demand forced an increase
to fifty-two before the season concluded.[22] While putting the finishing
touches to plans for that tour, Dickens adverted to his American dream
once more: "A faint outline of a castle in the air always dimly hovers
between me and Rochester, in the great hall of which I see myself reading to American audiences."[23] When the second season was over,
Dickens found the financial results so satisfactory that he felt "disposed
to devote his energies entirely to reading in the autumn and winter
months,"[24] but whether in England or America was the unresolved
issue. Another letter in June 1867 to the long-expectant Fields once
more raised hope: "I am trying hard so to free myself, as to be able to
come over to read this next winter! Whether I may succeed in this en-

deavor or no I cannot yet say, but I am trying HARD." With an eye to publicity, Dickens went on to caution Fields, "So in the mean time don't contradict the rumor."[25]

It was not only the success of the second Chappell tour that prompted Dickens to revive his American proposal but also the evident willingness and apparent ability of Americans to enter into specific and lucrative contracts. The willingness had long been manifest, but Dickens had been burned by Thomas Coke Evans' inability to follow through on the terms of his 1859 contract to purchase advance sheets of *All the Year Round,* an agreement witnessed by W. H. Wills and Wilkie Collins (but not, significantly, by Forster, who even then distrusted Americans). The postwar boom in the North coincided with renewed interest in Continental literature and the rise of enterprising publishers who were far more reputable than the scurrilous yellow journalists of 1839–42. The *New York Ledger* had paid one thousand pounds for the short story "Hunted Down" before the war, and during the fighting Harper and Brothers purchased advance sheets of *A Tale of Two Cities* for the same sum. Now Ticknor and Fields in Boston offered one thousand pounds for *A Holiday Romance,* to run in their magazine *Young Folks,* and the Honorable Benjamin Wood of New York proposed to pay the same amount for the story that eventually became *George Silverman's Explanation.* Dickens' reply to Wood was published in the *New York Sunday News* and picked up in literary columns all over the United States, so that by mid-April 1867 everyone knew that Wood's manuscript was "to be ready . . . by the first of August *at latest.*"[26]

Further, by May 1867 Dickens was beset with worries. At the conclusion of his second set of Chappell readings, he faced mounds of work: "I am so hurried that it is with great difficulty I can find time to get at [revisions and new Preface for the Charles Dickens edition of] Dombey. Between the New Edition, Correspondence, A.Y.R., and all other cares, I have as much to do as I can manage. Last night I was so tired, that I could hardly undress for bed."[27] No doubt the prospect of taking off for America and leaving some of these chores behind was momentarily appealing. At the same time, as he calculated the size and incapacity of his family, and set it against his probable estate and current expenses, Dickens grew anxious about money. "Expenses are so enormous," he told Georgy, "that I begin to feel myself drawn towards America, as Darnay in the Tale of Two Cities was attracted to the Loadstone Rock, Paris."[28] Trying to win Forster round to endorsing an American excursion, Dickens assured his friend that nothing would induce him to go unless he were convinced "that what I could get by it, added to what I have got, would leave me with a sufficient fortune." Not that Forster should imagine the trip to be pleasurable—Dickens exaggerated his prospective miseries to emphasize that the tour would be a duty, not a pleasure: "I should be wretched beyond expression there.

My small powers of description cannot describe the state of mind in which I should drag on from day to day."[29] Not, in all likelihood, what Dickens honestly expected to feel, but all too prophetic of the actual event.

Allowing rumors to circulate of Dickens' impending visit multiplied the offers. Mr. Grau, who had become wealthy and respected as the impresario of Madame Ristori and other artists, offered to deposit bonds at Coutts in any amount to guarantee Dickens' contract. James Fields and a group of private Boston gentlemen proposed to deposit ten thousand pounds in England against receipts, and take no profit, if only they might have the honor of being Dickens' sponsors. "Every American speculator who comes to London," Dickens told Forster in May, "repairs straight to Dolby, with similar proposals."[30] Thus excited, even Chappell joined the bandwagon for America. The time to go, Dickens concluded, would be immediately after the Christmas number of *All the Year Round* went to press, for waiting another year would delay the tour until the American presidential elections, an obviously unfavorable time. (He did not anticipate the impeachment proceedings of February–May 1868 that coincided with, and slightly impaired, his enterprise.)[31] His mind more than half made up, he rejected Wills' and Forster's urgent counsel to the contrary, and by 13 June had resolved to send Dolby to America to scout out the territory, to locate suitable halls, and to determine convenient dates.[32]

Thus several forces converged to quicken interest in going to America to read: the success of the English readings, the large sums of money in prospect, Dickens' own financial state, the urgings of some of his friends in England and abroad. In a list of reasons for going which he sent to Wills, Dickens mentioned another consideration: "I . . . believe that an immense impulse would be given to the C.D. Edition by my going out."[33] The American sales of Dickens' last edition were unquestionably stimulated by his visit, so that he profited both from the readings themselves and from the additional books the readings sold. But the plan to visit America also complicated his relations with American publishers and threatened to turn the triumphal progress into a fiasco. We must now interrupt our chronological narrative to look more closely into the past history of Dickens' American publications.

— *3* —

The only Authorized Publishers of Dickens's Works in America.—
T. B. Peterson and Brothers, *New York Tribune*, 4 May 1867[34]

Dolby specifically denies that he was sent ahead because of fears concerning lingering resentment against Dickens for his earlier American writings: "There was no anxiety whatever about public feeling in America, and the 'American Notes' and 'Martin Chuzzlewit' had no more to do with Mr. Dickens's calculations than if they had never been written."[35] He is wrong. Neither side had forgotten the earlier quarrels. Up to the last minute, Forster records, Dickens "had not been able to clear off wholly a shade of misgiving that some of the old grudges might make themselves felt."[36] The *New York Times,* editorializing on the occasion of Dolby's arrival in August, assured Dickens of a "kindly reception" and predicted that his visit would meet "at once with a pecuniary success and a personal reception both flattering and friendly." America had changed much in the intervening period and had "no small room for petty grudges." The *Times* asserted that "we have really forgotten all about *American Notes.*"[37] Eight days later the *New York Tribune* concurred.[38]

But at least one American paper was not slow to revive past complaints. James Gordon Bennett, founder of the *New York Herald,* reprinted on 3 September the stories that the *Herald* had carried in 1842 concerning Dickens' reception, and three days later sneered that in the *Notes* and *Chuzzlewit* Dickens the "driveller" gave "his own measure in attempting to give ours . . . show[ing] himself blind . . . and able only to see and describe the pitiful and the mean." However, the *Herald* continued, this "Homer of the slums and back alleys" planned to return not in order to write further but, instead, to be "a show" and "reap his pecuniary harvest in reading what he wrote in his better days."[39] Bennett told Dolby that the "second coming of Dickens" would succeed only if "Dickens would *first apologize* to the American public for the 'Notes' and 'Martin Chuzzlewit.' "[40] In a less than helpful gesture of support, he immediately reprinted, in the "Triple Sheet" for Sunday, 15 September, "Choice Excerpts" from *American Notes,* just in case his compatriots had forgotten Dickens' earlier sentiments. And in an editorial on the succeeding page, the *Herald* endorsed the visit with arch ambiguity, concluding that the *Notes* had been no more severe than Americans were customarily on one another: "Sometimes [Dickens' remarks] are a little ill-natured; but are we to require an amiable spirit and an even temper of every travelling Englishman who writes about us?"[41]

Bennett's jeers may have yielded publicity, but they did not significantly alter America's affection for Boz. On the occasion of Dickens' arrival in Boston, the *New York World* assured its readers that "there need be no fear as to the welcome which Charles Dickens will receive in America. This welcome will be as cordial, as general, and as deep as the admiration which all educated Americans feel for [this] writer."[42] A month later, on 16 December 1867, in anticipation of the second series of readings in New York, the *Times* reiterated its earlier assurances: "However galling certain paragraphs of Mr. Dickens may have been in their day, the present generation cannot forget that it owes to that gentleman an irredeemable debt of gratitude."[43] And on another occasion, the *Times* wrote, "Whatever sensitiveness there once was to adverse or sneering criticism, the lapse of a quarter of a century, and the profound significance of a great war, have modified or removed."[44]

It was not, in fact, from the quarter of *American Notes* and *Martin Chuzzlewit* that the principal threat to Dickens' reception lay, though as we shall see he took care to defend that flank as well. Instead, Dickens became embroiled in an angry exchange of letters and charges concerning who were his "authorized" American publishers, and how much his American "rights" amounted to. With a reading tour in the offing, the prize was well worth the contest, in terms of both sales and prestige. It was fought out in the pages of a dozen journals and entailed discussions of international copyright, the economic status of the professional author, and the viability of American publishers' self-regulated competitive practices.

There were basically four contenders for the honor of being Dickens' authorized American representatives: Carey, Lea and Blanchard, and T. B. Peterson and Brothers, both of Philadelphia, Harper and Brothers of New York, and Ticknor and Fields of Boston. Henry C. Lea recalled in 1867 that his predecessor had paid Dickens £50 in 1838 "in acknowledgment of the success of his work."[45] A year earlier, in 1837, Henry Charles Carey had sent to Mr. Samuel Dickens a draft for £25 for the first three (of five) parts of the Philadelphia *Pickwick;* the money, he explained, "we beg you will accept not as a compensation, but as a memento of the fact that unsolicited a bookseller has sent an author, if not money, at least a fair representative of it."[46] Carey and Lea were the first American firm to make a systematic effort to pay foreign authors for American reprints and advance sheets, although Harpers quickly followed suit, binding Bulwer by payments of £50 per volume for his advance sheets.[47] Dickens declined Carey's first offer but accepted double the amount the following year. Carey was not just throwing money away. He hoped to secure an agreement with Dickens for advance sheets to the next novel, for then, even if another publisher, planning to print from an early copy of the English edition, advertised the title as "in press," by trade courtesy Carey's claims would be honored and enforced above all others.

He was not altogether successful. Bentley claimed the right to control *Oliver Twist,* so Carey sent £60 to the publisher, and £50 to Dickens, for the manuscript of the latter portions of that novel.[48] Following up his advantage, Carey instructed his English agent, John Miller, to treat with Dickens for advance proofs of *Nickleby,* but Miller didn't act on his instructions, and Dickens couldn't have sent the proofs anyway, because he was "rather behindhand than in advance" with his copy.[49] *Nickleby* found favor in America through several different editions; at the same time *Bentley's Miscellany,* including all Dickens' contributions, was reprinted by William Lewer and his wife Jemima, later Mrs. Joseph Mason.[50]

When *Master Humphrey's Clock,* to be issued in weekly numbers to foil the pirates, was announced, Dickens tried to secure it to Lea and Blanchard by contracting for stereos to be shipped in time for simultaneous publication on both sides of the Atlantic. However, his letter to Philadelphia was delayed, and in the meantime hapless Mr. Miller, eager to make up for earlier mistakes, independently arranged for early proofs of each number at £2.10 each, totaling £112.10 for the *Shop,* and £107.10 for *Rudge.* Lea and Blanchard had been willing to authorize a much larger payment, up to £300, but had wanted proof at least thirty days in advance. That, of course, Dickens could not supply; finding the weekly numbers too difficult to manufacture on short notice, the Philadelphia publishers settled for issuing the *Clock* in twenty monthly parts instead. Thus between 1838 and 1841 Dickens had received some £330 from an American firm, either in tribute to his genius or for advance sheets. From the perspective of 1867, Henry C. Lea admitted, with its "enormous sales and plentiful greenbacks, these sums may not appear large, but in the fearful depression of business before and after the fall of the Bank of the United States, they were as much as any house could afford to pay. Within twenty-four hours after the appearance of each number it was re-printed bodily in a dozen newspapers, whose readers thus obtained it for nothing, while rival editions were rapidly brought out in the style of the cheap publications which sprung up about that time."[51]

Piracies within the American trade, and journalistic reprints, plagued American publishers as well as English authors. At no time were press ethics lower than during the early 1840s, when a deep depression in publishing was offset by rowdy journals that vied to publish the latest scurrilous gossip. During his first American visit Dickens was victimized by these papers, which he mistakenly took to be representative of the entire press. The inevitable adverse response to *American Notes* and *Martin Chuzzlewit* in the States was merely another instance of the journalistic abuse Dickens had legitimately criticized in those volumes. As a result, Dickens determined to put the pirates down wherever they practiced, whether on the Continent, where he had some hope of success, or in America. He lobbied for the passage of Talfourd's 1842 Copyright Act and worked to stop the importation of pirated editions into Canada.[52] He sent a famous circular letter to leading English authors stating that he would never again "enter into any negotiation with any person for the transmission, across the Atlantic, of early proofs of anything I may write," and resolutely forswearing "all profit derivable from such a source."[53]

Though his resolution lasted less than a decade, it helped to finish off one American publishing house and establish another as Dickens' representative. Lea and Blanchard prepared mightily for Dickens' American tour by issuing the earliest collected edition of his works in twenty volumes. But the fierce competition during and after the visit eroded trade courtesy and gave an advantage to New York houses from which the Philadelphia firm could not recover. *American Notes* had an enormous sale that utterly engulfed Lea and Blanchard's modest edition of five thousand, which, with a portrait for twenty-five cents and without for half that price, was added as No. 21 of their collected edition.[54] Without any special arrangement for advance sheets, they had to take their chances along with the competition, which was better situated, in New York, to whip up copies of *Dombey* and *Copperfield* from an English edition fetched at a run from the packet steamer at the dock.

Thus the 1840s were an interregnum for Dickens' American representatives. Yet his novels continued to sell well: a minimum of 175,000 copies of *Dombey* were taken in various editions, and John Wiley and G. P. Putnam shared in publishing the American part issue of *David Copperfield*, set from the English one. Slowly, however, the powerful house of Harper consolidated its position, and "became in a sense, though not formally," as Peter S. Bracher shows, "Dickens' official American publisher."[55] The Harper brothers had enormous resources behind them and began laying out large sums for advance proofs, which Dickens, despite his earlier letters, in the fifties once again began accepting. As publishers of *Harper's New Illustrated Monthly Magazine,* and later of the *Weekly,* they used Dickens as a circulation builder. Not only did they crib from *Household Words* and *All the Year Round,* but they also secured advance proofs of the latest serial novel to run alongside other periodical material. They contracted to pay £5 for *The Haunted Man,* £20 per part for *Bleak House,* £250 for *Little Dorrit,* £1,000 each for *Two Cities* and *Our Mutual Friend,* and £1,250 for *Great Expectations.*[56] At the outset they were almost forestalled by Rufus Wilmot Griswold, editor of the rival *International Monthly Magazine,* who sent one of his publishers over to England to offer $2,000 for advance sheets. Another unfortunate emissary, he went to Bouverie Street instead of to Tavistock House and was told by Bradbury and Evans that Dickens, wrapped up in private theatricals, contemplated no new serial. He left empty-handed, while Harpers, through their London agent Sampson Low, went directly to Dickens, who accepted Griswold's price, prematurely announced in the *New York Evening Post,* but Harpers' contract.[57] *Harper's* circulation increased throughout *Bleak House*'s run, reaching 118,000 per month; Henry C. Carey calculated that no fewer than 250,000 copies were supplied to American readers in one form or another.[58]

Competition forced Harpers into progressively more businesslike arrangements with its authors, and no writer benefited more than Dickens from the resulting arrangements. But Harpers was not above imitating the unsavory practices of its competitors. T. L. McElrath, the son of Horace Greeley's partner, paid $1,500 for advance sheets of *Hard Times,* scheduled to run in *Household Words.* Harpers, which had been mining the pages of Dickens' weekly with and without acknowledgement ever since its start, simply pirated the novel without payment or comment.[59] A few years later, when *All the Year Round* was announced, Harpers eventually negotiated a contract to reprint from advance sheets at £250 a year, but (as we have seen) not before Thomas Coke Evans tried and failed to issue the magazine in its entirety on his own.

Harpers could offer such large sums for Dickens' writing, even though they did not guarantee exclusive copyright, because of an arrangement which the firm had with T. B. Peterson and Brothers. In 1851 Petersons consolidated their position as the leading publisher of Dickens' works in volumes, by purchasing all the stereos, steels, and woodcuts owned by a half-dozen publishing houses. From Getz, Buck, and Company they obtained the plates that Lea and Blanchard had disposed of,[60] from Putnam they bought those which had belonged to Wiley and Putnam before the dissolution of their partnership,[61] and from Stringer and Townsend and Jasper Harding they got still other materials.[62] They then began issuing various editions, in prices ranging from a quarter per volume to five dollars, until by 1867 they had produced twenty-three different uniform editions. To augment and bring up to date their list, they joined with Harpers in purchasing the advance sheets and also bought Harpers' stereos and woodcuts, laying out nearly $9,500 for six novels and some "Christmas Tales," which they issued in volumes following periodical publication and then added to the various collected editions.[63] These investments were not always immediately repaid: the volumes of *Two Cities,* issued by Petersons after the novel was serialized in *Harper's Weekly,* did not sell.[64] But in collected form, the works obtained an immense circulation. Petersons believed, with considerable justification, that they were Dickens' authorized American firm, and their advertising stressed their claim.[65] "In the absence of an international copyright," the firm explained to its public in 1867, "it has always been held that the house which purchased the advance-sheets from an English author had the equitable right to the exclusive use of his works in the United States. . . . We supposed, when we purchased these plates, that we were buying the equitable right (as against any other American publishers) to reprint these works; and it was always regarded in the trade that we had acquired such a right."[66]

Not everyone regarded Petersons with such respect. Hurd and

Houghton competed in the fifties and sixties with two illustrated editions: the Riverside edition (the name survives in Houghton Mifflin's Riverside series), twenty-six volumes crown octavo illustrated in part on steel from designs by the original artists, and the Household edition, fifty-three volumes at $1.25 or $2.50 per volume, illustrated by F. O. C. Darley and John Gilbert. Possibly anticipating a Dickens tour, Hurd and Houghton announced at the beginning of April 1867 a new, inexpensive edition, called the Globe (to suggest Dickens' equality with Shakespeare, no doubt), to be completed in thirteen volumes with all the Darley and Gilbert illustrations, and sold for $1.50 each. During the forties Stringer and Townsend had reportedly offered to pay Dickens for advance sheets and had been turned down as a result of his resolve not to deal with American pirates; Hurd and Houghton in the sixties tried to arrange to pay Dickens a share of the profits in their Household edition, but Dickens declined, "considering himself debarred by his agreement with Messrs. Harper and Brothers."[67]

Not only did American publishing houses print their own collected editions of Dickens' works, they also took large quantities of the collected editions published in England. The Library edition, an incorrigibly feeble venture until Frederic Chapman consolidated all the volumes published by Bradbury and Evans with those from Chapman and Hall, added illustrations, raised the price, and then deeply discounted for bulk orders, exemplifies Yankee demand for Boz. Ticknor and Fields took 5,700 volumes of the unillustrated edition, then came back for at least 6,750 more of the illustrated version prior to 1867, and a whopping 52,000 (2,000 complete sets) during the American tour. Other houses did a more modest, but continuing, business: D. Appleton and Company; J. B. Lippincott and Company; Little, Brown, and Company; and Charles Scribner and Company. These collected editions, and the promise of a new one from Chapman and Hall commencing in 1867, prompted Ticknor and Fields to issue, on their own, the Diamond edition, launched in the spring of 1867 with "an immense sale." "It is a wonderful tribute to the genius of Dickens," the *Publisher's Circular* commented on 15 May 1867, "that a new generation of readers buy these new editions with an avidity equal to that of their seniors years ago."[68]

— 4 —

The only authorized publishers of [Dickens'] works in America.—
Ticknor and Fields, *New York Tribune*, 18 May 1867[69]

It was the efforts of the new boy in town, Ticknor and Fields, to establish their legitimacy as Dickens' publishers, that precipitated the troubles of 1867. The potential market was huge, a large part would gravitate to whatever firm clearly enjoyed Dickens' confidence, and additional advantages in sponsoring and assisting in the reading tour might accrue to the authorized firm. The jockeying for position started as early as 16 March 1867, when Fields saw in the *Boston Evening Transcript* an advertisement by T. B. Peterson and Brothers for their "Author's American Edition of 'Dickens.' "[70] In this notice, Petersons claimed to be, in conjunction with Harper and Brothers, "the only Publishers in America of the works of Charles Dickens, that have ever paid anything for the Manuscript and advanced Proof-sheets of his various works," citing as evidence their payments of "Five Thousand Dollars in Gold" for the advance proofs of *Our Mutual Friend* and a like sum for each of Dickens' "other late works."[71] The claim was, in a way, not true: Dickens had received money from Carey, Lea, and Blanchard and from Harpers, and had made money from the sale in America of collected editions published in England. In another sense, however, it was accurate: before 1867 no other American house had contracted with Dickens for publication, in the United States, of his collected works. Concerned that their own negotiations to secure those rights might be jeopardized or nullified by Peterson's statement, James T. Fields hurriedly sent a letter to Dickens, enclosing a copy of the offensive notice, and asking for a contradiction.

Before he received Fields' letter, Dickens, on 2 April, inscribed a testimonial to the firm of Ticknor and Fields declaring that they "have become the only authorized representatives in America of the whole series of my books."[72] That seemed to cover both editions printed in England and distributed in the States, and those that originated in America. Dickens may by this date have signed some kind of contract, and acknowledged the Boston firm's plan to pay him for their Diamond edition which they were issuing. That would explain Fields' alarm on seeing Peterson's advertisement in the *Boston Evening Transcript*. On the same day, 2 April, in order to boost sales of *Our Mutual Friend* in the Ticknor and Fields edition, Dickens praised Sol Eytinge's plates: "They are remarkable for a delicate perception of beauty, a lively eye for character, a most agreeable absence of exaggeration, and a general modesty and propriety which I greatly like."[73] On the eighth of the month, Dickens received two hundred pounds from Fields for his share in the profits of the first volume of the Diamond edition. In reply, Dickens praised the "honorable" conduct which had made him "retrospectively as well as prospectively—a sharer in the profits of your Diamond Edition of my works. This act of justice on your part, enhanced in my estimation by its having no parallel in my experience, and by the delicate manner of its discharge, binds me to you as my American Publishers, whose interests are identical with my own."[74]

Dickens' implication that no other publisher had offered a comparable "act of justice" received widespread attention. The *New York Tribune,* evidently quoting an earlier communication, alleged on 10 April that Dickens had commended Ticknor and Fields to one of his American correspondents: "I think you know how high and far beyond the money's worth I esteem this act of manhood, delicacy, and honor. I have never derived greater pleasure from the receipt of money in all my life."[75] That set the cat among the pigeons. The *Philadelphia Press* (for which the notorious Robert Shelton Mackenzie worked) picked up the story on 12 April and cited in contradiction Harpers' payments for the last three novels and the two thousand dollars spent for sixty-four original designs engraved on wood for the initially unillustrated *Tale of Two Cities.* Three days later George W. Childs' *American Literary Gazette and Publisher's Circular,* another Philadelphia publication, carried both the *Tribune* story and the *Press* amplification.

Ignorant of the furor in America, on 16 April Dickens wrote once again to his Boston publishers, this time "to contradict any such monstrous misrepresentations" as had appeared in the clipping sent him several weeks before, and which he had finally received. The sole basis of truth to the allegation that he received money from firms other than Ticknor and Fields were "two irrelevant facts"; first, that Harpers had, as Petersons claimed, purchased advanced sheets of the last three novels for simultaneous serial publication, and second, that Hurd and Houghton had recently bought from Chapman and Hall one hundred sets of the illustrations to *Pickwick,* specially printed on India paper; which according to the account books yielded Dickens a profit of £22.14.[76] Concluding, Dickens asserted that "in America, the occupation of my life for thirty years is, unless it bears your imprint, utterly worthless and profitless to me."[77]

When Dickens' compliment to Ticknor and Fields was reprinted in London in the *Pall Mall Gazette* on 7 May in the course of a notice decrying the lack of international copyright, Sampson Low, as Harpers' London agent, wrote to dispute Dickens' assertion:

Now, having myself as the agent of Messrs. Harper and Brothers paid to Mr. Charles Dickens many thousands of pounds for and on account of his works, when no other publishing house had paid anything, I do not think such payments should be wholly overlooked in the exuberance which he feels at being put into the possession of this additional honorarium from American publishers. Messrs. Harper do not seek from Mr. Dickens any such acknowledgement to be used by them as a public advertisement, but they have a right to claim from Mr. Dickens exemption from the only inference to be drawn from the communication, that his claims upon them have hitherto been disregarded.[78]

At the same time, Henry C. Lea, surviving partner of Carey, Lea, and Blanchard, wrote on 10 May to Childs about the allegation originally printed in the 25 April issue of the *Nation* and reprinted in the 1 May edition of *Publisher's Circular,* that Dickens had got nothing for his copyrights in America prior to *Bleak House.* "The positiveness of this assertion had induced me to look over some old memoranda of transactions connected with Mr. Dickens's novels," Mr. Lea wrote in the most gentlemanly letter of the whole fracas. "As there seems to be quite a lively discussion in progress between the American publishers of those works, and as the house which I represent was the original and, for many years, the sole publishers of them as a series, perhaps a few jottings on the subject may not be without interest."[79] He then retold the story of his firm's relations with Dickens, incidentally contradicting the report that Stringer and Townsend were the first firm to treat for advance proofs, since Lea and Blanchard, no doubt with the success of their similar arrangement with Bulwer in mind, tried the same thing with Dickens as early as *Nickleby.* Childs duly carried the letter in the next issue of the *Publisher's Circular,* 15 May.

The revelation therein that Dickens had been paid as early as 1838, while not news to Petersons, nonetheless prompted them to write on 20 May to Harpers for an exact account of that firm's payments. The next day Harper and Brothers replied, listing £3,900 paid for five novels. Petersons promptly despatched a letter to Childs setting forth their reasons for being considered since 1851 "the only authorized publishers in America of the works of Charles Dickens." After reviewing the history of their dealings, they concluded: "We contend that, under the circumstances, we are the owners of all the rights ever possessed by Carey, Lea and Blanchard, and Harper and Brothers. It appears, also, that in place of Charles Dickens never having received anything from this country, he has been paid liberally, considering the absence of any international copyright. Further, we suggest that it is a very doubtful proceeding on his part, in the face of these facts, to offer to sell to any other house in America, privileges which, it appears, he had sold before."[80] Childs gathered up all the correspondence, from Dickens' 16 April letter through Sampson Low's, Petersons', Harpers', and Lea's, and ran them, with editorializing, under the head "The Dickens Controversy," in the 1 June 1867 issue of the *Publisher's Circular.* The editorial rubbed salt into an open wound:

> We regard this letter of Mr. Dickens as ungenerous, if not dishonest. Would anybody suppose, upon reading it, that the writer had actually received £3,900 sterling, nearly $20,000 in gold, from a single American firm . . .? Why does Mr. Dickens ignore that fact? Why does he say that "in America the occupation of my life for thirty years is, unless it bears your imprint,

utterly worthless and profitless to me?" Are £3,900 received within
the last "thirty years," such trash as to be "worthless"? or has
that large sum melted away so as to be profitless"?—not taking
into account various respectable sums received from Lea and
Blanchard, and other publishers. Even if we suppose that Mr.
Dickens measured his words with a micrometer, and is speaking strictly and solely of "collected editions," we cannot help
thinking that a frank and gentlemanly nature would not have
failed to recognize voluntary liberality as respects *particular*
works, even if it did not, in form, extend to *collected* works. It
would have been in much better taste if Mr. Dickens had not
sought to cover up and suppress the fact that he had received
very large remittances from a single publishing house in this
country. Yet this very fact he coolly pronounces *"irrelevant."*
Were £3,900 ever before "irrelevant" to an author, unless in
view of a prospective speculation? We do not care to dwell on
this matter.

But of course the editor did care to dwell on it, and the scolding continued for another half page, concluding with heavy irony that because
Dickens had forgotten to include payments for two earlier novels in his
Harpers' calculations, totaling £650 in his "irrelevant" £3,900, he was
"only within about seventeen per cent. of the truth, which is pretty fair
for a novelist." The connection between Childs, Petersons, and Mackenzie was close, and their attitude toward Dickens at times similar;
when Petersons published Mackenzie's *Life of Charles Dickens* in 1870,
they reprinted an edited version of the 1 June "Dickens' Controversy"
as an Appendix.

The quarrel over "authorization" extended to the editorial and ad-
vertising pages of the leading journals, and to the title pages and adver-
tising inserts of the numerous collected editions of Dickens' works. At
the end of June, the *New York Tribune* ran an editorial also called "The
Dickens Controversy" which directly disputed the Childs-Petersons
claims. Citing Dickens' published correspondence with Ticknor and
Fields, the editorial reasoned thusly:

Mr. Dickens's meaning is plain enough: it is that Ticknor and
Fields are the only publishers who pay him a share of the
profits on the sale of his works in America. If he has received
certain sums from other houses it is not in recognition of his
rights as an author, but as an equivalent for a certain specified
service, that is to say, for his furnishing a copy of his book to
them sooner than to anybody else. The Boston firm say in effect to Mr. Dickens: "We make money off the product of your
brain, and it is only honest that you should have a part of it."
The Petersons say: "Someone is sure to take your book; let us
take it first and we will give you so many dollars." To pretend

that a payment like this is in the nature of a copyright, and that Mr. Dickens, having sold the advance sheets of a book to one house, has no right to consent to its subsequent publication by another, is simply absurd.[81]

In the same issue of the *Publisher's Circular* as the "Dickens Controversy," Ticknor and Fields reran their long May advertisement claiming that "they are henceforth *the only authorized publishers of his works in America.*" To substantiate their assertion, they included the text of four letters from Dickens, the two written on 2 April, the one of 8 April thanking them for the share of profits in the Diamond edition, and the notorious one of 16 April. In the same issue, Petersons took out an advertisement on the next page saying theirs were *"the best and cheapest editions in the world."* At the same time, to retain their customers against the competition, Petersons reduced the price on all their collected editions of Dickens' works. Ticknor and Fields fought back, bolstered, no doubt, by the news Dickens sent two days later that he really was trying to clear the calendar for a winter American tour: "Understand that I am really endeavoring tooth and nail to make my way personally to the American public, and that no light obstacles will turn me aside, now that my hand is in," he assured Fields in the conclusion of his 3 June letter quoted much earlier in this essay.[82]

From the moment the news leaked out, Dickens was besieged. Quite rightly, he feared that if his specific plans got abroad, speculators would ruin them by buying up all the tickets for resale at fantastic prices, by charging outrageously for rooms, and by doing such other mischief as would bring his whole enterprise into disrepute.[83] While waiting for first-hand reports from Dolby, who sailed for America on 3 August, Dickens wrote new prefaces to *American Notes* and *Martin Chuzzlewit* for the Charles Dickens edition, in which he mildly defended his version of "Hamerica," but softened it by pleading that he had always been prejudiced in favor of the United States (*Notes*), and that the American sections of *Martin Chuzzlewit* were deliberate caricature. "As I had never, in writing fiction, had any disposition to soften what is ridiculous or wrong at home, so I then hoped that the good-humoured people of the United States would not be generally disposed to quarrel with me for carrying the same usage abroad." American editorials, following his lead, with similar reasoning helped to mollify any feelings still ruffled and to dampen the squib prepared by Bennett and the *New York Herald*.

The presence of Dolby in America confirmed the hovering impression that Dickens would come, as many papers reported, and raised the faint hope that Dickens' presence would lead finally to American passage of a reciprocal copyright agreement.[84] New York publishers helped Dolby to make suitable arrangements and whipped up their readership with any gossip about Dickens. In August a story went round, gaining in detail and exaggeration with each retelling, that Dickens was so critically ill his surgeons were sending him to America for an enforced rest. This preposterous tale, though based in part on the fact of Dickens' generally delicate health, caused him no end of difficulty; overwhelmed with letters from concerned friends, he wrote to the *Times,* the *Athenaeum,* the *Sunday Gazette,* and Fields asking that the story be flatly contradicted. To one friend, F. D. Finlay of the *Northern Whig,* he certified "that the undersigned innocent victim of a periodical paragraph disease which usually breaks out once in every seven years (proceeding from England by the Overland route to India, and per Cunard line to America where it strikes the base of the Rocky Mountains and rebounding to Europe, perishes on the steppes of Russia), is NOT in *a critical state of health,* and has NOT consulted *eminent surgeons,* and never was better in his life, and is NOT recommended to proceed to the United States for *cessation from library labour,* and has not had so much as a head ache for twenty years."[85]

Suitably mangled, but with the essential message intact, even this private correspondence found its way into the newspapers.[86] And on 13 October 1867 the *New York Times* reported in an editorial that "the London journals tried hard to kill [Dickens] the other day, by circulating mysteriously alarming reports about the state of his health, but he publicly contradicted them in the tone of a man resenting a personal insult."[87]

Dolby returned with good news in late September, and by the twenty-fourth Dickens had reduced the argument for going to America to seven headings, "The Case in a Nutshell."[88] In essence, Dickens figured he might net £15,500 from the eighty readings alone. No other calculations entered into this "case," though he was clearly aware of how advantageous his visit might be to the sales of his collected works. Despite the opposition of Wills and Forster, Dickens was resolved, and after a few days' deliberation, he telegraphed to Ticknor and Fields the cryptic message "Yes." Whatever fears Dickens may have had about the character of his American reception had been dissipated by the size of the earnings he might accrue in five months' time. The new boys had finally secured the prize they had sought for a decade.

— 5 —

Literary rights are "a kind of property which is at once the most precious, the easiest stolen, and the worst protected."—James Parton, *Atlantic Monthly,* October 1867[89]

There was little danger that Dickens would founder on the rock of international copyright. Most American houses now believed it in their interest to be secure from piracies of foreign authors by less scrupulous competitors, and authors saw the value of protected foreign rights. A major article on the subject by James Parton, the most famous biographer of his day, appeared in the October 1867 *Atlantic Monthly*.[90] Even before it was printed, it was talked about. Two weeks earlier the *Publisher's Circular* announced that the essay was being "indit[ed]" among "the Vermont hills,"[91] and the *New York Tribune*'s monthly preview of periodicals singled it out for special mention. Parton was praised for "his peculiar sagacity of perception, and sparkling nimbleness of style," and for "giving a hackneyed theme a fresh hold on the attention of the reader by his novelty and vivacity of statement and illustration."[92] There was also mention and praise of Parton's article, along with quotations from it, in editorials on international copyright that appeared in the *New York Herald* on 7 October and the *New York World* on 22 October. Not all readers were so moved; Henry C. Carey issued a second edition of his *Letters on Copyright* early in 1868 and penned a special preface in which he disparaged Parton's article: there is nothing in it "beyond a labored effort at reducing the literary profession to a level with those of the grocer and the tallow-chandler."[93] But most found Parton's argument that reciprocal copyright conventions benefited all parties sensible.

All the publishing houses, even Harpers, Parton believed, were in favor of international copyright. In its absence, American writers as well as foreign ones were robbed, as Dickens had pointed out in 1842 without being heard.[94] Parton estimated that Harriet Beecher Stowe had lost $200,000 rightfully hers from the phenomenal success in Europe of *Uncle Tom's Cabin,* because there were no agreements regulating her copyrights abroad. Mr. Macmillan subsequently assured Parton that if international copyright had been in effect Longfellow would have gained an additional £40,000 or $250,000 from the sales of his works in England.[95]

Further, lacking the protection of the law, American publishers who purchased advance sheets could not be certain of profit, for the courtesy of the trade couldn't be enforced. Within forty-eight hours of Harpers' publishing a Dickens installment in one of their magazines, two or more other editions, set up from the Harpers text, would appear at a cut price. "We have not the least doubt," Parton mentioned in passing, "that Mr. Peterson honestly thought he had acquired a right, by fair purchase, to sell the property of Charles Dickens in the United States as long as he should continue in business, and then to dispose of that right to his successor."[96] But of course subsequent events proved Petersons wrong, in fact if not in law or custom.

Parton hammered home his point that the absence of reciprocal agreements hurt Americans. Citizens who invented something were protected internationally by patent laws, but citizens such as Mrs. Stowe and Mr. Longfellow who wrote or published books, poems, or plays were not. The same was true of scholars, whose labors—as in the case of Motley's *History of the Dutch Republic* and Bancroft's *History of the United States*—might consume years and thousands of dollars, yet yield sums insufficient to cover basic expenses.

Another aspect of Parton's argument also struck home. American publishers had frequently sent foreign authors payments for works reprinted in the States, but foreign publishers seldom reciprocated. This charge, a startling reversal of the situation as we know it from Dickens' perspective, may very well be true; if so, it speaks to the generosity of those same American publishers so frequently vilified by writers viewing trade relations from a European perspective. In support of this point, Parton reprinted a letter from Mrs. Eliza Lynn Linton that had appeared in the 29 June 1867 issue of the *Athenaeum,* complimenting Harpers for having sent her, "quite unsolicited, a money acknowledgment for reprinting in their cheap series two of [her] novels. . . . At a time when so many complaints are being made of American publishers, it is pleasant to be able to record this voluntary act of grace and courtesy from so influential a house."[97] Parton commented: "Complaints, then, are made of American publishers! This is pleasant. We say again, that, after diligent inquiry, we cannot hear of one instance of an English publisher sending money to an American author for anything but advance sheets."[98]

Parton took pains to demonstrate that on the whole American publishers had good relations with their authors and strove to meet their requirements, even when unscrupulous journals pirated foreign materials and ruinously undersold those that paid. "It is the grossest injustice to hold American publishers responsible for the system of ill-regulated plunder which they have inherited, and which injures them more immediately and palpably than any other class, excepting alone the class producing the commodity in which they deal."[99] Though his defense is strident, it rings true at many points; but his rhetoric was vulnerable, despite the *Tribune's* praise for its "sparkling nimbleness" and "novelty and vivacity of statement," to Carey's censure that he reduced "the literary profession to a level with those of the grocer and the tallow-chandler."

What is striking about the article as a whole is its confidence in the proposition that international copyright would be beneficial to American letters. When Dickens delivered his first speech on the topic in Boston on 1 February 1842, he had made the same point, but America was not ready to hear or concede it. "You have in America great writers—great writers—who will live in all time, and are as familiar to our lips as household words," he told his audience then. "I take leave to say, in the presence of some of those gentlemen, that I hope the time is not far distant when they, in America, will receive of right some substantial profit and return in England from their labours; and when we, in England, shall receive some substantial profit and return for ours." Dickens' argument was not so narrowly parochial and self-interested as the papers later portrayed it to be: he spoke for the simple justice of the thing, not for "heaps and mines of gold." But "there must be an international arrangement in this respect," he concluded; "England has done her part, and I am confident that the time is not far distant when America will do hers. It becomes the character of a great country; *firstly,* because it is justice; *secondly,* because without it you never can have, and keep, a literature of your own."[100]

Parton's article could not alone dissipate all the lingering antipathy towards Dickens for his earlier stand, but it was indicative of the virtual unanimity of major American publishers on the topic. At the end of a review of the first reading in New York, the *World* concluded: "So far as Mr. Dickens is concerned, this [tour] is after all only a quiet way of coming, in part, by his own. We refuse to enact laws of international copyright by which the men who create wisdom and wit for us on the other side of the Atlantic may be protected in the fruits of their labor; and happy, therefore, is the writer whom Nature, having made him a speaker also, has endowed with the faculty of charming out of us through our ears some measure of the justice which we ought to establish for him out of our hearts, in statutes and in laws."[101]

There was, however, one off-key voice in the chorus. An editorial in the *New York Herald* on 13 December 1867 disagreed: "Dickens wanted to secure a copyright law that would enable him to get fifty cents or a dollar on every copy of his books sold in this country. . . . He did not get his money through copyright, but he got a good sum through round abuse [in *American Notes* and *Martin Chuzzlewit*] of the people who refused the copyright."[102] James Gordon Bennett, in the midst of handing management of the *Herald* over to his son, missed no opportunity to stir up controversy around Dickens and to undermine chances for a successful tour. As early as September, when other journals were responding to Dolby's announcement of another series of readings with assurances of welcome despite *American Notes* and *Martin Chuzzlewit,* the *Herald,* as we have seen, carried extracts from the offensive works introduced by slanderous editorials. Those were the first of dozens of similar vindictiveness that appeared in the *Herald* before and throughout Dickens' tour.

On 27 October 1867, three weeks before Dickens' arrival in Boston, an editorial appeared entitled "Mrs. Yelverton and Mr. Dickens."[103] In it, Bennett drew a parallel between these two "eminent lecturers" on the advent of their tours. Marie Theresa Yelverton née

Longworth (1832?–81) had recently cultivated publicity in America in order to gain sympathy and support for herself as a betrayed and abandoned wife set on getting her husband back from the woman he now professed to love and had, in Mrs. Yelverton's eyes, illegally married. In April 1857 she had married William Charles Yelverton, fourth Viscount Avonmore (1824–83); in June 1858 he left her and married another woman. In October 1859 she sued in a London probate court for restitution of conjugal rights but was denied. In July 1864 a majority in the House of Lords affirmed a Scottish court's annulment of her marriage. She took her case to the public, in 1867 to the American public. Among the parallels the *Herald* drew between her and Dickens was that "both of them . . . have suffered from the restrictions of British law upon the victims of matrimonial infelicities." In an editorial two days later, Bennett warmed to his comparison. Dickens, he noted, will read from his novels; Yelverton from love letters to her estranged husband written, she explained in a letter to the *Herald* on 22 October 1867, "by the silvery moonbeams that light the shores of the classic Mediterranean . . . or by the still more mystic shores of the Bosporus, in sight of the very tower where Hero pined until Leander breasted the treacherous wave."[104] Dickens "will report the result of his studies of low life in London"; Mrs. Yelverton "will lift us into the ethercalized atmosphere of love."[105] With such difference of purpose and "the proverbial deference of Americans to the magnetism of petticoat influence" in mind, Dickens "should meet with a formidable rival in Theresa Yelverton."[106] A latter-day "Homer of the slums" has his appeal but will pale against this "burning Sappho" with "her golden hair, her blue eyes, and her clear complexion," who like her ancient predecessor, "loved and sung," and who "stood, a few years ago, on the Leucadian rock from which Sappho made her legendary leap" but chose "like a sensible Englishwoman . . . a longer but safer leap across the Atlantic."[107] Bennett's mock-heroic language, cued by Yelverton's hilarious excesses, was a coded message that contained the essential though unstated parallel: Yelverton and Dickens were two Britishers out for American money, ludicrously lionized by the toadyistic and gullible American public.

That hidden theme surfaced in the *Herald* coverage of Dickens' arrival in Boston. An editorial on 21 November 1867 reported that Dickens' transferral from the grounded steamer *Cuba* deprived seven thousand Bostonians of "the opportunity of welcoming him with the usual demonstrations of toadyism. . . . To make amends for the loss of a chance to take the horses from his carriage and to hand him up to Parker's, the Bostonians . . . besieg[ed] the book store of his publishers" and "created a furor unequalled since that excited by his arrival in the same city twenty-five years ago."[108] The Boston correspondent to the *New York World,* whose coverage of these events appeared on 21 November 1867, remarked on the drunkenness of many of those ready "to bow down and worship" Dickens.[109] The correspondent, "a sort of natural teetotaler" himself, noted as well that Dickens reportedly "imbibe[d] a cup of tea, or something else" upon arrival at Parker House. Bennett outdid even this when his imagination hit its stride on 26 November in a follow-up editorial. The *Cuba,* he said, "was almost swamped as the crowd rushed on board to see the stateroom in which Mr. Dickens slept, and the dirty linen was stripped from the berth as the first sheets of his second American voyage."[110] To prevent Dickens' escaping New York's welcome as he had Boston's, Bennett elaborated a plan for a triple guerdon of citizens around the city, all gentlemen of the city to serve in the first cordon, "all the scum of New York" in the third. "Running the gauntlet of the very thin first line, through real personal ability to avoid such material as it will be composed of, and escaping even the second line, he must naturally fall into the hands of the third." Boston shall not, declared Bennett, "beat us in the deification of Dickens. No matter how inferior a man's origins or how low his tastes, provided he has superior talent in developing those tastes, we always elevate him higher than Boston can ever dream of." These personal insults are variations on the theme sounded first in the phrase "Homer of the slums," and though they are incidental to the tirade against a toadyistic populace and a rival city, they must have left Dickens, if he read them, none too sure of his success or his safety.

Other journals counseled their fellow citizens differently on the proper mode of welcoming the Inimitable—not with uncontrolled enthusiasm, unrestrained intrusions on his privacy, unreasonable demands on his time and energy, and "noisy and obtrusive demonstrations," but rather with "sincere and gentlemanly greetings."[111] At first, between the misadventures of docking in Boston and the curiosity of the public, Dickens feared a repetition of earlier annoyances. The waiter at the Parker House had left the door to Dickens' private sitting room partly ajar, and promenaders in the corridors peeked in at the great man while he ate his meal. Dickens' temper flared, and he complained to Dolby, "These people have not in the least changed during the last five and twenty years—they are doing now exactly what they were doing then."[112] But the manager soothed his chief's ruffled feathers, and subsequent events proved that indeed manners had improved, and Dickens was accorded the privacy, courtesy, and rest he required.

In New York a reporter for the *World* provided readers with the numbers of Dickens' rooms at the Westminster Hotel, almost as a challenge, in the midst of an article describing Dickens' assiduous cultivation of privacy. The writer himself had been close enough to observe that the subject "did not use the mustard during the entire time occupied by him in eating his dinner, . . . a significant fact and worthy of note."[113] Apparently, few readers if any took up the challenge. The next day, the *World* reported that Dickens, unlike other famous visitors, "is suffered to overcome us as calmly as a summer-cloud, goes to his hotel in peace, eats his dinner uninspected, and makes his bow before a crowded house of interested spectators at Steinway Hall as tranquilly as if he were only Albert Smith preparing to lead Cockney-dom up Mont Blanc."[114]

Most beneficial to Dickens' spirits were the receipts that poured in, until greenbacks piled up on the table in such an untidy heap that Dickens thought they looked "like a family wash." Dickens' initial amazement at advance sales was occasioned not by avarice, he assured Dolby, but by "the compliment paid to him by the American people— for up to that time very few . . . had any idea what the Readings were like."[115] "Nothing can possibly be more splendid than our prospects here," he reported to Chappell. "They are quite bewildering."[116] No doubt the enthusiasm of the crowds cheered Dickens; no doubt he did his best, often under extremely trying circumstances as he suffered through a bitterly cold winter and a prostrating catarrh, to give them their money's worth. But no doubt the profits propelled him onward as well.

The public was certainly aware of them. Before Dickens arrived, one cartoon entitled " 'Improved' Readings in America," showed Dolby commanding "in advance, the American public to do reverence to . . . Boz's hat, previous to its being passed around to collect their cash. The flunkey's [*sic*] obey. William Tell—Bennett—and others resist." One of these patriotic gentlemen thumbed his nose at the hat. Dickens returned the compliment to "Hamerica" in another cartoon published on the eve of his departure for home the following May, which shows him carrying off thousands of American "NOTES." The pun which he used in the title of his earlier book now redounded upon him. Another cartoon returned to the theme of Dickens' greed. The following conversation between Dolby and his chief takes place before a billiard table heaped with greenbacks:

> Dolby.—"Well, Mr. Dickens, on the eve of our departure, I present you with $300,000, the result of your Lectures in America."
> Dickens.—"What! only $300,000? Is that all I have made out of these penurious Yankees, after all my abuse of them? Pshaw! Let us go, Dolby!"[117]

Ticket speculators, despite Dolby's efforts, pushed up prices beyond the limits Dickens had set, and laid him open to further charges of profiteering. In such a predicament he and Dolby were sitting ducks. Bennett, the likely hotshot, was unexpectedly restrained and sympathetic. An editorial on 14 December 1867 on the mishandling of ticket sales concluded that "Mr. Dickens and Mr. Dolby are in bad hands, and the sooner they recognize it and amend the matter the better they will stand in the regard of all."[118] An editorial in the *Herald* three days thereafter stated that though Dolby and Dickens were "in hot pursuit of dollars," they did not seek "to get them in this case by unfair means."[119] On this particular issue, the *New York World* delivered the low blows. *World* editorials of 9 and 12 December aired suspicions that Dolby was in collusion with the speculators. According to an editorial on the ninth, "an unknown man . . . representing that he had been sent by Mr. Dolby" called at the printer hired by Dolby to print the tickets for the lecture series with an order for more tickets. The printer grew suspicious and printed only one ticket, which "the stranger seized" and "left the place hurriedly." When questioned, Dolby was "very reticent about the matter."[120] An editorial on the twelfth warned that the success of the lecture tour depended on a quick solution to the problem because "to make access to these agreeable readings a matter of early rising, constitutional vigor, diplomatic tact, and financial audacity, will be to kill the goose which is both expected to be and is perfectly ready to lay any number of golden eggs for Mr. Dickens and Mr. Dickens' *impresario*."[121] Dolby came directly under fire in a *World* editorial on 14 December for his scheme to frustrate speculators by registering prospective ticket buyers. That Dolby should descend from "the serene heights where he reposes" to call his "minions" to the task of registration was proof of the severity of the problem. But "Dolby *ex machina*" was no solution. The public could fend better for themselves. "Let Dolby retire into the gloom from which he has emerged."[122]

Dickens made quite a lot of money out of his American readings. "There can be little doubt," Peter Bracher concludes, "that indirectly his steady popularity in America, fed by large circulation of his books through Harper publications, helped make the reading tour of 1867–68 a highly profitable enterprise."[123] Conversely, the reading tour sparked sales of his collected editions and the Ticknor and Fields Reading edition.[124] In 1859 Dickens had told his Swiss friend de Cerjat that "the readings in the country have opened up a new public who were outside before; . . . [and] his public welcomes are prodigious."[125] Anticipating a similar expansion of audience and demand in America eight years later, American publishers laid in tremendous stores of Dickens' works, until, as Forster says, "his novels and tales were crowding the shelves of all the dealers in books in all the cities of the Union."[126]

Preparations began at least two years before the actual tour. In order to explain in March of 1866 why he had spent in the preceding half year almost £3,000 on reprints of the Cheap and Library editions, Dickens' publisher Frederic Chapman reported, "I find that it is necessary to keep a larger stock than we have been in the habit of keeping as I expect to receive frequent orders from America."[127] The twenty-three editions published by Petersons, the three from Hurd and Houghton, and the Diamond edition from Ticknor and Fields, which sold from 12,000 copies of *Pickwick* down to 2,000 of other titles, hardly satisfied the demand. Reorders from America of the collected editions published by Chapman and Hall continued unabated; we have noted that Fields took 2,000 complete sets of the illustrated Library edition in less than a year. "Even in England," a New York journal confided with pardonable exaggeration, "Dickens is less known than here."[128] In September 1858 *Harper's Weekly* insisted that Dickens was really more widely circulated in the States than in the United Kingdom;[129] he was serialized in magazines that sold between 100,000 and 200,000 each month and were read by many times that number, he was distributed free with newspapers, and his books appeared in countless versions retailing from pennies upward and printed in orders that ran to the tens of thousands. Ironically, largely due to the absence of any reciprocal copyright convention, Dickens became the largest selling author in the history of American publishing.[130]

— 6 —

There is a point on which Dickens and Dolby should not be misunderstood. . . . Money is what is wanted, and let it take any shape, it will be welcome.—*New York Herald*, 13 December 1867[131]

But the story we have been telling has reached an anticlimax. We began by proposing that Dickens' second American visit might have been shipwrecked by the same damaging controversy that nearly capsized his first, and we have concluded with a statement that he was the best-selling author in America. We have suffered through a long spell of squalls and thundershowers, but no deluge, only a sudden gust of wind heralding his second coming, then sunshine all the way. What happened was less a failure of narrative than a fortuitous collocation of circumstances that deflected or aborted criticism. It is difficult to find evidence for why something did not happen, but we can at least speculate with some assurance about the reasons for the comparative lack of hostility toward Dickens in the public and the press throughout his reading tour. First, and overriding all the others, was simply the magnitude of his fame. It was too great to be resisted, Longfellow believed, and Horace Greeley set it against the limited financial rewards Dickens had garnered from his writing: "The fame as a novelist which Mr. Dickens had already created in America, and which, at the best, has never yielded him anything particularly munificent or substantial, is become his capital stock in the present enterprise."[132] Since Dickens was no longer parodying American institutions, but British ones, in the States he suffered less from political opposition than he did after 1853 in England.[133]

Second, the shrill and unprincipled journals that had fought circulation was during the early 1840s, and used Dickens as a principal victim, had largely disappeared, and American publishing was grounded on a much more genteel and stable base. The *Herald* regularly and the *World* occasionally tried to whip up animosity, but in general all the leading figures in the trade supported Boz: the list of guests present at the farewell dinner, chaired by Greeley, reads like a who's who of American publishing.[134]

Third, Dickens carefully controlled his relations with the media. While still in England, he softened his criticism of America in new prefaces to the Charles Dickens edition. In his reply to Lytton's toast at his London farewell banquet, a speech well covered in the American press,[135] Dickens took pains to pay tribute to the "immense accumulation of letters from individuals, and associations of individuals, all expressing in the same hearty, homely, cordial, unaffected way, a kind of personal interest in me," that influenced his decision to go abroad, and "to see for myself the astonishing change and progress of a quarter of a century over there, to grasp the hands of many faithful friends whom I left upon those shores, to see the faces of a multitude of new friends upon whom I have never looked, and last, not least, to use my best endeavour to lay down a third cable of intercommunication and alliance between the old world and the new."[136]

While on tour, Dickens refrained from making public statements about contemporary issues. Since his visit was confined to the North, he had no particular occasion to speak out against slavery, though he thought privately that emancipation was merely a party trick to get votes. Public manners he thought decidedly improved, and newspapers likewise more civil and forbearing. Concentrating on work and his health, he made no effort to write up his experiences for subsequent publication. That decison, as well as Forster's poor health and unremitting opposition, helps to explain the lack of color and interest in his communications home.

The most striking exercise of Dickens' restraint was over the question of international copyright. In the midst of his tour, Representative Baldwin of Massachusetts, a member of the Joint Congressional Committee on Library, reported that a bill for reciprocal copyright agreements had been recommitted. To lobby for the bill, which some privately thought bad, but better than nothing, several publishers formed an International Copyright Association in February 1868. Even before Dickens' arrival in the States the press had confidently expected "that Dickens, who takes a deep interest in the question . . . , will have a conference with the principal publishers of New York on the subject, which has been and is a serious matter with authors, English and American."[137] But when the time came to speak out, Dickens remained silent, "on the ground," Dolby reports, "that he felt the case to be a hopeless one, as the Western men, in his opinion, were too strong for the legitimate publisher in the East. He gave his reasons why the passing of such an Act would be a matter of difficulty; as in his 'experiences he never found any people willing to pay for a thing they could legally steal,' and so he declined losing any time over the subject."[138] Disheartening fatigue and cynicism made him reluctant to take part in a stale controversy.

Finally, the public was aware of Dickens' illness. Each electrifying performance seemed a triumph of will over infirmity. Forster appends a characteristic account of Dickens' entry to the farewell banquet:

> At about five o'clock on Saturday the hosts began to assemble, but at 5:30 the news was received that the expected guest had succumbed to a painful affection [sic] of the foot. In a short time, however, another bulletin announced Mr. Dickens's intention to attend the dinner at all hazards. At a little after six, having been assisted up the stairs, he was joined by Mr. Greeley, and the hosts forming two lines silently permitted the distinguished gentleman to pass through. Mr. Dickens limped perceptibly; his right foot was swathed, and he leaned heavily on the arm of Mr. Greeley. He evidently suffered great pain.[139]

The *Herald,* swinging away till the end, carried a less heroic version of the event:

> Rather wearily "Boz" made his way from stair to stair supported by an implement greatly in vogue among disabled soldiers. In other words, "Boz" limped badly, and had all the appearing of what would be termed in Wall Street, and in a pecuniary sense, a "lameduck."
> At the landing, Mr. Greeley seized the gouty gentleman frantically by the hand. . . . "Boz" was escorted into the parlor by Mr. Greeley, in the exact center of which he paused, wiped his forehead significantly, and took a long breath—obviously dazed and half frightened. . . . Here several of the members of the fraternity stepped forward to his support as if in anticipation that he might faint.[140]

Such criticism as the public desired to level against Dickens was usually deflected to Dolby, his capable and long-suffering manager. The ticket speculators, whose most ingenious contrivances were generally foiled by Dolby's forethought, wrote anonymous letters and articles of the most abusive kind. Dolby's nickname among his friends, "P.H.," was suggested, he explained in his book, by a reference in the *New York World* to "pudding-headed Dolby."[141] Dickens went hardly anywhere, seldom dined out, refused all invitations to attend dramatic renditions of his works, even declined to attend parties given by his closest friends. Dolby, to the contrary, went everywhere, was visible and on the line to all complainants, made all the arrangements with hoteliers and impresarios, auditorium managers and ticket sellers, railways and coaches. The *Herald* grumbled on 13 December 1867: "Dickens is apparently to stand aside and seem to do the dignity—not to be mixed up with filthy lucre—and Dolby is to chaffer over the price."[142] Managing celebrities was a fairly new line of work in 1867; in this as in so many other ways, Dickens' preeminence caused revolutionary changes in the status of author. By sending Dolby in advance to pave the way, Dickens retained his popularity, an aura of powerful distinction, and leisure to rest from his exertions, without sacrificing, in the minds of his clamorous public, any of his affection for the common people.

The banquet at Delmonico's on 18 April afforded Dickens his only opportunity to speak out extensively on his changed view of America. He began by paying tribute to the working members of the press, at whose invitation he was present, adverting to his own training as a journalist. He went on to express, in the most flattering terms, his appraisal of the country that had been his host for four months: "I have been [astounded] by the amazing changes that I have seen around me on every side—changes moral, changes physical, changes in the amount of land subdued and peopled, changes in the rise of vast new cities, changes in the growth of older cities almost out of recognition, changes in the graces and amenities of life, changes in the Press, without whose advancement no advancement can be made anywhere. Nor am I, believe me, so arrogant as to suppose that in five-and-twenty years there have been no changes in me, . . . and that I had nothing to learn and no extreme impressions to correct from when I was here first. [*A voice—'Noble,' and applause.*]"[143]

He then detailed the character of those changes, in a passage subsequently added as a Postscript to the Charles Dickens edition of *American Notes* and printed under the heading "A Debt of Honour" in the 6 June 1868 issue of *All the Year Round:* "I have been, in the smallest places equally with the largest, . . . received with unsurpassable politeness, delicacy, sweet temper, hospitality, consideration, and with unsurpassable respect for the privacy daily enforced upon me by the nature of my avocation here, and the state of my health. This testimony, so long as I live, and so long as my descendants have any legal right in my books, I shall cause to be republished. . . . And this I will do and cause to be done, not in mere love and thankfulness, but because I regard it as an act of plain justice and honour."[144]

Dickens took back with him to England not only an altered view of America, but also a considerable portion of that fortune bequeathed to his family at his death two years later. Total receipts for the seventy-six readings[145] came to $228,000; expenses before and during the trip for Dolby and Dickens, for James Osgood and a staff of three, for halls, tickets, and advertisements, for a 5 percent commission to Ticknor and Fields (one of those perquisites of being Dickens' authorized American representatives), for hotels, transportation, meals, medication, and tips, reduced the net take to nearly £38,000. But since Dickens distrusted American currency after the war, he insisted on exchanging bills for gold at a 40 percent discount, so that his final profit amounted to only £19,000,[146] less than one-fifth of what the *New York Herald* predicted he would make off with: "We will send him home with a hundred thousand sterling."[147]

— 7 —

If there had been international copyright between England and the States, I should have been a man of very large fortune, instead of a man of moderate savings, always supporting a very expensive public position.—Charles Dickens to James T. Fields, "early in October" 1867[148]

But even £19,000 was a sizeable amount of money to get from a country of pirates. Clearly much had changed in twenty-five years; clearly the fears expressed on both sides of the Atlantic prior to the visit were exaggerated, and, where real, were dissipated in the warmth of the mutual affection exchanged between Dickens and his audiences during that frigid winter of 1868. He was, on the whole, treated well by American publishers and editors, and had been for some years prior to his journey. Indeed, if one looks at the record of American publishers and Dickens with a neutral eye, one sees a fairly respectable history, despite the abuses of 1842 and of the *Herald* in 1867, and the refusal of Congress and the American people to enter into any form of reciprocal convention covering literary properties. Even with these handicaps, Dickens made far more money from America than he did from Germany or France, where his books were published under agreements. Setting aside the pirates, who operated with impunity on both sides of the ocean and caused Dickens at least as much grief in London as in New York, the American firms of Carey, Lea and Blanchard, Harpers,

Ticknor and Fields, and even Petersons tried to observe trade courtesy, to remunerate Dickens fairly and in some cases freely for his works, and to deal straightforwardly with what was, at the least, a fluid and confusing situation. There was lots of unacknowledged borrowing, even in Harpers' magazines, either directly from Dickens or from his journals; but there were lots of acknowledgments too to this seemingly inexhaustible source of imagination—even some that were unwarranted: Mrs. Gaskell's story "Lizzie Leigh" was attributed to Dickens.[149]

By 1867, through authorized and unauthorized efforts, Dickens was as widely known in the United States as any living writer, English or American. There may be some justice to his complaint that with international copyright he would have been a man of large fortune, instead of moderate savings. But there is also truth to the fact that the second American tour, though threatened with the same kind of public controversy that had blighted the first, was phenomenally successful, that it netted Dickens directly more than 20 percent of his estate, and indirectly through the sale of his collected works several thousand additional pounds. In fairness, it is time to recognize that however "worthless and profitless" Dickens' American rights may have seemed to him when he wrote to Fields in October 1867, within less than a year they had proved very valuable indeed.

James A. Davies

STRIVING FOR HONESTY

An Approach to Forster's Life

JOHN FORSTER'S *Life of Charles Dickens* was his last completed literary biography, written during much mental and physical stress. It was also the last of several book-length studies of Dickens published immediately after the novelist's death. This essay is about the implications of such obviousness; it argues that the biography can be better understood and appreciated by relating it to Forster's other literary-biographical work, to the main circumstances of his personal situation, and to earlier biographies of Dickens.

During the 1830s Forster began a biography of Goldsmith; it was published in 1848 and followed by an extended version in 1854. While this work was proceeding he also published essays on Dryden, Churchill, Defoe, and Foote. "Sir Richard Steele" appeared during 1855, the year in which work began on a life of Swift originally envisaged as a paper in the *Quarterly Review.*[1] As a group these studies illustrate a consistent literary-biographical approach shaped by several basic influences. Those of his mentors, Charles Lamb and Leigh Hunt, and of his friend, Bulwer Lytton, partly explain Forster's choice of subjects while associating them with the idealization of writers and a concern for the dignity of literature.[2] Also, Forster had been trained as an advocate before turning to weekly journalism; the eighteenth-century studies were written at the height of his career as a commentator, editor, and reviewer, the lawyer-turned-journalist well practiced in undermining opposing points of view and in presenting partial impressions. The tenor of the times, the numerous pressures on biographical truth, was the strongest force of all.

Thus, Forster's work is both aggressively polemical and judiciously slanted, the former quality seen at its most extreme in the essay on Churchill. This opens with a full-blooded attack on Churchill's editor, William Tooke: "It would be difficult to imagine a worse biographer than Mr Tooke. . . . But though Mr Tooke is a bad biographer and a bad annotator, he is a worse critic. . . . Whether he praises or blames, he has the rare felicity of never making a criticism that is not a mistake."[3] Damning evidence is supplied and the attack extended to expose Tooke's factual and grammatical errors. Here is Forster the reviewer, "Pungent . . . of the Exterminator,"[4] the savage critic of Edwin Forrest's acting and Ainsworth's Jack Sheppard.[5] Boswell on Goldsmith; Scott and Hazlitt on Defoe; Macaulay on Foote, Steele, and Swift; Cooke on Foote; Jeffrey and Johnson on Swift—these are other targets. Frequently Forster's work seems that of a biographically inclined Tom Cribb.

As for judicious slanting, this involves suppression, distortion, and, for us, revealing comparisons with modern authorities.[6] Goldsmith's envy, coarseness in company, extravagant gambling, and failure to honor contracts; Churchill's hatred and harrying of Smollett and vindictive satirical attacks on the man who thwarted him of his father's living, his participation in the rites at Medmenham Abbey, the hedonism of his epitaph; Defoe's uncontrollable anger; Foote, fat and flabby, leaving his estate to his illegitimate sons; Steele's heavy drinking, homicidal dueling, monetary marriage, illegitimate children, and flagrant dishonesty; Swift as absentee parish priest and congenital misanthrope—all are silently omitted from Forster's pages.

Whitwell Elwin noted that Forster "could scarcely bring himself to recognize that moral meannesses could coexist with majesty of intellect, or that a man, who was a genius in his books, could out of his line be inferior to ordinary mortals";[7] Fonblanque wrote to Forster: "Your office of righting wronged reputations is a noble one."[8] Such comments point accurately to the nature of Forster's work, yet he did not write simple hagiography. Despite the suppressions even the most favorable account, that of Defoe, does not quite "extol his hero throughout":[9] Forster does indicate Defoe's imaginative limitations, such as his failure, often, to appreciate qualities that transcended "the merely shrewd, solid, acute, and palpable."[10] Churchill was given to "violent extremes . . . carrying a hatred of hypocrisy beyond the verge of prudence . . . to the very borders of licentiousness."[11] Steele was improvident; Foote, "the heedless, light-hearted coxcomb,"[12] often indulged in cruel public mimicry of the famous; Goldsmith was too often the dandy, too often impulsive, too often foolishly oversensitive; Swift sometimes wrote coarsely and abusively.

But such faults, argued Forster, resulted either from spontaneity (Churchill and Swift splendidly carried away in the heat of literary and political battle, Foote enraptured by his own creativity, Steele and Goldsmith tempted by the good things of life or into ill-afforded kindness) or from unpropitious circumstances, the latter clearly seen in Forster's comment on Churchill: "The stars do not more surely keep their courses, than an ill-regulated manhood will follow a misdirected youth." Churchill's riotous life was the consequence of "a marriage most imprudent—most unhappy," contracted too early in life as a reaction to parental pressure to enter the church. Similarly, Defoe's limitations were linked to his "Presbyterian breeding," and Goldsmith's faults further explained by reference to his unhappy childhood, the boy persecuted because of ugliness and seeming stupidity: "It was early to trample fun out of a child; and he bore marks of it to his dying day." The insults and brutality of college life also cast a "shadow . . . over his spirit, the uneasy sense of disadvantage which obscured his manners in later years."[13] In contrast, the silent suppressions relate to faults both socially dishonorable and indicative of basic personal deficiencies, faults hard to excuse or condone, and too often occurring when the spontaneous became the uncontrolled.

Forster's *selection* of material is also governed by recognizable principles. The eighteenth-century studies illustrate the Romantic fallacy that the nature of the work reflects the author's character: for example, Steele's *Tatler* "could have arisen only to a fancy as pure as the heart that prompted it was loving and true,"[14] and Forster wrote to Bulwer: "I question . . . that effects declared to be almost universally good and even fascinating, and especially to the young, could possibly have been produced by a man who sat down with a 'deliberately malignant' design. I don't believe it of any one—and especially I deny it of Swift."[15] But, though Forster considered that his subjects produced idealistic and morally sound literature, they were generally regarded as an unlikely band of paragons, the main biographical problem being clearly put in a letter from B. W. Procter: "You must be so tired and perplexed with your labour, in trying to make out a good character for Mr. Jonathan Swift."[16] The solution involved the concept of "essential character," an inviolate core of innate goodness expressed by the author's works. Hence Forster's description of Goldsmith: "His existence was a continued privation. . . . But . . . he passes through it all without one enduring stain upon the childlike purity of his heart," and frequent assertions that Goldsmith "looked into his heart and wrote."[17]

Closely allied to "essential character" is Forster's idea of genius: "To charming issues did the providence of Goldsmith's genius shape these rough-hewn times. It was not alone that it made him wise enough to know what infirmities he had, but it gave him the rarer wisdom of turning them to entertainment and to profit. . . . It lighted him to those last uses of experience and suffering which have given him an immortal name."[18] And, from Forster's account of Dryden composing *The Fables:* "It was thus amid the most grinding incidents of poverty, and in immediate contrast to the remorseless and close-shut coffers of the publisher, that the superabundant wealth of the poet's genius overflowed all restraints at last, and, regardless of such things as Tonsons in the world around it, poured itself freely forth to gladden future generations." [19]

Inviolate itself, literary genius transforms circumstances and reassures its possessor. Such ideas may partly reflect the influence of Carlyle's lectures on "The Hero as Man of Letters," which Forster attended and from which he quoted in the life of Goldsmith; Carlyle, like Forster, insists on the writer's "inward sphere" of superior moral qualities expressed by the literary work. But there is one important difference: Carlyle's mystical rhetoric is absent from Forster's work. Whereas, for example, Carlyle envisages literary genius as "continually unfolding the Godlike to men," [20] in Forster's scheme, to use only the quotations immediately above, it "shaped" and "overflowed." Such words are more matter-of-fact than transcendental, for Forster's literary-biographical method associates the Romantic with, if not the ordinary, at least the *socially* desirable.

The latter is heavily stressed. Above all, Forster's writers are indomitable: Goldsmith "shows to the last a bright and cordial happiness of soul, unconquered and unconquerable," Foote has "a fulness and invincibility of *courage* . . . which unfailingly warded off humiliation," Churchill a compelling fearlessness. They are men of integrity: what Forster wrote of Swift ("He had nothing in him of the hired scribe, and was never at any time in any one's pay") [21] applies to all his subjects. Despite intolerable financial pressures they wage ceaseless war against hypocrisy and corruption.

> He [Defoe] did not stand at the highest point of toleration, or of moral wisdom; but with his masculine active arm, he helped to lift his successors over obstructions which had stayed his own advance. He stood apart and alone in his opinions and his actions from his fellow men; but it was to show his fellow men of later times the value of a juster and larger fellowship, and of more generous modes of action. And when he now retreated from the world Without to the world Within in the solitariness of his unrewarded service and integrity, he had assuredly earned the right to challenge the higher recognition of posterity. He was walking toward History with steady feet; and might look up into his awful face with a brow unabashed and undismayed. [22]

Limitations and virtues are indicated, but the passage is most important as an example of the assertive, angular, muscular, almost uncouth language typical of these studies and embodying a main principle of Forster's approach. His writers *strive*, and even though general recognition, let alone monetary reward, is rarely gained, yet such massive perseverance *forces* praise from the discerning contemporary and from posterity. Such work offers a literary-biographical equivalent to the "Epilogue to Asolando," or literary heroes fit for Samuel Smiles. They are also fit for Forster himself because he endows them with his own qualities: Forster, too, was indomitable, courageous, a man of integrity, and a striver after literary fame and power. His real-life relationships were often strained because he sought to transform friends into self-portraits. He was more successful with the dead.

The stress on the socially commendable is a manifestation of the influence of Hunt, Lamb, and Bulwer: the eighteenth-century studies combine to present literary history from Dryden onward in terms of the desire of writers for social acceptance and just rewards. Dryden was "the first writer of any significance who composedly faced the world on the solid and settled basis of literary pursuits. . . . Literature was his trade: he not only lived upon its wages, but was never ashamed to own it. . . . It was a man's own fault, after this, if he was thought disreputable because he wrote for bread."[23] Defoe, Steele, and Swift represented the next stage: "At the critical moment when the people were rising into the first importance, men who could best use the pen found themselves best able to influence and persuade them. Speakers to either Lords or Commons had no such influence, for the reporting of debates was unknown, and their speaking remained within their four walls. What the orator now is, the writer was then, with the world for his audience."[24] Though Forster's fascination for "the party of literary politicians"[25] of Queen Anne's time came naturally to one who, as *Examiner* editor and general man-of-letters, sought to become a Victorian equivalent, it was not uncritical: dependence upon the whims of politicians and the promises of office made literary men, despite their achievements, little better than slaves. And even though Defoe, Steele, and Swift were men of integrity, literary men as a class lost their reputation through associating with corrupt and scheming politicians.

For Foote, Churchill, and Goldsmith, matters did not improve: "It was, in truth, one of those times of Transition which press hardly on all whose lot is cast in them. The patron was gone; and the public had not come. The seller of books had as yet exclusive command over the destiny of those who wrote them; and he was difficult of access; without certain prospect of the trade wind, hard to move." Literary men had lost both high office and influence and were still slaves, though now controlled by the bookseller: "the Man of Genius . . . must descend in the social scale" and, again despite exceptions, " 'man-of-letters' became the synonyme [*sic*] for dishonest hireling."[26]

Goldsmith's life of poverty and misery, chronologically the last of Forster's eighteenth-century studies, is offered as an example of how not to treat literary genius, Forster departing from his biographical brief to argue that mid-Victorian England needed to recognize such genius without patronage or other degradation. This recognition was not a question of money, for "the public have quite altered these matters since the days of Dryden. Their direct interference has placed upon a basis entirely different the whole question of literature and literary pursuits. A writer of any merit is now as little dependent on the generoisity of a publisher, as on the more degrading charity of a patron."[27] Rather, the concern was for social respectability, as is made clear by Dickens' reaction to *Goldsmith:* "The gratitude of every man who is content to rest his station and claims quietly on literature, and to make no feint of living by anything else, is your due for evermore."[28] The "dignity" theme unifies all Forster's literary-historical work.

After 1860 and the publication of *Biographical Essays,* Forster turned from literary biography to seventeenth-century history only to be recalled by Landor's death in 1864. Very reluctantly he prepared to honor a long-standing promise to write the life of his friend. Forster was in poor health and had other books to write, including the much-deferred *Swift* and a new life of Strafford. He was in his "Podsnap" period, married to a wealthy widow, installed in a Kensington mansion, long retired from journalistic controversy, a historian with an honorary doctorate from Trinity College Dublin, one of Her Majesty's Commissioners of Lunacy, and Very Highly Respectable. Landor had been a wildly impulsive and increasingly embarrassing friend whose scandalous behavior in old age had led Forster to pack him off to die in Italy. Forster's own part in the exiling, concerned more for the proprieties than for the welfare of a senile eighty-three-year-old, had been far from praiseworthy.[29] There were also libel laws to be considered.[30] The assignment was far from attractive.

Much of *Walter Savage Landor* is very dull, and consists of arid summaries of Landor's works, long illustrative quotations, extracts from correspondence offered without comment. But it is of interest for two reasons. First, and for the first time, we see Forster applying his biographical principles to the life of a close friend. Polemical attacks on Landor's critics, suppression and falsification of material,[31] some attempt to explain Landor's faults in terms of his undisciplined childhood and early freedom from monetary cares, the basic pattern of struggle and worldly failure, part of Landor's works offered as evidence of "the nobler part of his character," the attempt to stress socially acceptable qualities, all remind us of Forster's earlier studies. So, too, does the language of undaunted striving: "To the end we see him as it were unconquerable. He keeps an unquailing aspect to the very close, has yielded nothing in the duel he has been fighting so long single-handed with the world, and dies at last with harness on his back."[32]

Second, despite the similarities, there are crucial differences in

Forster's approach. Even though he indicates Landor's good qualities, such as his ability to inspire affection and his "pervading passion for liberty," now he is openly critical of the essential character both of his subject and his subject's literary works. Landor's failure properly to educate his children ("such nonsense . . . Such a fool's paradise") and his desertion of his family ("more for his own sake than for theirs") are condemned unequivocally as expressions of an extreme and damaging egotism, and even though libel laws prevented explicit mention of Landor's improprieties, such as the seduction of Nancy Jones and the old man's scandalous relationship with sixteen-year-old Geraldine Harper, Forster does hint strongly at these. And, in Landor's work, Forster detects basic flaws, writing, for example, of *Gebir,* that "impetuosity, want of patience, is as bad in literature as in life."[33]

Further, and not only because of personal faults and literary defects, Landor was hard to associate with the "dignity of literature" theme; "Landor wrote without any other aim than to please himself," knew nothing of the hardships of the author by profession, and refused to write for pay. The biography's real hero is Southey, "the representative man of letters of his day";[34] Forster prints his correspondence and eulogizes his character. The "dignity" theme is thus carried into the nineteenth century but at the expense of Landor's reputation. Forster preserved his own by presenting himself, in *Walter Savage Landor,* as the man who furthered Landor's literary career and sought to keep his friend out of trouble; Landor was grateful but not always obedient; he begged Forster to be his biographer. Here is the predictable (because partial) reaction of Forster-as-Podsnap and a contrast to the treatment of Landor, to the more insistent fact that at that point in his life when Forster seemed more likely to purvey whitewashed distortion he began to incline toward honesty.

Walter Savage Landor appeared in 1869; in 1870 Dickens died and Forster began "the inexpressibly sorrowful task"[35] of examining Dickens' letters. His health was appalling, his serious illnesses including rheumatic fever, rheumatism, bronchitis, gout, a liver complaint, skin diseases, and, in 1872, "frightful attacks of giddiness and sickness." He was "hurried and harried" on the asylum circuits of the Lunacy Commission, often traveling in dreadful weather. His last surviving sister died in 1869 and was followed by Dyce, Maclise, Fonblanque, Bulwer, and Macready, before *The Life of Charles Dickens* was complete. In December 1870 he wrote to Bulwer: "The joy is gone out of my life—but I struggle on much as I can, with no certainty from day to day."[36]

The state of Forster's "now" must have tempted him to sentimentalize the biographical "then." The idealizing tendency of Forster's approach to literary subjects, the constraints of libel laws with many principals still alive, the support of Georgina Hogarth and Dickens' daughter Mamie, the early appearance of significant studies of Dickens by Hotten, blandly uncritical, and Sala, adulatory,[37] Forster's own affection for and admiration of his dead friend, his own Respectability, would seem to make such temptation irresistible.

Most modern critics agree that Forster succumbed. Notable exceptions are the Leavises, who appear to assert the straightforward and candid nature of Forster's presentation: "Forster . . . gives us the sense . . . of being really inward with Dickens's personality and character, and without being concerned to make out a case by 'interpreting' his subject."[38] The Leavises' views are enthusiastically restated by Elliot Engel who, misleadingly, suggests that they are widely accepted.[39] But other commentators divide into two groups defined in terms of their reactions to the succumbing. The first group considers that Forster made an effort to tell the truth and achieved a certain truthfulness before idealizing pressures prevailed. Thus George H. Ford points to Forster's valuable insights into Dickens' complex character, yet concludes that Forster's desire "to paint an accurate portrait of one of his closest friends" could not be and was not reconciled with the "idealized conception of Dickens' character"[40] that dominates the biography. Sylvère Monod reminds us that Forster "did not use a tone of uniform praise. . . . Self-centredness, vein of hardness, intellectual limitations, are all there"; but, in the end, Forster "said about as much as he thought he could say after his life-long friendship and with a good many of the family still around him."[41]

Group two is less inclined to stress Forster's good intentions, and views him, more simply, as a successful idealizer. K. J. Fielding notes Forster's exclusion of uniquely personal reminiscence, considers he evades such controversial issues as the separation and Dickens' relations with his wife, and sees the whole as the distorting "biography of a friend."[42] Gerald G. Grubb states that "almost everything of any consequence which Forster omitted was the result of deliberate design, not of ignorance, . . . [to] keep alive the public idolatry of Dickens, and to please, insofar as possible, the conflicting elements of Dickens' own family."[43] Madeline House and Graham Storey differ from Grubb only in their assessment of the nature of Forster's idealism: "He was . . . concerned not simply with the public image . . . but with the truth, as he conceived it. The *Life* contains numerous small distortions of fact, but paradoxically these distortions were in the interest of a larger, or ideal truth."[44] Alec W. Brice makes much the same point but explains it in terms of a "Romantic theory of biography": original materials were manipulated or altered so that, in F. R. Hart's words, quoted by Brice, they would "accord more closely with . . . [the biographer's] intuitive grasp of his subject."[45] Group two is completed by Edgar Johnson and the implications of his massive biography: the reminders of what Forster must have known but carefully suppressed.[46]

The Leavises' view, based as it is on the fallacious idea that only inept modern biographers offer "interpretations" of their subjects, can be set aside, with Engel's championing, as undiscriminating. This present essay seeks to relate to the other modern critics. Like them, it accepts that Forster idealizes; unlike them, it does not believe that idealization is the biographer's main aim. And whereas the most favorable commentators treat Forster as being truthful and perceptive only up to a point, this essay emphasizes that Forster does face the consequences of his perceptivity. In other words, this essay, in arguing that, despite idealizing pressures, Forster sought valiantly to convey the truth, aims to reverse the view of Ford and Monod. Or, to put matters in yet another way: modern critics, with their stress on Forster's "deliberate design" in the interests of idealization, offer implicit support for a view of the *Life* as illustrative of the principles that govern Forster's eighteenth-century literary studies, but it is now suggested that the study of the latter, and of *Landor,* in relation to the *Life,* is the best way of demonstrating that, in the *Life,* Forster's biographical approach has changed.

The change is not absolute, for, to an extent, the *Life* is another work by a slanting polemicist and partial advocate. As has been clearly demonstrated elsewhere, documents were edited and falsified to stress the lively, sparkling side of Dickens and to remove vulgarisms or the cutting response. Some socially damaging facts were suppressed, such as Dickens' dandyism, the extent of family sponging, antagonism toward the established church, and the depth of his pessimism about the condition of England.[47] Forster is again able to assert, more plausibly because of the suppressions, the Romantic relationship between author and work: much of the latter taught "the invaluable lesson of what men ought to be from what they are" and reflected "that inner life which essentially constituted the man."[48] The associated concept of inviolate genius is, here, socialized by Forster to stress both Dickens' indomitable spirit and integrity, and those of his qualities attractive to hearth and home: Dickens the family man, the lover of regularity and order, and Dickens the hearty extrovert, never bookish, never highbrow, fond of riding, of walking, of amateur dramatics, the irrepressible companion, the good friend, the philanthropist. To this extent Dickens is assimilated into Forster's "composite literary man," Daniel Richard Dickens, perhaps, or Charles Oliver Defoe.

But the *Life* reveals what *Landor* revealed, that whereas, when writing of the long-dead, Forster could impose ideas (about biography, literary men, personality) upon all his material, when writing of his friends the immediacy of their lives' truth drew him toward honest revelation, to a fundamental change of emphasis apparent in *Landor* and intensified in the *Life.* In the former, Forster faced facts but had to draw back from complete disclosure; in the latter, despite some local bias and falsification, so far as the key incidents are concerned Forster not only faces facts but also seeks ways round obstacles to explicitness.

The contrast between the *Life* and Forster's earlier works shows the change in his principles. Such change is underlined when Forster's treatment of key topics is contrasted with the work of Hotten and Sala, the most important pre-Forster biographers of Dickens. Thus, Hotten's treatment of Dickens' childhood and youth simply refers to his "education at a good school" and his boyhood reading of "the standard works of the best authors";[49] Sala is more certain but equally inaccurate: "He had not been born in poverty, but in a respectable middle-class family. He had never known—save, perhaps, in early youth, the occasional 'harduppishness' of a young man striving to attain a position—actual poverty. . . . He had no terrible experiences to tell. . . . From youth to age he lived in honour, and affluence, and splendour."[50] Only Forster knew the truth, and Engel has skilfully shown, with special reference to Dickens' childhood and youth, that "one way of understanding the value of Forster's work is to discover how much information about Dickens it revealed which was completely new to the Victorian reader."[51] But most impressive is the use Forster makes of this unique material. Dickens' autobiographical account is linked to the rags-to-riches theme of the *Life,* as the source of "the fixed and eager determination, the restless and resistless energy, which opened to him opportunities of escape from many mean environments, not by turning off from any path of duty, but by resolutely rising to such excellence of distinction as might be attainable in it"; it is also the beginning of the countertheme, the relationship between the early humiliations and Dickens' persisting and ultimately self-destructive faults of character: "A too great confidence in himself, a sense that everything was possible to the will that would make it so, laid occasionally upon him self-imposed burdens greater than might be borne by any one with safety."[52] The purely pathetic and sentimental potential of the account is manfully resisted.

The presence of theme and countertheme supports Monod's and Ford's assertion that Forster's approach is not simply uncritical. But the consequences of such explicit statements, in particular the rigorous tracing of character flaws, are also faced with some frankness. And when sufficient frankness is not possible Forster resorts to a kind of fearless implication: documents are printed and arranged so that they seem to speak for themselves. We can see this in a minor way in, for example, Forster's treatment of Dickens' relations with Richard Bentley. Though Forster refrains from explicit condemnation of Dickens' lack of moral awareness in his disputes with the publisher, he does print the letter in which Dickens admits to having foolishly accepted the poor terms to which he was now objecting, refers to his (Forster's) "no small difficulty in restraining him from throwing up the agreement altogether," thus implying where at least some right lay, before appealing, with slight ambiguity, for a "considerate construction to be placed on every effort made by [Dickens] to escape from obligations incurred in ignorance of the sacrifices implied by them."[53]

Again, and without comment, Forster offers much quite startling evidence of the morbid side of Dickens' imagination: for example, he does not delete Dickens' thoughts of the drowned, in *The Old Curiosity Shop,* with "the stars shining down upon their drowned eyes," or Dickens' description of his eagerness when in America to "see the exact localities where Professor Webster did that amazing murder." Forster retains Dickens' thoughts of Mary Hogarth, including his friend's reaction to Mrs. Hogarth's death that meant he could no longer be buried next to daughter Mary ("I cannot bear the thought of being excluded from her dust"), and Dickens' strange and emotional dream of Mary Hogarth's apparition urging Roman Catholicism upon him. The last incident draws from Forster direct references to "trying regions of reflection" that trouble men of genius, and to Dickens' "disturbing fancies."[54]

Forster allows such incidents to offer evidence of Dickens' obsessive and insensitive single-mindedness. This use of the frank and the implicit in developing the countertheme is most clearly and importantly seen in his handling of two key topics—Dickens' marital troubles and the reading tours. Once more, we are helped to see the changed emphasis in Forster's work by contrasting it with Hotten's and Sala's. Hotten attempts to whitewash the marital troubles: brief references to the *Household Words* "manifesto" and to "a misunderstanding . . . betwixt Mr. and Mrs. Dickens, of a purely domestic character—so domestic— almost trivial, indeed—that neither law nor friendly arbitration could define or fix the difficulty sufficiently clear to adjudicate upon it. . . . We trust the reader will think we act wisely in dropping any further mention of it."[55] Sala is pompously vague: "He chose . . . to make the fact of his domestic troubles public; although into the circumstances thereof he did not enter. But he published . . . a vehement vindication of himself from some attacks, or some scandalous imputations so wildly improbable in their nature, and so obscure that their very existence was ignored by ninety-nine out of every hundred men and women who began to wonder at the passionateness of his defence. . . . Nothing more need or can be said. . . . Those who have a right to speak, have not spoken; and the world has no right to enquire into the mystery—if any mystery there be—nor will have, any time these fifty years."[56]

Forster is more candid. He illustrates Dickens' developing unhappiness, analyzes his state of mind in 1858, and sees Dickens' inability properly to consider others and his impulsive and restless behavior as

manifestations of the too-great concern for self and the fierce determination to get what he wanted that were legacies of the early hardship:
Forster criticizes the "manifesto" and the writing of the "violated letter," and states: "Thenceforward he and his wife lived apart. The eldest son went with his mother, Dickens at once giving effect to her
expressed wish in this respect; and the other children remained with
himself, their intercourse with Mrs. Dickens being left entirely to
themselves."[57] Forster writes with impressive compassion and events
force from him the haunting phrase and some fine sentences: "There
was for him no 'city of the mind' against outward ills, for inner consolation and shelter. It was in and from the actual he still stretched forward
to find the freedom and satisfactions of an ideal, and by his very attempts to escape the world he was driven back into the thick of it."[58]
The moving imagery and rhythms appropriate in their anguished awkwardness suggest both Dickens' predicament and his biographer's sincere sadness. Nonetheless, Forster goes as far as the libel laws allowed
and at the end of "Volume the Third" he prints Dickens' will.

Hotten had remarked that "After his [Dickens'] wishes had been
put into legal form by his solicitors, he copied out the entire document
in his own handwriting."[59] Hotten then quoted Dickens' description of
Georgina Hogarth as "the best friend I ever had," his instructions for a
quiet burial, and his expressions of religious faith. Forster, however,
prints the will in its entirety, an inclusion almost certainly unique in
Victorian biography. In doing so he is able to give Ellen Ternan due
prominence as first legatee and the recipient of a generous bequest and
is able to remind his readers of his own role as Dickens' "dear and
trusty friend" and an executor of the will. Further, the will provides a
penetrating insight into Dickens' thinking and household arrangements
by contrasting Georgina Hogarth, his children's "ever useful self-deny-
ing and devoted friend,"[60] with Mrs. Dickens, the unhelpful benefi-
ciary of Dickens' postmarital financial generosity. The will is a cruel
and bitter document, final suggestive testimony of those faults of character that aggravated the separation. Its inclusion circumvents libel laws
and other pressures to demonstrate the strength of Forster's desire to
tell the whole truth, and to undermine such criticism as, for instance,
that of K. J. Fielding that Forster offers only "the vaguest outline"[61] of
the separation story. Even Edgar Johnson's great biography can offer
little more on Dickens' domestic feelings at this time than can be de-
duced from the material Forster supplies.[62]

Finally, the reading tours: Hotten records without comment that,
in 1858, Dickens began to read "professionally, and as an avowed
source of income,"[63] and cites dates and subjects during his narrative.
Sala's main concern is with the "Sikes and Nancy" reading, questioning
the "taste and the usefulness of the display," criticizing Dickens for

some overacting, and summing up: "[Dickens gained] by these performances many thousands of pounds, but losing, I am afraid, many years
of the life which he might have reasonably hoped to attain."[64] Forster
begins with Dickens' request for his opinion, restates his opposition to
the readings ("It was a substitution of lower for higher aims; a change
to commonplace from more elevated pursuits; and it had so much of
the character of a public exhibition for money as to raise, in the question of respect for his calling as a writer, a question also of respect for
himself as a gentleman"),[65] and then, once again, ascribes Dickens' dis-
regard of all arguments against the tours to the defects of character
consequent upon his traumatic upbringing by repeating his earlier
comments about Dickens' hard and aggressive confidence and fierce
determination. Having expressed his disapproval, Forster then devotes
over a quarter of "Volume the Third" to descriptions of the tours,
mainly in Dickens' own words, that exhibit significant changes of emphasis.

Thus, during the early days, Dickens' letters concentrate on places
and people; there is nothing like the accounts of income in the chapter
on the second series: "On the 18th I finished the readings as I pur-
posed. We had between seventy and eighty pounds *in the stalls,* which,
at four shillings apiece, is something quite unprecedented in these
times. . . . The result of the six was, that, after paying a large staff of
men and all other charges, and Arthur Smith's ten per cent, on the
receipts, and replacing everything destroyed in the fire at St. Martin's
Hall (including all our tickets, country-baggage, cheque-boxes, books,
and a quantity of gas-fittings and what not), I got upwards of £500. A
very great result." Succeeding references to "Hunted Down," that "its
principal claim to notice was the price paid for it," and to "two brief extracts from letters of the dates respectively of the 8th of April and the
28th of June will *sufficiently describe* the London readings,"[66] the extracts referring exclusively to box-office takings and the possibility of
taking more, show Forster suggesting potently that, for Dickens, mon-
eymaking now came above all else. During the American tour Dickens'
letters reduce people to numbers, are much obsessed with occurrences
that might decrease takings, such as the activities of speculators, and
crow over the eclipse of competition. At the end of that chapter Forster
offers a detailed analysis of American takings and earnings and, only
four pages later, quotes Dickens' own similarly detailed account of the
great financial triumph. A report of the "Last Readings" then follows,
but now dominated by Dickens' dreadful ill health.

Forster had been literary adviser to Chapman and Hall, and to several popular writers, continuing as Bulwer's valued associate until the
latter's death in 1872. His special talent was the understanding of popular taste and reaction. Because of this it is hard to accept G. H. Ford's

opinion that "Forster was simply overwhelmed by the difficulties of writing about a contemporary to whom he had been too closely attached,"[67] particularly if we recall his controlled use of material in the eighteenth-century studies and considered attempt at honesty in his life of Landor. It seems odd to deny that Forster knew exactly what he was doing in the *Life,* when he reprinted the will and organized his documents to suggest that Dickens killed himself for money. Forster is no longer the restorer of wronged reputations but a biographer valuing integrity in the face of mealy mouthed pressures.

This last is underlined as we recall Forster's own abiding obsession with the "dignity of literature," and the unifying progress from Dryden through the essays to Goldsmith and on to Southey that seems, in the early stages of the *Life,* to be completed by Dickens: "He would have laughed if, at this outset of his wonderful fortune in literature, his genius acknowledged by all without misgiving, young, popular, and prosperous, any one had compared him to the luckless men of letters of former days, whose common fate was to be sold into a slavery which their later lives were passed in vain endeavours to escape from. Not so was his fate to be, yet, something of it he was doomed to experience."[68] But the shining jewel of the literary profession, the man who, through the good influence of his books and the example of his life, seemed to be forcing "writer" and "gentleman" into permanent juxtaposition, not only began writing books that attacked the very foundations of the society whose acclaim Forster wished literary men to receive but also took up with an actress half his age, separated from his wife, and made much money through nonliterary, ungentlemanly, and obsessively self-destructive activities. Forster's chagrin must have been intense, yet, amidst disappointed hopes and crumbling theories, he sought valiantly and ingeniously to be truthful to life.

A final brave consequence is Forster's treatment of his own role in Dickens' life. As is well known, Forster also manipulated and falsified documents to emphasize Dickens' reliance upon him and to counter the fact that the two had been less close in later years.[69] There is, as G. H. Ford has shown, a long tradition of regarding the biography as an expression of Forster's egotism: "The Autobiography of John Forster with Recollections of Charles Dickens." Ford himself stresses that "in the biography itself, it is the egotism which is especially evident."[70] But the traditional view is too simple. Fielding notes that Forster sometimes suppressed complimentary references to himself in Dickens' letters;[71] Grubb concludes that, in the extant letters, Forster "omitted or toned down most of the passages in which Dickens expressed his deep regard for his biographer, most of those in which he expressed his dependence upon him as a critic, most passages in which Dickens undertook to thank him for his services as a mediator."[72] Forster could have said

very much more about the overall effect he had on Dickens' work, and
he says little or nothing about, for example, the platform and support
he provided for Dickens in the *Examiner,* and the way he brought
Dickens into London literary life. Self-aggrandizement is thus an inadequate description of his approach. We see further that Forster's treatment of himself is consistent with his treatment of Dickens: whereas, in
treating his friend, a more localized idealizing is countered by a general
emphasis on frankness and implicit revelation, so, in treating himself, a
carefully controlled stress on his own importance is at least balanced by
what can, perhaps, be called a policy of dissociation. It is hard to agree,
for example, with the Leavises, that Forster was simply concerned "to
give himself greater importance in relation to Dickens in the eyes of his
world,"[73] when, after the closeness and affection of the early relationship, Forster is almost anxious to show how frequently Dickens ignored his advice. Forster advised against Dickens taking the editorship
of the *Daily News,* against separating from his wife, against making a
public statement about the separation, against giving paid public readings, against the tour of America, against the inclusion of the
Sikes/Nancy reading. We are allowed to see only too clearly that he may
as well have kept silent. The resemblance to his role in *Walter Savage
Landor* is considerable, but with the difference, again marking the
changing emphasis, that Forster's treatment of himself in the *Life* is of a
piece with the treatment of his subject.

John Forster has not been regarded as an honest biographer of
Dickens; certainly, he falls short of modern scholarly practice. But his
approach has been misunderstood, his achievement underrated. In the
spectacle of an aging, ill, and saddened man seeking to reject all applicable biographical precedents, telling much and, when unable to tell
more, implying much more, there is the kind of heroism, the undaunted attempts at obstacles, the striving toward commendable goals,
that Forster very often portrayed in his writer subjects. There is much
to be said for such an opinion as Longfellow's: "To write the life of a
dear friend just gone, must be a task almost too painful. How fearlessly
and well you have done yours I need not say. . . . You give an exact
portrait of Dickens, and have had the courage not to conceal some
things that others might have hidden, but which make the likeness true
and lifelike."[74]

Earle Davis

DICKENS AND SIGNIFICANT TRADITION

THE GROWTH of Dickens from the status of supreme entertainer to serious analyst of society is one of fiction's most interesting stories. When he first began constructing *Pickwick Papers* in 1836 (we recall that he was twenty-four years old) until his publication of *David Copper-field*—say about 1850—he invented a remarkable number of best-selling narratives which seized and gripped the sensibilities of a vast reading public, and almost always for purposes of reading pleasure and escape into romantic make-believe.

Most critics suspect that the greatest fiction goes beyond amusement and suspense into the realm of significant analysis of human problems, that is, philosophy, politics, ethics, psychology, social relationships, or whatever makes readers think seriously. This accomplishment is rarely reached by entertainment alone (no matter how good the story is—as a story). Nor is significance attained merely by tacking a simple moral purpose on to the action. There is always the possibility that life may be selected or distorted so that the good always suffer or the bad reach prosperity, or vice versa. Fielding achieved greatness primarily by ironically defending the opposite of what he believed to be true. Jane Austen and Emily Brontë used other means, but they achieved significance. The point with reference to Dickens is that he started out a remarkable storyteller and ended a social analyst who invited his readers to judge Victorian society. It is this significance which elevates him to eternal literary importance.

Dickens' basic appeal in his earliest novels was humor founded firmly upon the exploitation of eccentricity. His caricatured immortals form a spectacular panorama, from Mr. Jingle and Sam Weller to Mrs. Gamp and Mr. Micawber. Most of these characters were memorable for their individual manners of talking, speech which often was decorated with repeatable tags of expression, mannerisms which stamped them forever on the reader's memory. Farcical involvement in ridiculous situations added to the effect of light entertainment, and so it became natural for anyone who in real life sees a sufficiently peculiar individual to say that he is just like a character out of Dickens.

We who know Dickens well realize all this; we know how he involved his eccentrics in standard melodramatic action, how his plot conflicts resembled the stereotyped examples which had been the traditional materials of stage and previous romantic fiction. He also investigated highly sentimental scenes and asked his readers to shed tears as well as laugh. He drew upon the grotesque and the suspenseful elements of the tale of terror. He utilized Gothic atmosphere, occasionally borrowed from the lore of history, experimented with mysteries, described crime and murder, and the remarkable narrative accomplishment of alternating these resources made sure that he held the attention of his reading public no matter what its other interests.

The climax to the career of Dickens the entertainer was the publication of *David Copperfield*. Surely the autobiography of the boy whose life story derives in some part from Dickens' own experiences, told with breathtaking appeal in the early chapters which are transfigured by the use of the wise but childish first-person, reaches a stunning height for the novel which takes us into and out of the real world. When he was in our world, his characters and backgrounds were very exact, even photographic. Santayana once said that "the secret of this new world of Dickens lies . . . in the combination of the strictest realism of detail with a fairy-tale unreality of general atmosphere."[1]

Certainly generations of Dickens-lovers have been willing to spend years in worship of the great entertainer, alternately enjoying the novels because of the comedy or the sentiment or the melodrama. Most of the typical worshipers have been less amused by the later novels, ostensibly because the eccentrics were not quite so funny, but often because Dickensians felt that the materials were suddenly more complex, that the plots became more serious and heavy, that the tone achieved darkness rather than light entertainment. It was more fun and less demanding to be Pickwickian than to live in the bleaker atmosphere of intense social analysis.

Dickens did not suddenly become a serious critic of Victorian society without having previously shown signs of criticizing the ills of society. He had from the earliest tales definite opinions about the things he found wrong in his world. He made the farcical tone of *Pickwick Papers* deepen toward the end with a moving picture of the nauseous debtors' prison. He attacked poorhouses and big city delinquency in *Oliver Twist*. He made a sally against vicious schools for boys in *Nicholas Nickleby*, against the horrible living and working conditions experienced by the victims of the Industrial Revolution in *The Old Curiosity Shop*, against religious intolerance in *Barnaby Rudge;* and he had pilloried egotism and hypocrisy in *Martin Chuzzlewit*. It is safe to suggest, however, that all this was primarily added to appeal to reader interest and entertainment.

In any case his selection of social evils in need of reform looks from the distance of the twentieth century to be relatively negligible in comparison with the accomplishment of pure enjoyment on the part of the reader. It is a kind of natural, unthinking enjoyment. The reader can say, along with Dickens, "How awful many of these conditions were! Is it not interesting to read about them! But of course most of this is in the past! We do not need to do anything about things today!" We know, for example, that even by the time Dickens was writing *David Copperfield* the debtors' prisons were gone. The Industrial Revolution produced all kinds of hardships for the working classes, but labor is in pretty good shape today after a long bargaining struggle with management. Or we may say that the humanitarian opinions expressed by Dickens are generally admirable, but they are dated and important mainly in retrospect; they escape significance but supply a record.

Consider the effect of *Oliver Twist*. Philosophically Dickens can be said to be attacking the utilitarian position of the reformers of his day who thought that charity and handouts to the poor (some form of welfare or the dole) allowed them to live comfortably without working, sponging on their more deserving neighbors. People must be encouraged or forced to work, said Adam Smith and Bentham, not sit lazily in comfort derived from government handouts. If people are in real need, put them in poorhouses where they will be kept alive but not treated so well that they will want to stay there. The young Dickens saw that this political and economic philosophy must depend upon there being enough jobs with fair wages; otherwise society condemns many victims to penury, hardship, vice, or even revolution. The Reform Bill did not guarantee anything like full employment or prosperity; rather it condemned many of the poor to inescapable suffering.

Put this way, Dickens' position in *Oliver Twist* seems familiar. Enlightened nations are coming to believe that they need to care for the poor and aged, that there ought to be enough jobs for those who are willing to work or should be encouraged to do so. We still argue about the proper administration of welfare payments to the unemployed, no matter what the year or the day.

Nevertheless the effect of *Oliver Twist* as a novel does not endure primarily as a document of social criticism. Anyone who has enjoyed its transformation into motion picture or musical comedy must feel that its basic appeal is romantic, melodramatic entertainment. Oliver is a fairy-tale hero, morally noble in his refusal to do wrong, an innocent exploited by villainous persecutors. He is not exactly a real-life person but an allegorical character in constant difficulties, finally being rescued to happiness and security after undergoing a variety of ordeals. Mr. Bumble is not primarily an ogre but a fine stage-actor who makes us laugh at the way in which he keeps the orphans from eating properly or enough. Fagin, the sinister manager of delinquent juvenile London thieves, is more funny than vile, particularly when he calls on the mannerisms of the vaudeville Jewish comedian. The Artful Dodger is an attractive pickpocket who beguiles us with his art. Even Nancy is a prostitute with a heart, capable of singing rhythmical songs like "Ooom-pa-pa!" It is all fine make-believe, replete with cops and robbers sequences, and although it has reference to social evil, it is not exactly serious art unless of course you believe that entertainment without thought is the goal to be desired. The moral point of the novel achieves the end which would be praised by Aesop or Hans Christian Anderson. The good end happily and the bad are punished. Dreams are fun, but only Freud asserted that they have prime significance.

Little of this is to Dickens' discredit. He had a natural ambition to reach a wide reading public and he wanted to make money. He knew instinctively that concessions must be made to what the public wants and would buy. He was consistently advised by his friend, the critic John Forster, a man who had his finger on the pulse of popular demand. It is possible to interpret all the novels up to *David Copperfield* as examples of partial conflict between serious purpose and reader enjoyment for its own sake. Entertainment was always supreme, although the author must have felt many times that he ought to be able to entertain and challenge his readers intellectually at the same time. But publishing the tales in weekly or monthly installments also tempted him to change his original intentions in the course of developing his basic plans, depending on how the parts were selling. He did not originally plan the story of Little Nell so that it would end in dripping sentimentality, but after Forster suggested that it would sell, he carried the whole thing to its somber conclusion. Many of the later novels endured changes in intention, usually to try to increase sales.

It is in *Martin Chuzzlewit* that we find the most interesting evidence of the conflict between commercial arrangement and artistry. Dickens planned the projected novel in more detail than usual, intending to have his various characters and incidents illustrate a central attack on hypocrisy. After the first monthly numbers appeared, sales dropped alarmingly. He consulted with Forster and shifted his outline, introducing Mrs. Gamp to enliven the comedy and sending young Martin to America on the theory that criticizing Americans would restore reader interest. As a result most Dickensians remember Mrs. Gamp for her delightful verbal rambles with the mythical Mrs. Harris, and not because she was a vicious example of the untrained practical nurse.

The amusing hypocrisy of Mr. Pecksniff lives on for its encounters with farce, certainly in excess of any emphasis on his serious deficiencies in understanding or charity. Even the change of heart eventually experienced by young Martin (or for that matter *old* Martin too) resembles the devices of arranged melodrama rather than real life. But the novel still revolves several strands of plot in a kind of planned alternation, since each division of action has connection with the others, all of them emphasizing Dickens' original purpose of castigating hypocrisy.

After *Martin Chuzzlewit,* Dickens went through a period of experimentation with some unusual narrative devices and forms. These are illustrated by the short seasonal tales called *Christmas Books.* The most famous of these is, as everybody knows, *A Christmas Carol.* The moral fable is the regeneration of Old Scrooge, who changes from hardhearted businessman to kindly boss after he sees visions of his dead partner Marley and the three ghosts who visit him. In *The Chimes,* written a year later, Dickens let loose a measured blast at the insufficient methods society uses to aid the poor and alleviate economic difficulties experienced by the masses in the 1840s. He gave this latter tale two endings, a supreme example of catering to public taste which presumably would reject the realistic ending.

Dickens' serious criticisms of society were materially influenced at this period in his development by the writings and opinions of Carlyle. He shied away from the position being expressed by Marx and Engels, the rejection of capitalist economy which reached climax in the Communist Manifesto of 1848. Dickens had always objected to traditional capitalism, Adam Smith, Malthus, and the utilitarians. Carlyle presented a kind of middle position between two extremes, one which Dickens interpreted as calling on humanity to be tolerant and charitable, to work hard to improve things, and to attempt better national understanding of the economic problems of all the people—meaning probably that he hoped the capitalistic system would work quite well if nobody cheated and the rich were willing to aid the poor without consistently exploiting them. Even Carlyle thought that this hope was a little elementary,[2] but it was embodied in *Dombey and Son,* where the selfish businessman reaches ruin and unhappiness before he, like Scrooge, reformed and became benevolent—perhaps a little late, since he had to lose son, wife, and fortune before he saw the light. In an effort to sell this interpretation of economics, Dickens decorated his novel with another sentimental death, that of Little Paul Dombey, and invented a number of amusing eccentrics like Captain Cuttle and Mrs. Skewton to keep his readers happy while they presumably absorbed his serious purpose. The effect was again an artistic mixture, like most of the early Dickens novels, stimulating at times, funny, sentimental, and melodramatic.

David Copperfield turned out to be mainly entertainment. As a novel it derived from an experiment the author made starting to write his own autobiography in the manner of the early romanticist Holcroft. The first part of the novel, specifically the beginning fourteen chapters, allowed him to let himself go in creating a host of eccentrics, from the Peggottys and Barkis and the Murdstones and Aunt Betsy and Mr. Dick to the inimitable Micawbers. Eventually he inserted a number of plot sequences, all of which explore romantic passion or Victorian standards of sexual relationships. The various strands necessarily revolve about David (he is telling the story), thus providing unity even though there was occasional difficulty in supplying motivation or even telling exactly what happened (Steerforth's seduction of Little Emily is the main case in point) whenever David himself was not present. The novel begins remarkably, holds to a narrative standard which is often extraordinary, tails off a little, then exhibits flashes of inspired narration which keeps its general accomplishment very high indeed. But the level is still entertainment: delightful caricature, slimy villains, predictable melodrama, silly adolescent love, and the smug underlining of Victorian moral standards.

It is true that there are occasional serious insertions in the novel. The hazards of child labor in the bottling factory, the deficient schoolteaching of the time, the debtors' prisons, the ridiculous inefficiency of the law and legal practice, even the kind of prison where criminals were given ease and comfort at the same time that the honest poor suffered and starved outside prison walls—all these matters find emphasis. His novels up to this time thus indicate that Dickens could not forget the serious problems of society even while he was trying to tell a good story which would only incidentally refer to real social difficulties. For many readers this has been enough, but through the years after Dickens died, the number of worshipers varied enough for his reputation to fall below that of more intense novelists. In the first opinions of critics like George Lewes, Anthony Trollope, or Henry James, Dickens was merely "Mr. Popular Sentiment."[3]

The long step to complete seriousness began with *Bleak House,* 1852–53. From this point on, the total effect of Dickens' novels changes (it is fair to except *A Tale of Two Cities* and perhaps *Great Expectations,* certainly *Edwin Drood*) to an emphasis on a consuming social purpose. He was at the height of his creative powers when he conceived the way in which he could entertain his readers by centering all his narrative devices on a theme which would reflect something important to say about Victorian social health. Since his judgment was in conflict with popular attitudes (those probably held by his readers anyway) he necessarily lost some of the carefree narrative ease which so often previously had allowed him to insert a character or a scene which would entertain. It has been suggested that his marriage was breaking up and that his personal unhappiness soured him. It has also been charged that about this time he became acquainted with Wilkie Collins, as a result changing the arrangement and organization of his novels to a greater concern for suspense and intricate plot complications. Neither of these influences appears to be a sufficient cause for his dark interpretation of social evil, although both had some part in intensifying his interest in the serious issues of his world, the consequent suffusing of his narratives with a social microcosmic pattern.[4]

Up to this time we note that his fictional techniques had depended upon many resources, and that he often jumped from one to the other in telling his stories. There was caricature and farce; the development of his action by dialogue and speech mannerisms; melodramatic arrangement of plot materials; the occasional appeal of sentiment or horror. He had also utilized his opportunities to attack what he conceived to be error wherever he saw it, in people and in institutions. Artistically he had, as it were, alternated or contrasted these narrative resources according to his inspiration of the moment or in response to what he thought were the demands of his reading public. Gradually or naturally, depending on how one judges his genius, he came to the practice of organizing his complex tales around a center—a definite theme, or what might be called a contrapuntal arrangement of various episodes, sequences, and technical experiments which were all related to a central thesis or idea. He had made his first steps toward this method in *Martin Chuzzlewit,* emphasizing the ills of hypocrisy; in *Dombey and Son* he showed the ego and selfishness of the economic system by criticizing the typical business tycoon; in *David Copperfield* it was Victorian morality as displayed in the proper or improper relationships of the sexes in and out of marriage. Historically it is important to note that Dickens is the first novelist to attempt this involved technical method of developing the large-scale novel where every character or bit of action reflects a central thesis.

Bleak House first illustrates the mastery of this technical arrangement, a purpose which was greater than an attack upon hypocrisy, ego, intolerance, or even the Poor Law. He wished to make an all-inclusive charge against social institutions and customs which interfere with human happiness. Dickens' intent was to arrange all of his narrative weapons, which previously had been used primarily for entertainment, to bolster his analysis of the ills of Victorian society. This is a matter of degree in arrangement.

His assault turned out to be epic in its breadthwise cutting through many levels of the novel: the incapacity of the legal system and the artificialities of caste; the abuses of economic competition and the stupidities of religion, education, and politics; the nauseous city slums and the homes of pyramiding capitalists, the inefficient nobility, the incapable ruling classes, and the do-nothing legislators. Dickens thought that little could be done to make this world better unless the public was informed and used personal initiative to establish better conditions in the future.

Pervasive obsession with social decay allied itself to his basic plan for *Bleak House*. He saw intense suffering around him; the widespread poverty of masses of people and the festering ghettos of London sickened him. In the past he had attacked results; now he wanted to center on causes. The focus of injustice in England seemed to him to be the very institution which was established to remove injustice—the law itself. Obviously law, in its ideal intent, should aid and protect individuals against exploitation and injustice, but by Victorian times it had come to stand for the exact opposite of its intention. Remember that this was a conclusion separated from the criminal code (Dickens saw injustices in this area too); it had to do primarily with the Court of Chancery which dealt with financial legal matters. This point has occasionally been misunderstood, as if the satire of *Bleak House* were concerned only with an isolated example of unfair legal procedure, exaggerated in Dickens' usual manner of caricature, farce and incidental distortion, long since reformed. Dickens' central purpose, however, goes far beyond the Jarndyce Will case (where the entire vast estate was eaten up in costs without any of the principals profiting—only the lawyers). It is fair to point out that the case does not seem to have been an exaggerated example of unbelievable legal injustice.[5]

The Court of Chancery, the lawyers, the technicalities of muddling · procedures, and the general inequities of legal practice were supported by the general public and particularly the elected Parliament which Dickens thought represented stupidity. Society and its governing body were responsible for the law and court procedures. Assuredly society and Parliament were ultimately to be credited with the general state of England's economic health. Victorian England pretended to be extremely moral; the truth of the matter was that Victorian morality hypocritically permitted and encouraged pretense, injustice, and immorality. In Dickens' last novel, *Edwin Drood,* we find perhaps the most illuminating statement of this point in all his writing. "It is not enough," says Mr. Sapsea, "that justice should be morally certain; she must be immorally certain—legally, that is."[6] And, as Edgar Johnson remarks, "It [*Bleak House*] regards legal injustice not as accidental but as organically related to the very structure of that society."[7]

There are two main courses of action in *Bleak House,* one told in the authorial omniscient third person, the other through the first-person-feminine point of view expressed by the heroine, Esther Summerson. These are alternated every two or three chapters. The action at first concentrates upon the Chancery Court, then shifts to high society and the Dedlock family, eventually ending with the mystery of the lawyer Tulkinghorn's murder. Dickens devised a large number of contrasting intrigues or strands of action to illustrate his thesis that Court of Chancery procedures threatened or ruined the prosperity of anyone involved in law cases. The exception was the lawyers who profited from court action at the expense of the litigants. The Jarndyce Will case (appealed and retried continuously, never settled) is the first example. But there are also the cases involving Mr. Gridley, the mildly mad Miss Flite, and others. Dickens intended to show that these cases were not exceptional, but usual, the result of general neglect of honest legal practice. The nauseous slums were usually dependent upon money tied up in cases like the Jarndyce affair. But all this makes lawyers wealthy, from Conversation Kenge to Mr. Vholes to Mr. Guppy to the monstrous Tulkinghorn, each illustrating a different degree of perversity and evil.

This is the first time that Dickens had drawn his main plot materials from life rather than from the melodramatic tradition usually depicted in his fiction. He did not forget the need to entertain, of course, and he seems not to have been able to avoid dipping into the resources of folklore for purposes of reader enjoyment. When Mr. Krook blows up of spontaneous combustion, Dickens thought that the symbolism involved would justify his borrowing from the miraculous. Mr. Krook's shop, full of odds and ends, uselessly cluttered, the bones of clients in the corners, is a symbolic court of Chancery. Legal malfeasance needs to blow up, so Dickens makes it happen.

The Dedlock section has two parts. The essential situation depends upon the mystery of Lady Dedlock's past, the illegitimate child she had believed dead, and the gradual uncovering of her guilty secret by the family lawyer, Tulkinghorn. This melodramatic sequence then develops into what is the first mystery story in English fiction in the "Whodunit" sense. Tulkinghorn is murdered and a detective or police officer unravels the mystery of how, why, and by whom it was done. Inspector Bucket is England's first detective in a full-length novel.

The artistic effect of this large-scale masterpiece depends upon whether its central purpose is intensified by the many illustrations supplied. The two courses of action are interlocked through as many duplications as seem possible. Many of the characters in both areas are connected. The general disease which infects Victorian England is symbolized by the very name of Dedlock; it spreads from the law to society to Parliament to the economic system, even to orthodox religion.

Parliamentary ineptitude comes in for special satire when Dickens criticizes the Boodle-Coodle-Doodle clan, the ruling class which approaches the job of running the country with complete inefficiency except for keeping in office. Dickens' contention is that the disease of the social structure of England spreads from the slums to the law courts to the churches to the manor houses to the halls of Parliament. It is a virulent pestilence, nowhere more nauseous than in high places.

Curiously enough *Bleak House* is the first Dickens novel which experiments with symbolism to any serious degree. It appears to the modern critic that he had not quite worked out an all-inclusive verbal idea for a selected symbol, but he made the first approach to the narrative concept of organizing his various characters and plots around his central purpose, then decorating them all with a single symbol—varied, but repeated and recurrent. The atmospheric background for much of his tale illuminates and intensifies the effect of his central indictment. Over the pages of the novel hovers a perpetual fog which surrounds the spiritual darkness of the Court of Chancery and all its works. The rain and mist of foul weather rot away the Dedlock mansion and all it stands for in fashionable decay. Fog constitutes atmospheric imagery, and Dickens thought that the best example should be the decay and combustion of Mr. Krook and his shop, a symbolic representation of the eventual hoped-for collapse of legal injustice.

He intended that this symbolism should extend to the Dedlock circle and high society in general. The slums are at one end of the story, Chesney Wold at the other—both surrounded by bleak mist: "It is but a glimpse of the world of fashion that we want on this same miry afternoon. It is not so unlike the Court of Chancery but that we may pass from the one scene to the other as the crow flies. Both the world of fashion and the Court of Chancery are things of precedent and usage; over-sleeping Rip Van Winkles, who have played at strange games through a deal of thundery weather; sleeping beauties, whom the knight will wake one day, when all the stopped spits in the kitchen shall begin to turn prodigiously."[8] Fog creates a "bleak world," and Dickens named the home of John Jarndyce "Bleak House." The kindly and likable guardian of Esther Summerson could not separate himself completely from the lawsuit and was affected by all the ill winds that blew from the court, even though he tried to aid all those who suffered from exploitation. Shaw in a later day borrowed Dickens' bleak intention and substituted the adjective *Heartbreak.*

One must not forget that Dickens was not writing a moral tract, but was intending to construct an entertaining masterpiece. The ideal was to amuse and to stimulate his readers simultaneously. Any story which flirts with propaganda or purpose is in danger of losing serious reader attention, since real life can be falsified to bolster the author's opinion, thus alienating the reader. Dickens certainly did not intend to sacrifice entertainment to his thesis, rather than each should intensify the other. His most impressive eccentrics may be Miss Flite, Grandfather Smallweed (the moneylender), and the Reverend Mr. Chadband. But there are many more: Harold Skimpole, Mr. Boythorn, Volumnia Dedlock—the reader can take his pick. The lawyers add their brilliant presentation, the mellow, rounded, meaningless rhetoric of Conversation Kenge, the glove-peeling hypocrisy of Mr. Vholes, the technical redundancy of Mr. Guppy, the inhuman deadliness of Mr. Tulkinghorn—all of them are fascinating villains. Dickens used caricature and farce to underline his purpose, and occasionally he was completely successful, for example when he portrays Mrs. Badger, the lady who impresses the memory of her previous husbands upon Mr. Badger so that he will glory in his own comparative lack of conspicuous sufficiency.

The murder of Tulkinghorn and its solution do not necessarily contribute to the central thesis, except as an aftereffect. But they add reader-suspense and the sensational unraveling of carefully prepared complications. Dickens had never previously produced a plot so well prepared and artfully revealed at the last. If the reader is not distracted by Esther's heightened goodness in narration, the two points of view used in the novel intensify each other. Each narrative manner exposes different segments of diseased, bleak, foggy Victorian society. The essential satire is doubled or multiplied rather than separated. Our conclusion has to be that *Bleak House* is more powerful than anything Dickens had previously written. Perhaps it is more powerful than any novel anyone else had written.

Hard Times and *Little Dorrit* followed *Bleak House* in chronology and serious intention. The shorter *Hard Times* is a bitter indictment of Victorian social and economic practice and it clearly spells out many of the author's beliefs. It is tempting for some modern critics to praise *Hard Times* overmuch because the purpose seems clearer, as if the fact that the author has a point overrides the necessity for illustrating the point artistically. As an example, note that George Bernard Shaw praises the novel enthusiastically for its opposition to Adam Smith and utilitarian economics. Strangely enough, F. R. Leavis felt at one time that *Hard Times* was Dickens' best novel because he said it was "a completely serious work of art."[9]

But the fact is that there is some narrative insufficiency in the novel, less effective humor, less powerful melodrama. The symbolism is the natural smoke and haze which hover over Coketown, and this resembles the fog and mist of *Bleak House*. If we are in any doubt about Dickens' opinions, *Hard Times* illuminates our understanding. He is arguing for what he conceives to be justice to both capital and labor, for cooperation, for some kind of positive action in economic matters which would avoid the possible road to revolution. Labor needs to be more equitably rewarded, he says. Perhaps this makes the novel "more serious," and it aims at significance. But the entertainment and storytelling arts owned by Dickens must be said to falter in some degree. It is not as balanced or as intense as *Bleak House*.

The opposite effect is illustrated in *Little Dorrit*. If there is a weakness here it is overcomplexity. The author is vindictive about the fools and idiots, the exploiters and the usurers, the proud and the self-ish, the bigoted and evil members of typical Victorian society—perhaps more than ever before. This is his darkest novel. But he manages to revolve the narrative sequences and characters about his central hub of denunciation at the same time that he decorates his pattern with a specific symbol: prison bars, bolts, bonds, chains, and the like. The central idea is his feeling that most of society is fettered by established custom and the strangling restrictions of self-sufficient possessiveness.

Prison walls extend themselves to outworn but securely established customs, to decayed traditions, to unbending religious orthodoxy, to the specific chains of caste, position, and the locked doors of fashionable society, even to the stone walls and barred windows of political privilege. He devised an overlarge scenario for his project, inventing no less than six distinct plot sequences to "weave his pattern," as he says in his preface. The main plot concerns the Dorrit family, and he elaborately contrasts the family at first in prison for debt, then snatched into extreme affluence by an unexpected fortune. Along with the Dorrits are the Clennams, Mrs. Clennam being a prisoner in body, business, and soul. Her son, Arthur, however, is shown learning to escape from his bonds. Mrs. Clennam lives in a creaking old pseudo-Gothic mansion which eventually collapses like the fabled "one-hoss shay," producing a kind of parallel for the spontaneous combustion of Mr. Krook in *Bleak House*.

The third sequence concerns government inefficiency. The red tape of the Circumlocution Office is hopelessly entangled since the ruling Barnacle tribe have learned "how not to do it." Today we are likely to call this kind of thing government bureaucracy. Perhaps the most venomous attack of Dickens upon economic evil attaches itself to the story of Mr. Merdle, the pyramiding capitalist, banker, and financier. Mr. Merdle is a real prisoner of money and power, his abilities tied to sharp dealing in every kind of financial manipulation, everything that is permitted to the laissez faire system where the smart operator can beat the odds and pile up a huge paper fortune. This involves interlocking corporations, price-fixing, and the ways in which cartels can be formed and manipulated. Mr. Merdle finally failed and took millions of investors with him. But in the meantime he buys and sells social and political privilege. He seems to have a peculiar physical malady which must be his conscience. He commits suicide at the last when his economic house of cards collapses as completely as does the old Clennam house.

The fifth and sixth sequences are less distinct, perhaps less important. But they add their emphasis to the pattern. They concern Mr. Casby, the slum landlord, who is served by the pixie servant Mr. Pancks;

and then there is the Meagles family which Dickens uses as another instance of the utilitarian castelike example of society in chains. All six strands of plot are interwoven in the novel, and Dickens uses most of the devices which previously had been turned to entertainment alone. He is challenging the reader to look seriously at the question of whether England's financial and social structure is in danger of falling to pieces as the Clennam mansion does; whether the manipulations of businessmen at the expense of the public will always reach the dark days of collapse when the stock market falls, heralding depression, as did the Merdle enterprises; whether the government or Parliament will ever have sense and idealism enough to remedy the crying defects of the country; whether we will ever escape from the prison bars of modern unchecked free enterprise, the public-be-damned practices.

It is still fiction, of course. The dark effect of the author's opinions is occasionally lightened, but not much. Flora Casby is one of Dickens' most successful talking women (there had been Mrs. Nickleby and Mrs. Gamp before her), but the level of eccentricity is not as high as in more popular novels. He is more concerned with the fact that enlightened nations ought to encourage inventors and scientists like Doyce, certainly that they ought not to be restrained economically by legislation dedicated to one class alone—not the entire nation. When Arthur Clennam is talking to Ferdinand Barnacle about the collapse of Mr. Merdle's financial empire, he expresses the hope that people will be wiser in the future. Pessimistically Dickens makes Barnacle say: "My dear Clennam. . . . Have you really such a verdant hope? The next man who has as large a capacity and as genuine a taste for swindling will succeed as well. Pardon me, but I think you really have no idea how the human bees will swarm to the beating of any old tin kettle; in that fact lies the complete manual of governing them."[10]

Still, Dickens says that escape from the prison walls of false social standards to the tolerant happy land of justice for all rests mainly upon individual desire and capacity for improving the world as a result of trial and error. He never suggests a formula like socialism or communism or tyranny or benevolent autocracy. But he hopes dimly that an incompetent governing class can be replaced; society must provide fair opportunities and rewards by decent means; worn-out institutions must come down as must prison walls; the caste system, hypocritical Puritanism, selfish economic exploitation, must collapse some day. Human brains and will power are our only hope for social betterment. Doyce says to Clennam at the end of the novel: "First not a word more from you about the past. There was an error in your calculations. I know what that is. It affects the whole machine, and failure is the consequence. You will profit by the failure, and will avoid it another time. I have done a similar thing myself, in construction, often. Every failure teaches a man something, if he will learn; and you are too sensible a man not to learn from this failure."[11]

The next two novels, *A Tale of Two Cities,* and *Great Expectations* go back in some degree to the old requirements of entertainment at the expense of serious purpose. For some readers, that is an advantage. There were reasons for this shift in narrative effect, some of them personal. Dickens had finally separated from his wife (it has always intrigued me that he discovered incompatibility after having ten children). In his involvement with his public image he tried to justify himself in print, publishing in his magazine a tasteless and self-serving explanation of his personal affairs which alienated many of his friends, including his financial backers. So he imperiously abandoned *Household Words* and transferred its editorial staff, format, and custom to a new project which he called *All the Year Round,* financed by himself.[12] In his desire to establish the sale of this new venture he threw himself into the construction of two novels which he could print and thus increase sales for the magazine. This need constituted a kind of recession from his new artistic purposes. Obviously he always intended to be serious in some measure and to insert significant materials into whatever he wrote.

It is probably clear that *A Tale of Two Cities* is not typical Dickens. It is historical (borrowing from Carlyle's *French Revolution)* and a fine melodramatic story. It manages to build up one of his most effective climaxes in the final guillotine scene where Sidney Carton sacrifices his life for Charles Darnay, the man who had won the girl both loved. It is interesting that its dramatic and suspenseful action has caused it to be selected for compulsory reading by thousands of American high schools (lately there has been a turn to *Great Expectations)* where generations of youthful readers have reacted to a novel which is not really a fair sample of the lasting accomplishments of Dickens. Among its untypical characteristics were a change in narrative method, fewer eccentric characters and less humor, the action developed by description rather than conversation, and certainly a sparse selection of alternate or contrasting plots.

It is true that the effect is more concentrated, and it also plays with some interesting symbolism. Dickens took the idea of *resurrection,* or the concept of being "recalled to life," as a recurrent theme, evolving it in many sequences and even in portrayal of individual characters. Dr. Manette is recalled to life from the Bastille, and Sidney Carton is regenerated from uselessness to dedication by his love for Lucy. The most interesting small use of this symbolism is perhaps in the presentation of Jerry Cruncher, the grave robber who digs up and sells dead bodies to the medical profession, but who also beats his wife for "flopping" or praying for him while he is on his grisly adventures, particularly if he fails. The climactic guillotine scene makes excellent emotional use of the resurrection lines taken from the Bible or the funeral service.

It would have been possible to examine the French Revolution in a large significant sense, something parallel to the accomplishment of Tolstoi in *War and Peace,* showing what happens to a country in the throes of violence. Dickens obviously thought that evil social and political practice had driven the exploited French people to rebel against their masters. As a result, the people got out of hand and destroyed good and bad things indiscriminately. The Defarges in the beginning represent rejection of the bad old regime, but at the last they are just as evil in their desires for revenge. Dickens seems to have felt, like Joseph Conrad, that revolution never really improves things. He is certainly warning England that "it can happen here, and you will not like it."

Generally speaking, therefore, *A Tale of Two Cities* is entertainment, suspense, and melodrama. *Great Expectations* comes closer to significance, since it is the story of a young man who is drawn into snobbery and incapacity by expectations of inheriting wealth and social position. The novel uses symbolism in the sense that many characters and events show the variety of influences which "great" or false expectations exert on British society. Obviously the author criticizes those who depend on position, money, caste, or pretense rather than sincere effort devoted to making the most of whatever status one is born into or can attain by honest work. Pip, who tells the tale, appeals to most readers who often say that this novel succeeds in entertaining and challenging us at the same time that it depicts the development of an interesting hero who goes through phases of incapacity to final distinction of character. Pip certainly is Dickens' most successful "round" character, and despite his snobbery is likely to worm his way into our esteem before the tale is done.

There is a small problem. Dickens supplied two endings for the novel, the original one in harmony with his purpose, showing Pip and Estella separating forever, the substituted and printed one providing a kind of semihappy conclusion where the two might eventually get together. Whatever his reasons for changing his original conclusion, we are justified in supposing that his serious purpose was not so important to him that he would really insist on it if his readers did not like it. This is one of a number of small reasons for concluding that while *Great Expectations* has artistic merit on a high level, yet it was a step back from the extraordinary impact of *Bleak House* and *Little Dorrit.*

He did develop a technical narrative trick which he apparently borrowed from Wilkie Collins. This device led the reader to expect a wrong interpretation of the action, in this case the source of Pip's expected inheritance, then suddenly supplied a different explanation which surprised everyone. Note that he followed *A Tale of Two Cities* in the weekly magazine with Wilkie Collins' *Woman in White,* then printed *Great Expectations.* The Collins novel was perhaps the most spectacular example of that author's involvement with suspense and misdirection of reader expectations. One supposes that Dickens felt the need to compete, as he did in his last novel, *Edwin Drood,* following Collins' *The Moonstone.*

Now we come to *Our Mutual Friend.* This last completed novel may be Dickens' most remarkable accomplishment in terms of his analysis of Victorian society. It was in the *Bleak House-Little Dorrit* model, returning to the panoramic plan which presented several sequences of action woven round a central pattern of purpose. He also fashioned a number of characters around interlocking symbols. Specifically he portrayed London, England, wallowing in the muck and filth of a city which might be said to represent hell on earth. In modern times he would certainly have chosen a more suggestive title for this novel. One likes to imagine "A Moundfull of Dust," "Disposal," "The Wasteland," "Ashes to Ashes," "Trash Collection," "All the Queen's Horses," "Garbageways," "The Slime of Time," "The Organs of Defecation," "Cloaca Revisited," "Scavenger's Wake," or even a single four-letter word for excrement.

The specific symbol of filth offered him the opportunity to expose forcefully most of the things he found wrong with his world. It is easy to mention filth as an expletive, one supposes, but Dickens adds the idea that too many people value whatever is rejected by the body rather than spiritual goals. The ideal man should prefer the things that live eternally, not cling to that which decays. From Parliament to wealthy mansions to business houses to slums—in every part of London he saw mankind straining and struggling over what he thought was a dung heap trying desperately to produce money or whatever could be measured in pounds and shillings.

The quintessence of his symbol was the cesspool of the Thames, draining off the sewage from the wasteland of London; its parallel form was dust, trash, and garbage. His pen became a kind of excretory organ spouting out a sizzling cover for all the festering values that are produced by money, the "awful offal" of Victorian standards of life. Writers have rarely expressed such an extreme of disgust.

There are three courses of action which make use of his symbol, although the third one has sometimes confused the casual reader. One plot centers about the longshoremen who make a living by salvaging the wreckage that floats down the Thames and who sometimes rob the bodies of the drowned floaters; the second plot derives from a fortune made in the "dust collection" of the metropolis, the youthful heir to this fortune pretending to be dead in order to find out whether or not he wants to marry the girl who was, by his eccentric father's will, a necessary part of his inheritance. The son had been out of the country and knew nothing about the girl. The third plot centered first on two pretenders who married each other, each expecting to live from the money supposedly possessed by the other, neither having any—and this last plot then introduced a number of rich or hoping-to-be-rich characters who represented some form of filth in business and society, since they all live off the leavings of other people.

The suspense in the narrative tends to center about Harmon (the young heir who is "Our Mutual Friend"). Dickens invents a devious sequence of events which allows him to pretend to be someone else while he investigates the character of Bella Wilfer, the girl he is supposed to marry. Bella (a willful girl, note) is given one of those problems which George Eliot so loved, to choose between true attraction (she falls in love with Harmon, thinking him penniless) and financial security. Bella makes the right choice, of course, and when she decides to marry Harmon we know that she will get the money too.

The other romantic plot concerns Lizzie Hexam, the plain, unsophisticated, working-girl type, who has character if not social position. She has two lovers, Eugene Wrayburn and Bradley Headstone, one a ne'er-do-well upper-caste lawyer who lives mainly on a family allowance, the other a teacher who resents the fact that his profession is low in the social scale (also the economic scale). Bradley (Dickens did not exactly like teachers and preachers, remember) develops a kind of manic-depressive obsession against his rival for Lizzie. He eventually plots to murder Eugene, attacks him, and throws him into one of London's sewage canals. Poor Lizzie tries to run away from her problem, since she loves Eugene and thinks he will not marry her. After she saves his life (coincidence) he decides on his deathbed to marry her and recovers after all. Both these romantic sequences have melodramatic connections and derive from the general idea of entertainment allied to suspense.

Dickens also invented another example of misdirection in presenting Mr. Boffin, who inherited the dust-and-trash fortune after Harmon's supposed death. The eccentric old father apparently left a number of wills, and a certain Silas Wegg (another eccentric out of Dickens' earlier novels) tries to blackmail old Boffin, since he claimed to have found a later will in the trash mounds. These melodramatic sequences are cited because they accompany many small strands of action which supposedly emphasize the symbolism of filth and excrement. The admirable characters, in the author's opinion, are those who attempt to get out of the conditions of social stagnation dominated by economic greed.

It is the symbolism rather than the plot materials which makes the novel impressive. Obviously the Gaffer-Hexam-Rogue-Riderhood plot derives from the scavenger-floating body business of the Thames. The Harmon-Wilfer-Boffin plot depends on the money made in dust-trash-garbage collection. The third plot, involving the Lammles, the Veneerings, the Podsnaps, and various other snobs, supplies a parallel. This last group represents those who live in social filth, each member showing his dedication to the excremental false values of Victorian England. All the group that gathers at the Veneering table live from an inherited or manipulated income, at someone else's expense. This means living from shares, dividends, stock gambling, insurance, inherited property, or the diddling of values in the marketplace. They prey on and live from the misfortunes of others, says Dickens. All this presents a dim view of traditional capitalism and free enterprise, of course.

The symbolic theme is occasionally very successful in small sections. For example there is Mr. Venus and his shop, a place which contains a collection of salable objects intended to nauseate the ordinary reader. Mr. Venus sells skeletons, stuffed animals, unborn babies in jars, all the paraphernalia of a man who makes a living from that which is dead or liable to decay. He supplies bodies for medical dissection too. He also joins Wegg temporarily in his blackmail attempt on Mr. Boffin, and Wegg is one of Dickens' finest offensive eccentrics. He has a wooden leg, and his original member had been amputated and sold to Mr. Venus. Wegg eventually buys it back, and it does not seem to be overstating the case to suggest that the author used another grotesque instance of showing how people value the things which are discarded by the body.

The characters who try to find redemption from the lust for money are the ones Dickens admires. Mr. Boffin refuses to succumb despite his pretense of degeneration. Apparently he does this to influence Bella in picking the right man. Harmon values sincere love more than inherited fortune. Old Betty Higden prefers to work rather than give in to charity and welfare. Wrayburn decides not to marry money but to turn below his class to Lizzie Hexam, although it takes the murderous attack by Headstone to nudge him over the edge of decision.

We suppose that Dickens was on the side of hope rather than despair. But the artistic accomplishment of the novel depends upon the significance of his symbolic thesis. Dust pile and sewage, economic misery and social standing based essentially on filth, stolid and stupid complacency with a world which permits all that is evil under heaven—truly Dickens creates a kind of inferno. Furthermore this inferno exists among us who live, not as punishment after death. He retains his deepest scorn for a world which is satisfied to remain in its filth: "My lords and gentlemen and honorable lords, when you in the course of your dust-shoveling and cinder-taking have piled up a mountain of pretentious failure, you must off with your honorable coats for the removal of it, and fall to the work with the power of all the Queen's horses and all the Queen's men, or it will come rushing down and bury us alive."[13]

The artistic miracle of Dickens' fictional accomplishment is that an absorption with essential human questions grew out of narrative techniques which he had followed to the ends of entertainment for its own sake. We can always read him for the story alone, although his sentimental scenes and some of his melodramatic plots are not always as absorbing as they once were. But the greater implications of the late novels, the patterns and the symbols, the challenge to the reader, all go past simple enjoyment. Perhaps it requires a later generation to see something like the disgust which would make Dickens name two characters Murdstone and Merdle after the implications of the French *Merde.* Surely the greatest accomplishment as a novelist for all seasons and time is the utilization of his entertaining devices to the analysis of a serious criticism of life. This means that he became a significant novelist, not merely a supreme entertainer. *Bleak House, Little Dorrit,* and *Our Mutual Friend* reach that plateau where enjoyment and thought attain the highest artistry, the combination of tale-telling and social analysis which will continue to make Dickens' reputation glow and sparkle down through the years.

David Paroissien

DICKENS AND THE CINEMA

IN THE years following Edmund Wilson's revaluation of Dickens' achievement, critical and scholarly studies proliferated since 1941 to the extent that they have become, in the words of one observer, " 'The Dickens Industry.' " Typical of the productivity implied by this remark is the work of Earle Davies, Edgar and Eleanor Johnson, William Axton, Robert Brannan, and Robert Garis, all of whom share an interest in Dickens' connection with the nineteenth-century London stage.[1] Perhaps challenged by Dickens' remark in 1870 to Herman Merivale that he "fancied that he knew the name of every play that had been acted for years," these critics have explored, but not exhausted, how Dickens' novels were affected by what George H. Ford calls "his life-long exposure to Victorian melodramas and burlesques."[2]

The consequences of this passion, its impact on the structure, style, and characters of the novels, Dickens' knowledge of drama as both spectator and performer, and his success or failure in combining the two genres will continue to interest scholars for some time. Meanwhile, the intensity of the debate should not blind us to some important corollary questions: irrespective of further attempts to establish degrees of theatrical influence, how far can we go in attempting to equate the technique of the dramatist with that of the novelist? Aside from reservation with Robert Garis' suggestion of mechanical trickery implied by his comparison of Dickens' art to the conjurer's, "an illusionist" with his "version of pulling rabbits out of hats," how useful is it to assess, as Garis does, his style solely with respect to a concept of "Style as Theatre"?[3] As a novelist, can Dickens' vision be inherently theatrical; are the modes of manipulating and persuading the same for dramatist and novelist?

If too much stress on the theatricality of Dickens' style blurs the difference between the two media, one can cite the interest in Dickens and narrative film as a corrective. Although all three resemble each

[68

other insofar as they are narrative arts with a temporal form, the affinity between the nineteenth-century novel and narrative film is stronger than that between novel and play. For the dramatist, communication is essentially auditory; the dramatic conflict is structured through scenes and acts and developed primarily by dialogue. By contrast, both novelist and film maker project their characters and the narrative conflict through a series of pictures of events, temporally or spatially arranged to make their audience see.

To acknowledge this difference is not to deny the use of dialogue and sound in film and novel; the purpose is to emphasize the importance of descriptive writing to the novelist. Unable to stage conflict, portray characters in costume, and employ carefully prepared sets, he must rely on his ability to evoke mental images to make his reader see. Setting and descriptive passages, therefore, serve as essential components of the writer's narrative art and means of characterization.

It is to this aspect of the novelist's craft that the film maker responds with understanding; herein lies the value of looking at Dickens' art from a different perspective. Skilled at making visible the nuances of thought, adept at rendering characters palpable through images, and accustomed to dealing with scenes and places in concrete, perceptual terms, film makers' interest in Dickens is worthy of note. Accordingly this essay will examine the following issues: how does one account for Dickens' cinematic appeal? what influence has Dickens had on narrative film? and how can literary criticism benefit from a filmic analysis of his style?

— 2 —

The first step in accounting for Dickens' cinematic appeal is to mention the frequency with which his works have been adapted. Drawing on the research of Anna Laura Zambrano, we know that every novel in the canon, including three Christmas stories, has been filmed. These productions, which constitute a microcosmic history of film from the primitive one-reelers of the first decade of the twentieth century to the latest in animated cartoons and musical extravaganzas, have attracted such directors as D. W. Griffith, George Cukor, David O. Selznik, Alberto Cavalcanti, David Lean, and Delbert Mann. To date, more than eighty versions of the novels and short stories have been made, with *Oliver Twist, A Christmas Carol,* and *David Copperfield* among the most frequently adapted.[4] The significance of these adaptations lies chiefly in their quantity, which illustrates how Dickens, more than any other classic novelist, has provided the screen with so much raw material. Why this is so is a complex issue.

Some explanations call attention to public taste. As early as 1932,

Q. D. Leavis scornfully summarized Dickens' novels as " 'laughter and tears' " and suggested that his and Hollywood's exploitation of the formula accounted for the popular success of both, including, presumably, film versions of the novels.[5] More recently Taylor Stoehr restated the film industry's interest in Dickens with less acerbity.

> Our main palliative—the great art form (such as it is) of the twentieth century—has been the movies, and it is therefore not surprising that Dickens' novels should have so much in common with them, and should have proved so notably translatable into the film medium [writes Stoehr when comparing the nineteenth-century appeal of Dickens's "dream" world to the popular appeal of motion pictures today]. . . . Even the accompanying circumstances are the same: the star system corresponds to the public adulation of characters like Little Nell or Sam Weller, who call up so powerful a response in their audiences that they are taken as real people; the Saturday-night movie, like the appearance of the latest serial installment, renews the fantasy world as regularly as the night offers its dreams; even the cult of Hollywood has its parallel in the topographers and travelers who keep the Dickens Fellowship going, unwilling to give up the notion that their dream world somewhere has a magical equivalent in reality.[6]

Appealing folk heroes and heroines, laughter and tears, nothing with a "message"—proved formulas for profit. They are all abundant in Dickens' novels awaiting the alert film maker who knows, as Russell Baker wrote in a column questioning the sensibilities of the critics full of praise for Lina Wertmuller's *Seven Beauties,* that "movies probably can never be more than entertainments for the child imprisoned in the oldest of us."[7]

By concentrating on the extrinsic factors likely to attract the film industry, neither Leavis nor Stoehr concedes in their comments the possibility of a more substantive affinity.[8] Nevertheless, if we come back to the role of descriptive writing, which, we noted, is an important way of distinguishing the novelist's art from the dramatist's, a second explanation occurs.

Dickens' ability to evoke environments is well known to all who read him; and E. D. H. Johnson expresses what is often thought when he writes: "Indeed, the most lastingly memorable quality of the novels may well be their atmospheric density, wrought from the stylistic brilliance of the descriptive writing."[9] What is clear to readers and critics is felt more acutely by film makers, for whom training and craft reinforce an innate sensitivity to visual perception. Thus it is not surprising to find the Russian film theorist and director, Sergei Eisenstein, praising

Dickens' use of "atmosphere" to reveal the inner world and ethical countenance of his characters and suggesting the secret of Dickens' success ("as well as the cinema's") lies in his creation of an extraordinary plasticity. The observation in the novels is extraordinary—as is their optical quality.[10]

The impossibility of Dickens' foreseeing a comparison of his art with the cinema's is irrelevant to Eisenstein's analogy; dramatically his observation underlines the very effects Dickens sought to create and of whose importance he spoke in the novels and letters. One noticeable example occurs as early as 1841 when Master Humphrey theorizes about the power of "external objects" to impress the mind. "We are so much in the habit of allowing impressions to be made upon us by external objects," explains the narrator of *The Old Curiosity Shop*, "which should be produced by reflection alone," that "without such visible aids," the plight of others often escapes us. Had he been forced to imagine Nell "in a common chamber," he muses, "with nothing unusual or uncouth in its appearance," instead of surrounded by "the heaps of fantastic things" at the curiosity-dealer's warehouse, he would have been less impressed with her strange and solitary state. With "these helps to my fancy" crowding on his mind, Nell's condition was brought "palpably before me."[11]

Later in his career the experienced novelist advised the novice Emily Jolly on the same point: "An air of reality" is imparted to people, scenes, and houses "in the colouring throughout" and by "little subtle touches of description." Without them, he warned in his letter commenting on the manuscript she had submitted to him for criticism, there is no "attendant atmosphere of truth" and rather than believe in the protagonist, the reader will see "the heroine . . . for ever exploding like a great firework without any background; she glares and wheels and hisses, and goes out, and has lighted nothing."[12]

Dickens never made this mistake himself; moreover he was "absolutely certain" that such writing, far from being "a peculiarity of mine," ignited the particles of truth and life in fiction. As he tactfully reminded Charles Collins after reading a novel he sent to *All the Year Round* for possible serial publication: "Rely upon it, the story is altogether in want of touches of relief, and life, and truth. It is greatly too much in the manner of the stories of about the time of the Essayists; it does not hang well together, it is not easy; and there is too much of the narrator in it—the narrator not being an actor. The result is, that I can *not* see the people, or the place, or believe in the fiction" (*Letters*, III, 137–38).

The warning to Charles Collins about the dampening effect of telling instead of showing provides a useful measure of Dickens' own narrative practice; it also affirms what novelist and film maker have in common. To paraphrase Conrad's address to his readers in the preface to "The Nigger of the Narcissus," Dickens believed that the aim of fiction was to make one's audience feel, hear, and see; and that the presentation of people and places through "pictures," "images on the brain," was far more effective than the discursive reporting of Collins' narrator. Commmenting on his own art, Dickens confided to John Forster how he created his fictive world: " 'I don't invent it—really do not—*but see it,* and write it down.' " Good writing, as Herbert Read reminds us, is "VISUAL:" on these grounds novel and film unite.[13]

— 3 —

So far our investigation has focused on the preliminary stage concerning reasons for Dickens' cinematic appeal. The number of adaptations and the optical quality of his imagination present a prima facie case for an affinity between novel and film; the next task is to look at the deeper implications of their reciprocity. Let us, therefore, return to Eisenstein, who was the first to examine Dickens' influence on narrative film and argue that "the first shoots of American film esthetic" had a literary source: Dickens and the Victorian novel (p. 195).

The intermediate link in this surprising connection ("What could be further from films! Trains, cowbowys, chases . . . and *The Cricket on the Hearth?*"), is D. W. Griffith; in taking it up, a glance at the practice of early film directors is useful for understanding Griffith's innovative role and how Dickens' novels, through Griffith, are relevant to the development of film. Writing of the form of narrative film before Griffith began his career with American Mutoscope and Biograph in 1908, his biographer, Robert M. Henderson, comments that the filmmaking process of selecting, combining, and arranging shots, now known as editing, did not exist. "Each scene was photographed with the camera in a fixed location," explains Henderson. "The scene was played exactly as it would have been on stage. The actors were photographed in what was to become known as a medium shot with all of them visible in their entirety. Entrances were made, as on the stage from left to right. There were about twelve scenes in the film, and each film was a single shot."[14]

Within five years this method of constructing narrative films was radically altered by Griffith. By dividing a scene into sections or "shots," demonstrating that the duration of a shot need not depend on its natural action but could be lengthened or shortened for dramatic effect, varying the distance between viewer and scene within the same scene, and developing editing (the process of assembling shots into sequences and organizing the sequences into the completed film), Griffith established the basic principles of film composition.[15] The result, as

Robert Richardson notes in *Literature and Film,* was to separate film from theater. No longer a fixed and passive recorder of the events staged before it in a single visual area, the camera became mobile, thus making possible a distinctly cinematic form capable of narrative art of a high order. "A film was to be composed of all sorts of shots taken from all sorts of angles and distances": what gave the finished product its coherence, Richardson continues, was not "consecutive action in a fixed locale" as in theater, "but a logic or continuity created by the sequences into which the shots were joined together."[16]

Early film audiences, however, accustomed to the single long shot or medium shot of the static camera, were less appreciative of the narrative innovations popularized by Griffith. When the first close-ups appeared, spectators familiar with the stage view felt cheated by the camera's preempting their freedom to select whatever area of the stage they chose to concentrate on. Unable to see the actors in their entirety they expressed their disapproval by stamping and shouting: "Show us their feet!"[17] Similarly, Linda Arvidson Griffith reported the discussion in the studio when Griffith experimented with parallel plot construction. Preparing for a scene in *After Many Years,* 1908 (his first version of *Enoch Arden*), Griffith suggested showing Annie Lee waiting for her husband's return to be followed by a shot of him on a desert island. "It was altogether too distracting," objected his colleagues. " 'How can you tell a story jumping about like that? The people won't know what it's about.' " To which Griffith replied: " 'Well . . . doesn't Dickens write that way?' " (pp. 200–201).

This anecdote, together with Griffith's more detailed testimony to a London *Times* reporter in 1922 about Dickens' role in the evolution of his narrative craft, provided Eisenstein with the clue for investigating the seemingly improbable connection between the "trains, cowboys, and chases" of American cinema and the fictive world of Dickens.[18] Prompted by Griffith's remarks, Eisenstein turned to the novels, where he found abundant evidence of the "film indications of Dickens" in his use of: close-ups, dissolves, frame composition, "the alteration of emphasis by special lens," "cut-backs," parallel editing, and a basic montage structure that, in viewpoint and exposition, was very close to the cinema.

Confronted by this impressive accumulation of "future film exponents," Eisenstein saw the danger of pursuing the analogies to the point of losing their conviction and charm by "slid[ing] into a game of anecdotal semblance of tokens" (p. 213). Instead, he concentrated on how the new form of film narrative united with certain aspects of the older form of fictional narrative and avoided trying to "prove" Griffith's borrowings from Dickens.

Eisenstein's case for their interrelation rests on the common ground he saw in the method of narrative construction and the "principle of building . . . [known as] *montage*" shared by film and novel (p. 204). By *montage* Eisenstein meant in this context: 1) a method of assembling a series of shots related by time, place, and situation to form a sequence; and 2) in a more theoretical film sense, an analytical method of editing that broke down an idea into its constituent parts and then constructed an episode in which the whole sequence depended on the exactness of the fragments.[19] Supporting his assertion that Griffith arrived at montage through the method of parallel action and that he was led to it by Dickens is the presence of both kinds of montage in the novels: the montage of parallel action and "montage exposition."

Turning to chapters xiv through xvii of *Oliver Twist,* in which Oliver is captured by Nancy and Sikes as he returns some books to the bookseller's on behalf of Mr. Brownlow, Eisenstein praised Dickens' skillful alternation of the different social groups portrayed in the novel and cited his interlocking of the sequence in which the characters converge separately around the protagonist as a classic example of "a montage progression of parallel scenes." Of particular relevance to early film makers was Dickens' practice of moving back and forth and juxtaposing fragments of the story—Brownlow and Grimwig sitting in silence with a watch between them awaiting Oliver's return; the thieves drinking at The Three Cripples; Oliver making his way to the bookstall; Bumble preparing to leave for London on business—so as to convey the simultaneity of these fragmented yet interrelated events.

The importance of the "sudden shiftings of the scene, and rapid changes of time and place" was further enhanced for the film maker, Eisenstein thought, by the narrator's interjection of "Dickens's own 'treatise' on the principles of this montage construction of the story" (p. 223). Pausing at the opening of Chapter xvii, the narrator reflects: "It is the custom on the stage, in all good murderous melodramas, to present the tragic and the comic scenes, in as regular alternation, as the layers of red and white in a side of streaky bacon." The hero in despair, in the next a comic song; the heroine in danger, a funny chorus. Although the changes may at first appear absurd, the narrator counters: "The transitions in real life from well-spread boards to death-beds, and from mourning weeds to holiday garments, are not a whit less startling"; furthermore, he adds, these "shiftings" are not only sanctioned in books by long usage, "but are considered by many as the great art of authorship."

This " 'treatise,' " Eisenstein suggested, "could not have escaped the eye of the patriarch of the American film"; Griffith openly acknowledged his debt to Dickens and "very often his structure seems to follow the wise advice." Montage, Eisenstein concluded, "played a most vital role in the creative work of Griffith and brought him his most glorious successes" (p. 224 and p. 204). The counsel was also opportune; Dickens' observation and practice in *Oliver Twist* evidently provided a literary precedent without parallel in film and reinforced Griffith's commitment to experiments until his ideas gained greater acceptance.[20]

In addition to Dickens' use of parallel montage in *Oliver Twist* as a narrative device for increasing dramatic and emotional tension by exploiting the contrast of various story lines, Eisenstein noticed in the same novel a second kind of montage: "a prototype . . . of montage exposition" that, in the hands of the skilled film maker, could provide an even more significant means of artistic expression.

The structure of parallel montage, Eisenstein contended, was inextricably linked to the dualistic outlook of bourgeois society, where social issues are perceived simply *"as a contrast between the haves and the have-nots"* (p. 234). The only outcome of this antithesis, as presented by Dickens and Griffith, he continued, was the liberal's "hypothetical 'reconciliation' " of the two parallel lines of the rich and the poor as they crossed at infinity.[21] Alternatively, by emphasizing the dynamics implicit in juxtaposition, Eisenstein theorized that film continuity could advance through a series of shocks and conflicts (thesis, antithesis) to a synthesis where a new relationship was possible. Collision, in his view, ought to lie at the heart of montage; by confronting the spectator with the juxtaposition of dissimilar things, the artist could propel the audience forward to a deeper level of understanding, one consistent with the principles of the dialectic materialism of Marx and Engels in whose writing Eisenstein sought confirmation of his theory and practice.[22]

It was Dickens' ability in his set pieces to jolt the reader's mind with "montage-cluster[s]"[23] that impressed Eisenstein and accounted, he thought, for the novelist's success in conveying the "head-spinning tempo of changing impressions" that characterize his "dynamic (montage) picture[s]" of urban life (pp. 216–17). Citing the description of Sikes and Oliver traversing London at dawn, Eisenstein demonstrated how there was more to it than the "frightfully literal and catalogue-like" writing that Dickens abhorred.[24] To make his point, he broke down the chapter into units, assigned to each a shot number as if it were a shooting script, and added the following explanation:

How often have we encountered just such a structure in the work of Griffith? This austere accumulation and quickening tempo, this gradual play of light: from burning street-lamps, to their being extinguished; from night to dawn; from dawn to the full radiance of day . . . this calculated transition from purely visual elements to an interweaving of them with aural elements: at first as an indefinite rumble, coming from afar at

the second stage of increasing light, so that the rumble may
grow into a roar, transferring us to a purely aural structure,
now concrete and objective . . . with such scenes, picked up *en
passant,* and intercut into the whole—like the driver, hastening
towards his office; and, finally, these magnificently typical details, the reeking bodies of the cattle, from which the steam
rises and mingles with the over-all cloud of morning fog, or the
close-up of the legs in the almost ankle-deep filth and mire, all
this gives the fullest cinematic sensation of the panorama of a
market. (P. 216).

Eisenstein's approach to the description of Smithfield is instructive;
by looking at Dickens' technique from his perspective, one notices that
there is more to the novelist's method of seeing than simply cataloguing
details about the filth, stench, noise, and crush of the market. The concern for compositional design evident in the play of dark and light, the
interweaving of visual with aural elements, and the use of fragments or
close-ups to present those aspects of the scene he regarded as most
expressive, all suggest a control and manner analogous to that of the
film director, who, in breaking up a scene into its selected significant
parts, confounds our senses and stuns and bewilders us by thrusting his
artifact "directly under [the spectator's] nose." This impact, argues Ivor
Montague in his analysis of the camera's power, comes from the film
maker's showing "the spectator *nothing but* the aspect of the depicted
phenomenon he desires to emphasize at a given moment. The close-up,
for example, derives even more expressive significance from what it
excludes than from what it discloses. It enables him to make his communication with absolute clarity and precision, since the spectator cannot see anything else of the phenomenon depicted but the aspects the
director chooses to show him, in the order and for the duration chosen
by the director."[25]

The method of "the discontinuous image," as Stanley J. Solomon
calls the camera's eye when distinguishing its movements from those of
the eye in real life, is all the more emphatic because "each frame of the
shot excludes all sorts of irrelevant details."[26] In real life we perceive
objects differently; impressions are received by the mind more ran-
domly, without the selecting, ordering, and arranging that characterize
the camera's way of seeing. As a result, the film spectator becomes an
ideal observer seeing through the director's art only those aspects of
life which are the most expressive and the most characteristic. To vary
Henry James' dictum slightly, "Life being all inclusion and confusion,
and art being all discrimination and selection," the film maker searches
out his tiny nugget "washed free of awkward accretions" normally received by the eye.[27]

It is the search for clarity and precision that characterizes Dickens' most effectively written set pieces, where every detail chosen is a significant one and each image is selected with the artful precision of a meticulous director. Take, for example, the opening of *Little Dorrit,* where the staring sun, through its very intensity, produces a series of reflected images from which emanates a total sense of Marseilles on a fierce August day. Staring out of "the fervid sky," the sun is stared back in turn by "staring white houses," "staring white walls," and "staring white streets," "staring tracts of arid road," and "staring hills," as the narrator assembles highly selective units dealing next with the harbor—boats without awnings "too hot to touch," "ships blistered at their moorings," stones of the quays not cooled for months—and then back inland to convey a faint sign of habitation: "horses with drowsy bells," "recumbent drivers," and "exhausted laborers in the fields." Throughout the passage the repetition of the key word "staring" marks off successive shots and renders the whole a perfectly orchestrated shooting script with shifts in tempo from sun-induced stasis to the sudden movement of a lizard, contrasts of color (foul black water within the harbor, beautiful blue sea without) and texture (smooth water, rough stone walls), and a continuous interplay of light and shade that climaxes with the "villanous prison." Marseilles burning in the sun; the City of London awakening; Chancery wheezing in the fog; Magwitch standing before Pip in the lonely graveyard—cities, streets, and people never emerge all at once in a lifeless tableau to be taken in at a glance. Each appears piece by piece in a series of carefully constructed fragments, which, when fitted together like so many pieces of a jigsaw puzzle, provide a total impression of the scene Dickens wished to create.

— *4* —

More than ten years ago Ada Nisbet closed the "Craftsmanship" section of her bibliographical essay on a century of Dickens criticism with the judicious note that Eisenstein's essay "makes a major contribution to the study of Dickens as artist and literary craftsman."[28] By concentrating on Eisenstein's emphasis on the importance of background and setting to films and novels and his comments on the relationship of film and fictional narrative, the foregoing pages have attempted to demonstrate what that contribution is. As a film maker, Eisenstein was particularly sensitive to the use of setting: used effectively by directors and novelists, relevant details, shots, close-ups and montage exposition serve as indispensable components for the expression of ideas, attitudes, and the created world of the artist. *Mise-en-scène* is also crucial, Eisenstein noted, to the depiction of a character's "inner world and ethical countenance"; nowhere is this truer than in the imaginary world of Dickens. Whomever we select—Mr. Venus surrounded by Hindu babies in bottles, buttered muffins, stuffed canaries and loose teeth; Mrs. Clennam before the fire in an airless room, with the heat drawing the smell of black dye out of the crepe of her dress and the bierlike sofa on which she was sitting; Miss Havisham in her withered bridal gown contemplating speckle-legged spiders running in and out of her cobweb-covered wedding cake—each character emanates from the page, bringing, like the rum-soaked Mr. Dolls, their own atmosphere with them. Without it, their authenticity would be challenged, our belief unwillingly suspended, and the individuals dismissed as Dickensian exaggeration. Taken to its extreme, this is also the device of the German expressionist film makers of the 1920s, who used details of setting to depict a character's state of mind. Twisted rooms, strangely formed windows, unexpected angles of light, the stool of a threatening, unreasonable town official six or seven feet high, and the constantly turning arm of the organ grinder at the fair; an English Cathedral Town, a massive grey square tower, a rusty iron spike, clashing cymbals, ten thousand scimitars flashing, thrice ten thousand dancing-girls strewing flowers—Robert Wienee's *Cabinet of Dr. Caligari* (1919) and the opening paragraph of Dickens' *Mystery of Edwin Drood* (1870)—both attempt to convey the chaotic impressions streaming through the disturbed mind of the film's narrator, Francis, and the novel's protagonist, John Jasper, and render in concrete, perceptual images the consciousness of two superbly portrayed schizophrenics.

Obviously Eisenstein was not the first to call attention to so integral a part of Dickens' craft; in 1906 G. K. Chesterton remarked that "it is characteristic of Dickens that his atmospheres are more important than his stories."[29] To admit this, however, is to deny neither the sensitivity or the authority Eisenstein's film training gave his literary perception; on the contrary, his comments epitomize the need to turn to optical technology when analyzing this aspect of his style. Furthermore, the urge is not a new one: though coming no closer to moving pictures than to ancestral toys of the cinema like Thaumotropes, Stroboscopes, Zoetropes, and partially-revolving lantern slides, Dickens' contemporaries yielded to the same compulsion. As early as 1839, Richard Ford was writing in the *Quarterly Review* that "Boz sketches localities, particularly in London, with marvelous effect; he concentrates with the power of a camera lucida"; by the middle of the century, the metaphor had become an essential part of the critic's vocabulary. Hence George Eliot's praise of Dickens' facility of copying "with the delicate accuracy of a sun-picture"; R. H. Hutton's definition, in part, of Dickens' genius as "a power of observation so enormous that he could photograph almost everything he saw"; and H. F. Chorley's comment that Dickens "possess[ed] the immediate power of the daguerreotype." As if in agreement with John Ruskin, who noted in a letter to his father that Dickens' "powers of description have never been enough esteemed,"[30] critics, it seems, were determined to remedy the omission with the compliment of likening his graphic ability to that of the camera.

In a recent essay Leon Edel comments on the relationship between the camera and the novel with respect not to Dickens but to Balzac, Tolstoy, Flaubert, and James: "Wherever we turn in the nineteenth century we can see novelists cultivating the camera-eye" and seeking to become a camera not as a static instrument but as the camera "possessing the movement through space and time which the motion-picture camera has achieved in our century."[31] Just how cinematic Dickens' movements were, we know from Eisenstein's analysis of the structural device of the montage progression of parallel scenes and montage exposition. Perceptively, he isolated both the organizing principle of *Oliver Twist* and that of Dickens' narratives in general. Integral to the parallel scenes of progressive action is the technique of contrast, one which Dickens absorbed from both "good murderous melodramas" and more sophisticated sources like *Tom Jones,* and one which he eventually refined and developed into what Edmund Wilson called a new genre: "the detective story which is also a social fable."[32]

On the significance of "sudden shiftings of the scene" in the later novels, however, Eisenstein's ideology foreshortened his critical insight: evidently constricted by his Marxist theories, he was unable to appreciate that Dickens' artistry and philosophy developed beyond the "streaky bacon" dualism of *Oliver Twist.* From *Dombey and Son* (1846–48) onward, Dickens shifts locales not simply for the suspense and excitement arising from the juxtaposition of heterogeneous social groups: the rapid transitions become the very means by which he conveys the concept of the interdependence of the rich and the poor, the high and the low, whose collective fate is linked not hypothetically at infinity but practically in the present. To take an example from *Bleak House,* it is the social and moral implications of the "connexions" that should engage the reader's imagination, not the mystery, a point which is underscored by the narrator's deliberate challenge: "What connexion can there be," he insists, "between the place in Lincolnshire, the house in town, and the Mercury in powder, and the whereabout of Jo the outlaw with the broom?" Ghost stories, sexual misconduct, spontaneous combustion, murder, and a breathtaking chase—each propels and sustains the reader's narrative interest through a bewildering series of apparently disconnected events; but at every turn in the multiple catastrophes each is subordinate to the novel's social concerns and a reminder that *immediate* action was necessary. Should the point be missed, there are explicit warnings: "There is not an atom of Tom[-all-alone's] slime, not a cubic inch of any pestilential gas in which he lives, not one obscenity or degradation about him, not an ignorance, not a wickedness, not a brutality of his committing, but shall work its retribution, through every order of society, up to the proudest of the proud, and to the highest of the high. Verily, what with tainting, plundering, and spoiling, Tom has his revenge."[33]

However, if Eisenstein remained scornful of the implication of the "connexions," the locales inhabited by the characters curiously brought together "from opposite sides of great gulfs" are depicted in visual terms which undoubtedly met with his approval. The fog of Chancery one implacable November afternoon, the rain at Chesney Wold, the grease and soot of Krook's Rag and Bottle Warehouse, the dust of Tulkinghorn's legal chambers, or the pestilential filth of Tom-all-alone's—each fragment is made visible and palpable: viewing from the perspective of a crow skimming over the leaden London sky, we learn to share, with the narrator, the meaning of the pieces we see spread before us. Eisenstein urges the reader of literature to a fresh alertness to the visual quality of Dickens' writing; one hopes that the magnitude of Dickens' collected works, together with the extensive literature film criticism is building up, does not discourage those who are proficient in one to ignore the other.

Thomas J. Rice

BARNABY RUDGE

A Vade Mecum for the Theme of Domestic Government in Dickens

IN RECENT years most Dickens criticism has focused on the darker side of his imagination, as an understandable reaction to the overly simple, yet popular, view of Charles Dickens as a "Father Christmas" figure or as an impassioned defender of the home, the hearth, and the happy family. Similarly, the common view of Dickens as the unconscious, spontaneous artist has been modified considerably by close analyses of his intricate craftsmanship and by resourceful studies of his methods of composition. These two perspectives on Dickens as dark visionary and master technician, however, are not necessarily complementary. While Dickens is often a radically original artist, modifying and expanding the techniques of fiction he inherited, I would argue that his attitudes and opinions, even his "imaginative vision," rarely deviate widely from the accepted mores of his age. (Here, the comparison with Shakespeare is inevitable, though commonplace.) In *Barnaby Rudge* (1841), for example, Dickens employs an extraordinary complex of analogous relationships, parallel actions, and symbolic patterns to articulate a fundamentally conventional, edifying moral.[1]

Throughout his career Dickens cultivated his reputation as a domestic novelist. His fiction relied extensively upon the family for its subject matter and was especially tailored for the eyes of all members of the fireside circle. In later years his advocacy of literature which would instruct and delight the women, the young ladies, and the children of the audience, as well as the gentlemen, was formalized into a "Household Words" rule of decorum for himself and for contributors to his journal. Dickens' preoccupation with the domestic situation in his work and his psychically healthy veneration of the family in his life and in his fiction have been too easily taken for granted simply because they reflect the conventional attitudes of mid-Victorian England. We tend to forget, however, that conceptions of the family, its role in society, the relationships among its members and its proper governance, have changed markedly in the last century. Dickens' views of the family demand examination and assessment *because* they are conventional.

Dickens' novels share with the greater part of his audience a concern for protecting the sanctity of the home. The unhappy home environment is certainly his most frequent plot device, and his stories regularly conclude either with the establishment of a new order or with the restoration of household harmony. If Dickens' fascination with fragmented homelives is the result of his own unfortunate family relations in childhood and maturity, the reunited domestic circle is both a form of personal wish-fulfillment and a spiritually uplifting ideal for his readers. Beyond this, there is little direct, informative discussion of household government in his fiction. While most of his opinions on domestic subjects are available, implicitly, in his satires of inadequate and incompetent parents, or of disorderly and impertinent children, only in *Barnaby Rudge* does Dickens comment explicitly, through action, character, and theme, on the nature or operation of the ideal family and provide us with the standard against which we can measure the inadequacies of the Chuzzlewits, the Jellybys, or the Pockets. Dickens' analysis of domestic roles and his ingenious analogical and structural explorations of the family in *Barnaby Rudge* present a complete and coherent picture of his ideas on home management, a virtual handbook of his views on the full spectrum of household relationships. *Barnaby Rudge* provides us a unique vade mecum for the theme of domestic government in Dickens.

It seems clear that Dickens planned *Barnaby* to embody an impressive variety of family situations and to illustrate many of the notions of prudent domestic government he shared with his contemporary audience.[2] Dickens deviates slightly from his characteristic fictional attacks on social injustice in favor of a more moderate affirmation of the established order. The fundamental conservatism of *Barnaby's* social views is consistent, moreover, with its theme of political moderation.[3] The reasons Dickens chose to reinforce, rather than to modify, his readers' preconceptions are not complex: *Barnaby Rudge,* from its inception, was to be his first "three-decker" novel, his calculated appeal to the intellectual readership that scorned "penny dreadful" literature and that sought more "improving" writers, such as the admirable Sir Walter Scott.[4] As a historical novel, *Barnaby* was intended to draw the immediate attention of Scott's audience, to rival his reputation in his own field. As a prudent delineation of the most accepted views of family governance, it was to appear intellectually and morally substantial.

The term "domestic government" best describes Dickens' chief social theme in *Barnaby Rudge* and suggests the most significant, and most acceptable, dimension of his appeal to popular concensus. Dickens grounds the analyses of his various family groups on the commonplace analogy between the domestic and civil spheres. He assumes, as would his readers, that the household, as the basic social unit, reflects and determines the welfare of the nation. Although the hierarchical structure of society had weakened considerably under the Whig ascendancies and the "great chain of being" idea provoked doubt rather than certainty by early Victorian times, the concept of the family as the mirror and the determinant of society still had a traditional validity. Thus Dickens' political and social themes are closely interrelated not only by their shared conservatism, but also by this direct correlation between the public and the private worlds. Dickens literally and figuratively brings his political message *home,* for he pivots the two-part structure of the novel on the civil-domestic analogy. Only recently the familial crises in *Barnaby Rudge* have been dismissed as "more or less irrelevant to the novel,"[5] yet such a judgment overlooks Dickens' efficient fusion of his political and social themes through an analogy that would not have easily escaped his contemporary readers. Unfortunately, the complexity and the dexterity of his analogical technique may be missed by the reader who is unaware of the familiar assumptions about household rule in early Victorian England. A close study of the theme of domestic government in *Barnaby Rudge* will clarify some of these assumptions, demonstrate a significant unifying element in the novel and, by virtue of its comprehensiveness, provide us with a basic outline of Dickens' conservative view of the family.

— I —

Barnaby Rudge is a divided novel. Approximately one-third of its contents is devoted to the development and the interaction of five family units, while the balance of the narrative concerns the historical events which embroil the entire cast. Dickens deliberately separates the private and the public material by inserting a five-year hiatus between these two parts, yet a closer inspection reveals considerable foreshadowing of the riots of 1780 in the opening chapters and a continued exploration of the domestic themes, through analogy, in the civil section. By so dividing the novel Dickens invites, rather than discourages, the sensitive reader to seek a connection between its apparently disparate parts. The principal household situations presented include one of the few intact families in Dickens' work (the Gabriel Vardens), the "widow" and child (Mrs. Rudge and Barnaby), the widower and son (John and Joe Willet, John and Edward Chester), the orphan (Emma Haredale and Hugh), the stern stepfather (Geoffrey Haredale), the Dickensian father surrogate (Varden to Sim and to Barnaby), and the mysterious parent (Rudge and Chester). Dickens considers within this framework the relationships between parent and child, husband and wife, and master and servant. The landed-gentry Haredales and the impoverished Rudges represent broken families who have suffered alike from sins against moderation, and they are situated, significantly, at the extremes of the novel's social spectrum. Between the two poles, and under the shadow of their domestic fragmentation, Dickens places the remaining households: the Willets, the Chesters, and the Vardens. Each of these groups illustrates a specific thesis on household government, from the ambiguous revolt in the lower middle-class Willet home and the unequivocally righteous rebellion in the upper-class Chester family, to the clearly unjust upheavals in the idealized, middle-class Varden circle.

Barnaby Rudge opens with an upset in the natural order which prefigures later rebellions.[6] The theme of domestic insurrection is firmly established in Solomon Daisy's tale of Reuben Haredale's murder at the hands of his servant (Rudge), and it is effectively reinforced by a violent storm outside the Maypole tavern, a sympathetic upheaval of the elements. As the parallel familial disorders are developed, Rudge periodically reappears as an ominous, everpresent symbol of depravity. Not only Rudge's, but *all* the localized private revolts have their logical extension in the massive public uprising of the Gordon Riots. Each individual rebellion can be attributed to a specific problem in household government. In the second part of *Barnaby Rudge,* Dickens introduces the corresponding political dimension of each domestic problem.

Throughout the novel Dickens seeks a definition of the just revolt, a concern he shares with his contemporary Carlyle. The elements of right rule are probed in his treatment of the conflicting claims of authority and liberty, the relative duties of family members, and the sacrosanct blood-relationship between parent and child. The civil equivalents for these issues are the conflict between government and individual rights, the duties of the state and its citizens, and, implicitly, the sacred tie between king and subject. Of course Dickens considers the Gordon Riots a treasonable rebellion; yet his treatment of injustice in home government promotes a partial sympathy for at least one of the rioters' grievances.

The Haredale and the Rudge family groups serve complementary purposes in Dickens' development of his theme. Since the original crime of the Haredale murder occurred twenty-two years before the novel's opening, the two households involved are poignant illustrations of the ultimate effects of insurrection. Both families are fragmented. The murderer has deserted his wife and child and is believed dead. Emma Haredale has been orphaned and is living with her guardian uncle. Geoffrey himself lives in, and forces upon Emma, a seclusion from the society that erroneously suspects him of his brother's death.

The deterioration of the Haredale fortunes is figuratively conveyed in the disintegration of the family estate, the Warren: "It was a dreary, silent building, with echoing courtyards, desolated turret-chambers, and whole suites of rooms shut up and mouldering to ruin. The ter-race-garden, dark with the shade of overhanging trees, had an air of melancholy that was quite oppressive. Great iron gates, disused for many years, and red with rust, drooping on their hinges and over-grown with long rank grass, seemed as though they tried to sink into the ground, and hide their fallen state among the friendly weeds. . . . There was a sombre aspect even on that part of the mansion which was inhabited and kept in good repair, that struck the beholder with a sense of sadness; of something forlorn and failing, whence cheerful-ness was banished. . . . It seemed a place where such things had been, but could be no more—the very ghost of a house, haunting the old spot in its old outward form, and that was all" (101–2).

The devastation of the Haredale property, a clear projection of its owners, is firmly associated with the fruits of another rebellion of ser-vant against master through the verbal echoes of the lost Eden, "whence cheerfulness was banished." In the second part of *Barnaby Rudge,* Dickens unites Barnaby with his demonic father and diverts the mob to Chigwell to complete the destruction of Warren. The crime of Rudge, therefore, exactly prefigures the civil riots. The long-suffering Haredales have been crippled by Rudge and are nearly destroyed by the satanic political conspiracy of Chester and Gashford.

The Rudge family, too, feels the effects of the original crime. As the heir to the sin of his father, Barnaby is inevitably, if unwittingly, en-ticed to a repetition of the offense. The inexorable logic of this little morality play uncharacteristically puts Dickens in a position implicitly supporting the doctrine of natural depravity. However, Barnaby is ex-onerated from any responsibility for his actions through his idiocy, the added stigma of his father's crime. Rudge's obsessive guilt, Haredale's unfeeling and biased objection to Emma's love affair with Edward Ches-ter (the son of the man who has slanderously implicated him in his brother's death), and Haredale's monomaniacal pursuit of the mur-derer are all, similarly, the final fruits of the original sin. Against this somber background Dickens carefully delineates the moral, social, and political dimensions of simultaneous rebellions in the Willet, Chester, and Varden households.

— 2 —

The relationship of John Willet and his son Joe illustrates the tenu-ous balance between the claims of authority and liberty in government. In his presentation of the Maypole household Dickens examines the relative duties of father and son, the limits of parental power and the demands of filial obedience. Old John, a tyrannical father, and Joe, an imprudent son, are equally guilty of disturbing the domestic peace. Joe threatens to upset the natural order ("We'll see whether boys are to govern men, or men are to govern boys" [230]), while his father continually diminishes his natural right of liberty. Once the balance of normal household power is upset, a confrontation becomes inevitable. Unlike the other domestic rebellions, there is no real sense of justice or criminality in the characters' actions. When the ambiguous issues raised by the Willet situation are extended to the civil sphere in the second part of *Barnaby Rudge,* they create a similarly equivocal response in the reader's attitude toward the Gordon Riots.

Old John's government of his son is a plainly absurd absolutism which may be appropriate for an infant but not for a reasoning adolescent. Despite Joe's age "it pleased his father still to consider [him] a little boy, and to treat [him] accordingly" (6). Willet's advice to his son initially seems prudent: "What do you mean by talking when you see people that are more than two or three times your age, sitting still and silent and not dreaming of saying a word?" yet this impression deteriorates rapidly: "When I was your age, I never talked, I never wanted to talk" (8). Joe, in turn, is not sufficiently mature to make Willet's inept government totally unreasonable. He is a likeable, but overly talkative, querulous, and indiscreet fellow. His impudent replies to his father, while perhaps deserved, show a lack of filial reverence, an unwillingness to honor his parent and to endure his obstinacy. Joe flatly rejects Varden's counsel "to bear with his father's caprices, and rather turn them aside by temperate remonstrance than by ill-timed rebellion. . . . [he] politely intimated his intention nevertheless of taking his own course uninfluenced by anybody" (24). Joe's insubordination eventually leads to a house arrest, or as Willet malappropriately expresses it, a "patrole." Invoking a political metaphor, Dickens describes the excessiveness of this punishment, the abuse of parental authority which incites further disobedience:

> Old John having long encroached a good standard inch on the liberty of Joe, and having snipped off a Flemish ell in the matter of the parole, grew so despotic and so great, that his thirst for conquest knew no bounds. The more young Joe submitted, the more absolute old John became. The ell soon faded into nothing. Yards, furlongs, miles arose; and on went old John in the pleasantest manner possible, trimming off an exuberance in this place, shearing away some liberty of speech or action in that, and conducting himself in his small way with as much high mightiness and majesty, as the most glorious tyrant that ever had his statue reared in the public ways, of ancient or of modern times. (228)

Significantly, when Joe's resentment finally explodes it is directed
not at his father, but at one of Willet's "Maypole cronies," Tom Cobb.
Joe rightly distinguishes between Willet's and Cobb's relative authority:
"These things are hard enough to bear from you [father]; from anybody else I never will endure them any more" (231). Dickens carefully
preserves the reader's partial sympathy for Joe by diverting his revolt
away from his father, thus avoiding an unspeakable crime against nature.[7] This special veneration of the relationship between parent and
child, in fact, is the key to Dickens' view of domestic government. Even
the idiot boy Barnaby instinctively recognizes the sacredness of the
blood bond between father and son.

> "Ah! I know! You are the robber!"
> He said nothing in reply at first, but held down his head, and
> struggled with him silently. Finding the younger man too
> strong for him, he raised his face, looked close into his eyes,
> and said,
> "I am your father."
> God knows what magic the name had for his ears; but Bar-
> naby released his hold, fell back, and looked at him aghast.
> Suddenly he sprung towards him, put his arms about his neck,
> and pressed his head against his cheek. (478)[8]

Sir John Chester's villainy in *Barnaby Rudge* is, on the other hand, com-
pounded by his inhuman rejection of both his sons.

For Dickens, and for his contemporary audience, the tie between
parent and child was as sacrosanct as the covenant between God and
mankind, or between the king and his subjects.[9] Any violation of this
natural bond was considered so serious that the parent was traditionally
given the power of life or death over his child. The legal penalty of
death for striking one's parent was rescinded only in the late 1830s.[10]
Admittedly this prerogative was rarely, if ever, exercised; nevertheless,
it indicates the general reverence for the family bond. Although Joe
avoids the damnable crime of violence against his father, he does raise
his hand against his father's authority. He has profaned the hospitality
of the hearth. When Joe runs away from home to avoid punishment
for his action, he compounds his sins against the domestic order. The
recruiting sergeant appropriately introduces Joe to the new world of
outcasts he has joined, men capable of patricide: "The serjeant rejoined
with many choice asserrations that he didn't; and that if his [the
sergeant's] own father were to say he did, he would run the old gentleman through the body cheerfully, and consider it a meritorious action"
(236). In the highly moral world of *Barnaby Rudge* it is necessary that
Joe suffer more than exile for his offenses. He therefore loses the arm
he has raised in rebellion.

Willet's authoritarian home rule is uniquely indebted to the contemporary Evangelical theories of domestic government which receive
much less sympathetic treatment from Dickens elsewhere in his fiction.
Old John is definitely not a religious enthusiast (no tavernkeeper would
be); however, he does see himself as the Evangelical "god" of his
hearth, a god of wrath. His program for Joe's upbringing can be compared with that of Susanna Wesley for her famous sons John and
Charles: "As self-will is the root of all sin and misery, so whatever
cherishes this in children, insures their after-wretchedness and irre-
ligion: and whatever checks and mortifies it, promotes their future
happiness and piety. . . . So that the parent who studies to subdue
[self-will] in his children, works together with God."[11] Unfortunately,
too often the Wesleyan formula was distorted by the overly zealous
parent who confused the will of God with his own, and generations of
Englishmen were raised by arbitrary and unreasoning parents like Willet, "a father of the good old English sort" (228). The most frightening
example of the autocrat father in Dickens' fiction is Mr. Murdstone,
David Copperfield's Evangelical stepfather; Willet differs from Murdstone only in religion and the tone of presentation. In *Barnaby Rudge*
Dickens' conscious moderation enables him to see some validity in, and
the necessary authority of, the strong father figure.

As a comic character Willet is made far less threatening and more
sympathetic than David's wicked stepfather. The difference in age between the child David and the young man Joe transforms a night-
marish situation into an absurdity. Like David, Joe is imprisoned, but
Dickens never shows him being "knocked about" by his father. Willet
remains a pompous fool, trying to the reader's and his son's patience
perhaps, yet too harmless to encourage fear. Thus the catastrophic attack on the Maypole by the rioters inspires disgust, not satisfaction.
John's failings are many, but they do not deserve this sort of retribution. The destruction of the Maypole, like that of the Warren, strikes us
as a tragic waste. There is a stability in the "John Bull-ish" Willet that is
attractive as well as oppressive. Like the Warren, his household is a
projection of himself:

> All bars are snug places, but the Maypole's was the very snug-
> gest, cosiest, and completest bar, that ever the wit of man de-
> vised. Such amazing bottles in old oaken pigeon-holes; such
> gleaming tankards dangling from pegs at about the same incli-
> nation as thirsty men would hold them to their lips; such sturdy
> little Dutch kegs ranged in rows on shelves; so many lemons
> hanging in separate nets, and forming the fragrant grove al-
> ready mentioned in this chronicle, suggestive, with goodly
> loaves of snowy sugar stowed away hard by, of punch, idealised
> beyond all mortal knowledge; such closets, such presses, such

drawers full of pipes, such places for putting things away in hollow window-seats, all crammed to the throat with eatables, drinkables, or savoury condiments; lastly, and to crown all, as typical of the immense resources of the establishment, and its defiances to all visitors to cut and come again, such a stupendous cheese! (151)

This absolute orderliness may be restrictive, yet it offers substantial rewards and is certainly preferable to the chaos of rebellious disorder.

The despotic John Willet is spared from Dickens' and the reader's wrath because his obtuse home government may be prudently circumvented. As a form of civil policy, however, such authoritarianism is far more menacing. In the second part of *Barnaby Rudge,* Willet is given a political "double," the magistrate, who gains no corresponding sympathy. In establishing a connection between Willet's family role and that of the justice of the peace, Dickens reflects one of the most common precepts of domestic theory. As John Angell James observes in his popular and influential *Family Monitor* (1833), the parent is "the supreme magistrate of [the] household, and cannot have a right idea of [his] situation, without considering [himself] as appointed to *rule.*"[12] The country justice of *Barnaby Rudge,* "a thoroughbred Englishman" and "a genuine John Bull," is directly paralleled to John Willet in several respects. Both are highly esteemed by their neighbors for their no-nonsense rule. The magistrate's friends "all agreed . . . that it was a pity there were not more like him, and that because there were not, the country was going to rack and ruin every day" (357), while Willet's Maypole cronies similarly argue that "it would be well for the country if there were more like him" (228). The justice tyrannizes over his wife, the "book learner," who differs from Joe only in her submissiveness. Both the magistrate and Willet are firm advocates of corporal punishment and imprisonment. This country magistrate would remain an absurd figure, a hard-drinking, hard-riding, "Squire Western" Tory, were it not for his influence on Barnaby's fate. Unlike Willet, he threatens a fatal miscarriage of justice. His testimony in court "turned the wavering scale against poor Barnaby" in maintaining that the idiot "was sane, and had, to his knowledge, wandered about the country with a vagabond parent, avowing revolutionary and rebellious sentiments" (574).

A second, vital link between Willet's domestic authoritarianism and national policy becomes apparent in Dickens' handling of the capital punishment issue in *Barnaby Rudge.* Old John's confidence in this "enlightened" treatment of petty offenders as evidence of "how wide awake our government is" (87) allies him with the supporters of that "constitootional" officer Ned Dennis, the hangman: "He remembered the great estimation in which his office was held, and the constant

demand for his services; . . . he bethought himself, how the Statute
Book regarded him as a kind of Universal Medicine applicable to men,
women, and children, of every age and variety of criminal constitution;
and how high he stood, in his official capacity, in the favour of the
Crown, and both Houses of Parliament, the Mint, the Bank of England,
and the Judges of the land; . . . he recollected that whatever Ministry
was in or out, he remained their peculiar pet and panacea, and that for
his sake England stood single and conspicuous among the civilised nations of the earth" (567–68). The amoral and ignorant hangman represents capital punishment itself, a degenerate policy which has lost both
its moral justification and its value as an object lesson through indiscriminate use. It is a "dreadful and repulsive penalty," Dickens writes,
"which never turned a man inclined to evil, and has hardened thousands who were half inclined to good" (500). This abuse of civil authority is equivalent to the excessive parental reliance upon corporal punishment, "a parental kick, or a box on the ears, or a cuff on the head,
or some little admonition of that sort" (228–29).

The public significance of Willet's heavy-handed home discipline is
again clarified by his evangelical heritage. Susanna Wesley's program
for parents tended to sanction the ready application of the rod in con-
trolling children: "Break their wills betimes. . . . Whatever pains it
cost, conquer their stubbornness; break the will, if you would not damn
the child. . . . Therefore (1) Let a child, from a year old, be taught to
fear the rod and cry softly. In order to do this, (2) Let him have nothing he cries for; absolutely nothing, great or small; else you undo your
own work. (3) At all events, from that age, make him do as he is bid, if
you whip him ten times running to affect it."[13] Although this advice
was tempered with warnings against indiscriminate chastisement and
punishment in anger, Mrs. Wesley's disciples were not always so merciful. In fact, some disciples of the "spare the rod and spoil the child"
philosophy further advocated Mr. Murdstone's favored tactic of deferred punishment, to give the child a full opportunity to dread the
event.[14] Not only did this form of mental cruelty have disastrous psychological effects on the child, but its dissassociation from the crime
negated any positive, educational value in the penalty. Throughout his
fiction and occasional prose Dickens demonstrates a special fascination
with the condemned criminal's dread of the gallows (e.g., Dennis' scene
in chapter lxxvii), as well as the guilty child's corresponding fear of
the rod (e.g., David's agonized anticipation of his flogging, *David Copperfield,* iv). In *Barnaby,* Dickens particularly attacks the inadequacy of
capital punishment as a lesson for the potential criminal, the spectator
at public executions. Representing the unredeemed witnesses, the "hardened thousands," are Dennis and Hugh. Both are intimate with the
gallows by profession and by experience, yet neither is deterred from

his criminal behavior. Rather, it is strongly implied that their familiarity with capital punishment is the primary cause of their rascality. The hangman's work has so brutalized him that he sees execution as an end in itself, an art which exists for its own sake. Hugh, an "edified" spectator at his mother's hanging, likewise illustrates the destructive impact of this "dreadful and repulsive penalty." The contagion of the gallows has tainted Hugh, and he is destined to be hanged. His fate is clear to his fellows and to Hugh himself. Only the reader is tempted to question its inevitability.

In the private sphere Willet misinterprets his parental duty to correct his child, for the sake of his soul, by approaching punishment as the privilege of authority. His chastisement is indiscriminate in its failure to distinguish between major and minor offenses and in its substitution of the rod for reasoned admonitions. Willet has, in effect, misused his parental responsibility to superintend Joe's moral education. Likewise, the failure of the civil powers to eradicate crime at its sources and their excessive reliance on capital punishment as a brutal object lesson are abuses of governmental duties. As the rebellious son is the ultimate result of John Willet's authoritarian home rule, so also is the renegade Hugh, as he says, "the ripened fruit" of the "black tree," the gallows (596). The state's preoccupation with punishment for crime, rather than with its prevention, and its failure to proportion the penalty to fit the offense are merely logical extensions of perverted ideas in domestic government. Indeed, the English nation at the time of the Gordon Riots had arrogated the power of life and death over its citizens as a God-given privilege and had abused it accordingly. If the Riots of 1780 were motivated by this issue alone, Dickens would have been a more sympathetic historian. His equivocal treatment of Joe's revolt, his obvious relish in the storming of Newgate and the other riot scenes, and his relenting characterization of Hugh indicate a personal identification with this particular grievance which, in part, accounts for his ambivalence toward the mob. However, Newgate was not the Bastille, and the Gordon Riots were not the French Revolution. The riots also represented a moral and a social chaos abhorrent to Dickens. Their full nature is clarified in the domestic and the civil development of the Chester and the Varden households.

— 3 —

The revolt of Edward Chester against his father, Sir John Chester, is established as a deliberate contrast to that of Joe Willet. Here there is no ambiguity, no shared responsibility for the event. Chester is a viciously inadequate father, while his son is dutiful to the last. Dickens finds no possibilities for humorous development of their relations, and

he adopts a somber tone of moral earnestness. Again the themes of
parental authority, the relative duties of father and son, and the sacred
bond between parent and child are introduced. Earlier in life Sir John
had abandoned his illegitimate son Hugh, and during the novel he disinherits his legitimate son Edward. Dickens has Chester clearly reaffirm
both these rejections of the parental bond near the end of the narrative. Varden says,

> "I KNOW that you anticipate the disclosure with which I am
> about to end, and that you believe this doomed man, Hugh, to
> be your son."
> "Nay," said Sir John, bantering him with a gay air. . . .
> "Think better of it, sir, when I am gone," returned the lock-
> smith; "think better of it, sir. Although you have, thrice within
> as many weeks, turned your lawful son, Mr. Edward, from
> your door, you may have time, you may have years to make
> your peace with *him*." (580–81)

Chester's callous indifference toward Hugh's fate compounds the inhu-
manity of his denials of fatherhood: "Extremely distressing to be the
parent of such an uncouth creature! Still, I gave him very good advice.
I told him he would certainly be hanged. . . . There are a great many
fathers who have never done as much for *their* natural children.—The
hairdresser may come in, Peak!" (582). Chester preserves his cosmetic
appearance and disguises from himself his own responsibility for
Hugh's destruction.

Sir John's treatment of his "lawful" child Edward is the focus for
one of the most damning indictments of the vicious parent in Dickens'
work. To disinherit a child in the eighteenth (or nineteenth) century, to
sever all legal and economic ties, was a profoundly religious as well as a
social act. Since the parent was viewed as the god of the household, his
formal dissolution of the natural relationship with his offspring, "quite
a holy kind of bond" as Sir John observes (94), and his abandonment of
all hopes for the child's eventual reformation were logically and doc-
trinally analogous to the damnation of a soul.[15] When he dismisses his
son, Chester properly assumes this role of the final Judge, bidding
Edward to "go to the Devil, at my express desire" (246). However, his
lack of moral justification makes Chester a depraved parody of the
Godhead, an anti-Christ. Only the most grievous of circumstances, such
as the striking of the parent, could warrant the condemnation of the
child.[16] To disinherit without sufficient cause was a heinous, unnatural
sin against the "holy" bond of the family. As they are presented by
Dickens, Chester's unjust dismissal of Edward and his symbolic disin-
heritance of Hugh are clearly his greatest crimes.[17] Edward disobeys
his father's command to marry unscrupulously, to become a "fortune

hunter," and Dickens explicitly justifies his revolt. His refusal to comply
with his father's dishonest demand is sanctioned by the single exception
to the commandment of filial obedience: the submission of the child to
the parent in all things was superseded only by his duty to God. When
these obligations conflicted, when the parent ordered a sinful act, the
child was bound by conscience to refuse.[18] "It is sad," Edward reflects,
"when a son, proffering him his love and duty in their best and truest
sense, finds himself repelled at every turn, and forced to disobey"
(245).

In composing Chapter xxxii, the final conference between Chester
and his son, Dickens carefully establishes the theological justice of Edward's revolt and the sacrilegious nature of Sir John's actions. Initially
Chester rejects his parental identity: " 'Ah father!' cried his son, 'if—'
'My good fellow,' interposed the parent hastily, as he set down his glass,
and raised his eyebrows with a startled and horrified expression, 'for
Heaven's sake don't call me by that obsolete and ancient name' " (243).
Chester's denial of fatherhood as a meaningless label is reinforced by
his cold, rationalistic rejection of love itself: "About to speak from your
heart. Don't you know that the heart is an ingenious part of our formation—the centre of the blood-vessels and all that sort of thing" (243).
While Chester is adept at ornamenting his conversation with an occasional pious platitude when it is advantageous, his sincerity is undermined by a pointed echo from his pseudoscientific denial of the spirit:
"Remember, if you please, your interest, your duty, your moral obligations, your filial affections, *and all that sort of thing*'" (244, emphasis
mine). The devil is fond of quoting Scripture, and Sir John is equally
ready to cite the tenets of domestic government. Edward, however,
convincingly defends his own moral values. He recognizes and rejects
his father's cynical materialism as he defends his disobedience in precisely the terms which sanction it, his spiritual duty to a higher power:
" 'The curse may pass your lips,' said Edward, 'but it will be but empty
breath. I do not believe that any man on earth has greater power to call
one down upon his fellow—least of all, upon his own child—than he
has to make one drop of rain or flake of snow fall from the clouds
above us at his impious bidding. Beware, sir, what you do'" (245).
Chester, so warned, disinherits his son with full knowledge of his own
injustice. Edward remains the model of the virtuous son throughout
the novel, attempting to reconcile his father and superintending his
half brother's burial. The retribution for his revolt is negligible, a
meaningless loss of honor among his father's fashionable set. It is more
pertinent to speak of Dickens' retribution for Chester, the instigator of
revolt both in his family and in the state: his last provocation, his en-
ticement of Haredale into a duel, results in his death.

As has been his method with the Haredales and the Willets, Dickens' description of John Chester's living quarters symbolically reflects, with similar poetic justice, the nature of the occupant. The hypocritical Chester lives in an *apartment,* in the insubstantial "Paper" buildings, not in a home at all. Sir John offers his son a household which lacks a solid foundation, just as he represents a life-style which, based on preserved appearances, is intrinsically empty and potentially destructive. Thus he is often presented in a state of studied dishabille amidst an elegant but chaotic disarry of clothes and covers, inhaling an artificial atmosphere: " 'Here, Peak. Bring some scent and sprinkle the floor' " (181). Chester is despicable to the fastidious Dickens as much for this thinly veiled chaos as for his attempted perversion of his son's education. In his parental role as teacher he actively exhorts Edward toward a hollow life of hypocrisy, cautioning him against a "squeamish and moral" code of behavior. He has tried to breed him "upon a careful principle" of artificial gentility: "the very manner of your education, I assure you, maintained by credit surprisingly" (120). Edward recognizes that he cannot maintain such an aristocratic life-style without self-compromise: " 'From my childhood I have been accustomed to luxury and idleness, and have been bred as though my fortune were large, and my expectations almost without limit. The idea of wealth has been familiarised to me from my cradle. I have been taught to look upon those means, by which men raise themselves to riches and distinction, as being beyond my breeding, and beneath my care. I have been, as the phrase is, liberally educated, and am fit for nothing. I find myself at last wholly dependent upon you, with no resource but in your favour' " (116–17).

Dickens clearly intends that Chester be recognized as a disciple of, and a surrogate for, Lord Chesterfield, Philip Dormer Stanhope, in this attempt to mold his son. The similarity in their names, the parallel incidents in their careers (e.g., the clandestine loves of their sons, the frustration of their educational programs, their illegitimate children, and their concern for their gentility, even in death), and the shared preoccupation with appearances would have made the identification immediate for a generation that knew Chesterfield's *Letters to His Son* as a standard handbook both for etiquette and for epistolary style.[19] Sir John's Chesterfieldian superintendence of his son's lavish education is flawed, nonetheless, for somehow Edward has developed a sensitive conscience. Perhaps as Dickens' Victorian answer to the decadent cynicism of the enlightened pragmatist, he cultivates in Edward the quite impractical virtues of independence, self-respect, and self-help. The frustrated Chester is left apostrophizing, " 'My Lord Chesterfield, . . . if I could but have profited by your genius soon enough to have formed my son on the model you have left to all wise fathers, both he and I would have been rich men' " (173). Dickens' attack upon the hypocritical, genteel Chester is a characteristic nineteenth-century response to the abuses of rationalism; it is also a valuable admonition to his contemporary audience whose children, like themselves, were being raised upon Chesterfield's morally seditious *Letters*.

Sir John Chester's domestic government, like Willet's, has its equivalent in the civil sphere; however, Dickens clearly demonstrates that Chester's political machinations endanger rather than support the ruling powers. By emphatically separating Chester from the ministry in office at the time of the Gordon Riots, indeed, by making him one of the prime movers of rebellion in the family and in the nation, Dickens effectively dissociates the rioters from Edward's just revolt and associates them with the irreligious, self-serving aristocrat. To give Chester a civil counterpart, Dickens simply elevates him during the novel's five-year interval to Sir John Chester, M.P., to act as his own parliamentary representative.[20] Dickens conveys Chester's political decadence by again appealing to the reader's moral sensibility. His rationalism, as contemptible to Dickens as its nineteenth-century descendant, Benthamism, denies man's spirituality, his natural affections, "and all that sort of thing." His gentility is construed as a lack of industry, a negation of the Samuel Smiles self-help ethic. To Chester self-reliance is improper, indicating vulgarity or "a tendency to prose" (117). His success in gaining a parliamentary seat is achieved not through his own honest energies, but through political chicanery to obtain legislative immunity (302).

Chester's chief political role in *Barnaby Rudge* is that of the heartless, Machiavellian conspirator. He is a symbol of political manipulation and hypocrisy in authority for the sake of his own self-aggrandizement. He is serenely unconcerned by the individual fates of his victims. As he ignores the execution of his bastard Hugh, so also, in the domestic sphere, would he have dismissed Edward: if he "were awkward and overgrown . . . I should have exported [him] to some distant part of the world" (119). Although Chester serves quite well as his own civil equivalent, he, like Willet, is provided a political "double" who first appears in the second part of the novel. His fellow conspirator, Lord Gordon's secretary John Gashford, is similarly distinguished from the governing powers and is an active agitator of rebellion. Dickens uses several techniques to reinforce the political and symbolic alliance between Chester and Gashford, but his most effective and most readily apparent device is the series of parallel, clandestine meetings between the rioters and the provocateurs which punctuate the historic section of the book. Chester's consultations with Hugh are juxtaposed to "Muster Gashford's" with Dennis, Sim, and Hugh. Both men successfully divorce themselves from their agents while instigating the major actions of the riots. Chester and Gashford are similarly self-serving. As Chester attempts to use his sons for his own advantage in private life (Edward to marry well, and Hugh to gather intelligence), Chester and Gashford both exploit the rioters to achieve their public and their private ends. The two men alike determine their political opposition to Catholic emancipation (the ostensible catalyst for the Gordon Riots), on an identical personal motive, their mutual hostility toward the Roman Catholic Geoffrey Haredale.

Sir John Chester's principles, at home and in office, represent Dickens' concept of the rule of an elitist, decadent aristocracy. His cynicism and his egocentricity are the logical political extreme of Louis XIV's *"L'état, c'est moi"* credo. However, Chester's moral degeneracy had no historically valid equivalent within the English government at the time of the Gordon Riots. While there may be some ambiguity in Dickens' presentation of the riots, there is certainly no suggestion of their possible justification. At worst the national government was at times as authoritarian and as obtuse as John Willet, yet never as self-centered and deliberately malicious as Sir John Chester. It is Gabriel Varden's domestic situation which directly parallels the actual state of the nation.

— *4* —

The disorder of the Gabriel Varden household corresponds exactly to the Gordon Riots. The full nature of the uprising, its combination of mass discontent, political conspiracy, and religious bigotry is reflected in the chief threats to Varden's domestic government: the violent rebellion of his apprentice Sim Tappertit, the seditious behavior of his servant Miggs, and the provocative religious enthusiasm of his wife Martha. Although Sim, Miggs and "Mrs. V." never combine forces, they all systematically undermine Gabriel's authority, violating their "indentures" as apprentice, servant, and wife. At the beginning of the novel the unrest is sufficiently advanced to elicit comparison with the Haredale, Willet, and Chester circles. Unlike these three families, however, the Vardens, like the state, suffer open rebellion only during the second section of the novel. But Gabriel's household mirrors more than the political situation. Its three crises also complement those of the Haredales, the Willets, and the Chesters. Sim's attack on the locksmith evokes Rudge's murder of Reuben Haredale; Migg's impertinence develops the less pleasant, insubordinate side of Joe Willet's character; and Mrs. Varden's attempt to vindicate her actions toward her husband is based on the same grounds as have justified Edward's filial disobedience. The Vardens, therefore, both embody the clearest analogue to the public upheaval and reinforce much of the parallel domestic argument of *Barnaby Rudge*.

The servant's household status and rules for behavior were similar to those of the child. He was commanded to honor and to obey his

master in all things, yet he was also expected to cultivate the special virtue of humility. Samuel Stennett, in his *Discourses on Domestic Duties*
(1800), particularly emphasizes the servant's obligation to understand
completely his place in the domestic order:

> Now, although servants are upon an equality with their masters
> in regard of nature, and may be superior to them in respect of
> ability for the business they undertake, yet their condition in
> life is vastly inferior. . . . It is contrary therefore to all idea of
> truth, equity, and decency, for a servant to conceive of his mas-
> ter as his equal, and to treat him as such. For persons in this in-
> ferior station to affect authority and dominion is evil "for
> which," the wise man tells us, "the earth is disquieted and
> which it cannot bear" [Proverbs, XXX, 21–22]. . . . The ser-
> vant ought therefore to give honour to whom honour is due, to
> cherish in his breast an unfeigned esteem for his master as his
> superior, to address him on all occasions most respectfully, to
> carry himself in his presence with all humility and reverence, to
> listen in silence to his commands, to comply submissively with
> his will, and on no account to dispute his just authority over
> him.[21]

It is strongly implied that the "disquieted" earth, and hearth, in *Barnaby
Rudge* is largely caused by the affectation of authority by persons of "inferior station."

Sim Tappertit contemptuously disregards each of the domestic
duties he is supposed to cultivate. His insubordination grows from
surliness and abuse of the substitute grindstone, early in the novel, to
open defiance during the riots. He surreptititously escapes, with a
forged key, for nocturnal visits to the Barbican cellars where he casts
oaths of "vengeance, complete and terrible" on the "Tyrant Masters"
(65). However, it is primarily Sim's absolute failure to recognize his
place, his exaggerated self-esteem, which determines these and his
other infidelities. Vanity is, so to speak, the "humor" of his character.
Sim sets his eyes, literally and figuratively, on the master's daughter, although she is above him in height and in station. He arrogantly bears
himself as an equal toward the aristocrat Chester, which is clearly impertinent, if ironically appropriate, behavior. The deluded Tappertit,
in fact, advances the notion through his society of apprentices that
their lowly situation is of recent date and unconstitutional: "The captain . . . told him how that under the same Constitution (which was
kept in a strong box somewhere, but where exactly he could not find
out, or he would have endeavoured to procure a copy of it), the 'pren-
tices had, in times gone by, had frequent holidays of right, broken people's heads by scores, defied their masters, nay, even achieved some

glorious murders in the streets, which privileges had gradually been wrested from them, and in all which noble aspirations they were now restrained" (65). Simon's upward striving is accompanied by a rejection of his trade, a disgust for manual labor which contrasts sharply with the cheerful serenity of the "harmonious locksmith," the willing service of Joe Willet, and the enthusiastic self-reliance of Edward Chester. Sim hastens to remove "from his face and hands all traces of his former work" (33) and invariably protests that any task assigned him is unconnected with his "indenters." Tappertit's absurd pretense of gentility, which is unmistakably evoked by his appropriate name (a "dapper tomtit"?), is one facet of his overall self-delusion, his blind vanity, and his failure to recognize his place in the natural order.

> Sim, as he was called in the locksmith's family, or Mr. Simon Tappertit, as he called himself, and required all men to style him out of doors, on holidays, and Sundays out,—was an old-fashioned, thin-faced, sleek-haired, sharp-nosed, small-eyed little fellow, very little more than five feet high, and thoroughly convinced in his own mind that he was above the middle size; rather tall in fact, than otherwise. Of his figure . . . he entertained the highest admiration; and with his legs, which, in knee-breeches, were perfect curiosities of littleness, he was enraptured to a degree amounting to enthusiasm. (33–34)
>
> These thoughts [of his person and his order] always led him to think what a glorious engine the 'prentices might yet become if they had but a master spirit at their head; and then he would darkly, and to the terror of his hearers, hint at certain reckless fellows that he knew of, and at a certain Lion Heart ready to become their captain, who, once afoot, would make the Lord Mayor tremble on his throne. (34–35)

Sim thus aspires to that unbearable "evil" Stennett has described, the revolutionary arrogation of "authority and dominion" over his superiors.

Sim's distorted vision of his station in the social and in the domestic order fundamentally distinguishes his revolt from those of the exasperated, but moderate Joe Willet and the soberly thoughtful Edward Chester. Like Joe, he rebels violently; however, his explosion is directed at his governor, Varden. His assault upon Gabriel is less serious than a son's attack on his father, since no supernatural bond exists between master and servant. Nevertheless, it is a direct and serious threat to domestic order which recalls Rudge's murder of his master. Sim's offense is softened by the comic presentation of his feeble, inebriated attempts to pummel the massive locksmith; yet, Tappertit suffers the harshest reprisal of all the rebels: the loss of his precious legs. The painful retribution for Sim's actions and the direct correlation of his revolt with the drunken assaults of the mob indicate that Tappertit's rebellion is both the least just and the most like the Gordon Riots. The only blame that could possibly be assigned to Varden must rest on his hesitation to control his apprentice. If he errs, it is through a flexibility of judgment, a benevolent trust in human nature which contrasts favorably with the authoritarianism of Willet and the cynicism of Chester. Significantly, the English government also was criticized for its failure to react promptly and decisively to the Riots of 1780.[22] The Varden household thus reflects both the nature of the riots and the manner of their treatment. As the shock of the agitator's violence forced the government, finally, to action, so also does Sim's revolt move Gabriel to reassert his authority over the remaining sources of domestic chaos, Miggs and Mrs. Varden.

Migg's role in Dickens' development of his theme does not demand extensive commentary. She testifies to the remarkable complexity of *Barnaby Rudge*'s analogical structure and symbolism in the number of characters she parallels.[23] She acts as a reflection both of Sim, as an undutiful servant, and of Chester and Gashford as an agitator of domestic chaos. Her hypocritical evangelism accentuates the distorted values of Mrs. Varden's religious enthusiasm. Moreover, Joe Willet's worst trait is heightened and explored, for comic effect, in her impertinence. Yet she does act out her own drama of insubordination—she thwarts the locksmith during the riots by destroying his last defense, his trusty firelock (482). Miggs throws her support to the rioters: "Personal considerations . . . sinks into nothing, afore a noble cause. Ally Looyer! Ally Looyer! Ally Looyer, good gentlemen!" (546). When commanded to "hold her tongue directly" she launches into an elaborate "self-assertion" which, while meant to be "ironical," is an accurate summation of her proper, neglected station in life.

> "Ho, gracious me!" cried Miggs, with hysterical derision. "Ho, gracious me! Yes, to be sure I will. Ho yes! I am a abject slave, and a toiling, moiling, constant-working, always-being-found-fault-with, never-giving-satisfactions, nor-having-no-time-to-clean-oneself, potter's wessel—an't I, miss! Ho yes! My situations is lowly, and my capacities is limited, and my duties is to humble myself afore the base degenerating daughters of their blessed mothers as is fit to keep companies with holy saints but is born to persecutions from wicked relations—and to demean myself before them as is no better than Infidels—an't it, miss! My only becoming occupations is to help young flaunting pagins to brush and comb and titiwate theirselves into whitening and suppulchres." (546)

A little religion is, evidently, a dangerous thing. But Miggs is confused about more than her scriptures and her "situations." Within the Varden household she has created disorder by giving her allegiance, questionable though it may be, solely to the mistress and by systematically frustrating the requests (and defenses) of Gabriel. Miggs' reinforcement sustains Mrs. Varden's militant Protestantism, a departure from her characteristic good nature. As Miggs ultimately puts her distorted evangelism before her domestic obligations, so also do the rioters exploit a false religious cry of "No-Popery" to justify their attack on the civil establishment. Consistent with this inversion of the natural order, Miggs is superficially loyal to the lady of the household, the family's moral guardian, and rebellious toward the master, the governor of the home. Through the influence of Miggs, Mrs. Varden too has set "church" against "state," creating conflict between her and her husband's place in the order of domestic relationships.

The traditional wifely duty of submission, though frequently ignored or circumvented in every age, was predicated on the same commandments to love, honor, and obey that determined the conduct of the child.[24] The husband, father, and master was not simply the head of the family, he was the center of the domestic universe, "the sun that shone upon them all: the centre of the system: the source of light, heat, life, and frank enjoyment in the bright household world" (612). In the Varden home the roles of husband and wife have been dangerously reversed and "disquiet" is the predictable result. Gabriel's natural authority is thwarted by Mrs. Varden's invocation of God's higher power. He submits to her whims and contrariety out of respect for her "Christian conscience." The parallel to Edward's defiance of his father is incomplete, however, because Varden neither commands nor indulges in sinful behavior. His chief faults, to his wife, are his unchristian fondness for a bumper of ale and his service in the godless militia. While drunkenness and murder are violations of any ethical code, ale and military service could be considered evil in themselves only by the most rigorous code of ethics. Dickens, and the greatest part of his audience, would consider Mrs. Varden's scruples incidental, rather than central, to Christian morality.

"Mrs. V's" preoccupation with Christian appearances and with peripheral matters of conduct betray both a blindness to true Christian action and a susceptibility to deception in the name of religion. She fails to recognize her husband's merit, and she is manipulated by the seductive religious persuasions of Chester and of the Protestant Association. Gabriel reasserts his authority when he realizes that the rioters and his wife have abused religion for evil ends, either for sectarian persecution or for domestic domination: "But recollect from this time that all good things perverted to evil purposes, are worse than those which are naturally bad. A thoroughly wicked woman, is wicked indeed. When religion goes wrong, she is very wrong, for the same reason"

(394). Mrs. Varden clearly echoes the false religious enthusiasm of the Gordon Riots, as Tappertit symbolizes the chaotic insubordination of the mob. Miggs, as both an undutiful servant and a puritanical hypocrite, forms an effective bridge between them.

Although Gabriel's latterly forceful home rule represents the actions of the English government at the time of the riots, he is also provided with a political counterpart for the sake of the novel's structural symmetry. The blind Sir John Fielding, "a bold and active magistrate" (469), symbolically reflects Varden's benign obliviousness to the escalating disorder in his family, as well as his ultimate aggressive response. As a representative of the ruling powers, Fielding defies the mob like Varden (by imprisoning rioters, including Barnaby and Rudge, in the face of threats), and he suffers similarly for it in the attack on his home (511). However, it might be more accurate to say that Gabriel's civil significance is much more generalized than this. Unlike John Willet and John Chester, who represent individual factions or political abuses, Gabriel Varden embodies Dickens' vision of the entire well-intentioned, moderate middle class which initially observes and eventually confronts the threats of national chaos. His station in life and principles of conduct earn the final allegiance of both Joe Willet and Edward Chester, his fellow heroes. His class standing and moderate attitudes reflect the station and perspective both of Dickens and of his contemporary audience. The locksmith's home is a projection of its owner's middle-class modesty and commendable sense of order, yet it also symbolizes the fundamental stability and good health of the nation.

> It was a modest building, not very straight, not large, not tall; not bold-faced, with great staring windows, but a shy, blinking house, with a conical roof going up into a peak over its garret window of four small panes of glass, like a cocked hat on the head of an elderly gentleman with one eye. . . .
> With all these oddities, there was not a neater, more scrupulously tidy, or more punctiliously ordered house, in Clerkenwell, in London, in all England. There were not cleaner windows, or whiter floors, or brighter stoves, or more highly shining articles of furniture in old mahogany; there was not more rubbing, scrubbing, burnishing and polishing, in the whole street put together. Nor was this excellence attained without some cost and trouble. (30–31)

Varden, the archetypal Englishman, rules his pleasantly eccentric little nation with moderation, benevolence, and justice. His good nature may be abused, and a miniature Gordon Riot might temporarily devastate his household, but his judicious response restores the balance of the body domestic. So also may the English "Constitution," with all its "oddities," temper political authority for the sake of individual liberty, but it too is able both to withstand attack and to facilitate a just and a merciful return to order. Consistent with his conservative intention for *Barnaby Rudge,* Dickens presents a virtually uncritical hymn of praise to the middle-class, its station, its values, and its great invention: the "English Constitution." Thus Dickens explores in *Barnaby Rudge* only those domestic and social ills which he and his moderate audience could universally deplore. The urgency of his attack on the "Bloody Code" for public execution is diminished considerably by the fact that it had already been substantially revised in the 1820s. Wisely, he resists suggesting any explicit, and therefore controversial, remedies to contemporary problems.

To complex network of familial situations Dickens creates in *Barnaby Rudge,* together with their balancing political parallels, both provides a symmetrical, unified structure for the novel and emphatically illustrates the most important symbolic meaning of the family for Dickens: its civil significance. Although by no means the only concern of the book, the theme of government makes *Barnaby Rudge* a coherent and powerful novel, Dickens' first sustained achievement in fiction. But *Barnaby* offers the reader of Dickens more than these immediate rewards. Its full articulation of the domestic-civil analogy enlightens our appreciation of individual scenes and entire novels within his canon, from the Murdstones' coup d'état in *David Copperfield* to the attack on Political Economy through the Gradgrind household in *Hard Times.* *Barnaby Rudge* is both a concise expression of contemporary ideals of familial rule and a vade mecum for the theme of domestic government throughout the works of Charles Dickens.

Arlene M. Jackson

REWARD, PUNISHMENT, AND THE CONCLUSION OF *DOMBEY AND SON*

THE ENDINGS of Victorian novels often seem to be plot contrivances based on an unconvincing belief in an optimistic future, or as an answer to the moral expectations of the audience. Jane Eyre marries a maimed but now manageable Rochester, and only after the convenient death of his mad wife; Eleanor Bold marries Mr. Arabin after misunderstandings have been cleared away and the obsequious Mr. Slope has departed the scene; Dobbin finally marries Amelia Sedley after the unfaithful George dies on the battlefield; Walter Hartright marries Laura Fairlie while Count Fosco and Sir Perceval meet violent deaths. The benevolent characters can begin their happy "future" after obstacles are cleared away, and often after the just dispensation of rewards and punishments. Rewards, usually defined as fortuitous acquisition of wealth or a desirable marriage, and punishments in the forms of public exposure, banishment, imprisonment, and even violent death by accident or by legal sentence, seem based on the belief that life can be easily dichotomized and that rewards and punishments will be and can be parceled out to those who deserve them.

Actually, even in most of the novels mentioned above, considerably more realism lies within the ending than might seem apparent from a cursory view. Jane Eyre senses at the end the Victorian woman's limited arena for the exercise of power; Amelia knows Dobbin does not really love her; and Becky Sharpe's future seems most unpleasant, especially to the reader who sympathizes with Becky's general plight in Victorian society. The highly intelligent, loyal but homely Marian looks on from the outside as Walter and Laura begin their married life—and the reader wonders what Walter can respond to beyond Laura's rather frail beauty. There are other problem endings in Victorian fiction, as well as these. Dorothea Brooke marries Will Ladislaw and must learn how to adjust to limited aspirations. (On the other hand, Maggie and Tom drown together and thus avoid the problem of living out difficult deci-

[103

sions.) Can Bathsheba Everdene really be contented with the tranquil, slow, and somewhat inarticulate Gabriel Oak? Thus, the endings of many Victorian novels contain a most painful reality—a sense that all is not right and cannot be made right—and this reality does not lie very far beneath the surface of the supposedly optimistic or morally just ending.

Dickens' works have not appeared in the above examples—and Dickens, of course, is most vulnerable to the charge of plot contrivance and of playing to his audience as he disposes of his characters according to their just deserts. *Pickwick Papers* ends with several suitable marriages; Oliver Twist finds love and identity, not to mention fortune; Nicholas Nickleby marries Madeline Bray, luckily become an heiress; Newman Noggs finds family love because of his constancy; Kit marries Barbara, and Mr. Garland aids him to a successful future. On the other hand, Ralph Nickleby hangs himself, as does Bill Sikes; Fagin is executed; Quilp drowns as he attempts to escape from the police. (The deaths of Nancy and Nell serve sentimental or melodramatic ends, and Nancy's horrible death only emphasizes the depravity of Sikes.) *Barnaby Rudge,* too, ends with a dichotomized picture of rewards and punishments: they go to those who deserve them. Of course, Dickens is primarily interested in a great many other issues than rewards and punishments: in the unmasking of roguery and evil, in the defining and understanding of human virtues, in a variety of social issues, particularly when they relate to man's avariciousness for material goods or unconcern toward fellowman. With all the richness of Dickens' fiction, however, we are still left with the dichotomized endings, with rewards and punishments. Such endings do not square with what we know of the world's reality.

An additional problem in Dickens' early works is that the rewards and punishments seem parceled out because of the author's sense of justice, usually with little preparation, and therefore credibility, within the text itself. When rewards and punishments are too easily dichotomized, and when rewards and punishments are given to characters from the author's (and in this sense *external*) hand, rather than prepared for through the probabilities of character or situation, the novel's psychological and moral realism can be questioned.

But in the Dickens' canon, there is an increasing sense of darkness and complexity, and the endings of the later novels do not fail to reflect this change. Even so, as G. W. Kennedy points out, "The important common structural feature in the endings of Dickens' novels is the presence of a private domestic sanctuary in which the surviving benevolent characters are able to find permanent refuge."[1] The refuge concept in the later novels must be qualified somewhat, notes Kennedy. The earlier novels, however, clearly celebrate a golden time of ageless-

ness: a reward for those who have remained faithful to moral standards in spite of their various trials or temptations.

This new, golden world also describes the ending of *Dombey and
Son,* where the white-haired, grandfatherly Dombey and his family
circle celebrate a new order of things. The ending as a whole indicates
an escape into a new order of time, as seems clear from the specific
scene at the Midshipman, when the long-hidden bottle of precious
Madeira emerges into the golden sunlight.

I wish not to deny the mythic aspects in *Dombey and Son* but to
point out the considerable reality present within the novel's conclusion.
Dombey and Son, in fact, is the first of Dickens' novels to achieve a psychological reality in its conclusion. That reality is based on the probabilities of character and situation which slowly and steadily develop from
the novel's early pages. This psychological reality has not been understood very well, possibly because of problems in interpreting the novel's
major female characters, Florence Dombey and Edith Granger, and in
accepting the final disposition of Paul Dombey, Sr. The shaping of the
novel's final reality, furthermore, does have a strong moral pressure
from the Victorian world in general and from Dickens' own views on
the family. The work of art is never without shaping, external pressures, however, and we should understand them for what they are—
the novel's enriching context. These external pressures on the probabilities of character and situation, have, in fact, a reality of their own.

There are several significant points to be made about *Dombey and
Son*'s conclusion. First, the rewards and punishments are not so easily
or clearly dichotomized. There is, in addition, a new way of defining
reward—a perspective that Dickens uses in later novels, such as *Great
Expectations.* Quite simply, in *Dombey and Son* Dickens reveals his belief
that moral recognition leads to psychological "wholeness." What is just
as important, there is preparation from within the text for the various
dispositions of character. *Recognition* depends on a strong confessional
scene for each of the three major characters, an arrangement that is
too parallel to be coincidence. Each confessional scene, furthermore, is
the culmination of a set of recurring images: the darkened room for
Dombey, the family image for Florence, and the image of prostitution
for Edith. Each image creates and conveys psychological responses
which, together with the nature and extent of the confession itself, justify the character's situation at the novel's end.

The dispensation of rewards and punishments in the ending has
been defined in various ways: mysterious, unpleasant, implausible, or
unjust, depending on how each character is interpreted. Is Dombey's
domestic refuge, for instance, a reward or punishment? How plausible
is the destruction of the proud, commercial man who is now "swal-
lowed up" by sentimental Florence, obsessed with the "need to be

loved"?[2] According to this view—one which still considers the image of
the white-haired man surrounded by family as highly unpleasant—is
this really a fair ending for a man who, after all, has done nothing
wrong?[3] Doesn't the Dombey we know from earlier events deserve "a
more complex fate"[4] than this condemnation to a woman's world of
tears and love?

On the other hand, if the final position of Dombey is considered as
a reward, isn't it too much of a reward for a man who has spent his
adult years as a cold businessman, seventeen of those years in active
and unreasonable rejection of his daughter? How can the reader accept
Dombey's final peace and happiness in the company of daughter, son-
in-law, grandchildren, and assorted friends (very assorted) like Sol
Gills, Captain Cuttle, and Mr. Toots?

The Jungian suggestiveness of Florence "swallowing" or overwhelming Dombey is a tempting interpretation, but the image pattern
surrounding Dombey himself runs counter to such a reading. The ice
images associated with this character convey the seriousness of his emotional deficiency toward every other person in the novel except young
Paul, and he is actively injurious to Edith's well-being, as well as to
Florence's. What Dombey has done is to fail to recognize the individual
worth of other human beings, and he suffers the penalty of the failure:
a disintegration of personality, marked by his suicide attempt. Dombey
achieves wholeness at the novel's end, but he can never be the same as
he was before. His broken spirit, his loss of his vigor and initiative,
added to his earlier losses of business and house, even his honor, is
punishment for misdeeds. His psychological peace is a reward, however, and he has earned the reward as well as the punishment. The
confession scene and the recurring images of the darkened room prepare us to accept the seemingly implausible change in Dombey's character, and thus to accept Dombey's reward, highly qualified though it
is.

That Dickens was aware of the problem inherent in Dombey's conversion is apparent in his preface. He first explains that "correctly observing the character of men" is a rare ability, and that the two most
common mistakes in observing and judging character are "the confounding of shyness and arrogance . . . and the not understanding
that an obstinate nature exists in a perpetual struggle with itself."
Then, in a defensive tone, Dickens explains: "Mr. Dombey undergoes
no violent change, either in this book or in real life. A sense of his injustice is within him all along. The more he represses it, the more unjust he necessarily is. . . . It has been a contest for years, and is only
fought out after a long balance of victory" (p. xv).

In her landmark study of the novel, Kathleen Tillotson gives
strong and absolute support to Dickens' concept of Dombey, and points

out much of the preparation for change that Dickens included throughout the novel. In Chapter xxxv, for instance, Dombey's feelings for Florence rise to the surface as he watches her sleep. Those feelings again appear during his restless wandering through the empty house, after Florence has left him. The Dombey-Florence relationship is the central theme of the novel, believes Tillotson,[5] and thus these instances of Dombey's feelings for Florence become extremely important for understanding how Dickens prepares for Dombey's conversion. There are other proofs of Dombey's hidden depths, however, and they are more central to his position as individualized character, and not just to his role in the father-daughter relationship.

Three major plot events, occurring near the novel's end, affect Dombey to the extent that his "conversion" seems to depend primarily and much too abruptly on them. The dishonor brought by Edith and the fall of the House of Dombey shake his existence, but it is not until he realizes that Florence has indeed left him that he becomes aware of personal guilt. Dombey directly confronts his responsibility: "He was fallen, never to be raised up any more. For the night of his worldly ruin there was no to-morrow's sun; for the stain of his domestic shame there was no purification; nothing, thank Heaven, could bring his dead child back to life. But that which he might have made so different in all the Past—which might have made the Past itself so different, though this he hardly thought of now—that which was his own work, that which he could so easily have wrought into a blessing and had set himself so steadily for years to form into a curse: that was the sharp grief of his soul" (839).

Two earlier events, however, also prepare for change: the death of Mrs. Fanny Dombey, which opens the novel, and the death of young Paul. These events also serve to harden Dombey's heart toward Florence, and thus reveal Dombey's complexity. Still, Dickens' handling of these earlier episodes demonstrates his conscious preparation for Dombey's change. The novelist's intention becomes apparent through what immediately follows each of these episodes: a special scene of recognition that takes place in Dombey's darkened chambers.

The most important external sign of Dombey's struggle, in fact, lies in his relationship to his place of residence. Because of its moral suggestions, the Dombey house is primarily an emblem of the Victorian commercial man, solid and opulent in its massiveness. Within that house exists another emblem: the darkened chamber of Mr. Dombey's private rooms. After each crisis of his life, Dombey retreats to his rooms, to sit in darkened isolation. With one exception to be noted later, the narrator is careful not to follow Dombey into those rooms, presumably out of sympathy and respect for the privacy of the bereaved, for instance, or for the man who is in intense personal pain.

Much of the reader's understanding of Dombey's internal state is indirect because of the narrator's refusal to pursue Dombey into the darkened room, but Dickens' use of "ice" images in describing Dombey also contributes to this sense of distance. The "master keys" of Dombey's soul, Dickens writes, are parental interest (for his son Paul) and ambition frozen "into one unyielding block" (47).

As early as the death of Fanny Dombey, Paul Dombey, Sr., shows a sense of loss—not for his own sake, but for that of his infant son, who now must grow up without a mother: "Mr. Dombey had remained in his own apartment since the death of his wife, absorbed in visions of the youth, education, and destination of his baby son. Something lay at the bottom of his cool heart, colder and heavier than its ordinary load; but it was more a sense of the child's loss than his own, awakening within him an almost angry sorrow" (15). The sorrow was for the child's loss, not his own, and the anger was for the humiliating necessity of hiring a nurse. Richards is hired, the funeral for Fanny is over, most of the furniture in the unused rooms of the house covered up. Dombey sits in his own rooms, observed from a safe distance by Richards: "she began to entertain ideas of him in his solitary state, as if he were a lone prisoner in a cell, or a strange apparition that was not to be accosted or understood" (23).

That these scenes are not meant to emphasize Dombey's bitter pride but to convey his loneliness and his great but misguided need for love becomes clear in a scene which follows almost immediately. Watching Florence with his infant son, Dombey remembers his dying wife and Florence embracing: "he could not forget that closing scene. He could not forget that he had had no part in it" (29). His sense that there was something here that he ought to have shared in, some dim sense of the love absent in his life, emerges; he feels that Florence knows something about him that he himself cannot explain, and with great perversity, the feeling emerges as a cold rejection of Florence's overtures. Dombey himself, however, has tried to make overtures to Florence, but the rigidity of a personality formed over so many years, and not to be broken or changed at will, dominates. Thus loneliness and pride, plus years of hiding his feelings behind an icy demeanor, keep Dombey from showing the vague feelings trying to break through is habitual coldness.

Young Paul's sad homecoming from school and his death provide more insight into Dombey's capacity to feel and also reveal more of the complexity in his psychological state—the darkened chambers, again, play an emblematic role in revealing the inner Dombey. One of the rare outdoor scenes which reveals this hidden side, however, occurs while Paul is still at school. Dombey often travels to Brighton and pathetically walks past the Blimber's house at night, waiting for Paul to grow up. This detail from Dombey's life reveals a kind of monomania about Paul and his part in Dombey's commercial life, but it also shows Dombey's great need to have someone on his side, someone to communicate with, to trust, and to love. The image of Florence does nothing to fill this need, and Dombey can be faulted for not seeing her potential in fulfilling the needs he has transferred to Paul. The Blimber episode stresses Dombey's needs, rather than Florence's rejection, and emphasizes Dombey's desire for love and companionship from Paul as well as his more crass desire for a son to carry on the family commercial tradition.

When Paul is taken home in his last illness, he asks Florence: "[Papa] didn't cry, and go into his room, Floy, did he, when he saw me coming in?" Florence shakes her head no, but Paul says, "I'm very glad he didn't cry. . . . I thought he did" (205). The implication here is a bit cloudy, but it would appear that Paul, and not Florence, has the greater perception. The implication is that Dombey did cry, or that Paul had seen or at least sensed something unusual—or even that Florence says no in order to reassure Paul, to keep him from becoming too sad. That Paul recognizes the relationship between Dombey's revelation of emotion and the darkened private chamber is significant as well.

The hiding of emotion (and the more important fact that there is emotion to hide) is clearly revealed after Paul's death. That night "the bereaved father has not been seen even by his attendant; for he sits in an inner corner of his own dark room when anyone is there, and never seems to move at other times, except to pace it to and fro" (239). The emotion becomes so intense that Dombey exchanges his own chamber for Paul's room, an exchange that will occur once again, when another emotional crisis arises. And, of course, immediately after the funeral, Dombey retreats again into his rooms, as other mourners move upstairs to the drawing room: "And what the face is, in the shut-up chamber underneath: or what the thoughts are: what the heart is, what the contest or the suffering: no one knows" (241). His evening walks past Blimber's, his tears at Paul's sad homecoming, his tears at Paul's death—all indicate an early Dombey capable of feeling. But Dombey manages to control, even to anesthetize feeling, until the external psychological signs are almost obliterated.[6]

Dombey's complexity is indicated in a following scene, when Florence goes into his room to share his grief and to comfort him. She sees he knows that she herself is lonely and grieving, but he rejects her; and then the narrator reveals anger at the uncalled-for rejection, not only for its own sake but because that rejection is based on Dombey's feeling that Florence's life makes Paul's death all the worse. After Dombey has spurned Florence, the narrator repeats four times: "Let him remember it in years to come" (chap. 18). Yet, after this scene revealing his cruelty, Dombey locks the door and cries for Paul in private. Ironically, he had seen himself, allied with Paul, as able "to have shut out all the world as with a double door of gold" (280). But now, isolated from the world of love, Dombey is left alone in his darkened room, a room which has become an emblem of grief and loneliness.

The image of Florence still troubles him, however, and so he asks himself, "What was there he could interpose between himself and it?" (283). The answer is Edith. While the marriage may be seen as his quest for an heir to replace Paul, it is also his search for love, whether he consciously acknowledges it or not, and it is a hedge against Florence, whom Dombey considers has been traded for Paul. Dombey recalls it was Florence, and not himself, who was called to the bedside of his dying wife, that it was Florence, not himself, who was first in his son's affections. Dombey thus sees Florence as his competitor in the quest for love. This motif of competition provides important insights into Dombey's psychology.

For a brief moment, Dombey believes he has Edith to himself, in spite of her coldness, and after returning from their wedding trip, Dombey shows a slight change in attitude toward Florence. (That Dombey has physically possessed Edith in their conjugal relationship may have misled him into thinking she is "his.") And this change seems present as Dombey sits in a darkened room (not this time his own chambers) and places a handkerchief over his face, pretending to fall asleep. The narrator then asks if he was touched by the sight of her: as he looked on, he "softened to her, more and more" (503). The name "Florence" is about to be spoken, when Edith appears, and the love so evident between the two women causes "a darkness" to appear on Dombey's face as his heart hardens toward both women. A large cause of his tyrannical treatment of Edith over the next two years is his desperation as he realizes he is powerless to dominate Edith and that, instead of Florence being the outsider, he himself is the unloved one. As will be noted later in considering Edith, Dombey also loses the physical dominance he had early in the marriage with Edith. Even though Dickens veils his material, it is apparent that Edith is withholding from Dombey his "rights" over her body, particularly toward the end of their two-year marriage, and this sexual loss underscores the absence of love in his life.

As Dombey sits in his darkened rooms, he blames Florence for his unhappy relationship with Edith, and, even as this idea festers, "a vague yearning for what he had all his life repelled" (lvi) comes upon him, but his pride wins out, and so he hates her. The more Edith and Florence reveal their love for each other, the more Dombey seeks to oppress Edith with his tyranny and pride. Dombey's fall from his horse becomes an effective symbol of his inability to control Edith, emphasizing the loss of his sexual prowess (as it will look to the world, since she

soon runs off with another man), but it also forecasts a fall from
pride—and thus a changed Dombey. The source of that pride had
been his position in the Victorian world as man of fortune and husband of the beautiful Edith Granger. Both are lost to him—and by
him.

At various stages of Dombey's life, and as early as the death of
Fanny and then Paul, the darkened room has been an emblem of his
frozen, deadened emotions, of his proud and willful isolation. It has
also been a place where Dombey could hide his deepest and most
tender emotions, uncertain or short-lived as they seem to have been.
After the news of Edith and Carker, and then of his firm's bankruptcy,
the darkened rooms become more clearly a refuge from pain. After the
news of Edith's flight, Dombey rushes off in immediate pursuit, but
soon returns to his rooms, "where he trod so heavily that [Florence]
could hear him walking up and down from end to end" (665). Now the
rooms are his place of pain.

After rejecting his daughter's love, Dombey remains in the darkened room, suffering the shame bestowed by the world's opinion of a
man who has lost his wife to another man, and becomes oblivious to the
practical world around him, while his servants become dissipated. "The
world. What the world thinks of him, how it looks at him, what it sees
in him, and what it says—this is the haunting demon of his mind. . . .
When he is shut up in his room at night, it is in his house, outside it,
audible footsteps on the pavement" (716). Dombey thus uses the darkened room to hide his pain from the world's eyes. After the bankruptcy, Dombey once again turns to the darkened chamber as refuge
from the world's opinion. And then, finally, the rooms are also the setting for Dombey's ultimate rejection of Florence, when he strikes her
on their threshold after she has come to comfort him.

From this point on, the darkened rooms become an emblem of
conscience, an emblem that will gradually expand to include the entire
house. Alone in his room, with memories of what he had done to
Florence now and in the past, after the death of Paul, Dombey's conscience at last becomes active. As this process begins, Dombey realizes
that, of his three great calamities of worldly ruin, domestic shame, and
rejected parent, the one calamity that for which he must bear direct
and single responsibility is his treatment of Florence. "He knew, now,
what he had done" in his rejection of Florence and her love. And so he
"let the world go from him freely. As it fell away, he shook it off." Thus
Dombey accepts responsibility for his actions. The stab of recognition
Dickens as narrator calls the "sharp grief of [Dombey's] soul" (840). Yet
the narrator cautions that the process is far from over, for if Dombey
had heard Florence's voice in the next room, "he would not have gone
to her."

Now the darkened room as emblem of conscience enlarges into the dark and empty house, through which Dombey walks at night, alone with his memories. In one poignant scene, Dombey lies down on the floor in Paul's room and weeps for all that he has lost. The scene is several times repeated in his wanderings. Finally, Dombey's remorse becomes so great that he nears suicide but is saved by Florence's appearance. As Dombey clasps Florence he tries to speak, and at last unburdens himself: "Oh, my God, forgive me, for I need it very much!" (844). It is an open confession, revealing his self-knowledge. The failure to specify what he wishes to be forgiven implies he knows it is for everything.

This confession is the final step in the process of purgation or, in Dickens' metaphor, "thawing," as the last vestiges of the frozen, "unyielding block" break down before Dombey's suffering. The greatest impact on that block of pride has surely been from the most immediate events in his life, but Dickens reminds us that Dombey's "obstinate and sullen" nature has been undermined throughout the years by the contesting forces within him.[7]

With Dombey's acceptance of Florence's love, and with his confession (joined by hers, as will be noted), the darkness of his chambers is forever changed because of "the glorious sunshine that had crept in with Florence" (845). Metaphors of light, rejected by Dombey in favor of the darkness of isolation, the refuge of pain, and the gloom of guilty conscience, now dominate the novel through the sunlit, open beach. The icy, unyielding block of pride now gives way to the healing power of the sea, forecast by Dombey's tears as he begs forgiveness. Such images counter the sense that Dombey has been domesticated and overpowered by Florence. He has found the peace and love that he had been moving toward, however haltingly, throughout the novel.

Dombey's devotion to his two grandchildren and his love for Florence become the external signs of the new man. There is no darkened room, only the bright and open beach, where Dombey comes in contact with the waters of life-death, the natural processes involved with being human. Yet, even though he is surrounded by love, Dombey's future is not painted in glowing terms. It is hard to see him fraternizing with Sol Gills and Captain Cuttle, for instance, and Dickens is careful to omit such details, for Dombey's conversion is not so complete that he would be at ease with his new friends. (In the Madeira scene, Dombey's conversation with Gills and Cuttle is quite awkward.) Dickens chooses not to tell us much of the new man beyond the external signs of his position in Florence's household, but we are aware that Dombey is undeniably broken in spirit. He is not the man of power and presence he once was. His broken body means his future life will be neither long nor without physical suffering, and Dickens implies that his future will also be colored with thoughts of all the lost years. Thus, the happiness of Dombey's future is tempered with these extensions of the novel's concluding insights.

But before he projects this future, Dickens as narrator has continually reminded us of Dombey's complexity—the mixture of a man who knew what he was doing, but who could not refrain from doing it, a man toward whom, as Edith explains, we ought to have understood the causes that made him what he was: his great need for love, his sense of his own importance, fed by those around him as well as by the Victorian emphasis on money, possessions, and appearance, so cleverly parodied by Dickens through Mrs. Skelton, who is "put together" in the morning and then "falls apart" at night. Through using the darkened room to express the various states of mind, Dickens externalizes Dombey's psychology. These states of mind indicate the several recognitions of Dombey, and give evidence of Dickens' great care in developing character. When the hidden internal struggle breaks forth in the new Dombey at the novel's end, we ought not to be surprised. The process of Dombey's change had begun much earlier.

Florence shares in this final scene of family riches. With her husband Walter Gay by her side, and together with son, daughter, and father, Florence finds a reward for persevering through all the years of rejection and loneliness. She who had always sought *family* at last finds its reality. As the thoughtful, proper, and loving Victorian child, Florence resembles the Victorian ideal. Julian Moynihan, however, finds Florence a distinct danger to Dombey and finds feeling in Florence to be an engulfing sentiment, as sign of the "slackly feminine sphere of influence."[8]

In Dickens' text, however, Florence is not presented as a danger to Dombey, though she is usually seen in relation to sentiment—a Victorian ideal for young women but not for young men, unless they are deficient in intellect, as is Mr. Toots. (The ideal for young men is typified by the active Walter Gay: motivated by self-help, native ability, *energy,* joined with common sense and genial spirits). Indeed, Florence is not a danger but a victim herself—to feminine stereotyping, just as her real-life feminine counterpart was. In a sense, Dombey is a Walter Gay "gone wrong," and the world of feminine sentiment juxtaposed with the masculine action of a Dombey creates a basic tension in the novel. According to Nina Auerbach, "This schism between masculine and feminine spheres seems more fundamental to the novel's world than the usual division critics make between the 'money world' of the firm and the 'water world' of the Wooden Midshipman group."[9] But the tension is resolved in the end when Florence and Dombey are able to communicate, even though we do not know what they say to each other, after the confession scene.

Another problem in dealing with Florence is that the "fairy tale"

ending seems to stress the allegorical nature of her earlier characterization. According to A. E. Dyson, Florence is too allegorical and has to
remain so because of the novel's scheme of redemption. Dickens cannot
criticize Florence because she must remain unchanged in the process of
Dombey's redemption.[10] All of this emphasis on the destructive quality
of Florence's love is provocative and valuable interpretation, yet in
Dickens' scheme Florence is not destructive, and her role as Dombey's
redemptive agent must be qualified. Important as Florence is in Dombey's change, the process, as explained earlier, begins from the novel's
early pages. And Dombey's change hinges on his recognition and confession. Dickens is careful to stress Dombey's self-directed actions at
this crucial scene, though Florence's role is still very strong.

In many ways, Florence is not an interesting character, since she is
too saccharine and subservient to external forces. Dickens' technique
does not help her image, even after we understand the substantive burden placed on her by the Victorian (and Dickensian) concept of the
ideal. To a large extent, the characterization of Dombey determines
that of Florence. In order to leave us without doubt as to Mr. Dombey's
guilt, explains Kathleen Tillotson, Dickens created in Florence a character who would have to be universally loved.[11] And as Stephen Marcus
explains, Dickens placed another burden on Florence: his creed emphasizes the life of simplicity, where the exercise of the Will is seen as
aggressive.[12] Thus, Florence's perfection consists of long-suffering, innocence, and simplicity, associated with passivity. In addition, her characterization depends to a large extent on reflections from the male figures of Paul and Mr. Dombey, and even by way of contrast to the
energy and activity of Walter Gay. Such characterization almost always
means the individual psychology gives way to the counterpointed psychology. Because we have known Florence as a child, furthermore, we
continue to think of her in those terms, even when she has reached the
age of seventeen and has matured into a young woman. Passivity is an
important component in Florence's personality, but Dickens' technique
actually increases the sense of passivity in Florence.

Florence has been considered an unconvincing, allegorical character, primarily because of her redemptive quality (either dangerous or
unreal, depending on one's point of view) and because of her passive
perfection, again unreal and even annoying. Another major problem in
understanding Florence, one which I believe has never been adequately
examined, involves a most puzzling scene at the novel's end, in which
she confesses her own guilt.

On her knees before her father, Florence prays for forgiveness:
"Papa! Dearest Papa! Pardon me, forgive me! I have come back to ask
forgiveness on my knees. I never can be happy more, without it." The
narration surrounding this confessional speech reveals first Dombey's

surprise as he hears her. "Yes. His daughter! Look at her! Look here! Down upon the ground, clinging to him, calling to him, folding her hands, praying to him." Then, Dickens shifts the point of view from Dombey to the narrator, when the latter indignantly comments, after Florence's confession: "Raising the same face to his as on that miserable night. Asking *his* forgiveness!" (843). If Dombey is surprised, the narrator is upset that Florence should be in such a position before him. What is the purpose in having Florence confess something which the two "listeners" either do not expect or accept?

The confession scene seems grossly unfair to Florence. She has been faithful to her father for a longer period of time than could be thought humanly or realistically possible. If she is too good for belief, that is something quite apart from this scene and provides no reason for placing her in such a debasing, humiliating position. That *she* should need to beg forgiveness seems to be a total inversion. Must a child always give way to the parent, even when the child is right and the parent wrong? Why need Florence be put through such a confession before she can receive her reward? Florence's confession does not get as much emphasis as Dombey's either in the text itself or in textual commentary, yet it is quite important. Florence is not a destructive force—yet she is not perfect, either, and through the confession scene Dickens tells us that Florence has need of repentance, for she has rejected her father, and at a most critical time.

In the early parts of the novel, Dickens conveys Florence's suffering and innocence in a straightforward and sympathetic manner, but then when she at the age of fourteen visits the Skettles, Dickens begins to qualify her perfection. But first, Dickens counterpoints Florence's basic situation with a recurring image of "the family," as if to tease her with what cannot be in her young life.

Several family groupings are at various times presented to Florence's eyes: Sol Gills and Walter Gay; the Toodles family; the bargeman and his sickly child; the aunt and niece; as well as other, nameless sets of parents and children Florence observes during her stay with the Skettles. There are other groupings, of course, such as the Carkers, Edith and her mother, as well as Alice and her mother, the "Mrs. Brown" who kidnaps Florence. These last, together with Florence's own relationship with her father, are obviously deficient in love. (The Carker group is split, of course, and demonstrates love between sister and one brother, with a second brother outside the pale of the "family" image.) The earlier groupings, the ones directly presented to Florence, possess a surfeit of love; some, from the Gills-Gay set to the Toodles grouping, convey a love that includes Florence herself. These groupings have important roles in the novel, and their members are developed and individualized to a considerable extent.

One family image not individualized but used emblematically, a picture held out of reach, is the motherless family which lives across the street from the Dombey house. The "rosy children," who have moved into the house opposite the Dombeys while Paul and Florence have been away at Brighton, are not "immediately suggestive" of Florence's situation, for are four girls, but they are motherless as she is. Their relationship with their father, however, is extremely unlike Florence's. The eldest child, in particular, has a special place by her father's side. Florence's reaction on seeing the special love between father and daughter is to hide her face and weep for what was absent from her own life.

The Toodles family also offers a congenial picture of family life and reminds Florence of what she lacks, though she sees the family grouping but once, on the fateful day when she meets Mrs. Brown and is rescued in her wandering by Walter Gay. The Toodles family is functional in the plot, but other family groupings are used more as tantalizing and symbolic reminders to Florence of what she lacks and must strive to achieve.

A few years later, while visiting the Skettles, Florence observes the other children staying in the house, "children who were as frank and happy with fathers and with mothers as those rosy faces opposite home. Children who had no restraint upon their love, and freely showed it. Florence sought to learn their secret" (343). Then, Florence recalls Mrs. Brown whom she had met as a child. The old woman had robbed her, yet had spoken with love of her daughter. Another family reference occurs when, still at the Skettles, Florence meets one of the local workmen and his only child. His sickly and ill-mannered child receives her father's love in spite of herself. Florence is directly conscious of what *could be* when she contrasts this situation to her own life. Again, while at the Skettles, Florence meets an aunt and her niece, the latter an orphan who ostensibly has so much less than Florence, but in reality possesses a great deal more: her aunt loves her, and they have a relationship which enables them to share love, as well as gives them a perception into the deficiency in Florence's life. Florence overhears the words of the aunt to her niece: "not an orphan in the wide world can be so deserted as the child who is an outcast from a living parent's love" (346). Florence "wept long and bitterly" after hearing these words and resolved that, "however long the time in coming, and however slow the interval, she must try to bring that knowledge [of how much he really loved her] to her father's heart one day or other" (347). Each of these family groups, from the "rosy children," to the workman and child, to aunt and niece, reminds Florence of her own forlorn state, but also holds out a promise of what *ought* to be, and what could be.

An extreme complexity exists in Florence's own situation. While she consciously determines to be faithful to her father, to make him, as she believes, find his love for her, she has been unwittingly the cause of increasing his dislike of her. She had displaced him, as *he* believes, in the affections of his wife Fanny. (The terrible pain of this is indicated through his frequent recollections of Florence in the dying Fanny's arms.) Florence has also displaced him in Paul's affections: it was Florence, and not the father, who was called by his dying son. And when Edith becomes Dombey's wife, Florence once again deposes him from what he considers his rightful place as first in his new wife's affections. While Dombey has obviously misjudged Edith, it is true that from his own point of view, wherever he turns, Florence is there and seems to have usurped his rightful place. Florence, however, is unconscious of this. The irony of the situation is that Florence will have more obstacles to overcome even as she vows to persevere in her love for her father. As becomes clear to the reader, Florence herself is the greatest obstacle in her quest for Dombey's love. This grim irony creates a sense of hopelessness—in the reader, though not in Florence's own mind, for she is unaware of how her father is jealous of her easy capacity to give and receive love.

Florence's perseverance lasts until almost two years after Dombey's marriage, and thus two years after the Skettles' visit. Years of Dombey's neglect and rejection of Florence lay behind the two years of the marriage, when Florence had first been full of hope that a different relationship with her father would now be possible. Perversely, that hope was followed by two years of no change toward the better but, rather, a deepening of Dombey's rejection of her. At the end of those two years, Florence gives up trying to reach her father. The existence of that earlier hope makes her later recognition that much more empty. Dickens explains that Florence realizes she still loves her father, "but, by degrees, [she] had come to love him rather as some dear one who had been, or who might have been, than as the hard reality before her eyes. . . . Whether it was that he was dead to her, and that partly for this reason, partly for his share in those old objects of her affections, and partly for the long association of him with hopes that were withered and tenderness he had frozen, she could not have told: but the father whom she loved began to be a vague and dreamy idea to her: hardly more substantially connected with her real life, than the image she would sometimes conjure up, of her dear brother yet alive, and growing to be a man, who would protect and cherish her" (649). Dickens plays with the movement between real and ideal in Florence's recognition: she moves from the dream of Dombey's loving her to the reality of his rejection; then, Dombey and the reality of the concept "father" became unreality—vague, dreamy ideas. The vagueness is increased because of Dombey's self-exile in the darkened room.

The change in her attitude, Dickens tells us, had come upon her as gradually as "the change from childhood to womanhood, and had come with it" (649). By letting her father slip into "vagueness," by no longer seeing him as a reality, she rejects him and is thus abandoning her promise to be steadfast in loving him. She thus abandons the image of the happy family that she had resolved to create in her own life. No longer holding these "ideal" images, Florence at the same time becomes aware of her own sense of self, particularly of woman-self. This awareness makes her turn toward the real and, of course, prepares her for the love she will share with Walter Gay.

The quiet turning away from Dombey is countered in a highly dramatic action by Dombey himself when he strikes Florence. The act is a serious one, but Florence readily forgives him. Yet, that forgiveness is qualified by Florence's next move: "she fled from the idea of him as she had fled from the reality, and he was utterly gone and lost. There was no such being in the world" (680–81). Florence's act of rejection is an extremely serious one, equal in kind to her father's years-long rejection of her. Herein lies Florence's guilt: the negation of the *reality* of her father becomes a denial of the *idea* of his existence.

Familial love is an essential part of the Dickens code, and operates in all his novels. If fathers forget to love their children, it does not release the children from loving their fathers. Thus, Nell and Little Dorrit show constant love in the face of neglect, even when the parent (or grandparent) seems unworthy of such self-sacrificing devotion. These two Victorian children, in fact, do not falter as Florence does in the face of this enormous and binding responsibility. No matter how much Florence is rejected, she cannot in conscience react in kind. She must continue to offer her love and understanding, no matter how often it is spurned, even when Dombey strikes her down after the Edith-Carker episode. Here an earlier recognition ought to have forewarned Florence. The workman with the sickly child had not given up but persevered, even though his forbearance might seem to encourage the child's ill manners. The constancy of love is vital and remains so regardless of external circumstances. Yet Florence falters, and it is more than momentary, for her denial of Dombey's *reality* has occurred some two years earlier, when she had stopped thinking of her father as a fallible human being with needs and even excuses of his own, as Edith will later remind her. However sympathetic we might be to the reasons for Florence's rejection of Dombey, it is also true that she has abandoned her father in the time of his greatest need, as evidenced by his near-suicide.

Florence recognizes she has rejected the family image when she treats her father as if he were nonexistent. Her recognition occurs during the first year of her marriage with Walter Gay, particularly through her child's birth, but the specific, direct recognition remains hidden from the reader, as the events of this year are only summarized by the narrator. What we are given, however, is the result of that insight. The scene of reconciliation which follows Dombey's thoughts of suicide also becomes Florence's confession scene. Here she reveals she recognizes the seriousness of her actions, and her duty to love. "I know my duty better now," she admits. After her child was born, as she explains to her father, "and when I knew how much I loved it, I knew what I had done in leaving you. Forgive me" (844). Florence's understanding of family love is thus renewed by the birth of a child, and it is at this point that she perceives a most painful truth. Simply put, her duty is to love always. If this duty seems painful, it does not make the reality any less true.

The concept of duty, in Florence's case, is handled with serious-ness; it is handled differently in other parts of the novel. Mrs. Chick speaks of Fanny's duty to "make an effort" as she is on her deathbed; Alice Marwood speaks in bitter terms of the duty she had, measured against the duty others ought to have had toward her; Mr. Dombey speaks to Edith of duty—he must be "deferred to and obeyed." In Dickens' world, duty can be the basis of humor, can be associated with social consciousness, can be understood as a perversion. In its serious and straightforward sense, Dickens' code emphasizes that duty does not demand, but places on man the obligation to give. The distinction is a fine one, but important, for it lies behind Dickens' treatment of Florence's belief that she has been guilty toward her father and helps us to understand the author's reasoning behind the reconciliation scene.

Dombey, it is true, has the same duty to love, and he has violated this code over a much longer period of time. Dickens severely criticizes Dombey for this violation, yet there is also the sense here that sex-role stereotyping (and audience expectation), as well as Dickens' own views, operates to create distinctions between Dombey and Florence and their responsibility to love within the family grouping. That distinction serves to give some degree of guilt to Florence, for at least this one point in the novel. Like most Victorian authors, Dickens saw woman's identity in terms of family life. When Florence rejects her father, she rejects part of her self, though she is saved by her love for Walter Gay and their child. Men like Dombey can be seen in terms of what they do in the world of business as well as in personal and family relationships. Women like Florence (and Edith, though in strikingly different ways) are seen in relation to their role in the family group. Because Florence's world is so small and circumscribed, a failure in responsi-bility looms large, especially to Florence herself. For a Dombey, how-ever, responsibility is large but perhaps may not appear as great because the range of actions is so much wider than that of a Florence or Edith.

Compared to Dombey's continual neglect of the familial bond, Florence's fall seems slight, but the slightness is true only when we take into account the world of the entire novel. As far as her own narrow world is concerned, her act is significant and has gone on for a longer period of time than the one act of running away from her father after he strikes her. Thus, even though Dombey and the narrator express surprise or indignation at Florence's confession of guilt, their reactions serve the needs of high drama and do not negate Florence's confession. Considerable logic lies behind her admission of guilt. Dickens recognizes her essential goodness—there is never any doubt of this goodness—but he also wishes the reader to perceive the rightness of her confession. The reader may readily overlook Florence's fault, but Dickens does not, and it is because of his male position and role as father that he should demand complete perseverance from Florence while he is not proportionately as hard on Dombey.

In the major novels of Dickens' time, the plot line was not necessarily of the "they lived happily ever after" variety. *Jane Eyre, Vanity Fair,* the Palliser novels of Trollope—all presented the ending which stressed a right handling of things but also contained a strong tempering of happiness with a sense that things would never be the way they ought to have been. Of the three characters concerned here, Florence finds the greatest happiness at the novel's end, and that in her roles of wife, mother, and then finally of daughter (a reversal of the expected sequence). In the best of all possible worlds, Florence would deserve the rewards of family love, and even in an imperfect Victorian world, Florence's reward is possible, even if not probable. Yet I do not find this reward a real problem in Florence's characterization, since the image of family has been held before her throughout the novel, and Dickens prepares us to expect the withheld promise to become a reality and fulfillment, especially after the confession scene. Yet the happiness of Florence is not without its counterpart of sadness. The image of a broken Dombey, always in front of Florence, is this constant reminder, and Florence's reward is tempered with the knowledge that the years of lost love can never be regained.

Edith Granger Dombey's disposition at the novel's conclusion seems least satisfactory. In effect, Edith and Paul Dombey, Sr., have exchanged positions; as Dombey emerges from the darkened room, Edith enters its shadows. Dombey comes into the sunlight and meets with familial love, while Edith moves into darkness and meets a life of loneliness. Dombey knows he is unworthy of such happiness; Edith must believe she had earned the right to at least some happiness. Regardless of her desertion of Dombey, Edith has always been true to

Florence. Though she has protected the "orphaned" child from the machinations of her own mother and kept her out of Carker's way as well, however, Edith is banished to a corner place in the house of cousin Feenix. Edith herself describes this half life as a kind of death: "When you leave me in this dark room think that you have left me in the grave" (871–72). Dickens thus appears to be punishing Edith for her desertion of a husband rather than rewarding her for faithfulness to a lonely and unprotected child. Edith's faithfulness to Florence receives no reward, apparently, and by condemning her to exile, Dickens seems to create a basic injustice. What is most curious about Edith's seclusion from the public eye, however, is that she appears grateful for the darkness of her seclusion.

Dickens uses considerable space in his text for delving into the motives and responses of Paul Dombey, Sr., and for explaining Florence's hopes and disappointments. He spends much less time on the inner self of Edith Dombey, for while such "dark" women (women with a mysterious past, as Lady Dedlock in *Bleak House,* Miss Wade in *Little Dorrit*) fascinate him, he was not attuned to the psychological nuances of these women. He was able to capture, however, the anguished defiance of Alice Marwood-Brown, possibly because he kept her well into the background of his story, and stressed her anger rather than her depth. Dickens also could imaginatively re-create the fallen woman in her destitution (Emily in *David Copperfield*), the dependent woman in her long-suffering and wisdom (Esther Summerson in *Bleak House*) and the innocent woman in her goodness (Little Dorrit and Nell), but he was not sure of his ground when it came to the independent woman. Only later, with Bella in *Our Mutual Friend,* Rosa and particularly Helena in *The Mystery of Edwin Drood,* did Dickens show an understanding of the feminine character, apart from its particularized, familiar identity of mother, wife, daughter, or sister. Always, however, Dickens was fascinated by the Dark Woman and her secrets, though he was somewhat at a loss in re-creating them directly. Most often, Dickens uses an indirect method: physical positioning of the body, particularly of the hands, and the use of darkness as background for some of her appearances. Often Edith's cold demeanor must do service for psychological analysis. In some ways, Dickens is much more explicit in his handling of the prostitute Alice Marwood, and, through a suggestive parallelism, comments on Edith through this other female character.

Edith's characterization has long been considered unsatisfactory, in the sense that her actions and manner are viewed as unbelievable. Dickens was too intent on drawing the parallel between Alice and Edith, believes Cockshut, or possibly his guilt about his own sexual activities intruded into his creation of Edith.[13] Kathleen Tillotson, on the other hand, proposes that Edith is in the tradition of melodrama, "not a tragic heroine, but a tragedy queen. The curling lip, the flashing eyes, the burning brow, and the throbbing bosom monotonously recur with the phraseology that attaches to them; chapters in which she appears fall naturally into 'scenes', with all the stage direction supplied."[14] Edith's proud attitude is unreal, believes F. R. Leavis: "It is impossible to make moral sense of her attitude towards her marriage, and only in the world of melodramatic rhetoric could there be any illusion to the contrary. That Dickens, yielding in response to protests, should have changed his mind and saved her 'virtue' at the expense of the sensationally thwarted villain adds nothing essential—it couldn't—to the unreality."[15]

Yet the melodramatic mode of presenting this character ought not to blind us to Edith Dombey's psychological and moral realism. Like Miss Wade in *Little Dorrit,* one of Dickens' "dark women," Edith's past contains a suffering so great, perhaps, that it can only be suggested. Edith's first marriage and the death of her only child are referred to but not with any explicitness. We are aware, however, that these experiences have caused trauma too painful for full explanation. References to "Cleopatra's" machinations in marrying off Edith, indications that this mother has consistently believed that her daughter was an object for sale, continue to create the understanding that Edith's past has been filled with pain. Dickens further suggests that the result of that suffering has been a loss of belief in self and a negation of her own sense of human dignity.

In addition to pressing economic considerations, this loss of self-respect lies behind Edith's strangely passive acceptance of marriage with Dombey, a marriage that she admits to her mother is most abhorrent to her. Indeed, as she also clarifies, she has made no attempt to hide her distaste for marriage from Dombey himself. The parallels drawn between Edith Granger Dombey and Alice Marwood allow Dickens to imply that Edith has prostituted herself in her own context just as much as Alice has. In a scene previous to her marriage, Edith proclaims to her mother: "There is no slave in a market; there is no horse in a fair: so shown and offered and examined and paraded, mother, as I have been, for ten shameful years. . . . Have I been hawked and vended here and there, until the last grain of self-respect is dead within me, and I loathe myself?" Edith then refers to Dombey buying her as if at auction. The result, as she confesses, is, "I despise myself" (394). Her one consolation is that she had done nothing to lure Dombey into making the purchase.

Further insight into Edith's complex deprecation of self occurs in another scene just previous to her marriage, when she wanders through the Dombey house and pauses to regard her image in one of the broad, high mirrors. The reflection was that of "a woman with a noble quality yet dwelling in her nature, who was too false to her better self, and too debased and lost, to save herself" (423). Believing that her baseness was evident to all who saw her, Edith covers herself with a haughty pride—the only form of self-assertion she sees as possible in her position.

Edith's belief that she has sold herself in prostitution through the marriage agreement with Dombey is most evident in her relationship with Florence. Before the day of her marriage, Edith looks in on Florence, kisses the sleeping child, and cries the cry of lost innocence. Then, as Edith and Dombey leave on their "honeymoon," Edith shrinks from Florence's touch, again because she senses her own degradation, particularly apparent when contrasted with Florence's innocence.

Edith's marriage with Dombey has been a commercial transaction and makes her think of herself as prostitute. This marriage and her flight with Carker, which reiterates prostitution, are the most obvious external events in Edith's life, and in themselves would mark her as a woman of fascination, as well as melodrama. In between these two poles of her life are the two years of marriage with Dombey, and they are years filled with pain. While Dickens' reticence in dealing with domestic matters hides much from our eyes, the public pain surely suggests the greater, private agony of Edith Dombey. That pain is most apparent in scenes having sexual implications and reiterates Edith's own understanding of herself as prostitute, as "bought object."

Edith's suffering becomes more explicit after Dombey places the concept of Duty before her. He first refers to her duty to be hostess to his business guests. Later he refers to her duty to uphold his position before the world: "I consider it no unreasonable return for the worldly advancement that has befallen you. I require it as my right. In short I will have it." Edith begs Dombey for reconsideration—that they must recognize that each must travel a separate course, "so that, in the course of time, some friendship, or some feeling for each other, may arise between us." But Dombey refuses to listen and stubbornly says, "Madam, I cannot entertain any proposal of this extraordinary nature. . . . I place my reliance on your improved sense of duty, and more correct feeling, and better reflection, Madam" (568–69).

The scene is far too painful and personal to refer just to Edith's duty to uphold Dombey's good name in the social sphere. The innuendoes in the conversation, the ominous and humiliating presence of Carker, as well as the chapter title ("Domestic Relations") all point to Dombey's demanding sexual acquiescence from Edith—her duty as his lawful wife to have conjugal relations with him. The scene ought to be taken as a not-so-veiled reference to Edith's deferral and obedience to Dombey's marital "rights," and that basic message explains Edith's horror during the scene, but the fact that it is delivered in Carker's pres-

ence makes Dombey's treatment of Edith particularly onerous. The
public nature of Dombey's demand is a double insult, and is a perverted understanding of the concept of Duty. Edith's pained reaction
to this personal and sexual humiliation receives considerable attention
in the chapter, thus revealing the sympathetic attitude of Dickens in his
narrative persona.

Soon after, Mr. Dombey is seriously injured after falling from his
horse—a metaphor for his loss of control over Edith and his state of affairs in general, but the episode may also be taken in more specific sexual terms of the loss of potency or marital "rights" over Edith. Shortly
after his recovery, Edith withdraws from Florence, as it is apparent to
her what course she must follow. In order to assert herself, she must
leave Dombey. She shrinks from touching Florence, as she is all too
aware of how the world will regard her as runaway wife. At this point,
too, she sees herself as taking an action contrary to accepted mores—
but caught in the trap of increasing prostitution, Edith believes that
running away is less destructive of self than staying with Dombey as his
purchased possession. Edith has let Carker embrace her (an embrace
she deliberately allows so that Carker will think she is sexually attracted
to him), and after that touch, she does not allow Florence to come in
contact with her, again emphasizing that she recognizes what she has
become.

When Edith runs off with Carker and yet refuses to become his
mistress, her actions strike a number of readers as melodramatic and
unreal. In his study of the novel, for instance, A. O. Cockshut refers to
the refusal and raises the question: "It would be interesting to know
why" Edith refuses to be Carker's mistress.[16] But when Edith runs off
with Carker, it is not so much *with* Carker as *away* from Dombey. This
is a positive step toward asserting self and thereby regaining a sense of
her own dignity. (Refusing Dombey his conjugal "rights," if that is how
we are to read the "duty" scene, becomes the first step in Edith's
struggle, but it seems unlikely that Dickens was conscious of this interpretation.)

Edith's assertion of self in a sexual setting is more clearly and easily
handled by Dickens in the famous Dijon scene. After arriving at their
hotel, Edith refuses to let Carker touch her. When she lets him know
he is not to have his sexual "reward," Edith continues to assert self. The
melodramatic touches in the scene seem to be used as a kind of cloak
for the sexual meaning: the demand and refusal are such potentially
charged events that Dickens, for reasons of audience reaction or of
personal reticence, could not bear to present more openly. In such
cases, Dickens' technique is in danger of hiding all too well, but the
meaning here is discernible, especially when viewed in relation to Dombey's earlier reference to Edith's "duty." If the flight has been such an

important step in asserting her integrity, then of course Edith cannot allow Carker to touch her, since to have an affair with Carker would negate her flight from Dombey.

But Edith, too, must make her confession before peace can come. It is through Florence that the truth is wrung from her: "Guilty of much! Guilty of that which sets a waste between us evermore. Guilty of what must separate me, through the whole remainder of my life, from purity and innocence—from you, of all the earth. Guilty of a blind and passionate resentment, of which I do not, cannot, will not, even now, repent; but not guilty with that dead man. Before God!" (868). Edith does not wish reconciliation with Dombey; it is too late for that, and she is far too proud, even now. But to Florence's entreaties to reconcile with Dombey, Edith answers: "When he is most proud and happy in [Florence] and her children, he will be most repentant of his own part in the dark vision of our married life. At that time, I will be repentant too—let him know it then—and think that when I thought so much of all the causes that had made me what I was, I needed to have allowed more for the causes that had made him what he was. I will try, then, to forgive him his share of blame. Let him try to forgive me mine!" And then Edith's pride causes her to choose exile before society thrusts it upon her: "When you leave me in this dark room, think that you have left me in the grave" (871–72).

Audience expectation also plays a part in Edith's final disposition. In general, the conventions of mid-Victorian fiction do not allow the "fallen" woman to be redeemed, as she will be in the fiction of the latter part of the century. It appears quite probable, furthermore, that Dickens did not entirely realize what he had created in the person of Edith Dombey. Like Thackeray's Becky Sharp and Hardy's Eustacia Vye, Edith Dombey is a character whose complexity became too much for her creator to handle. Edith's psychology, in fact, possesses a complexity that Dickens seems only to half-understand. Part of this complexity is due to the shaping of the character's final end: Mr. Dombey and Florence, for instance, have rewards based primarily on the internal logic of the novel. The disposition of Edith, however, not only as internal logic but also the additional shaping pressure of audience expectation because the "fallen woman" concept is a more serious breach in Victorian mores than a cold, unloving father.

Mr. Dombey may be deficient in feeling, but he has always remained faithful (in letter, though not in spirit) to his marriage vows; Edith violates both letter and spirit, and has also been deficient in feeling, except where Florence is concerned. In addition, once Dombey is reunited with Florence, it would be too much for the novel's credibility for Dombey (and Dickens) to show a change of heart toward Edith. There is, after all, no blood relationship here as there is with Dombey's own child, and there has never been anything other than reciprocal coldness between Edith and Dombey. No structural or psychological basis exists for a union between Dombey and Edith at the novel's end. Any mutual concern for Florence Dickens carefully plays out in separate scenes between Florence and her father, or between Florence and Edith. And while Edith's love for Florence deserves some reward, her relationship with Dombey as her husband takes precedence, and denies her that privileged place.

Unhappily, Edith Dombey goes beyond the boundaries of moral action. She had earlier sold herself in marriage—an action she cannot forgive herself for—but now she has brought dishonor to Dombey by breaking the marriage bond and running off with another man. While she considers her honor intact because she has not allowed Carker to touch her after she has left Dombey, the public action of breaking and flaunting the marriage bond is such a serious action in Dickens' code that it cannot be forgiven.

But Edith's dark room is not necessarily a thorough and complete punishment, though its resultant separation from Florence certainly is. Instead, the dark room is a private place of peaceful, if gloomy, isolation, for the woman who saw herself always in terms of how others used her, from her earliest years, as she had bitterly informed her mother, to her being accounted as a possession wed by duty to Dombey, to her relationship with Carker who saw her as forbidden fruit— Edith has never been seen for herself. The many scenes which convey Edith's sense of herself as prostitute or as "unclean" provide important insight into her grateful acceptance of final seclusion from the world, and also prepares us for her final confession scene. As a counter to the earlier images and expressions of being "bought object," Edith now has the isolation necessary if she is at last to possess herself. Only Florence, of all the people in the world, has seen her as a human being with importance in that right, and it is because of Florence's understanding her that Edith comes to confess the truth of her experience with Carker and attitude toward Dombey.

Though Dombey and Florence have their final dispositions carefully prepared by Dickens and sanctioned by the confession scene as well as by the darkness, family, and duty motifs of the novel, Edith Dombey's disposition has, because of her continuing consciousness of what she is doing, a logical basis and an additional psychological complexity that make her into the most intriguing and believable character of the novel. The movement in *Dombey and Son* is that of the rising and falling tide, of the ocean as symbol of life and death. The structural rhythm of the novel indicates that as Dombey has passed from the darkened chamber into the light, so too will Edith. But for now, the isolation of the darkened room is the beginning of the healing process. Quite simply, Edith's story has not yet ended.

Through the disposition of the novel's three major characters, Dickens stresses the search for self, self-knowledge, and the recognition of the worth and needs of other selves. This is the realistic but rewarding knowledge that underlies the mythic celebration of two of the characters and makes Edith Dombey's domestic refuge more reward than punishment. In *Dombey and Son,* Dickens reveals an understanding of reward that distinguishes this work from earlier novels and prepares for the ever more painful realities of later writings.

Stanley Friedman

DICKENS' MID-VICTORIAN THEODICY

David Copperfield

ALTHOUGH SOME critics still see *David Copperfield* as an affirmative work, a story which, despite "dark shadows," conveys a "general impression . . . of light and fulfilment,"[1] various recent commentators assert that Dickens' most popular novel is essentially negative and grim. These readers emphasize David's revelation of his own weakness and offer harsh judgments: 1) Copperfield is a "lost, alienated" man unable to resist evil; 2) he has never resolved his childhood Oedipal conflict; 3) he evades obvious questions of his own guilt; 4) his "traditional consolations" are clearly unsatisfactory; and 5) his "prudential morality" does not adequately explain "intractable tragic elements in life."[2]

Even if we wish to avoid making *David Copperfield* another of Dickens' "dark novels," we must concede that the book includes a striking contradiction: the narrator is ostensibly presenting a record of triumphant survival, but he is certainly obsessed with death. Moreover, many other puzzles and paradoxes appear. A paean to effort, discipline, and perseverance, the story nevertheless questions the extent to which human beings can control their lives. Self-reliance is preached, but in times of crisis the protagonist depends heavily on others for financial or emotional support. Furthermore, David blends self-criticism with conceit, using self-pity to soften intimations of guilt. Openly didactic and moralistic, he strangely leaves us unclear about the actual lesson he derives from his experiences and makes us wonder whether his advice cannot be reduced to an absurd injunction asking everyone to work hard and be lucky.

These inconsistencies, however, are best understood as reflecting the mature David's complex philosophical and religious attitudes. Indeed, the entire narrative can be regarded as an attempt to determine whether effort or providence or chance is the decisive factor in this world, whether suffering can be redeemed, whether belief in divine justice can be reaffirmed. Various points suggest that Dickens intended the book as a theodicy, a text that will seem ironic only if we neglect its asserted conclusion. As J. Hillis Miller and Alexander Welsh have maintained, religious motifs are highly significant in *David Copperfield*,[3] and these critics' views are further supported if we examine closely a number of interrelated features: David's obsession with death; his awareness of guilt and moral responsibility; the novel's use of *déjà vu* and of Shakespearean drama; the work's autobiographical form; several references to *Robinson Crusoe;* and a few details that suggest the possible influence of Goldsmith's *The Vicar of Wakefield.*

— I —

From the start, we are confronted with puzzling elements, beginning with the full title: *THE PERSONAL HISTORY, ADVENTURES, EXPERIENCE, & OBSERVATION OF DAVID COPPERFIELD THE YOUNGER. OF BLUNDERSTONE ROOKERY. (Which He never meant to be Published on any Account.).* Despite one scholar's effort to distinguish among *history, adventures, experience,* and *observation,* the terms seem whimsically redundant.[4] Moreover, the appellation "the Younger" appears superfluous, for we soon learn that David's father has long been deceased and was evidently never well known. Similarly, "Of Blunderstone Rookery" is unnecessary, for the protagonist's name is not a common one, and we later realize that his published novels have made him the only famous bearer of that name. Finally, the use of the third person in the parenthetical clause suggests that the title as printed may have been prepared by someone other than David. Whether the latter is still alive, why he wanted his story to remain unpublished "on any Account," and why he wrote a book that he did not intend to publish are all obvious questions to which Dickens directs our attention. Are we to expect a guilt-ridden confession, a scandalous revelation? Or a tale of piety, a memoir that David composed for himself only or for the private edification of a few selected friends and relatives? For as one scholar, discussing the early tradition of spiritual autobiography, observes, many records of "self-searching and trial" were "kept or revised in presentable form for the sake of families, congregations, fellow-sufferers, or whatever group of readers the manuscript might reach, even by those who had no intention of publishing their lives to the world at large."[5]

The opening sentence augments our confusion: "Whether I shall turn out to be the hero of my own life, or whether that station will be held by anybody else, these pages must show." In John Barth's novel *The End of the Road,* the narrator is told by another character, "Everyone is necessarily the hero of his own life story,"[6] an idea that relatively few of us would challenge. But David Copperfield evidently does not know if he is the hero of his own life, and his narrative is presumably an attempt to satisfy his need to answer this question. Even though the word "hero" is ambiguous, denoting either the protagonist or the outstanding positive exemplar in a drama or story, the phrase "of my own life" perhaps relieves us of the problem of choosing between these meanings, for normal egocentricity may readily blend them. David's question, however, implies a fusion of self-centeredness and self-effacement. Ostensibly, his book is an exercise in self-analysis, an effort to discover his relationship to the events of his own life. Since the novel is not presented as a diary or ongoing record, and since the past tense leads us to assume that the author already knows what has happened, we infer that he feels disturbed by an inability to comprehend the significance of his experiences and that he hopes through writing to relive or reexamine his life in order to further his self-understanding. Through autobiography, David can organize his past, and, surprisingly, he feels a need to do this after having been married to Agnes for "ten happy years" (866), more than thirteen years having elapsed since the deaths of Dora and Steerforth. Late in the narrative, David refers to "the compact I have made with myself, to reflect my mind on this paper" (697). In bringing his mind's "secrets to the light" (697), even if only for his own perusal, he is revivifying his memory and achieving a kind of control over a past that evidently still troubles him. Indeed, David seems motivated by goals that Roy Pascal considers central to autobiography, a genre that serves as "the means to review one's life, to organise it in the imagination, and thus to bring the past experience and the present self into balance."[7]

While focusing his gaze on himself, however, David Copperfield, in his opening sentence, suggests uncertainty about deserving this attention and seeks to deny self-love and narcissism by asserting that his narrative was inspired by self-doubt.[8] But when we realize later in the book that these opening words have been written by a man who has gone from abused orphan boy to successful novelist blessed with angelic wife and blissful brood, we may wonder about the sincerity of this supposed self-questioning. Copperfield is not teasing us, however, and the fact that he never provides an explicit answer to his initial question is a sign, ironically, of that query's great importance to him, despite his material success.

In the novel's second sentence, Dickens suddenly shifts the tone from solemn to playful, hinting deliberate avoidance of the *in medias res* opening of heroic stories. David comes close to *ab ovo,* starting from the caul, and his whimsical manner provides security and reassurance, in contrast to the grim content of his words—remarks about predestination for ill luck.

The reference to luck immediately raises the question of what control a person can exercise over his life, a query integrally connected with the idea of a hero as a positive exemplar. For the word "hero" in this sense implies control and accomplishment rather than passivity. Although a hero may be subject to good or bad luck, he must also be a character responsible for his deeds, not a mere pawn at the mercy of fortune.

David's birth at the exact stroke of midnight on a Friday is the first of many reported coincidences; and coincidence itself, so strongly insisted upon by Dickens throughout his career, again leads us to questions about the extent to which we can direct events in our lives. Our own births, of course, we cannot arrange.

After the first four paragraphs, with their banter and lighthearted speculation about the power of a caul to provide protection from drowning, the narrator, who has been extremely unhurried, abruptly announces his wish not "to meander" and then records what he evidently sees as the distinguishing fact of his early years, if not of his entire life: "I was a posthumous child" (2). The bluntness shocks, for up to this point the easily loquacious remarks arouse little anxiety, except perhaps for the use of "poor" meaning "unfortunate" in reference to David's mother (1). This early emphasis on the death of David Copperfield the Elder is increased by the image of the white gravestone "lying out alone there in the dark night" (2) and by several remarks about the grave, comments appearing in important places—the end of Chapter i (12), near the beginning of Chapter ii (14), and toward the end of Chapter iii (42), the chapter concluding the first installment. Significantly, in two versions of Hablot K. Browne's etching included with Parts XIX–XX and intended to serve as the novel's frontispiece, the path at the right leads the viewer's eyes to gravestones that are visible through the trees.[9]

Throughout *David Copperfield* we find the problem and the flavor of death: in the words of Mr. Omer, the pleasant undertaker, " 'we are all drawing on to the bottom of the hill, whatever age we are, on account of time never standing still for a single moment' " (735). And the narrator, the mature David, includes in more than one-third of his pages either some direct reference to mortality or else a figurative expression using the idea of death. For example, he observes that the advertisement for his caul "was withdrawn at a dead loss" (1), and later, when commenting on a childhood fall from a seat in church, David tells us that he was "taken out, more dead than alive, by Peggotty" (15). Again and again, we find locutions like "dead sleepy" (16 and 76), "the death-blow at my peace" (53), "hushed as death" (89), and "as if the house were dead too" (248).

But, of course, more important than these figurative expressions are the novel's references to actual mortality. In the first number alone (chapters i–iii), we find not only the comments about the gravestone of David's father but also a remark about the supposed death of Betsey Trotwood's husband, the information that Clara Copperfield was an orphan, the recollection of the church tablet memorializing "Mr. Bodgers late of this parish" (15), the mature David's poignant affirmation that though his mother be now dead, his "remembrance brings her back to life" (24), Mr. Peggotty's use of "drowndead" to describe the fathers of Ham and Em'ly (32–33), a reference to the death of Em'ly's mother, and Mrs. Gummidge's frequent thoughts of her late husband, " 'the old 'un.' " No wonder that David, finding on his return from Yarmouth that his mother is not present to greet him, pathetically asks, " 'Not dead, too! Oh, she's not dead, Peggotty?' " (42).

These intimations of mortality from recollections of early childhood are more than supported by subsequent events in the novel. Six deaths figure importantly in David's story—those of his mother, Barkis, Spenlow, Dora, Steerforth, and Ham. The first death and the last three represent climactic points, while the loss of Barkis anticipates and makes possible—by delaying Em'ly's marriage—the "greater loss" of her seduction, and Spenlow's death functions, on the other hand, in what at first seems a positive way, helping to bring about the narrator's union with Dora. Significantly, there is a wide range in the ages of these six victims, the causes of their deaths, and the reactions of others: the very old Barkis and the youthful Clara and Dora expire slowly, while Spenlow, Ham, and Steerforth meet sudden ends, the first from "natural" causes, the latter two from accidents attributable to "nature."

Moreover, the novel's emphasis on mortality is even more extensive than most critics suggest. During the course of the story, the narrator briefly reports or mentions the deaths of his infant stepbrother, the first Mrs. Chillip, Traddles' uncle, the child Dora is bearing, Betsey Trotwood's husband, the second Mrs. Chillip's father, the second Mrs. Murdstone's mother, and Traddles' mother-in-law, as well as Dora's dog, Jip, and the crew of Steerforth's ship. And we are also made aware of demises occurring prior to the novel's opening. Besides being told about David's father and the relatives lost by the members of Mr. Peggotty's boat-home, we learn that Traddles' guardian is an uncle, the boy evidently being another orphan, and we subsequently find references, direct or indirect, to many departed figures who are only of tangential interest: Steerforth's father, the parents of the Micawbers' "Orfling," Mrs. Micawber's parents, Mr. Dick's father, Agnes Wickfield's mother, Uriah Heep's father, Annie Strong's father, Rosa Dartle's parents, Dora's mother, Mr. Pidger (the apparent suitor of Dora's Aunt Lavinia), Martha Endell's parents, the parents of the page employed by David and Dora, Agnes' maternal grandmother, and such dubiously real personages as Mr. Topsawyer (a prior customer of the waiter who dupes young David), the boy supposedly killed at Salem House, and Mrs. Crupp's previous boarder.

Still another feature in David's narrative is the vast number of situations in which characters anticipate the deaths of themselves or others, such remarks ranging from expressions of a serious death wish to mere speculation to mock threats of suicide. At least sixty of these morbid anticipations show the funerary interests of young David, of the mature narrator, and of other figures in the novel. Although Micawber's suicidal hints are ludicrous, the idea of self-destruction is treated very seriously when the disgraced Em'ly writes to Mrs. Gummidge, " 'Oh, if I was fit, I would be so glad to die' " (587), and when Martha, having gone to the river to end her life, begs Mr. Peggotty, " 'Stamp upon me, kill me' " (683). And character after character considers the future death of himself or others: Mr. Mell's elderly mother speculates about her aged companion, Mrs. Fibbitson; the kindly Clara Peggotty wonders whether Aunt Betsey will die and leave David a bequest; on the journey to Dover, David fears "being found dead in a day or two, under some hedge" (180); Mr. Wickfield thinks of his own or Agnes' death; Ham expresses premonitions about his end; Mr. Peggotty talks about whether he will die before finding Em'ly; Dr. Strong anticipates leaving Annie free; and Micawber, brief though his part in the novel is, comic though he almost always is, again and again foresees his death. His and the other characters' musings keep the theme of mortality before us.

Indeed, even extremely casual references move to this topic: Traddles comforts himself by drawing skeletons; in the home of Peggotty and Barkis, David finds a "large quarto edition of Foxe's Book of Martyrs" with pictures of "all kinds of dismal horrors" (148); the "goroo" man weirdly sings "The Death of Nelson" (185); the subject of Mr. Dick's "Memorial" is evidently the execution of Charles I; and when David chooses to prepare to become a proctor, his attention is, of course, directed to wills.

In addition to all of these direct and indirect cases of *memento mori,* we find a number of philosophical comments on death. Besides Mr. Omer's previously noted words about everyone's " 'drawing on to the bottom of the hill,' " David records such statements as Steerforth's unfeeling dismissal of Barkis' approaching death as " 'a bad job,' " but " 'the common lot' " (426), and Mr. Peggotty's belief that " 'along the coast' " life ebbs and flows with the tide, a suggestion that death is therefore a natural part of life's cycle (445). Mr. Omer later offers a similar view when he refers to himself as a man " 'drawing on to a time of life, where the two ends of life meet' " (735), a remark that "parallels" Hablot Browne's cover illustration depicting the circle from birth to the grave.[10] David himself, however, seems to emphasize in his own comments the relentlessness and the mystery of death: he calls the sound of coffin-making "the tune that never *does* leave off" (306); he later refers to death as "that great Visitor, before whose presence all the living must give place" (438); and he notices, before Barkis dies, how, "in the expectation of that dread surprise, all other changes and surprises dwindle into nothing" (442). This *surprise*—in Barkis' case, paradoxically *expected*—is even more disturbing when unforeseen, as in the instance of Spenlow's extremely sudden demise. Later, fearing Dora's death, David broods about "the many, never old, who had lived and loved and died" (742).

All of the foregoing details suggest that Copperfield is both attracted to and repelled by death. As various commentators have observed, the narrator's Oedipal fear of his dead father becomes hostility toward the living sexual rival, Murdstone, while desire for the mother is later reflected in David's choice of Dora as a mate.[11] For the guilt such feelings evoke, death would be an appropriate punishment to seek. But Copperfield also fears death, for him a relentless depriver. Just before Barkis dies, the narrator remembers Em'ly's "dread of death" (444), expressed when she mentioned being afraid of the sea: " 'I have seen it very cruel' " (34). Although David at the time replied that he was not frightened, he comments in retrospect, "I have no doubt if I had seen a moderately large wave come tumbling in, I should have taken to my heels, with an awful recollection of her [Em'ly's] drowned relations" (35). And David continues to fear death. In fact, the end of his narrative, with its prayer that Agnes, "pointing upward" (877), will be near him when he dies, suggests that this dread is the great problem remaining for the neglected orphan now become a famous and prosperous novelist, now recovered from the losses of first wife and older friend: how to face his own eventual death.

Copperfield, who claims on his opening page that he has not yet seen ghosts, unless he did so while "still a baby" (1), nevertheless may at times remind us of literature's most famous ghost-seer—indeed, Robert Ornstein's comment seems largely applicable to David: "Throughout the play Hamlet faces the most ancient and abiding philosophical problem: he must 'learn how to die,' i.e., how to live with the fact and thought of death."[12] David Copperfield, from his blunt statement, "I was a posthumous child," to his musings about the gravestone, to his responses when facing the losses of his mother, Dora, and Steerforth, to his final thoughts in the book, is immersed in death.[13] Moreover, the novel suggests that its protagonist can face his own mortality only by relying on religious faith as confirmed by feelings evoked in him by another human being, Agnes, whom he has always associated with the "tranquil brightness" of a church window (223). Despite his credo of "resolution and independence," David is, like the speaker in Wordsworth's poem, paradoxically reliant on "a leading from above" in the shape of another person. David's adoration of Agnes may at times seem to approach the sacrilegious, but Dickens does not want us to condemn this attitude and does *not* intend a moral like that offered by the narrator in *Jane Eyre:* "My future husband was becoming to me my whole world; and more than the world: almost my hope of heaven. He stood between me and every thought of religion, as an eclipse intervenes between man and the broad sun. I could not, in those days, see God for his creature: of whom I had made an idol" (chap. 24).[14]

— 2 —

Actual death, however, is not the only problem with which David is concerned, for his story is also in large part an account of his dealings with two "ruined" women: Em'ly and Aunt Betsey. There is, of course, significance in the use of the same epithet to denote loss of sexual innocence and of money, two commodities that help determine reputation. Similar penalties—the living deaths of prostitution and debtors' prison—face those guilty of sexual transgression or financial laxity.[15] In both cases—Em'ly's and Aunt Betsey's—David is largely responsible for both the ruin and the recovery. He introduces Steerforth to Mr. Peggotty's "family"; but David is the one who thinks of asking help of Martha—and Martha becomes the savior of Em'ly. To see David as totally ineffectual is to neglect Mr. Peggotty's expression of gratitude after Em'ly has been found: " 'Mas'r Davy!' said he, gripping my hand in that strong hand of his, 'it was you as first made mention of her [Martha] to me. I thankee, sir!' " (729). Less directly, Copperfield "causes" both his aunt's apparent bunkruptcy and the subsequent recovery of her money. For, as Traddles discloses, Heep's actions against Miss Trotwood are motivated primarily by hostility toward David; but the latter, after finding work for Mr. Dick and supporting Aunt Betsey by his own labor, acts as a catalyst in bringing rescue, even though Micawber and Traddles are the actual agents of Heep's defeat. First, there is the fact that Heep's employment of Micawber comes about not only as a result of the latter's advertisement but also because of " 'a mutual recognition' " (532), the two men having previously met through Copperfield. In addition, David's earlier friendship with Micawber seems to stimulate the latter's conscience and to invite his confidential disclosures. And, while the Micawbers have come to know Traddles without David's assistance, it is David to whom the conscience-stricken Micawber writes, asking that Traddles be brought, too. Significantly, Heep attributes his defeat mainly to Copperfield, whom he accuses of inciting the others (lii). Indeed, although Uriah's remarks may stem merely from his extreme hatred, Micawber and Traddles do seem to act as surrogates for David, who implies that he deserves some credit by asserting, "I felt devoutly thankful for the miseries of my younger days which had brought me to the knowledge of Mr. Micawber" (761).

These questions of David's possible guilt or responsibility and of his moral achievements are important, for they point to the novel's most encompassing problem—the question of human control over events. Although a novelist could hardly avoid some consideration—either overt or implicit—of this topic, the subject seems to receive an unusual degree of attention in *David Copperfield*.

The narrator's obsessive concern with death reflects the obvious fact that mortality is a problem beyond human control, unless one accepts the Stoic idea of suicide as a solution. But, besides the many references to death, numerous other details keep the theme of control foremost. Aunt Betsey cannot dictate the sex of Clara Copperfield's baby, and Mr. Dick cannot keep Charles I out of the Memorial. Murdstone seeks to dominate others, as does Creakle. In addition, Mrs. Steerforth and her son are locked in a contest of wills, Agnes perceives Steerforth's dangerous influence over David, and Heep strives to control Wickfield.[16] Although Micawber mentions the need to ready himself for "a spring" at an anticipated opportunity (407), he also frequently speaks of "circumstances" beyond "control" (701, 750, 806, 872) and waits for something to "turn up" (163, 168, 171, 174, 175, 257, 261, 407). And three characters—Spenlow, Mr. Dick, and Dr. Strong—are concerned with testamentary wills, efforts to exercise some kind of posthumous control.

Other features also contribute to the theme of control: the tagline "Barkis is willin' " affirms voluntary choice; Mr. Peggotty visits a tavern called "The Willing Mind," an establishment later patronized by Steerforth; and Copperfield refers to involuntary associations in his memory (30, 40, 228, 396), becomes a "captive" of Dora's (390), and later speaks of his "undisciplined"—or uncontrolled—heart (814). Moreover, his grandaunt urges him to develop a " 'will of . . . [his] own' " (275), and David at times consciously considers this question of control. For example, he is torn between regarding his discontent over Dora's not being his full partner as an unavoidable feeling, common to all men, and seeing the situation as a mistake that could have been averted (697). Earlier in the same chapter, he attributes his success as an author to what "nature and accident" had made him fit for, but he also endorses effort and perseverance (690), implying a belief in human ability to achieve at least partial control of life. But the control is only partial, and Mr. Peggotty's confidence in human power to direct events— "no wrong can touch my Em'ly while so be as that man [Ham] lives" (314)—is painfully disproved.

Two other features in the novel are also important in evoking wonder about this question of human control. First, there is the customary Dickensian insistence on coincidences of various kinds, coincidence being, by definition, beyond human control and therefore attributable to chance or providence.[17] In addition, there is a point that has attracted some attention in a few studies of *David Copperfield*—the narrator's recounting of two *déjà vu* experiences, both involving his feelings about Agnes. When Heep for the first time clearly discloses a desire for Agnes, David reports having "the strange feeling (to which, perhaps, no one is quite a stranger) that all this had occurred before, at some indefinite time" (381). The second incident takes place later in the narrative, when Micawber, after praising Agnes, suggests that he would have thought Copperfield romantically attached to her if the relationship with Dora had not been previously disclosed. David comments, "We have all some experience of a feeling, that comes over us occasionally, of what we are saying and doing having been said and done before, in a remote time—of our having been surrounded, dim ages ago, by the same faces, objects, and circumstances—of our knowing perfectly what will be said next, as if we suddenly remembered it! I never had this mysterious impression more strongly in my life, than before he uttered those words" (566). Jerome Hamilton Buckley offers the following comment on these experiences: "The feeling, twice related to the fleeting awareness that he [David] has neglected or misunderstood Agnes Wickfield, is accompanied by a certain bewilderment, a half-conscious sense of misdirection, intimating that he has misread the signposts of his life."[18] J. Hillis Miller, who sees the two experiences as "covert premonitions of the place Agnes is to have in David's life," observes that "at the time David cannot understand the divine hints, and is left to work out his own destiny."[19]

Several psychoanalytic discussions of the *déjà vu* phenomenon suggest additional possibilities, some of which seem applicable to *David Copperfield*. For example, one authority maintains that a *déjà vu* experience expresses "the wish for a second chance," coupled with "the premise that one does better with the second chance"—"*déjà vu* is a wish directed into the past and falsely experienced as a memory."[20] Another view sees the experience as a complicated defense against anxiety: a disturbing "memory, wish or fantasy which threatens to emerge is minimized as being unreal, dreamlike or already past" and therefore not a cause for concern because it is safely over or at least has once been surmounted and so may again be handled.[21] A third opinion expresses reservations about the possibility of finding "one encompassing explanation" for the phenomenon and describes a variation in which a patient used *déjà vu* experiences in "an attempt to control time" so as to avoid being "faced with . . . current problems and . . . required to make decisions and to change."[22]

If we regard each of these diverse theories as possessing some validity, several interesting explanations of David Copperfield's two *déjà vu* experiences may be considered. First, Heep's declaration of interest in Agnes may seem a *déjà vu* phenomenon to David because the latter has suppressed any sexual interest he has in Agnes and is therefore made uncomfortable at Uriah's indication that she can be seen as a desirable woman. Indeed, shortly after meeting Agnes, David found his feelings confused: "I love little Em'ly, and I don't love Agnes—no, not at all in that way—but I feel that there are goodness, peace, and truth, wherever Agnes is; and that the soft light of the coloured window in the church, seen long ago, falls on her always" (232). When he leaves Dr. Strong's school, David is careful to define for Agnes her future role and to exclude a sexual relationship: " 'Whenever I fall into trouble, or fall in love, I shall always tell you' " (276). And, later, Agnes is explicitly labeled " 'my good Angel' " (366) and " 'my dear sister' " (370). Furthermore, in this first *déjà vu* experience David may be responding to earlier perceptions of Uriah as a sexual figure, for we have been told of the phallic "snaky twistings" of Heep's "throat and body" (235) and of his subsequent "ascendancy" over Wickfield, the broken father figure (369).[23] David's first *déjà vu* feeling, therefore, may signify not only his wish to repress his sense of Agnes as a sexual being, but also his intuition that excluding her as an object of sexual interest was a mistake. David may be seeking through *déjà vu* to displace his own previously suppressed desire for Agnes onto Heep. Or David may seek through *déjà vu* to minimize the threat posed by Heep and thereby to lessen his own guilt at having done nothing to aid Agnes or her father. Finally, David may want "a second chance," an opportunity to be first to claim Agnes. Significantly, in the very next chapter David resolves the problem when he meets Dora and becomes "a captive," therefore unable to help Agnes by expressing sexual interest in her.

David's other *déjà vu* experience, in reaction to Micawber's surprise that romantic feeling had not been evoked by Agnes, may indicate Copperfield's wish that he had shown such interest or his awareness that such interest would have been very suitable for him. Aunt Betsey had recently hinted that the attraction to Dora might be a mistake (504), and Dora's refusal to see David after Spenlow's death had perhaps created doubts concerning her loyalty. Different theories of *déjà vu* may suggest either that David fears Heep as an intruding rival for Agnes' affection or that Copperfield subconsciously *wants* Uriah to remove Agnes by marrying her, since this would reduce David's guilt about rejecting her for someone who is less worthy but more attractive physically, more like David's mother. That these explanations are in some ways contradictory may be regarded as a sign of Copperfield's extreme confusion, for the narrator is aware of his ambivalence toward Uriah: "I was attracted to him in very repulsion" (383).

Interestingly, the first *déjà vu* experience occurs just after David has been seriously disturbed at Agnes' having seen him drunk and out of control and after a conflict has been created by her warning about Steerforth's bad influence; the second *déjà vu* experience happens just after Spenlow discovers the relationship with Dora, attempts to end it, and suddenly dies, sending his daughter into seclusion and David into depression, for which a journey to Dover is prescribed as a remedy. As Arlow observes, *déjà vu* phenomena appear to be stimulated by "states of fatigue, stress, illness . . . (factors which presumably favor regression or the emergence of repressed material)."[24]

Finally, prior to each *déjà vu* experience, David has occasion to recognize his emotional dependence on Agnes. After the dissipation, he assures her that she is the person whose good opinion of him he most values (366); and in the installment before the one describing the *déjà vu* feelings evoked by Micawber, David, depressed over his new financial plight, blurts out upon meeting Agnes, " 'There is no one I should have wished for but you' " (510), and has to be reminded that Dora, to whom he is already secretly engaged, should receive priority. Just after the *déjà vu* experience with Micawber, David must once more be told by Agnes that his "reliance" must be not on her, but on Dora (568).[25]

Despite the complexity of possible interpretations of these two *déjà vu* incidents, the phenomena clearly emphasize David's concern over whether he has in some way anticipated situations and yet remained powerless to control them. This theme of control also seems present in his description of an event preceding the important coincidental meeting with Steerforth in London—David's attending a performance of *Julius Caesar*. The narrator reports that his response to the play was pleasure at having "all those noble Romans alive before me, and walking in and out for my entertainment, instead of being the stern taskmasters they had been at school" (286). In other words, David can now, in a sense, control figures who had once dominated him. No further reference is made to this performance, except the narrator's point that what for him was " 'a delightful and magnificent entertainment' " evokes an entirely different reaction from Steerforth, who, after announcing that he has been " 'dozing and grumbling away at the play,' " asserts, " 'there never was a more miserable business' " (288). Nevertheless, the mention of *Julius Caesar* may remind us of themes that are emerging in *David Copperfield*. A tragedy presenting a kind of parricide, *Julius Caesar* includes a vengeful ghost, superstitions, the motif of suicide, and explicit concern with the question of human control. Although previous commentators have not, I believe, seen the reference to the play as a means of reinforcing motifs in *David Copperfield,* scholars have noted that rebellion against the father—present in *Julius Caesar* if we regard Brutus and Cassius as Caesar's "sons"—is an important theme in Dickens' novel.[26] As we have seen, too, the opening page of the narrative directs us to ghosts and superstition, while suicide—the mock threats of Micawber, the real attempt of Martha, Ham's eagerness to face danger—later emerges as another concern. Moreover, in *Julius Caesar* two extremely well known passages stress the theme of control. Cassius' assertion of the primacy of will, "The fault, dear Brutus, is not in our stars,/ But in ourselves, that we are underlings," is balanced by Brutus' lines, "There is a tide in the affairs of men,/ Which, taken at the flood, leads on to fortune," a view that blends the concepts of destiny and freedom.[27] Later in David's narrative, Mrs. Micawber seemingly alludes to the play in order to raise again the question of human control over outward events: "'I wish Mr. Micawber . . . to be the Caesar of his own fortunes'" (808).

When Dickens came years afterward to write *Great Expectations,* he was, of course, to make much fuller use of this "play-within-a-novel" device, employing *Hamlet,* as Fielding had done in *Tom Jones* (bk. 16, chap. v).[28] But, while David, unlike Pip, does not see a performance of *Hamlet,* his narrative contains frequent references to the play, reminding us of numerous thematic resemblances between this tragedy and *Julius Caesar* and also emphasizing various points in *David Copperfield.*[29] We have already noted the obsession with death in both *Hamlet* and David's story, as well as the "ghost" motif in each. Robert Fleissner considers David like Hamlet in being an introspective character with a cruel stepfather and a weak mother; finds parallels between Ophelia and Dora, Ophelia and Em'ly, and Hamlet and Steerforth; and also sees a verbal link between David's reference at the end of the first chapter to "the earthly bourne of all such travellers" and the "To be, or not to be" soliloquy.[30] Although some of these suggestions may be unconvincing, several do seem significant, and to these we may add a few other resemblances: just as Hamlet is upset by the proximity of merriment and grief—"The funeral baked meats/ Did coldly furnish forth the marriage tables"—so David, riding home to his mother's funeral, resents the flirtation of Minnie and Joram; moreover, while Hamlet causes the deaths of both his prospective bride and future father-in-law, David bears some responsibility for the death of Dora and perhaps also for that of Spenlow.[31]

In addition, the theme of control, important in all Shakespearean tragedy, receives an extraordinary amount of overt attention in *Hamlet:* from Laertes' assertion that Hamlet's "will is not his own" to the player-king's lines, "Our wills and fates do so contrary run/ That our devices still are overthrown," to the references to "a divinity that shapes our ends" and the "special providence in the fall of a sparrow," to Horatio's closing words about "purposes mistook/ Fall'n on th' inventors' heads," the theme dominates the play, while the most famous speech, the "To be, or not to be" soliloquy, dwells on a double paradox, the idea that the only way to control one's destiny is to end it by suicide and the realization that even suicide does not bring complete control, for anticipation of a hereafter must "give us pause."

Both *Hamlet* and *David Copperfield* seem to emphasize human inability to control outward events and even feelings and thoughts.[32] But David's story is not a tragedy, and the attitudes of both the protagonist and Dickens appear to counsel trust in a benevolent and powerful providence and also an awareness of the need for human effort. In *Bleak House,* Dickens' next novel after *David Copperfield,* such a belief is explicitly endorsed when John Jarndyce advises Rick Carstone, " 'Trust in nothing but in Providence and your own efforts' " (chap. xiii).

— *3* —

Even though David Copperfield emphasizes his own efforts (546 and 606–7), his narrative, as we have observed, concedes the limits of human control over events, especially in the story's concern with death, a problem that dominates much of the book. The protagonist's major crises involve bereavement—the losses of mother, wife, and friend— and David still must face the inevitability of his own future death. For this, his narrative itself is a kind of preparation, and the story therefore seems closely linked to the tradition of spiritual autobiography, a tradition that includes not only intense emotional experiences and careful meditation on these but also the recording of such feelings and such introspection. As various scholars have noted, the Victorian era was indeed marked by enormous interest in autobiography and self-scrutiny.[33] For John N. Morris, "the experiences recorded in nineteenth-century autobiography" may be seen as "secular counterparts of the religious melancholy and conversions set down in the autobiographies of earlier heroes of religion."[34] Moreover, as Vineta Colby comments, Victorian religious novels often seem indistinguishable from "the autobiographies, diaries, and confessionals that proliferated during the period."[35] And still wider relationships are suggested in Roy Pascal's claim: "The nineteenth-century novels that delve deep into childhood, from Dickens and the Brontës onwards, are unimaginable without the great autobiographies."[36] To such links, we may add another line of connection, one moving from Puritan autobiographies to the early English novels of the eighteenth century and then on to Victorian fiction.[37] Indeed, the overall picture reveals a tangled web of influences; but the web is important in alerting us to the religious element in both Victorian autobiography and fiction.

One noteworthy indication of Dickens' success in making *David Copperfield* resemble an actual autobiography is found, ironically, in a frequently voiced criticism of the novel. Edgar Johnson observes, "to some readers, David Copperfield himself seems to fade out of the picture as his story moves toward the time of his life when he is supposed to be writing it."[38] And we may recall George Gissing's comment, "To his [David's] autobiography let all praise be given—with the reserve that we see the man himself less clearly than any other person of whom he speaks."[39] But Roy Pascal, writing about autobiography as a genre, regards such "indeterminateness and unlimitedness" as typical: "there is always a core of darkness in the hero of the autobiography," "a lack of vivid impact in respect to the hero, not only to our view of him, but also in his own sight."[40]

In addition, a strong link between *David Copperfield* and spiritual autobiography seems to be suggested by David's anguish and guilt over the deaths of Dora and Steerforth. Considering Chapter lviii, "Absence," which describes the protagonist's journey abroad to face his grief, Jerome Buckley remarks, "Like other Victorians, David endures a dark night of despair before he finds hope and purpose and even true identity"—a " 'pattern of conversion.' "[41] Indeed, the extremity of David's sorrow appears attributable to guilt concerning the fates of Em'ly, Ham, Steerforth, and Dora, for Copperfield made possible the tragic events in which the first three were involved, and Dora's parting words to him suggest that his failure to hide his discontent deprived her of her will to live.

Still further links between *David Copperfield* and spiritual autobiography or religious fiction may be found in various references to Defoe's *Robinson Crusoe*, as well as in one of Copperfield's basic moral points, his insistence on the advantages of adversity. Describing his arrival in London en route to Salem House, David states that he was "more solitary than Robinson Crusoe" (72), and later, on finding his aunt and her baggage in his chambers, he compares her to "a female Robinson Crusoe" (497). In calling attention to these remarks, K. J. Fielding adds the point that "Yarmouth was the scene of Crusoe's first shipwreck as of Steerforth's."[42] Moreover, we find other references besides these and the inclusion of Defoe's novel in the list of readings that sustained the young David's "fancy" (55): on first taking up residence at Mrs. Crupp's, David likens himself to Crusoe (356); in the next installment, before first meeting Dora, Copperfield emphasizes his being "very much alone," "alone in the world," then tells of a legal proceeding in which "the evidence was just twice the length of Robinson Crusoe" (387), and, after subsequently becoming Dora's captive, remarks, "when Mr. Spenlow went home without me . . . , [I felt] as if I were a mariner myself, and the ship to which I belonged had sailed away and left me on a desert island" (397); finally, much later in the story, David returns to his old room at the Wickfields', "like a shipwrecked wanderer come home" (781).

Referring to the narrator's comparison at the beginning of Chapter xxiv, James Kincaid suggests that David Copperfield "is, in actuality, lost, alienated: more like the Robinson Crusoe he imagines himself to be . . . than he fully realizes."[43] But Kincaid seems to neglect the point that Defoe's narrative is a tale of *ultimate* triumph, not defeat. Indeed, Starr maintains that "a long tradition of spiritual autobiography" "probably reaches its fullest imaginative expression in *Robinson Crusoe.*"[44] Like *Robinson Crusoe, David Copperfield* is at times a story of loneliness and isolation, but primarily a narrative of effort, perseverance, and survival, preservation that seems miraculous.[45]

Both novels place paradoxical emphasis on the need for self-help and the importance of providential care. Both narratives convey anxiety and comfort almost simultaneously, for the protagonists discover that their misfortunes are ultimately beneficial, that man, though seemingly weak and alone, can help himself and may also look to providence for divine aid. Indeed, David explicitly credits "the mercy of God" for keeping him from becoming "a little robber or a little vagabond" (161). Moreover, although various critics see the death of Steerforth as providential retribution, the main emphasis in *David Copperfield* is on providence as a beneficent force, offering compensation for sorrow and pain.[46] The narrator's attitude seems like that expressed when Crusoe exclaims, "How mercifully can our great Creator treat his Creatures, even in those Conditions in which they seem'd to be overwhelm'd in Destruction. How can he sweeten the bitterest Providences, and give us Cause to praise him for Dungeons and Prisons."[47] Late in *David Copperfield,* Dickens thrice stresses the idea of the ultimate value of adversity. After Aunt Betsey's announcement of her ruin, David resolves "to turn the painful discipline of my younger days to account, by going to work with a resolute and steady heart" (520). Subsequently, as we have already observed, he feels "devoutly thankful" (761) for what we may, with a glance at the preceding quotation from *Robinson Crusoe,* call his "dungeon" days, his youthful miseries, since they made him acquainted with Micawber and eventually led to the latter's role as the agent of Heep's defeat. Finally, Agnes' letter advising David during his depression in Switzerland expresses the same moral: "She knew that in me, sorrow could not be weakness, but must be strength. As the endurance of my childish days had done its part to make me what I was, so greater calamities would nerve me on, to be yet better than I was; and so, as they had taught me, would I teach others" (815).

Although Agnes does not clearly indicate whether David is to teach through his fiction or his behavior or both, the concept she wishes him to promulgate is an important one in Dickens' life and art. For the expression "make me what I was" echoes a passage in Dickens' autobiographical fragment, a comment following the description of the blacking warehouse days: "I do not write resentfully or angrily: for I know how all these things have worked together to make me what I am."[48] Insistence on eventual compensation for unmerited suffering is characteristic of theodicy, though not restricted to it,[49] and David, in developing and expressing such a consoling faith, relies more and more on Agnes.

$$- \; 4 \; -$$

In the final double number of the novel, Chapters lviii–lxiv, Agnes is all but deified. One chapter title, "A Light Shines Upon My Way," clearly guides us to a religious understanding, for the light seemingly refers both to David's discovery that he may now have Agnes as his wife and also to Agnes herself as a spiritual guide. Of course, as many critics have observed, she has been invested throughout the novel with religious qualities.[50] James Kincaid, who seeks to discredit Agnes as a mentor, emphasizes her inability to protect her father from Heep and also attempts to link her with Miss Murdstone because "they are both keepers of the keys."[51] On this last point, however, Mrs. Leavis seems more convincing in suggesting that Agnes' ability to take charge of "the household keys" distinguishes her from David's mother, who was forced to surrender the keys to Miss Murdstone, and also from Dora, who sees the keys as a toy for Jip.[52] That an ability to take charge of the keys is not in itself a negative quality is clearly demonstrated by Esther Summerson in *Bleak House*. Similarly, Robin Gilmour's claim that Agnes, "as the chief agent in Aunt Betsey's attempt to turn him [David] into a 'fine firm fellow . . . ,' acquires all the unfortunate connections with which 'firmness' is already associated in our minds," neglects the interest of Dickens in setting up an apparent parallel in order to emphasize the contrast between Miss Trotwood and the Murdstones, a contrast ably discussed by Max Véga-Ritter.[53] We should also note that Aunt Betsey, despite her emphasis on *firmness,* is not firm toward her husband and regrets her treatment of David's mother (347), with whom she has earlier been linked—"(My aunt always excused any weakness of her own in my behalf, by transferring it in this way to my poor mother)" (274). Moreover, for Dickens, whether firmness is good or bad depends on its purposes and consequences. And the novel stresses that Murdstone, unlike Miss Trotwood, does not want others to be firm; he therefore seeks to make David's mother submissive (49), and both he and his sister see David's firmness in negative terms, calling him "obdurate" and "stubborn" (118), as well as "intractable" (209). Finally, any effort to disparage Agnes must contend with the fact that Dickens, in his working notes, refers to her as "the real heroine."[54]

Agnes' message is simple: "'I hope that real love and truth are stronger in the end than any evil or misfortune in the world'" (511). In the next number, when Heep seems even more threatening, she asserts, " 'There is God to trust in' " (579). Later, Agnes reminds David, " 'Remember that I confide in simple love and truth at last' " (613). In these remarks, as in the subsequent letter to David in Switzerland, the emphasis is on faith and patience. Agnes accepts this traditional credo even though it clearly does not always seem supported by events in this world. For, while Wickfield is eventually freed from Heep's dominance and is described by Aunt Betsey as " 'a reclaimed man' " (837), his sufferings have left him weak and subdued. Moreover, for the deaths of Dora and Ham there seems to be no consolation except that found through traditional Christian hope. But this is one of the novel's points, and those critics who find David's acceptance of such consolation unsatisfactory and ironic are simply refusing to accept Dickens' basic axioms.

Further understanding of Agnes' role may perhaps be found by considering Dickens' response to Goldsmith's *The Vicar of Wakefield*, another of the books that sustained the child David. Discussing "the influence of Goldsmith," Mrs. Tillotson observes that it "may be traced in the Christmas books (he [Dickens] planned the *Carol* to be 'about the length of *The Vicar of Wakefield*') and in the tone of some of his descriptions of humble domestic happiness."[55] On 29 March 1849, just about a month after beginning to write *David Copperfield*, Dickens, in a letter to Miss Burdett-Coutts, referred to Goldsmith's novel as a "book of which I think it is not too much to say that it has perhaps done more good in the world, and instructed more kinds of people in virtue, than any other fiction ever written."[56]

Indeed, Goldsmith was clearly on Dickens' mind during the planning of *David Copperfield*. Forster reports that in January 1849, when Dickens named his eighth child after Henry Fielding, Fielding's name was a late replacement for Goldsmith's.[57] And the preceding April, Dickens had read and praised Forster's biography of Goldsmith, a two-volume work dedicated to Dickens himself.[58]

Certainly, *The Vicar of Wakefield* expresses an ethos similar to David Copperfield's endorsement of the idea of ultimate compensation for suffering. We may, in fact, see Goldsmith's entire novel as a development of the aphorism used as the title of its twenty-fifth chapter: *"No situation, however wretched it seems, but has some sort of comfort attending it."* Of interest also is the fact that Goldsmith's narrative describes the vicar's search for a daughter who has been seduced by a false promise of marriage (chapter 17: *"The pursuit of a father to reclaim a lost child to virtue"*), a quest which seems to anticipate Mr. Peggotty's hunt for his niece.[59] But perhaps the main link between *David Copperfield* and Goldsmith's novel is the inclusion in each of a character whose faith serves to inspire others: in a sense, Dickens' vicar of Wakefield turns out to be the daughter of Wickfield. The similarity of the names is appropriate, whether or not Dickens consciously intended an allusion.

— 5 —

When David Copperfield begins writing his story, he has apparently already triumphed over the enmity of the Murdstones, the loss of his mother, and the deaths of Dora and Steerforth. Moreover, his idyllic marriage has been seen by him as a reward for disciplining his own heart (817–18, and 840). After ten years of wedded bliss, however, some problem has arisen that compels David to study in a careful manner the extent to which he has been previously able to master events and act as the "hero" of his own life rather than as a victim. The writing of his autobiography may be regarded as a search for reassurance that he can meet a crisis that now confronts him or else awaits him. As we have previously suggested, a future trial that perhaps troubles David is his own death. As the narrative progresses, he recalls that in his past difficulties he came to see the assistance of Agnes as crucial, that she served as a mentor who reinforced his religious faith. Moreover, Alexander Welsh has made the important point that Agnes is presented as "a familiar of death" and appears to intimate the possibility of transcending mortality.[60]

David's composition of his autobiography is effective therapy, for his story is one of triumph. Indeed, the narrative stresses the defeat of evil. Each major villain—Murdstone, Heep, Steerforth—strikes at David by harming a woman, but each culprit is punished. Steerforth's death is seen as retribution, while Heep's successful duping of Creakle should not lead us to forget that Uriah is soon to be transported for life as a penalty for bank fraud;[61] and the Murdstones, although they seem to be prospering, are not to be envied—Mr. Chillip endorses his wife's opinion that "'they undergo a continual punishment; for they are turned inward, to feed upon their own hearts, and their own hearts are very bad feeding'" (834).

Of course, this element of retribution, although supportive of religious faith, may not seem to be presented in specifically religious terms. Nevertheless, religious features figure strongly in four of the novel's five major climaxes: the rescue of Em'ly, the death of Dora, the drowning of Ham and Steerforth, and the marriage of David and Agnes. Only the defeat of Heep, which is basically comic, appears devoid of important religious details. In Chapter l, "Mr. Peggotty's Dream comes true," the narrator, discussing Mr. Peggotty's "solemn certainty of finding" Em'ly, remarks, "there was something so religious in it . . . that the respect and honour in which I held him were exalted every day" (714). And, after Em'ly is found, Mr. Peggotty exclaims to David,

" 'I thank my Heav'nly Father as my dream's come true! I thank Him hearty for having guided of me, in His own ways, to my darling!' " (723). We may recall Mrs. Gummidge's words earlier in the story, just after the discovery of Em'ly's elopement: " 'For you know the promise, Dan'l, "As you have done it unto one of the least of these, you have done it unto me" ' " (454). And religious terms also seem important in the accounts of Mr. Peggotty's wanderings (584–85) and of the meeting he and David have on the river bank with Martha (682–87).

One critic, however, while conceding that "the latter development of Mr. Peggotty is the event with the richest religious significance in the novel," insists that "even here this aspect is thin compared to weightier themes," and asserts, "In perspective the matter of religion is strictly marginal, though the lumping of evidence may temporarily deceive."[62] But at crucial times religion does seem to emerge as an important feature. For example, Agnes' pointing "towards Heaven" (768) and her words about Dora in the letter to David in Switzerland (816) soften the death of the child-wife with the promise of divine consolation; and in Chapter lv, "Tempest," Ham's submissive remark—" 'If my time is come, 'tis come. If 'tant, I'll bide it' "[63]—is made to seem Christian rather than merely Stoic by the addition of the words, " 'Lord above bless you [David], and bless all' " (793). Furthermore, as J. Hillis Miller observes, the marriage of David and Agnes is presented as a religious culmination.[64]

Nevertheless, two features may account for the feeling of some readers that religion is not of major importance in *David Copperfield*. First, Dickens keeps his religious motif in vague, general terms of Christian belief, emphasizing formal ritual and clergy only in David's childhood, once for satire of Miss Murdstone's grim views (52), and once for wholly serious consolatory purposes in the narrator's account of his mother's funeral. Moreover, *David Copperfield*, unlike *The Old Curiosity Shop*, emphasizes compensation on earth, rather than in heaven, for unmerited suffering—at least for most of the principal characters. The Australian success of Mr. Peggotty and his "family," the Micawbers, and even Mr. Mell is important for this reason.

Although many commentators have expressed incredulity at Micawber's triumph,[65] it need not be considered implausible. After the defeat of Heap, Traddles asserts of Micawber, " 'Although he would appear not to have worked to any good account for himself, he is a most untiring man when he works for other people' " (774). Moreover, in a *Household Words* article that Harry Stone ascribes to Dickens, the opinion is offered that Australia will probably grant success to anyone "who is willing to work hard."[66] Obviously, in Australia there was more need for labor, less competition, more tolerance, and therefore a greater likelihood of initial success augmenting confidence and incentive and leading to further achievement. Referring to Micawber, A. E. Dyson comments, "The colonial second chance was made for a man of his calibre." [67]

Interestingly, Mr. Peggotty attributes his own success in Australia to religious causes: " 'Theer's been kiender a blessing fell upon us,' said Mr. Peggotty, reverentially inclining his head, 'and we've done nowt but prosper. That is, in the long run. If not yesterday, why then to-day. If not to-day, why then to-morrow' " (868). The words resemble Ham's: " 'If my time is come, 'tis come. If 'tant, I'll bide it.' " And the echo hints that the blessing upon Mr. Peggotty is a compensation not only for his own virtue, but also for Ham's nobility and sacrifice. Even though Mr. Peggotty is talking about the prospering of his own "family," Micawber's success may also seem in part a reward for his selfless behavior in exposing Heep.

In first disclosing his plans to migrate with Em'ly, Mr. Peggotty talks of beginning " 'a new life' " in Australia. But the moral rewards and punishments in the novel do not, of course, seem wholly consistent. If we wish to justify Em'ly's being moved to deny herself marriage while Martha Endell accepts a mate, we may acknowledge that, since Martha lacked the love and care of Mr. Peggotty and Ham, her fall was less blameworthy than Em'ly's. Nevertheless, the ultimate fate of Em'ly, who, before her own disgrace, showed sympathy and kindness to Martha, can be considered cheerful only in relative terms. In addition, for Dora, for David's mother, and for Ham, pain appears undeserved, despite the weaknesses of the first two. Indeed, John Lucas aptly notices that Dickens minimizes Dora's death by making it "part of a quite amazing *tour de force*," "a multiple narrative" designed "to divert our attention away from Dora herself" by presenting in a short space many climactic events, including the rescue of Em'ly, the defeat of Heep, the deaths of Steerforth and Ham, and the migration to Australia. [68] Moreover, the fates of the other victims are also presented in a soothing way by Dickens and David. No matter how austere Em'ly's Australian life may seem, she has escaped prostitution, while Ham, who uses a denial that he is " 'tired of . . . life' " (738) to imply that he actually *is,* meets a death that he all but sought. Even for David's mother there is consolation, in that her demise returns her to her happier, pre-Murdstone self: "In her death she winged her way back to her calm untroubled youth, and cancelled all the rest" (133), the first verb suggesting angelic status, and the word "untroubled" glossing over orphanhood and early widowhood. [69]

Speculating on why Murdstone became acquainted with David's mother, Aunt Betsey refers to " 'the mysterious dispensations of Providence' " (213). But, if in *David Copperfield* the divine plan is not always comprehensible, the human need for faith in its existence is clear. Generosity, honesty, kindness, and determination are the qualities Betsey Trotwood encourages David to develop, and they win much for him—but they are not sufficient for him to live by; for these virtues cannot avert pain, guilt, and suffering both for himself and for others. Because no one can control more than a small proportion of events in his life, faith is needed, and Agnes becomes an example of the beauty and ultimate power of such faith. Her attitude resembles the active "trustfulness" with which Mr. Peggotty perseveres (714).

In the final book of *Paradise Lost,* Milton's Adam marvels at the divine power to provide ultimate compensation: "O goodness infinite, goodness immense!/ That all this good of evil shall produce,/ And evil turn to good" (12. 469–71). Although David sees himself less as transgressor than as victim, he is, as we have seen, not without guilt. In any case, late in his story, when Agnes accepts his proposal, he expresses similar gratitude and awe at the ultimate compensation he is receiving: "We thanked our GOD for having guided us to this tranquillity"—"I saw a ragged way-worn boy forsaken and neglected, who should come to call even the heart now beating against mine, his own" (863). As David repeats and repeats, Agnes is an angel, a mediator.

Michael Steig has discussed the importance of Hablot Browne's illustrations for *David Copperfield:* in Plate 1, "On the pulpit there is a bas-relief of Eve and the serpent, a commentary upon Clara's being tempted to her own destruction by Murdstone," and, in Plate 16, "over the door is a picture of Eve and the serpent, thus implying Steerforth's satanism, as well as a parallel between Murdstone-Clara and Steerforth-Emily (compare Plate 1)."[70] The third antagonist who harms David by ill treatment of a woman dear to him is Heep, whom Micawber labels " 'a—detestable—serpent' " (711). In addition, the novel presents three places as Edenlike: one of David's main memories about the pre-Murdstone days is of the garden, "where the fruit clusters on the trees, riper and richer than fruit has ever been since, in any other garden" (15); the boat-home of Dan'l Peggotty's "family" is for the child David an idyllic setting; and, later, when David is disturbed by domestic tribulations with Dora, he recalls "the contented days with Agnes, in the dear old house" (697). Moreover, Steerforth is clearly designated by Agnes as David's "bad Angel" (367), and the competition between Agnes and Steerforth for influence is emphasized by David's reference to each as a star: when drunk, he exclaims, " 'Steerforth, you'retheguidingstarofmyexistence' " (360), but near the end of the novel, he remarks of Agnes, "She, ever a star above me, was brighter and higher" (841).

Agnes, therefore, unlike Clara and Em'ly, is an Eve who ultimately resists diabolic plots and helps David to redeem himself. Early in the narrative, describing Murdstone's coldness on first becoming a stepfather, David remarks "God help me, I might have been improved for my whole life, I might have been made another creature perhaps, for life, by a kind word at that season" (46). He suggests here that the evil done him was irreparable, but such is not the conclusion indicated by the rest of the story. As John Lucas maintains, commenting on the protagonist's discussion with Mr. Chillip toward the end of the novel, "David's cool dismissal of the Murdstone firmness serves as extremely satisfying evidence of his attained growth, his ability to survive their baleful effect on him."[71]

Although David Copperfield never explicitly settles his initial question about being the hero of his own life, the answer is clear. He is the hero—or rather, he and Agnes, referred to in Dickens' notes as "the real heroine," serve together as the hero of David's life. For, like Milton's Adam and Eve, their "State cannot be sever'd," they "are one,/ One Flesh" (*PL* 9. 958–59). David, at the end of his narrative, is able to look forward unflinchingly to what he cannot control, for he trusts to a faith inspired by Agnes. Recalling Dickens' interest in fairy tales, we may find significance in Bruno Bettelheim's assertion that in such stories the formation of "a truly satisfying bond to another" is seen as the means by which a person may achieve "the ultimate in emotional security of existence and permanence of relation available to man," a state that "alone can dissipate the fear of death."[72] By emphasizing not any exceptional abilities he might have, but instead merely his effort and perseverance, traits that he suggests all might develop, David Copperfield establishes himself as Everyman, and his autobiography, by justifying the ways of God as seen in the events of David's own life, becomes a theodicy asserting eternal providence and counseling us to be guided by faith, virtue, patience, temperance, and love.

Bert G. Hornback

THE HERO SELF

THE FIRST sentence of *David Copperfield* is, for me, one of the greatest openings in all literature: "Whether I shall turn out to be the hero of my own life, or whether that station will be held by anybody else, these pages must show." There is an immediate sense of remove about the sentence, both in its sense and in its rhythm. The speaker is floating at some distance from these pages, or from the events these pages will detail. The narrative voice introduces itself to us as a voice, as a mind, as a reflective, recollective, observing consciousness: and it is that voice or mind or consciousness that attracts us.

Yeats could have been thinking of such a voice as this when he spoke of writing "with an emotion which I described to myself as cold."[1] *David Copperfield* is a passionate novel, a novel warm with life, rich in emotion and feeling. It is a novel of "powerful feelings," to use Wordsworth's phrase; but in a way that Wordsworth was hardly thinking of when he wrote his famous definition of poetry, these "powerful feelings" are curiously separate in this novel from the act of "recollection" going on.[2] What is recollected is deeply felt, to be sure; we can attest to that from our experience in reading the novel, and we can also point to Dickens' remark in his preface that "no one can ever believe this Narrative, in the reading, more than I have believed it in the writing" (xii). But at the same time that we recognize—and experience—the deep feeling of the recollections that are *David Copperfield,* we are also quite conscious of the act of recollection itself, of the recollecting mind at work: and it is cold but still intense, almost dispassionate but at the same time energetic and absolutely committed to its creative task.

The narrative voice in *David Copperfield* is so special *as a voice* that it becomes both the central character and the most memorable character in the novel. Of course, this is as it should be, since the novel is about David the artist, the recollector, the imaginer, and how he sees the world. All of the wonderful galaxy of characters who populate that world are extras, really: they are in *David Copperfield* as tests for David's imagination, as exemplary substances for him to imagine and comprehend.[3]

David the narrative voice calls attention to himself frequently; and as he is a voice more than a character or person, it is appropriate that he attract our notice not so much by what he says as by how he says it. It is the tone, the rhythm, the feeling of that opening sentence which attracts us, I think, long before the mysterious thing it says begins to sink in. The two long formal clauses introduced by "whether," the first one almost entirely monosyllabic, are followed by the heavy falling cadence of "these pages must show." If you scanned the sentence, it would look like this:

> Whether I shall turn out to be the hero of my own life,
> or whether that station will be held by anybody else,
> these pages must show.

That is not an arhythmical prose sentence; it is, rather, a remarkable creation of a rhythm. It will reappear several times during the course of the novel, as the form of a certain kind of rhetoric, a voice. The rhetoric is the rhetoric of reverie, of "retrospect"; the rhythm calls attention to the abstracted imagination that is doing the musing and recollecting and reviewing. It calls us back from the story to the storyteller: from the narrative to the narrative voice.

The question asked in the opening sentence—whether David will be the hero of his own life or not—is difficult on the first level because ordinarily we presume ourselves to be the heroes of our own lives, and thus we do not even *hear* such a question. True, I have my heroes—like Ted Williams, or Dickens, or my father; but they are *my heroes,* not the heroes *of my life.* I expect to be the hero of my life—automatically. But in his abstracted state as an imaginer and a voice, David begins by questioning this. He poses the question, however, not as David the character, or even as David the narrator (who is after all a character too in some way). He asks the question as the narrative voice: so that the question becomes, then, whether the imagination—abstracted, noumenal, looking at its phenomenal world—can become substantial and heroic. If David is to be "the hero of [his] own life," then the book called *David Copperfield* must become the life and the imagination its hero. How "these pages" can "show" this, can prove it, will be by creating a real phenomenal world for us, as readers, and by demonstrating the imagination's comprehension of that world.

The key, again, is comprehension. I am reminded of Dostoyevsky's *Crime and Punishment,* which in my translation is full of the word "understanding." Raskolnikov wants to "understand" it all, and everybody else in the novel wants him to as well. Dostoyevsky—so much influenced by Dickens, and so much taken by both *David Copperfield* and *Great Expectations*—started the Raskolnikov part of the novel as a first-person narrative. It went badly, of course, because Raskolnikov *does not* understand it all, which is why he has a fever. Much of the time he is—or has been—delirious, because he cannot comprehend Petersburg, cannot comprehend the world. For Dostoyevsky as well as for Dickens, the resolution of the world's madness is comprehension, understanding. David's comprehension of the world satisfies us at the end of his novel. It satisfies us, not with the world, but with him. The conclusion of *Crime and Punishment* offers us a very different experience. It is Dostoyevsky who "understands," not his hero. Raskolnikov understands the symbol for comprehensive acceptance of the world—kissing the earth in the Haymarket—but he may not in fact believe in what the symbol represents or be truly converted. Dostoyevsky is not convinced, certainly, that his hero believes what he should believe or that he understands enough to be saved. That is why he tacks on the Epilogue, and runs Rodya through everything—from alienation and fever to Sonia and relief—again, and tells us then that he is saved. But the Epilogue is not very satisfactory. What comes through most strongly for us as readers is Raskolnikov's need to understand, and it is in this need that we identify with him.

Raskolnikov and David are certainly far apart as characters, but they do share that need to know, to understand it all; and sharing it makes them almost brothers. Raskolnikov is actually more like Mr. Dick than David. Like Dick, he knows the world is mad, but cannot comprehend it; its madness is bigger and more complex than his mind. He is confused by his experience and observation of life and in such a state commits the murders which almost destroy him. For David, however, the need to understand is not dangerous. Petersburg fever does not become his fever; the world's madness does not make him mad. His experience of the world is imaginative, his observation of it an artist's observation. And from his imagination of the world, David creates himself. Edward Wasiolek, the editor of the notebooks for *Crime and Punishment,* quotes Dostoyevsky's final determination that *"the story must be narrated by the author and not by the hero,"* and continues, "In this way the action is given to the hero, and the consciousness and significance of the experience are given to the author."[4] In *David Copperfield,* the action is given to the other characters, and the consciousness and significance of the experience are given to the author—to David the narrator—*as* his heroism. Point of view creates the hero as he comprehends the world that "these pages . . . show."

It takes David nearly a third of the first chapter of his novel to get to its opening scene, on the day of his birth. More than anything else, the opening several pages serve to establish the self-consciousness of the narrator as a narrator and as a narrative voice, recollecting. He sets up the different sources of his narrative very carefully, scrupulously indicating to us how he knows what he knows. "I was born (as I have been informed and believe) on a Friday" (1) is an example of one kind of information, that which he receives at secondhand about himself. "I was present myself [at the raffle sale of my caul], and I remember to have felt quite uncomfortable. . . . [It] was won, I recollect, by an old lady" (2) is another: it is his report of his own memory. A third kind of information—and the most important—comes from David's pulling his memory of the past up into the present. It creates, in effect, that other dimension of this novel, the "story" of the narrative voice itself. "There is something strange to me, even now," David writes, "in the reflection that [my father] never saw me; and something stranger yet in the shadowy remembrance that I have of my first childish associations with his white gravestone in the churchyard" (2). This and other "shadowy" memories are really what *David Copperfield* is about, at its deepest level.

At the beginning of Chapter ii David writes of his earliest memory, of his mother and Peggotty as "the first objects that assume a distinct presence before me, as I look back, into the blank of my infancy" (13). He remembers them so particularly—his mother as all that she ever is, "with her pretty hair and youthful shape," and Peggotty "with no shape at all, and eyes so dark that they seemed to darken their whole neighbourhood in her face, and cheeks and arms so hard and red that I wondered the birds didn't peck her in preference to apples." He even remembers "the touch of Peggotty's forefinger as she used to hold it out to me . . . roughened by needlework, like a pocket nutmeg-grater"—and then he defends himself for the detail of this memory:

> This may be fancy, though I think the memory of most of us can go farther back into such times than many of us suppose; just as I believe the power of observation in numbers of very young children to be quite wonderful for its closeness and accuracy. Indeed, I think that most grown men who are remarkable in this respect, may with greater propriety be said not to have lost the faculty, than to have acquired it; the rather, as I generally observe such men to retain a certain freshness, and gentleness, and capacity of being pleased, which are also an inheritance which they have preserved from their childhood. (13)

The "power of observation" that David speaks of here is the same thing that Coleridge praises in trying to define Wordsworth's "genius";[5] and David's claim for himself here is very close to what Coleridge claimed for his fellow poet. The continuance of this power, David says, marks a man's character with "a certain freshness, and gentleness, and capacity of being pleased"; and these virtues become, for Dickens, the virtues upon which he would build heroic life. Clearly this "power of observation" is indeed—literally—a power: it is observation empowered by imagination.

Late in the novel David speaks of his method of writing as "the blending of experience and imagination" (664), and this is also what he has presented from the beginning as the method of his life. His closely observed past experience is what David remembers; and he finds—or creates—the meaning of these memories in the present through the power of his imagination. Thus this novel has its most significant meaning, finally, in the present from which and toward which the past is recollected. The meaning of *David Copperfield* is in the creation of David's heroic life: the life which becomes heroic as it achieves meaning and happiness.

Meaning and happiness are both important words, and both are related to imagination. For Dickens just as for Coleridge, the way the imagination creates meaning is metaphoric. It "dissolves, diffuses, dissipates, in order to recreate," for Coleridge; to find meaning, to create new knowledge, "it struggles to idealize and to unify."[6] And "all knowledge," he says, "rests on the coincidence of an object with a subject" or "mind."[7] The idealization or unification which the imagination seeks is that highest kind of knowledge through which the mind both holds together all the parts and relates itself to them. It makes the individual pieces of life—events, characters, places—coincide metaphorically with each other and with the self experiencing them, creating out of the conjunction what we call a life. By means of another metaphoric operation, then, that life is completed—raised to a higher level—in the conscious relation of the reflective self or "mind" to the world of its experience. This completion of life is what I call *comprehension:* the act of holding together joined with the act of knowing. In Dickens' terms—or David's—such comprehension is what is achieved by the successful "blending of experience and imagination": the details of experience closely observed are transformed by the power of the imagination into "ideal" or comprehended life.

The way the imagination creates happiness is perhaps more difficult to explain than the way it creates meaning, primarily because we do not usually think of happiness as being such a serious thing as it is for Dickens here. Throughout his career, Dickens seems to have thought of happiness and meaning as being different aspects of the same thing. If *meaning* is created when spirit informs matter, then *happiness* is created by the physical embodiment of spirit; that is, as meaning comes from the imagination's comprehension of the world of its experience, so happiness comes from the experience itself *as it is* comprehended. It is not simply that one is the life of the mind and the other the life of the body. Rather, meaning knows experience, and happiness is the phenomenal form or expression of what is known. In their "ideal" state, for Dickens, they are almost identical, as meaning represents wholeness and happiness is fullness.

Meaning is a word that belongs for the most part with the reflective, recollective point of view in *David Copperfield;* and for most of the novel happiness is a word that is used in relation to characters and experiences. The narrator David often focuses attention on his happiness or unhappiness, weighing and understanding his experience accordingly. Miss Betsey hopes that the young David will grow up "happy and useful," and those words appear together, then, over and over again. Agnes is "happy and useful"; David wants to become so. In the final chapter—entitled "A Last Retrospect"—David reviews his world in terms of the happiness achieved by its various inhabitants. Curiously, he does not tell us about his own happiness, directly. But in the last sentence of the preface which he wrote immediately after finishing *David Copperfield,* Dickens remarks that writing this novel has "made me happy" (Penguin ed., p. 45): and that statement, taken at its most serious value, can be read as David's as well as Dickens'.

It is easier to demonstrate how the writing of *David Copperfield* has made David useful than how it has made him happy. Late in the novel, as he and Agnes talk together about his work as a writer, she tells him: "Your growing reputation and success enlarge your power of doing good" (843). And Mr. Micawber writes to him from Port Middlebay: "Go on, my dear sir, in your Eagle course! The inhabitants of Port Middlebay may at least aspire to watch it, with delight, with entertainment, with instruction!" (872). The "power of doing good" is the power of the social critic, the teacher. Dickens has been a social critic, frequently but incidentally, in all of the novels before *David Copperfield,* and in the novels which follow this one he creates whole fictions which are criticisms of society. He has written and will continue to write novels which instruct as well as entertain, teach as well as delight. Dickens must be aware of the reference to the traditional function of art in Micawber's praise of David's writing; and the claim which this praise makes for David's art must be as seriously intentional as it is obvious. *David Copperfield,* however, is not itself just a novel of social criticism—or not such a novel in the way Dickens' other works are. The most important thing *David Copperfield* teaches us is David's life: his heroic life of comprehension.

Wordsworth ends *The Prelude* proposing "that the history of a Poet's mind/Is labour not unworthy of regard," and that this history has a high didactic value:

> what we have loved,
> Others will love, and we will teach them how;

> Instruct them how the mind of man becomes
> A thousand times more beautiful than the earth
> On which he dwells.[8]

David never makes a claim like this for himself or his work, directly; but the way the narrative voice insists that we focus our attention on David the mind tells us that Dickens has made an assumption much like Wordsworth's about the didactic value of "the history of a Poet's mind"—or a "Portrait of the Artist." Thus not only is David's writing this novel the most "useful" thing he ever does for himself, it is also the most useful thing he could ever do for us. This novel has made him the hero of his own life—and it has made that heroic self a model for Dickens and for us.

David is a model which no one—Dickens or us—ever lives up to, and in this he is unreal: "ideal," to use Coleridge's word. He has it all together, to use today's vernacular—and that echoes Coleridge's other word for what the imagination does, "unify." Art teaches and delights, traditionally; and as we all know, it doesn't teach us either to do anything or not to do anything. It teaches us itself: it teaches us what it is. Dickens is almost always a bad—heavy-handed, sentimental, even hypocritical—moralist; but he is a wonderful metaphysician. And here, because everything about this novel—everything about Dickens' creation of it—comes under the idealizing influence of David's successful attempt at heroism, there is almost none of that kind of moralizing social criticism that preaches against and punishes evil or rewards the good. The closest it comes to that is in Agnes' "hope," expressed in response to Heep, "that simple love and truth will be strong in the end, . . . that real love and truth are stronger in the end than any evil or misfortune in the world" (511), and David's remark to Uriah after his exposure, near the end of the novel: "It may be profitable to you to reflect, in future, that there never were greed and cunning in the world yet, that did not do too much, and over-reach themselves. It is as certain as death" (760). But neither of these remarks is, finally, a moralizing one. Agnes does not ask for "the principle of Good surviving through every adverse circumstance, and triumphing at last";[9] she hopes, rather, that love and truth may be strong enough for us to build our lives on, even in the midst of evil and misfortune. David's remark goes beyond this, to argue the essence of evil. Evil punishes itself, he tells Uriah, threateningly: it *is* its own punishment, just as he is his. Conversely, goodness is its own reward. Goodness comes from happiness, and is rewarded with happiness, naturally—and that, too, is "as certain as death"![10]

The clearest articulation of the metaphysical state of happiness in all of Dickens' works is in *A Christmas Carol*. When Scrooge goes out, after his conversion, into Christmas day, he finds that his change has changed the world. He becomes, Dickens says, "as good a friend, as good a master, and as good a man, as the good old city knew, or any other good old city, town, or borough, in the good old world."[11] It is as though Scrooge's new goodness is contagious, and Dickens can't stop writing the word; and the reason for this is that Scrooge has found, upon looking at the world this new morning, "that everything could yield him pleasure."[12]

Much more substantially than Scrooge, David achieves a perspective from which he can view the world with pleasure. Of course, this achievement requires a metaphysical conversion on David's part, too; the "trial by adversity" motif that runs all through Dickens' work quite literally requires of David—twice—that he recreate himself. The first time is after his mother's death, the second after Dora's. The self he recreates after Dora's death, through his experience of near despair and mystical regeneration in the Alps, is the artist-self who writes this novel. It is a self that has overcome, through sympathy, the selfish ego which feels and registers pain only as pain; and free now from that ego, that *person,* David becomes his selfless understanding of the world. The voice that narrates this novel for us comes into existence in Switzerland when, under the influence of "great Nature" David is reborn.

What happens to David in the Alps will be examined in detail in a future essay; for now I want to keep to the theme of David's heroic self. In tracing that theme we have come to the climax: the new self which comes into being in Switzerland will be the hero of David's life. Almost immediately upon his conversion, David sets out "to get a better understanding of [him]self" (818). To do this, he will reflect upon and recollect his past, recreating his life through the combined power of memory and imagination. Though he recalls sad things, they will bring him understanding now, not sorrow. Imaginative comprehension supersedes sorrow and pain. It is a pleasure of the soul: and David, who before "had had no purpose, no sustaining soul within [him]" (814), has now a new soul. And the soul, for Dickens, has the greatest "capacity for being pleased" (13) that we know. When the soul of a man is happy, Dickens says, "everything [can] yield him pleasure."[13] And if everything yields pleasure, then life is full, positively whole, and "ideal."

In this world we live in—that Dickens lived in—only the imagination, the soul, can create ideal life. The miracle of *David Copperfield* is that, as we finish the novel, we *believe* this ideal life—just as Dickens did. "No one," he wrote, "can ever believe this Narrative, in the reading, more than I have believed it in the writing" (xiv). But as we move away from the novel, and consider more carefully—more objectively—what David's achievement really is, we begin to qualify our appreciation of it, perhaps. And we begin to ask questions—Keatsian questions—about what is real here, the story or the storyteller? And what makes the storyteller a hero? Does memory only remember, or is imaginative recol-

lection a substantial and real recreation of life? Is life only fully life
when it is understood, when it is comprehended by the imagination? Is
the highest human pleasure truly in such comprehension? And is that
pleasure wisdom?

At several points in the novel David stops to remind us that this
book is a remembering. He speaks of his "life" as a "volume," and of
time and events that "will never pass out of my memory" (115), of
"days" that "occupy the place of years in my remembrance" (59).
Things from the past, he says, "are things not of many years ago, in my
mind, but of the present instant" (154). Sometimes he stops to wind his
memory up: "Let me remember how it used to be," he writes, introducing a typical scene at Blunderstone, "and bring one morning back
again" (53). Chapter xviii is entitled "A Retrospect," chapters xliii and
liii "Another Retrospect," and chapter lxiv "A Last Retrospect."[14] The
language and imagery with which Dickens introduces these chapters is
as interesting as the reason for their being set in such a format—and
the two are related. The first retrospect is introduced this way: "My
school-days! The silent gliding on of my existence—the unseen, unfelt
progress of my life—from childhood up to youth! Let me think, as I
look back upon that flowing water, now a dry channel overgrown with
leaves, whether there are any marks along its course, by which I can
remember how it ran" (265). The reflecting, retrospecting mind looks
at its past sympathetically but objectively, and recognizes that it was life
unconsciously experienced: "the unseen, unfelt progress of my life."
The recollection of that life, in the present, is a "silent" reproduction of
"unseen, unfelt progress." The past is dead—"now a dry channel over-
grown with leaves"—and yet through the imagination it can be turned
again to "flowing water." Importantly, then, the David who watches this
re-created stream of life not only recreates it as life—as a dramatic
scene for us—but also observes it critically, to discover "whether there
are any marks along its course, *by which I can remember how it ran.*"
Again, though the novel is made enjoyable for us as a dramatic experience by David's vivid and detailed re-creation of the past, the introduc-
tions to this and the other retrospect chapters show clearly that the past
is important to David only as it influences the present. Miss Betsey has
once advised him, "It's in vain, Trot, to recall the past, unless it works
some influence upon the present" (347); and this idea controls the
novel.

Chapter xliii begins: "Once again, let me pause upon a memorable
period of my life. Let me stand aside, to see the phantoms of those days
go by me, accompanying the shadow of myself, in dim procession"
(626). The real character is the present character of David, the voice
that we are listening to, the mind's eye viewing the past for itself and
revealing that past to us. "Let *me* stand aside," it says, to see the past as

"phantoms" and the past self as but a "shadow." The chapter ends with a repetition of this incantatory introduction: "I have stood aside to see the phantoms of those days go by me. They are gone, and I resume the journey of my story" (633). The spell is broken, and the novel returns to a more normal narrative mode. The self-consciousness relaxes—but the focus of the novel, which is closely linked to that self-consciousness, remains unchanged: the narrator resumes, not his story or his journey through life, but "the journey of [his] story"—as though his story were itself a character.

The third retrospect—chapter liii—is the chapter in which Dora dies. It is the shortest chapter in the novel. Rhetorically, it is the most intense. It begins: "I must pause yet once again. O, my child-wife, there is a figure in the moving crowd before my memory, quiet and still, saying in its innocent love and childish beauty, Stop to think of me—turn to look upon the Little Blossom, as it flutters to the ground!" (764). The first sentence stops us just as it does David. It is an unwilling stop—"I must pause"—and the unwillingness is underlined, almost dramatized in the sound and sense of "yet once again." There is a "moving crowd before [his] memory," but it moves separate from David the narrator and from us. The act of remembering stops David the narrator at the very beginning of the chapter. His pause here is one of intense consciousness, and the few short pages which follow will record not a progress of events so much as a sequence of emotional responses toward a climax. At the end of the chapter, when Dora has died, the remembered character David will be stopped, too—at the point of numbing emotional crisis which David the narrator already feels in his memory at the beginning of this retrospect: "It is over. Darkness comes before my eyes; and, for a time, all things are blotted from my remembrance" (768). In the interim between that first stop and this last, the narrator calls up the past into his present, and makes that brief last day of Dora's life exist again in his mind: "It is morning. . . . It is evening. . . . It is night. . . . It is over" (763–66).

What differentiates these retrospect chapters from the rest of the novel is their style—and their style, of course, indicates what is really different about them, the special relation between the narrative voice and its subject matter. As I have argued earlier, the focus of *David Copperfield* is on David's remembering, not on what he remembers. In the retrospect chapters what we see is memory enacted: a direct, dramatic representation of the act of remembering. The retrospects are all written in the present tense, and their scenes are more like tableaux than dramatic scenes. They have the quality of theatrical illusions, as though they are presented through a scrim. At one point, under the influence of an evening at the theater, David describes his meditation on the past in just such terms, as appearing "like a shining transparency, through which I saw my earlier life move along" (286). Later, in writing about his purpose in this novel, he revises the scrim figure so that the emphasis is on the illuminating eye rather than what is illuminated or the illumination itself. His intention, he says, is "to reflect my mind on this paper" (697). *David Copperfield* is the mind of its hero reflected on a screen, superimposed on the images of plot, character, and action. Or, to use the tableau metaphor again, this novel is the reflection of David's mind on the scene itself. The most intense examples of such reflection are the retrospects, in which David freezes the action, in effect, in order to recover and dramatize what the action felt like to him in its time. The experience of these chapters is the narrator's direct and conscious reexperience of feeling, of what he felt when he first experienced the action or event. Thus in those formal "It is morning. . . . It is evening. . . . It is night. . . . It is over" divisions of chapter liii, the antecedent of "it" is not really time, but feeling.

Though these retrospect chapters re-create feeling—are moving, emotionally intense chapters to read—they are still very different in their effect from other dramatic narratives. Again I think of Yeats' "emotion which I described to myself as cold" as a way of explaining the difference. The cause, I am sure, lies in the kind of appeal these retrospects make to us. Their appeal—their projected communication—is from mind to mind: from David's mind, experiencing emotion, to our minds. We are unaccustomed still to the mind's communication of feeling *as* feeling, comprehended. And it is difficult for us to accept the "ideal" comprehending David—David the narrator—as real.

David's mind presents itself to us in these retrospect chapters as that disembodied voice which spoke the novel's opening sentence. The purpose of that voice, or mind, is to create meaning and pleasure out of its life, its world, and through its power of recollection—re-collection, really—make that life or world full and whole. The final chapter of the novel, "A Last Retrospect," exists as a retrospect in part just to claim that purpose achieved. It begins:

> And now my written story ends. I look back, once more—for the last time—before I close these leaves.
> I see myself, with Agnes at my side, journeying along the road of life. I see our children and our friends around us; and I hear the roar of many voices, not indifferent to me as I travel on.
> What faces are the most distinct to me in the fleeting crowd? Lo, these; all turning to me as I ask my thoughts the question! (874)

This has been the "written story" of David's life. David himself is the center of attention: *I see me,* he says, *in my life, and I hear voices talking to me and about me as I go by.* The third paragraph of this introduction seems to change the focus to those voices, those "faces" in the "the fleeting crowd" around him. Actually, however, David the narrator's question is whom among the crowd *he* sees most clearly in *his thoughts:* "What faces are the most distinct to me . . . turning to me as I ask my thoughts the question." He presents them: Miss Betsey, Peggotty, Mr. Dick, Mrs. Steerforth and Rosa, Julia Mills, Jack Maldon, Dr. Strong and Mrs. Markleham, and then Traddles. Except for Traddles, for whom there is a short scene to be played, they are all presented in tableau. Then "these faces fade away, . . . shadows which I now dismiss"—and it is over.

What is left? David, and David's mind. What is real? Again, only David, and David's mind. The rest is shadow. It existed only in David's mind, as the substance of his imagination; it exists now only as this novel, called by David's name: *David Copperfield.* The ambition "to reflect my mind on this paper" (697) has been fulfilled; and "these pages," which must identify "the hero of my life," identify him by means of his reflection as a life, a world, called *David Copperfield.*

Richard Barickman

THE SPIRITUAL JOURNEY OF AMY DORRIT AND ARTHUR CLENNAM

"A Way Wherein There Is No Ecstasy"

AMY DORRIT and Arthur Clennam ultimately achieve a quiet, modest, secure resolution of their personal dilemmas that distinguishes them from *Little Dorrit*'s throng—"the noisy, and the eager, and the arrogant and the froward and the vain" of the famous closing paragraph. Their marriage consummates a spiritual rather than an erotic development and is sanctified by Christian symbolism, but it is not a transcendence of ordinary experience, not "Love . . . most nearly itself/When here and now cease to matter." It does not even escape from the urban here and now into the domestic enclave that closes almost every Dickens novel from *Pickwick* to *Bleak House*. The Clennams must attempt to survive and sustain the virtues they have come to represent in the uproar of the London streets, with no Divine grace to support them.

Yet the symbolism of a Christian spiritual journey is not inappropriate. Both Amy and Arthur submit to a process that resembles the severe spiritual discipline offered in the *Four Quartets*.

> In order to arrive there,
> To arrive where you are, to get from where you are not,
>   You must go by a way wherein there is no ecstasy.
> In order to arrive at what you do not know
>   You must go by a way which is the way of ignorance.
> In order to possess what you do not possess
>   You must go by the way of dispossession.
> (*East Coker*)[1]

The thorough alienation from personal relationships that characterizes the lives of both hero and heroine is gradually disclosed in the course of the novel. The process involves renunciation and loss, retrenchment,

[163

and quiet, determined, sometimes despairing persistence; it is a disclosure of fixed conditions that antedate the novel's action rather than an authentic development of characters or relationships.

As Arthur explicitly realizes during his confinement in the Marshalsea, his love for Amy discovers what was always there. To arrive where he is at that moment has indeed involved no ecstasy but rather shame, humiliation, anxiety, disgrace, dispossession, and finally illness and despair. And this condition of complete simplicity that is like a negative of Eliot's moment of exaltation has indeed cost him not less than everything: "Looking back upon his own poor story, she was its vanishing-point. Every thing in its perspective led to her innocent figure. He had travelled thousands of miles towards it; previous unquiet hopes and doubts had worked themselves out before it; it was the centre of the interest of his life; it was the termination of everything that was good and pleasant in it; beyond there was nothing but mere waste and darkened sky" (733).

Arthur and Amy have both had to get from where they are not— from the dreamlike European landscape that reveals "the unreality of [Amy's] own inner life" and Arthur's equally insubstantial roles as dispossessed son and failed business partner—to arrive where they are at the novel's end. They must go by the way of ignorance; Arthur unobtrusively, perhaps unconsciously, abandons his initial quest for knowledge about the family mystery. He learns none of the truth about the Clennams' fraudulent economic or sexual dealings, not even that Mrs. Clennam is not his mother. Amy, who decides to leave Arthur in ignorance of his family's secret history, is almost an emblem of unassuming, unquestioning acceptance. As James Kincaid has written, "the novel distrusts justifications and holds up the non-explaining Amy Dorrit as a reproof to all its other characters."[2] They must go—as Arthur's refusal to accept Amy's fortune, or Amy herself until she is poor again, suggests—by the way of dispossession.

In the great literature of the Christian spiritual journey, from the *Divine Comedy* to Book I of the *Faerie Queene* to the *Four Quartets*, the hero or heroine must acknowledge impotence, submit to a penitential discipline, practice humility, and abandon the last tatter of personal pride and faith in personal resources. *Little Dorrit's* hero and heroine follow this pattern point for point. But the typical Christian quest also leaves behind both the splendor and the wretchedness of the secular world—Florence, the dream of a secular Christian empire, chivalric ideals, the heroes and masters of Western literature, personal friendships, fellow passengers in the subway, the whole great House of Pride—for the final Christian goal must be transcendence. Here *Little Dorrit* is crucially different. Amy and Arthur cannot escape the limits of a blighted secular world. They must immerse themselves in the common conditions of social wretchedness, even as they both willingly enter its primary symbol, the Marshalsea Prison.

The typical Christian quest discloses a community of faith hidden in ordinary secular life but revealed to the hero or narrator. And, of course, this community is directed toward and sustained by transcendent spiritual realities: "And what the dead had no speech for, when living, / They can tell you, being dead: the communication / Of the dead is tongued with fire beyond the language of the living" (*Little Gidding*). In *Little Dorrit* the familiar pattern of the Christian quest becomes deeply ironic. Amy and Arthur initially attempt to regain participation not in a community of faith but in ordinary social existence. The attempt is all the more precarious and fragile because it is so unassuming and yet so basic to the novel's conception of a minimally decent life. But even this attempt is futile. What passes for social existence in this novel is largely fraudulent; so Amy and Arthur finally must try to create a social reality for themselves and their small circle of friends. Any more comprehensive or permanent idea of community seems a nearly unattainable ideal by the end of the novel.

Fraud is thus more than a particular social evil in *Little Dorrit;* it is the essential mode of social existence. Merdle is not simply a scapegoat for thousands of greedy or foolish investors; his situation is emblematic of a whole society. In his totally spurious social roles (economic wizard, gracious host, father, husband) and in the utter isolation and misery of his private self, Merdle is only one extreme instance of a social and psychological condition that grips nearly all the novel's characters in some form: Miss Wade, William Dorrit, and Mrs. Clennam, obviously; but also Frederick Dorrit; Pet and her parents after her marriage; Blandois in his association with Henry Gowan; Affery; Doyce and Pancks in their economic roles; Casby after he is shorn; and Tattycoram in her life with the Meagleses as well as her life with Miss Wade. Flora, Mr. F.'s Aunt, and the Plornishes provide comic instances that are, of course, not entirely free of real pathos. Even Amy and Arthur find themselves coerced into deception, however selfless and well intentioned. Amy habitually and elaborately deceives her father to support his illusions. Arthur is anxious to discover the shameful secret that taints the Clennam name, to make reparation but also to suppress it from common knowledge.

As Merdle's case suggests, routine social fraud is hardly the problem. Deception seems almost motiveless by ordinary standards of vice: greed, revenge, or even the more amorphous desire for power. Instead, there is an unacknowledged but pervasive fear of a void: no relationship seems genuine; no motive seems candid or worthy; no condition of life seems to satisfy human desires; there seems to be no ultimate purpose, or even a sustaining provisional purpose, to human existence. Under the burden of this condition, unable to express its misery to anyone else or, usually, even to acknowledge it to themselves, the novel's characters submit to fraudulent relationships and institutions, perpetuate them, and generate more.

In sharp contrast to all the other late novels of Dickens, all *Little Dorrit*'s own melodramatic mysteries and ominous prophecies ultimately prove as empty and fraudulent as the characters' personal lives. By the time the Dorrits gain their fortune, their characters are fixed beyond change. By the time the Clennams' secret is revealed ("a very silly secret," Chesterton called it), it has lost whatever psychological impact for the characters or thematic impact for the reader it may once have had.[3] The melodramatic flurry of action it precipitates is bogus, at least in terms of the novel's primary areas of stress and significance. The villains are summarily punished, but Flintwinch and Blandois have both become peripheral by this point. Mrs. Clennam lapses into a more complete paralysis; Amy is unaffected by the secret; Arthur remains ignorant of it.

Even more than the Clennams' secret, the secret of the Dorrits' wealth is thematically tenuous, as tenuous as the connection between the Dorrits and the Clennams through Frederick Dorrit's long-forgotten protection of Arthur's mother. Pancks' unlikely interest in families and inheritances, suddenly provided to justify his quest for the Dorrits' fortune, indicates how casually this plot development proceeds. As with similar mysteries in *Bleak House, Great Expectations,* and *Our Mutual Friend,* elaborate, lengthy, and tantalizing preparations precede the disclosure of the Dorrits' wealth, a disclosure finally made with melodramatic flourishes; but the effect is as anticlimactic as the revelation of the Clennam mystery. The experiences of the Dorrits in the second part of the novel demonstrate how little effect the wealth that Pancks discovers has on their characters, just as the Clennam secret neither helps nor harms any living character. But the reader discovers through both carefully designed anticlimaxes the void that *Little Dorrit*'s society conceals as its most carefully guarded secret. There is no equal to a Jaggers or a Bucket, no network of crucial secret connections that deserves an investigator of their acumen, power, and stature. The only "crimes" in *Little Dorrit* (excepting Rigaud's apparent cowardly murder of his wife) are business failures, fraud, and the analogous crime in romantic affairs, breach of promise; the central violent death, Merdle's, is suicide.

The novel casts its network of coincidence and interconnections over the surface of the narrative, in the form of intersecting journeys, metaphors of journeys, and solemn premonitions of the dark destinations of journeys; but the narrative methods participate in the fraud that draws the social world into spurious association. Because of the persistent, brooding sense of spiritual stasis, all the ominous predictions about momentous encounters between strangely assorted fellow travelers seem ultimately anticlimactic, if not actually bogus. Miss Wade first voices the dark portent of mysterious encounters on life's journey: " 'In our course through life we shall meet the people who are coming to meet *us,* from many strange places and by many strange roads,' was the composed reply; 'and what it is set to us to do to them, and what it is set to them to do to us, will all be done' " (25). This is very easy and indisputably correct prophecy. For all its tone of dark predestination (a tone Mrs. Clennam later revels in), it is based simply on the fact of chance meetings. And such general prophecy, here or in the narrator's later echoes, always proves true; for in any life there will be chance encounters of great significance, but their significance can only be determined after the fact. Such a warning is little more than projected hindsight.

In this novel Dickens has denatured the symbolic coincidences so important to *Bleak House* and *Great Expectations,* making the interconnections overt and superficial rather than secret, mysterious, and suggestive of crucial psychological relationships. At the time she speaks Miss Wade knows very well that she will meet the Meagleses again to their disadvantage; she knows that Pet loves Henry; she has even begun her entrapment of Tattycoram. Like almost all the other apparently coincidental relationships in the novel, this one is the product of very conscious contrivance. The secret bond between Pip and Magwitch or Esther and Jo helps elucidate a crucial psychological and social kinship, which the characters sense only dimly or not at all; the analogous bonds in *Little Dorrit* are nearly always carefully designed snares, which reveal the lack of significant relationship.

So the ominous prophecy is as bogus and as revealing as Madame Sosostris' casting of the Tarot deck, false in its immediate claims but arresting in its exposure of crucial images and themes, and more significant still in its suggestion that the very materials out of which the artist forms his creation are suspect. This is only one of a number of ways that the novel engages in morally instructive deception, as a subtle induction into the ambience of the characters' world. The subplot that concerns Doyce's invention is itself overwhelmed in the collapse of the Merdle enterprises; after so much expenditure of energy by the narrative as well as by Doyce, Meagles, and Clennam, the lapse of interest is a puzzling anticlimax. But the collapse of Merdle's scheme, of the Clennam house, of William Dorrit, and, by the time of the novel's composition, of the Marshalsea itself, should be instructive. Preoccupation with any social apparatus, from an invention to a ministry, distracts from the spiritual crisis that lies half concealed within every social venture. The novel's impostures sum up and elaborate conditions of existence that must be experienced with something of the particularity of ordinary life rather than denounced in the abstract. We must, in other words, have an imitation of the ways in which we succumb to destructive illusions before their exposure can be meaningful.

As all these manifest problems—economic, social, psychological, moral, and ethical—that initially preoccupy the novel's characters (and readers) gradually lose their significance, the major thematic symbols of *Little Dorrit* (prison, journey, labyrinth, and ruined city) begin to establish their control over plot, setting, and action. Although the symbolic patterns that emerge intersect in a number of different, important areas of meaning, perhaps their most important function is to establish a landscape for the spiritual journeys of the novel's hero and heroine and the spiritual paralysis of nearly all the other characters.[4]

The Marshalsea serves as an apt symbol for the common spiritual condition in *Little Dorrit,* a condition that levels social hierarchies and calls into question even the most enlightened moral perspective. It is a prison for debt not crime, and thus by extension for the whole tangle of spurious relationships and obligations that ensnare everyone in the novel's world. A fundamental suggestion of Christian debt appears in the allusions to the Fall and the Crucifixion that almost habitually color the descriptions of the Marshalsea. It is a prison with accommodations for families, with space to walk freely and no enforced regimen, and even that Dickensian necessity for a complete society, a tavern and club. In every way the Marshalsea seems to be a comprehensive model of life in the novel's world rather than a satire of particular social abuses.

The most maddening quality of debtor's prison gives it a unique range of symbolic spiritual reference: confinement is indeterminate because the prisoner, by the very fact of his existence in the Marshalsea, becomes powerless to work off his debts. Whatever the nuances of social gradation within prison society, the prisoners all suffer under this common doom. Thus, like the Fall, imprisonment levels all secular hierarchies, stresses one common, desperate spiritual condition, and eliminates all possibility of self-redemption.

Yet in a profoundly important paradox, the novel exposes the common condition of its haggard and anxious characters as an enervating freedom, also most directly represented in the condition of the Marshalsea inmates. The first expositor of this idea is suitably bleary-eyed, sodden, dirty, and disreputable. Dr. Haggage (an authorial stand-in of sorts, who literally brings the novel's heroine into existence) defends the circumstances that have made his moral and physical deterioration inexorable.

> "That a child would be born to you in a place like this?" said the doctor. "Bah, bah, sir, what does it signify? A little more elbow-room is all we want here. We are quiet here; we don't get

badgered here; there's no knocker here, sir, to be hammered at by creditors and bring a man's heart into his mouth. Nobody comes here to ask if a man's at home, and to say he'll stand on the door mat till he is. Nobody writes threatening letters about money to this place. It's freedom, sir, it's freedom! . . . Elsewhere, people are restless, worried, hurried about, anxious respecting one thing, anxious respecting another. Nothing of the kind here, sir. We have done all that—we know the worst of it; we have got to the bottom, we can't fall, and what have we found? Peace. That's the word for it. Peace." (63)

This may seem merely the defensive rationalization of a man too self-indulgent, weak, or perhaps simply too unfortunate (like Plornish) to succeed in the more stringent society that rings the Marshalsea. But as the novel persists in making the Marshalsea thematically as well as circumstantially central, the center of analogy for all the various social settings, Dr. Haggage's "profession of faith" becomes the private, unconfessed, unconscious creed of a number of motley prisoners who live outside the Marshalsea's walls. All find in the imprisonment a secret release from a still less tolerable condition: the anxiety of a social struggle that seems pointless and endless. Like William Dorrit, they find that the lock and key that keeps them in also keeps numbers of their troubles out. Imprisonment provides this freedom but it is, as William Dorrit's career demonstrates, the freedom of exile, abandonment, despair.

Dorrit has succumbed to Haggage's nostrum even before it is offered to him. And Amy seems to point the moral, unobtrusively and unknowingly as always, by the very nature of her existence. Her story, "handed down among the generations of collegians, like the tradition of their common parent" (68), offers an admonition similar to the story of the Fall and just as universally ignored by the collegians. Both the anxieties and the listless cordialities of social existence, from her father's degraded solicitation of—ha—testimonials to the lavish bosom of Mrs. Merdle and lavish fraud of her husband, appear in the light of her example as uneasy, self-indulgent diversions from the one immutable fact of spiritual bondage. In the same way, Amy's half-apologetic, half-explanatory approach to new collegians, "Excuse me, I was born here," suggests the condition they share with her whatever their personal status and prospects, as if all birth were imprisonment and all social relations the haggard routine of inmates.

The transplantation of the Dorrits to Europe effects no change in their individual characters and only superficial alterations in their way of life. But it does reveal, beyond this expected irony, how general that way of life is in society; it can not be eluded in the Swiss Alps or among the ruins of Rome, any more than Arthur escaped its influence in

China. The narrator, in the blatant rhetoric that distinguishes many of his direct satiric assaults on society, insists on the correspondence.

> This same society in which they lived, greatly resembled a superior sort of Marshalsea. Numbers of people seemed to come abroad, pretty much as people had come into the prison; through debt, through idleness, relationship, curiosity, and general unfitness for getting on at home. . . . They prowled about the churches and picture-galleries, much in the old, dreary, prison-yard manner. They were usually going away again tomorrow or next week, and rarely knew their own minds, and seldom did what they said they would do, or went where they said they would go: in all this again, very like the prison debtors. (511)

The straggle of English tourists who wander desolately through the ruins of Venice and Rome (even the monastery on the Great St. Bernard is described as a ruin) typify society in their utter, listless lack of purpose or even direction and their routine obeisance to idiotic forms. The point of the contrast between the novel's two parts seems clear: a social world adapted to private needs is a prison; a social world adapted to mass habits is a ruin of traditional values.

Like the "hosts of tongue-tied and blindfolded moderns" who grope through the ruins of Rome and Venice, social groupings everywhere are clumps of wretched individuals, caught in routine, hypocritical rituals that parody communal interests but leave them as solitary in private misery as if they were deaf and dumb. The characters who nurse a secret shame or grief or rage are only more extreme and obvious examples of this atomization of society, but they are abundant: Mrs. Clennam, William Dorrit, Miss Wade, Tattycoram, Mr. F's aunt, Mr. Meagles, John Chivery, Flintwinch, Affery, Rigaud. Ultimately Arthur and Amy join them, Amy in the wasteland of Europe, Arthur in his Marshalsea room. James Kincaid has said bluntly, but without overstatement, what a number of other critics have sensed: "Although the novel is, as Trilling says, 'more about society than any other of the novels' . . . it really repudiates the notion of society. *Little Dorrit* not only deals with human isolation but sees that isolation as largely inescapable; perhaps, in a dark sense, it is even better than community."[5]

The Bleeding Hearters as well as the swarm of Barnacles, the Merdle investors as well as the Marshalsea debtors, engage in social rituals as idiotic and stupefying as the labyrinthine tours led by the Mrs. Generals. The routines lack the impulse of radical, unconscious desires that quicken and complicate the social forms in *Great Expectations* and *Bleak House*. All that seems vital and natural, even at its most destructive, in *Bleak House* and *Great Expectations* is stifled and walled-in here, so thoroughly that only a few characters have retained a capacity to feel passion and fewer still the capacity to express it. The novel offers no course for energy: Mrs. Clennam is as thwarted in her self-righteous viciousness as Daniel Doyce or Meagles are in their benevolence. Even Miss Wade is reduced to posturing scorn, autobiography, and petty espionage rather than the revenge she so avidly seeks; the closest she comes to violence is the temporary seduction of Tattycoram, a surrogate for her chief enemies, Pet and Henry Gowan.

Although *Little Dorrit* is cross-hatched with more journeys than any other Dickens' novel since *Pickwick Papers,* this major plot motif and major symbol is as paradoxical as the prison symbolism. Travel might seem to elude both the confines of place and the more ominous, ingrained prison of self-repression. Yet the Dorrits' example holds for the whole novel: the prison proves infinitely transportable.

Travel in this novel is perhaps the loneliest, most dispiriting activity that still makes a pretense at social relationship. But the vision of society darkens even further as the prison and the journey merge to form the labyrinth: the "labyrinth of bare passages and pillared galleries" threaded on the Dorrits' mandatory grand tour; the maze of calculations Pancks is condemned to retrace for the rest of his life after the Merdle crash; the array of rooms Merdle wanders, imprisoned in his own house; and the narrator's most general metaphor for existence, "the multiplicity of paths in the labyrinth trodden by the sons of Adam" (557). A labyrinth is prison and enforced journey at once. If society is truly labyrinthine, then the only intelligent purpose of travel must be to escape it. This is both the motive and the fallacy of virtually every journey in the novel, to escape a particular oppressive social relationship or a more vaguely perceived general condition of society. It is a necessarily futile effort to elude a spiritual condition through a change of place.

Amy's Marshalsea birthplace, where her father reverted to childhood and she was thrust into premature motherhood, finds a complement at the midpoint of her career in the somber Roman palace where her father dies and she is abandoned. She will return to the Marshalsea, assume her old dress, and marry Arthur in the church next to the prison. The only possible accommodation with the prison seems by her crucial example to be acceptance of its ubiquity, even in the ceremony of marriage. Similarly, the only possible accommodation with the frustrated journey seems to be to acknowledge the futility of an ideal of social progress or even of social purpose beyond the domestic circle of a few friends and depleted family.

Only death offers an escape from this labyrinth. The choices open to the living are all ways of accepting it as an inevitable condition; at the worst giving up all struggle, nearly all consciousness, like Frederick

Dorrit; but even at the best retracing the tedious, tortuous journey to find a fixed moral perspective, as Arthur in his prison room discovers that Amy is the "centre of the interest of his life" (733).

During his first, accidental imprisonment in the Marshalsea, Arthur has a sudden insight into forces that are the antithesis not only of a fixed moral perspective, but of any human order. He has been pacing up and down in the Marshalsea courtyard, drawn into this prison routine as if he were born to it. His questing urge ("I want to know") has literally been shunted into mechanical oscillation or the repetitious motion of a caged animal. As his frustration intensifies, the blank walls force his gaze upward, and he glimpses a terrifying image that will recur throughout the novel as another major symbol of spiritual destitution: "The walls were so near to one another, and the wild clouds hurried over them so fast, that it gave him a sensation like the beginning of sea-sickness to look up at the gusty sky. The rain, carried aslant by flaws of wind, blackened that side of the central building which he had visited last night, but left a narrow dry trough under the lee of the wall, where he walked up and down among waifs of straw and dust and paper, the waste droppings of the pump, and the stray leaves of yesterday's greens. It was as haggard a view of life as a man need look upon" (90).

This image of the wilderness—in the storm-blown sky over the Marshalsea; in the wild flight of clouds above the wilder streets of London during Amy's first night outside the prison; in the ragged, rain-torn country about Chalons where Rigaud flees like Cain—though less obvious and less frequent than either prison or journey, is in some ways as important a thematic metaphor. It suggests that condition of terrifying freedom that both sedentary prisoners and travelers flee. And it suggests how close the chaos of spiritual dissolution and the rigidity of confinement actually are. John Lucas has written that "one of *Little Dorrit*'s concerns is with the impossible dream of freedom."[6] Yet whatever fantasies lure and harry the characters, in one way or another they all share a terror of freedom, choosing the narrowest cell in preference to an aimless chaos that offers "as haggard a view of life as a man need look upon." Imprisonment and travel are in this way equally fugitive in this world, a paradox most fully illustrated by the career of William Dorrit.

The flight from refuge to refuge always courses some version of the wilderness. Sometimes it is close to an actual wilderness—the plain near Chalons or the desolation of the Alps. Sometimes the wasteland has overrun the city—Calais described as a weed patch, the "shame, desertion, wretchedness, and exposure" of London at night, or the actual ruins of Rome.

The disposition of symbolic landscape suggests a microcosmic pattern of religious imagery that encloses the whole novel: Marseilles is a hellscape; the monastery atop the mountain is a frozen travesty of Heaven; and the sodden plains and roads that connect one to the other (tracing a tortuous course through England as well as across France and Italy) is a purgatory flattened out into a patternless maze. This is Dickens' bleakest satire of a society that has parodied its own deepest spiritual tradition and totally squandered the energy of its new secular faiths.

Amy and Arthur are spiritual questers in this wasteland. For all their differences from the other characters, they represent the unacknowledged need of their whole society. Unlike the Christian prototypes suggested earlier, however, they never achieve a conscious recognition of the general spiritual destitution, much less any beatific vision. Most ironic of all, they do not even know, until perhaps for a moment near the novel's end, that they are engaged in an elemental search.

Arthur's relation to his mother and Amy's to her father reveal the same kind of debilitating tangle of unconscious emotional needs that characterizes the other great novels of Dickens' last two decades (in Pip's relation to his patrons and Esther's to Miss Barbary, Ada, Jarndyce, and Lady Dedlock, for instance). Yet this novel, without minimizing the anxieties of ordinary psychological life in society, seeks to probe beneath them to disclose a more pervasive spiritual malaise. The kind of psychological conflict that forms the center of interest in *Great Expectations* and *Bleak House* is certainly valid and absorbing here, but as a symptom of the disorder rather than the disorder itself. Unconscious psychological conflicts have equal reality in *Little Dorrit* as in the two other novels—Dickens is describing the same culture with similar scope and penetration—but not equal validity. Like the multiple illusions that beguile and torment Red Crosse in Book I of the *Faerie Queene,* they are at once psychologically real and metaphysically false. In a crucial shift of Dickens' perspective, the psychological conflicts—conscious and unconscious—that preoccupy both the characters and the novel's action are ultimately exposed as sham. They are all diversionary maneuvers to escape acknowledging the spiritual squalor and despair that paralyzes the entire society. Mrs. Clennam's self-induced paralysis and William Dorrit's multiple pretensions are only the most obvious manipulations of this sort. Amy's domestic martyrdom and Clennam's obsession with the family's guilty secret are also strategies to circumvent a spiritual void, however admirable they may be in the light of the novel's overt moral standards. Their strategies are wholly unconscious and defensive, where their parents' strategies are partly conscious and aggressive, and this makes a crucial moral difference, of course. But—as in so many of Dickens' late novels, as in so much Victorian literature from the "Lady of Shalott" to the "Hymn to Proserpine"—the relevance of moral values to sustained psychological and spiritual crises is persistently questioned in *Little Dorrit*.

The spiritual crises of Amy and Arthur do not erupt into consciousness through a sudden melodramatic discovery of hidden relationship as in *Bleak House* and *Great Expectations*. Pip and Esther are terrified by the complexities of something strange and powerful in their own natures; Arthur and Amy are depressed by the simple fact that supposed relationships have gradually dissipated into nothing. Even Arthur's illness indicates the difference. Unlike the raging fever and vivid, terrifying dreams that seize Pip and Esther, Arthur's illness is "the despondency of low, slow fever." It leaves him in a half-conscious state of incoherent thoughts and jumbled, hallucinatory sounds. It is the ordinary course of life that assumes the character of a dream for Amy and Arthur, and the revelation comes only gradually and quietly to full consciousness.

In keeping with the novel's paradoxical use of prison symbolism, Arthur's "problem" at the beginning appears to him and to us not as imprisonment but as freedom, Dr. Haggage's kind of freedom. In every way he is adrift. He has none of Pip's expectations, none of Esther's settled responsibilities. After twenty years' absence he returns to an England that is like a foreign land to him. In retrospect, his years in China, his whole life, appear devoid of growth, happiness, sustaining purpose; and his future seems still more somber. His father has died, and his mother's stern rejection of all attempts at intimacy precludes any meaningful contact with her. He knows no one in England outside the Clennam household except Casby and Flora; and his meeting with her shakes him even more than the interview with Mrs. Clennam, destroying the one illusion of significant relationship that persisted through the long dreariness of his manhood. Family has been only a hated business to Arthur for years. Now, as if to seal his own estrangement, he resigns even his nominal interest in the Clennam firm. He has no profession, no friends, as little family as possible (still less than he supposes since Mrs. Clennam is not his mother), and, he thinks, no will to begin in his fortieth year to find such things.

Arthur is an anomaly among Dickens' heroes, as his age suggests in itself. For the hero to begin the novel in middle life and, more important, in a state of such weary depression suggests a major shift in Dickens' conception not only of maturity but of childhood. Arthur's childhood is as bleak as any Dickens hero's, though not so exciting (even Esther's quiet routine is violently stirred by Miss Barbary's stroke, staged, rhetorically at least, as a judgment from God); and it certainly has subdued his temperament to an almost somber sobriety and diffidence. Yet the events of his childhood are not dramatized, because his condition has in its deepest import no necessary relation to a particular childhood or to particular social conditions in Victorian England. Like another hero, Joseph K., he is caught in a spiritual crisis that over-whelms even the most basic of family relations and the profound effect they ordinarily seem to have on character. Like Joseph K. in his bed-room or Dante in the dark wood, Clennam awakens in the middle of his life to a condition deeply personal, involving and even arraigning his most intimate feelings and relationships, yet also autonomous and universal. Largely to establish this sense Dickens has Clennam return to England from a life in China that is a total blank in the narrative, a method similar once again to the disinterest in biographical origins that distinguishes the *Divine Comedy* and *The Trial*. Like the garret court of *The Trial* or the whole framework and substance of the *Divine Comedy*, the prison society of *Little Dorrit* seems to generalize the experiences of its hero as a condition of human existence, so that the details of his his-tory suggest the intersection of a particular, present time with an unchanging spiritual reality as well as the development of a unique in-dividual.

Amy's journey in Europe ends where Arthur's journey begins, in the flurry of countries and cities that fall into place about her as one vast ruined prison. Yet her condition then appears, like Arthur's at the opening of the novel, not as imprisonment but as disorienting freedom. Her father, like Arthur's, dies at the culmination of this development; but death is only the extreme point of their gradual estrangement, which has been widening since their change in fortunes, indeed since the death of her mother. From Amy's perspective the spurious free-dom of wealth reveals the lack of relationship hidden by the Marshal-sea. As soon as they no longer need her for their comforts, all the Dor-rits begin to desert Amy, troubled by the memories of Marshalsea life she unintentionally arouses (all, that is, except Frederick and he dies before he can be anything more than a faltering substitute for the fa-ther she never had). She grows as aware of isolation as Arthur does, though she is less openly despondent and less critical of her family.

Joseph Gold and several other critics have argued, in essence, that Amy escapes alienation by total acceptance of her prison and total com-mitment to others' needs.[7] Yet commitment that arouses no response in others and acceptance that has no consequence in human community surely resemble alienation, however Amy may redouble her love and service. In fact her condition of estrangement is so marked and so crucial to her place in the novel that it reaches her own consciousness unmistakably: "To have no work to do was strange, but not half so strange as having glided into a corner where she had no one to think for, nothing to plan and contrive, no cares of others to load herself with. . . . It was from this position that all she saw appeared unreal; the more surprising the scenes, the more they resembled the unreality

of her own inner life as she went through its vacant places all day long"
(463).

It is difficult to regard Amy at this moment, as F. R. Leavis does, as
the generator of reality in the novel, though she certainly exemplifies
the ability to endure quietly and serviceably the social void at the novel's center. Hillis Miller, like Trilling, sees her as "a human incarnation
of divine goodness" (though he goes on to say that divine goodness,
though "present in the novel, is unavailable"). But James Kincaid's
bleaker assessment seems closer to the novel's spirit than any traditional
Christian conception:

> The blessedness Amy Dorrit gives to Arthur has absolutely no
> effect on the surrounding society, and the clear sense is that
> the expansive social redemption envisaged by comedy is impos-
> sible. Society is seen simply as a collection of the harassed, and
> the real problem is not the comic one of rejuvenating society or
> finding one's place in it; one searches, rather, for a way to pu-
> rify oneself of the social taint. . . . The truly meek alone have
> a chance here and they only in so far as they renounce social
> membership. In *Pickwick* victory was seen as a release from
> prison; here it is seen largely as an acceptance of imprison-
> ment.[8]

As much as this formulation resembles Christian doctrine, the differences are again crucial. There is no spiritual reality in *Little Dorrit* to
replace the illusion of social community. Meekness, renunciation, purification, and acceptance lead perilously toward an absolute despair and
an absolute denial of both secular and spiritual life.

Amy moves slowly toward a realization of her situation that resembles Arthur's initial awareness. Although his psychological condition
holds our attention for most of the novel, Amy's development has
perhaps even greater thematic significance because she travels so far.
She is directly, unmistakably, contrasted with Arthur at the novel's
beginning. Arthur recognizes that his exile represents a condition of
alienation and that his life has been blighted—incurably he thinks—by
his parents. Amy scarcely has been outside the Marshalsea; and she
gladly, gratefully endures the selfish impositions of her father, without
any sense that she might have reason to complain. Arthur is a disin-
herited son, whose father and mother are dead. Amy has been forced
into unnatural adult responsibilities from early childhood, with a regimen of duty far more taxing than Esther Summerson's. She has become
the substitute mother for the entire family: "She took the place of eldest of the three, in all things but precedence; was the head of the
fallen family; and bore, in her own heart, its anxieties and shames"
(72).

Amy begins the novel exiled in her own family, almost wholly unconscious of her own needs, almost wholly without a sense of separate, personal identity. Arthur begins the novel fully aware of an identity that seems only to isolate him from others and to bring painful consciousness. Amy's development reveals a slow growth toward awareness of a radical spiritual disorder, even as Arthur's persistent anxiety reveals the effects of that disorder when it has settled into a way of life.

Their careers are thus complementary; Amy moves toward Arthur's state and in some ways beyond it, so that by the novel's end they have experienced an equality and maturity of development (and of narrative presentation) that make them the most convincing, admirable, and compatible couple in Dickens. Amy moves steadily and painfully away from that unquestioning acceptance of the prison that some critics have seen as "inner freedom";[9] she moves toward a condition—if not quite a conscious realization—that acknowledges the futility of total self-effacement without a transcendent faith. Unquestioning submission has drawn too near to the miserable rationalizations of her father, the emotional rigor of Mrs. Clennam and Miss Wade, the cynicism of Gowan, and the despair that almost destroys Arthur.

Love itself is nearly insupportable in this world where the self languishes in secret and the impulse to love is stifled or perverted within the family itself. As painful and dispiriting as Arthur's rejection by Mrs. Clennam is, Amy suffers a deeper and more protracted agony. Her sacrifices are not only unappreciated but even nurture the corrupt pretensions of her father, brother, and sister; and her love is forced into the humiliation of disguise and deception in order to support the most craven vanity. It is little wonder that the most resplendent fairy tale Amy can invent for Maggy presents existence as obscure, tedious, pointless labor, love as a secret to be hidden away in darkness, and the greatest virtue concealment of that secret until death. A. E. Dyson has written with fine precision and sensitivity about the wrenching nature of Amy's virtuous sacrifice:

> There could be few sorrows more harrowing than Amy's daily knowledge that the very qualities which make for dignity and honesty in life could only achieve her father's death. It is not only the ordinary desires and hopes of life that she has to surrender, but the intelligence and sensitivity of her innermost self. William Dorrit's one defensive weapon is the shield of gentility: take that away—all its shame, all its pettiness, all its hollowness—and he would die. . . . There is no possibility of self-knowledge leading, through crisis, to renewal; self-knowledge is the enemy always to be feared. It is not even therefore as though Amy's sacrifice was made to redeem her father: a stern moralist might even condemn the pretence.

More simply, her duty as she sees it is to keep him going. In a
intolerable situation she can make life barely tolerable for him
from hour to hour. But to do this she has to shore up the ruins
of his snobbery, to make his survival from the stuff of decay.[10]

To surrender the intelligence and sensitivity of her innermost
self—this is surely to strain virtue to the point of utter abasement and
humiliation, but it is as surely the risk Amy takes, without ever realizing
the implications of her actions. She has indeed almost no self to surrender at the time of the novel's opening action, as the continual references to her tininess, quietness, unobtrusiveness all suggest. Dyson is
again penetrating: "her virtue seems like almost total self-immolation."
The repression of personal desires and almost the sense of distinct, autonomous personality has been so thorough that Amy does not have
even those mannerisms that agitate Esther with intimations of stifled
urges.

Amy has initially no desire except to care for her father and, after
him, her brother and sister; Arthur's desires oppose his mother's will
and are wholly frustrated by her. Both must endure the sense of impotence and shame that their positions create, with so little possibility of
resistance that they must abandon personal pride and even a last resid-
ual trust in their human resources. Like Red Crosse at the House of
Pride, the hero and heroine of this novel are completely distinguished
from the worldly proud: Mrs. Gowan, Mrs. Merdle, William Dorrit,
Mrs. Clennam, Gowan, even Meagles with his smack of snobbery. But
like Red Crosse they find that a deeper, more insidious and almost
wholly pervasive pride must be renounced through an ordeal of humiliation, a pride that is nearly indistinguishable from human nature.

Although Amy reaches an awareness of the emptiness of her life in
the absence of all significant relationship, there is a strange passivity, almost a suspension of existence, in the process. Like Arthur im-
mobilized and half conscious in the Marshalsea room, Amy wastes away
and recovers almost as if the transformation were physical rather than
psychological. Neither realizes anything like the full significance of the
process they suffer: Amy never admits that her father was selfishly ex-
acting to the point of outrage; Arthur never fully recognizes the spiritual significance of his love for Amy. Passivity even in climactic recognition is, of course, typical of Dickens' heroes and heroines; yet the
feverish hallucinations of Esther and Pip express the effects of human
nature in conflict with itself and with the orders of consciousness and
society it has created. The illness Arthur suffers is like the wasting away
of Red Crosse in Orgoglio's dungeon, even as Amy's dreamlike, vacant
wandering through the abysses of her consciousness resembles the
plight of the abandoned Una. Both Arthur and Amy seem acted upon
by spiritual forces outside and in some ways opposed to their own per-

sonal natures. Their experiences thus touch on something beyond ordinary relationships and mental conditions in the secular world.

Like most nineteenth-century novels, *Little Dorrit* pivots its action and thematic development on courtship and marriage. But Amy Dorrit and Arthur Clennam suffer love as part of their spiritual agony, as a burden imposed upon them. Courtship and marriage for them retains only a tenuous connection with ordinary romantic love.

Because she can imagine no hope of its fulfillment, because love has been equivalent to wrenching sacrifice in her experience, Amy's love for Arthur causes her to withdraw further into self-effacing seclusion: "A change had stolen, and was stealing yet, over the patient heart. Every day found her something more retiring than the day before. To pass in and out of the prison unnoticed, and elsewhere to be overlooked and forgotten, were, for herself, her chief desires. To her own room too, strangely assorted room for her delicate youth and character, she was glad to retreat as often as she could without desertion of any duty" (290–91). The initial awareness of love so disorients and pains Amy that it finds repeated expression in emotional distress: when Arthur calls her "child"; when John Chivery tries to propose on the Iron Bridge; and when Maggy finds her crying in her room. For the first time in her life, Amy has a perspective which forces her to see the wretchedness of the Marshalsea, of her father's pretensions, of her own situation.

Arthur's realization of their love much later, even when he knows that it is shared, also suggests that love burdens and isolates in a society so alien to it. The revelation affects him like a "heavy blow": "his whole appearance that of a man who has been awakened from sleep, and stupified by intelligence beyond his full comprehension" (729). Accustomed to regard himself as an elderly man after his failure even to acknowledge his romantic interest in Pet, Arthur now sees himself as ruined and degraded. The difference in age, the social and geographical distance between himself and Amy, even the old habit of regarding her as a foster child join to make their love an intensification of despair rather than a consolation. So he thinks of Amy as the end point of his history, but as an end that is more like death than romantic consummation: "Looking back upon his own poor story, she was its vanishing-point. Every thing in its perspective led to her innocent figure. He had travelled thousands of miles towards it; previous unquiet hopes and doubts had worked themselves out before it; it was the centre of interest of his life; it was the termination of everything that was good and pleasant in it; beyond there was nothing but mere waste and darkened sky" (733).

The first consequence of this love for Arthur as for Amy is to draw him still further into solitude and wasting despair: "Imprisonment began to tell upon him. He knew that he idled and moped. After what he had known of the influences of imprisonment within the four small walls of the very room he occupied, this consciousness made him afraid of himself. Shrinking from the observation of other men, and shrinking from his own, he began to change very sensibly. Anybody might see that the shadow of the wall was dark upon him" (735). These are not in any sense the obstacles and reverses of fortune designed by the narrative to roughen the course of love for dramatic purposes. They express the character of the love between Arthur and Amy as a spiritual trial involving in reality and not simply in romantic hyperbole the whole of their lives, intensifying still further the quality of chastening, loss, and renunciation in this strangely somber romance. The prison walls that enclose both Amy and Arthur when they acknowledge their love, first in isolation and then together, suggest how bereft the spirit must be to even conceive love in the world of this novel.

The way this relationship subsumes the roles of father and daughter has often been noticed.[11] Arthur asks Amy to regard him as a father; she asks to be called Little Dorrit even after they have acknowledged their love. Arthur literally occupies the place of William Dorrit in the Marshalsea; and he compensates and expiates for Amy's father in a number of ways. From the beginning he offers her the love and tender protection that William Dorrit fails even to recognize she needs. Dorrit has erected only a precarious personal vanity as a defense against utter wretchedness, the shoddiest and flimsiest perhaps of all social pretensions. Arthur's notoriety after the revelation of Merdle's fraud serves as a surrogate punishment for Dorrit's hypocrisy, especially since he insists on enduring the disgrace of his financial ruin, in contrast to Dorrit's evasions. (To make this significance of Arthur's disgrace more apparent, the plot has contrived Dorrit's investment of his entire fortune with Merdle.)

The final chapter, however, reverses this relationship of father to daughter that has prevailed through most of the novel.

> Changeless and barren, looking ignorantly at all the seasons with its fixed, pinched face of poverty and care, the prison had not a touch of any of these beauties on it. Blossom what would, its bricks and bars bore uniformly the same dead crop. Yet Clennam, listening to the voice [Amy's] as it read to him, heard in it all that great Nature was doing, heard in it all the soothing songs she sings to man. At no Mother's knee but hers, had he ever dwelt in his youth on hopeful promises, on playful fancies, on the harvests of tenderness and humility that lie hidden in the early-fostered seeds of the imagination. . . . But, in the tones of the voice that read to him, there were memories of an old feeling of such things, and echoes of every merciful and loving whisper that had ever stolen to him in his life. (815)

Even the momentary ambiguity of "at no Mother's knee but hers," seeming to refer to Amy rather than to nature, reinforces the suggested relationship. Arthur acts as both father and child to Amy, as she is both child and mother to him. The plot of the novel avoids the conflict of roles and responsibilities that might naturally, openly occur in such a situation, through the death of William Dorrit and the paralysis of Mrs. Clennam. Amy and Arthur are thus freed, even abandoned, to the relationships they fulfill for each other. The revelation that Mrs. Clennam was only Arthur's stepmother emphasizes Amy's maternal role, especially since the knowledge and the decision to reveal or withhold it from an Arthur are bequeathed from Mrs. Clennam to Amy like a mother's guardianship, perverted by Mrs. Clennam, fulfilled by Amy. In good part Amy and Arthur are inseparable and isolated at the novel's end because they quite literally mean so much to each other.

John Wain and other critics have understandably questioned the emotional quality and significance of this marriage.[12] Ordinarily the strong desires Amy and Arthur have to be both parent and child to each other might make impossible demands on the marriage and arouse ambivalent responses in the reader. Yet the expected strain of incompatible desires is curiously absent from the novel's ending. The fact is that there are no erotic desires to conflict with the need to establish the earlier and more basic family relationships that never existed for either Amy or Arthur or to conflict with the still more pervasive, general, and basic desire for any relationship that nourishes the spirit.

The strain that does twist the rhetoric about Amy's motherly care into sentimental form comes not from psychological ambivalence but from the attempt to locate in nature an essentially religious perception. As so often in Dickens, the passage reveals its strength and its true polarities despite its confused motives and rhetorical strain. The sound of reading, already dissociated from the personality of Amy into a more abstract, almost spiritualized "voice," modulates into light too bright for natural perception: "When the voice stopped he put his hand over his eyes, murmuring that the light was strong upon them." Whether Hillis Miller is correct in arguing that Victorian fiction generally relates one self to another in "an attempt to satisfy religious longings . . . ways in which a man may seek to make a God of another person in a world without God," this scene in *Little Dorrit* surely modulates from domestic to religious desires. Similarly, Alexander Welsh's argument that the transformation of loyalty from the father to the husband enacts a ritual of salvation, offered as a general perspective on Dickens' fiction, holds true for *Little Dorrit*.[13]

In an extraordinary scene early in the novel Dickens has disclosed the possibility of sexual maturity for Amy only to suggest that it is the wrong sort of maturity for this novel's themes, not forbidden but irrelevant. The scene does not perversely tease us with inappropriate possibilities; it rather reveals the fullness of Amy's character and the fullness of the novel's understanding of human development. It suggests that ordinary sexual and romantic possibilities are renounced, not ignored, by the novel, a renunciation that both Arthur and Amy share. Like the suggestion of thwarted sexuality in the characterization of Mrs. Merdle and Mrs. General, Amy's encounter with the prostitute sensitively explores areas of mental life that lie outside the novel's main ground. Even as the erotic themes of Book I of the *Faerie Queene* or the carnal emotions Dante-the-character shares with Francesca, Brunetto, and Ulysses undergird the primary spiritual themes, these moments in *Little Dorrit* increase the stature of the characters and deepen the novel's own significance.

In this scene Amy has been thrust into the mean, dirty streets of London as a direct consequence of her late visit to Arthur's room, with no refuge, no protector, not even the protection of daylight. The plot connection suggests the relevance of the episode to her awakening love. The prostitute asks for a kiss from Amy as if it were a blessing, but discovers that the child is a woman disguised by her diminutive figure.

> "Why, my God!" she said, recoiling, "you're a woman!"
> "Don't mind that!" said Little Dorrit, clasping one of her hands that had suddenly released hers. "I am not afraid of you!"
> "Then you had better be," she answered. "Have you no mother?"
> "No."
> "No father?"
> "Yes, a very dear one."
> "Go home to him, and be afraid of me. Let me go. Good night!"
> "I must thank you first; let me speak to you as if I really were a child."
> "You can't do it," said the woman. "You are kind and innocent; but you can't look at me out of a child's eyes. I never should have touched you, but I thought that you were a child." And with a strange, wild cry, she went away. (175–76)

The prostitute's words suggest that Amy is at a point of transition from childhood to womanhood, that maturing involves a frightening loss of sexual innocence, and that the child who has almost imperceptibly become a woman may find refuge in the security of her family. The whole episode intimates the fears that accompany the growth of Amy's love for Arthur (whom she has just a moment before thought of, quite naturally, as a kind father).

The prostitute's viewpoint is her own and cannot be "read into" Amy's perceptions, conscious or unconscious. Yet her words have an obvious bearing on Amy's situation. The prostitute means simply: Take warning by my example; don't expose yourself to the depravity of the nighttime streets; return to the family that can protect you from the shame and brutality of my condition. But the brief encounter, with the lingering echo of the parting "strange, wild cry" carries further than this. The two women who are with Amy on this night suggest a crucial choice that she must make (or endure). Maggy, the hulking woman whose mental life halted at ten years old, offers a grotesque image, with her bald head and great white cap like a baby's, of thwarted maturity. (Flora is another regressive child-woman who attends Amy in other episodes, comically grotesque where Maggy is pathetic.) The prostitute offers an image of sexuality so fully, blatantly, and brutally expressed that it overwhelms the self even more than Maggy's retardation.

Amy of course finds another, more fortunate process of maturity, but as this episode anticipates, it is a way that avoids the perplexities of sexual development or the regression that, in Dickens' symbolism, disfigures not only Maggy but even Esther Summerson and, in a still earlier novel, prefigures the death of Little Nell.

Little Dorrit offers abundant instances of the failure of ordinary romance, not to suggest along the lines of psychoanalytic critics like Norman O. Brown that sexuality is inevitably warped and as inevitably warps society in the growth from childhood to adulthood, but rather to suggest the failure of the ordinary family to resolve an essentially spiritual crisis. Flora, Miss Wade, Arthur's mother and father, Pet, Mrs. Merdle, even Rigaud's murdered wife and Rugg's jilted daughter establish the prevailing pattern of failed romantic expectations and often real spiritual misery.

Esther's disfigurement and her ardent relations with Ada suggest a strong erotic element in her romance with Woodcourt, however submerged. The analogous plot development in *Little Dorrit,* involving the loss of Amy's fortune and Arthur's refusal to accept her aid or to consider marriage so long as she is wealthy, suggests a love distinct from sexual nature. The love Amy offers seems to sanctify the secular world, achieving a kind of *agape* that does not depend upon a transcendent faith.

"Will you let me show you [through the gift of her fortune to pay his debts] that I never have forgotten, that I never can forget, your protection of me when this was my home? . . . You will give me the greatest joy I can experience on earth, the joy of knowing that I have been serviceable to you, and that I have paid some little of the great debt of my affection and gratitude. . . . Pray, pray, pray, do not turn from your Little Dor-

rit, now, in your affliction! Pray, pray, pray, I beg you and
implore you with all my grieving heart, my friend—my dear!—
take all I have, and make it a Blessing to me!" (759)

The strained, even foolishly principled motivation for Arthur's refusal becomes meaningful once we realize that his scruples are in themselves a groping toward spiritual understanding, toward an idea of the
need to renounce all hopes for secular salvation, even if Christian hope
is more than his circumstances or the novel can promise. However confused or opaque his reasoning may seem, he expresses a sense of unworthiness true to his deepest understanding of himself and true also
to his role as a spiritual hero.

> "No, darling Little Dorrit. No, my child. I must not hear of
> such a sacrifice. Liberty and hope would be so dear, bought at
> such a price, that I could never support their weight, never
> bear the reproach of possessing them. . . . If, in the by-gone
> days . . . I had discerned a light that I see brightly now when it
> has passed far away and my weak footsteps can never overtake
> it; it I had then known, and told you that I loved and honoured
> you, not as the poor child I used to call you, but as a woman
> whose true hand would raise me high above myself, and make
> me a far happier and better man; if I had so used the opportu-
> nity there is no recalling—as I wish I had, O I wish I had!—and
> if something had kept us apart then, when I was moderately
> thriving, and when you were poor; I might have met your
> noble offer of your fortune, dearest girl, with other words than
> these, and still have blushed to touch it. But, as it is, I must
> never touch it, never!" (759–60)

The impact of Arthur's reply, the very figures of speech he uses,
present Amy as a kind of Beatrice or Una and himself as a ruined man
who has failed to recognize her truth, who has disgraced himself far
beyond any worldly reverses, and who deserves no second chance.

It is clear that narrow ideas of male and female roles do not taint
Arthur's conviction; he would accept Amy's fortune if he had recognized her merit earlier, a free recognition by a free individual, not the
enforced enlightenment of a desperate prisoner. His strongest plea is
that Amy see him as he is, that she expose her idealized image to the
reality of his condition as he perceives it. Arthur's humility is unfeig-
ned, intelligible, and closer to the novel's vision of human existence
than any other character's sturdy sense of self-respect.

Between this moment and the novel's ending, Arthur regains his
spiritual as well as his physical health; and Amy, of course, nurses him
in both recoveries. Like the changes in Pip's attitude toward Magwitch,

Arthur's growth toward acceptance of his unworthiness as a common condition of humanity is enacted symbolically rather than finding expression in the processes of conscious struggle. If the analogy holds between Arthur during this period and Red Crosse in the House of Holiness, Dickens' technique was never more appropriate to his psychological themes. By the time Amy reveals her poverty, Arthur has already gained the confidence in himself and, paradoxically, a sense of the necessity for dependence on others that makes their marriage possible. He has met and relinquished the same last, paradoxical refuge of pride that Red Crosse encounters through Despaire: fixation on his own unworthiness. And as Christian authors like Spenser and Dante have suggested through the swoons, wasting imprisonments, dreams, and visions of their heroes, this process involves the unconscious mind at a depth beyond any credited by most psychoanalytic theorists (Jung and his followers are of course the most important exceptions).

So the loss of Amy's fortune ratifies rather than produces the change in Arthur, just as the novel's avoidance of a personal encounter between Arthur and Blandois after Amy has offered her love and her fortune suggests that the depth of humiliation has been reached, that Arthur is recovering, that Blandois will be destroyed in this process even as he was symbolically created by Arthur's frustration and shame.

Little Dorrit ends in the calm and dignity of a beautifully phrased passage: "They went quietly down into the roaring streets, inseparable and blessed; and as they passed along in sunshine and shade, the noisy and the eager, and the arrogant and the froward and the vain, fretted, and chafed, and made their usual uproar." The frantic thronging streets are quieted by the firm regularity of cadence and the simple diction. Each raucous set is isolated, suspended, and balanced by the conjunctions, so that the repeated "ands" have their own determined anaphoric effect. The final phrase almost casually dismisses all this sound and fury, not in contempt or even in resignation, but with a sense of serenity, order, and happiness in human relationships that will survive in the midst of any social uproar.

The lucid beauty of the passage can make us forget that the novel's dilemma has not been the furor of social unrest or the personal oppression of the arrogant, the froward, and the vain, but rather the solitary wretchedness of cells and spare rooms, the sense of social and spiritual emptiness that even the most virtuous, the quietest, and the humblest have felt. In an important thematic sense, the novel ends in irresolution, with the spiritual crisis suspended in domestic happiness (a type of ending that has even more representative significance for our time than for Dickens').

Amy and Arthur find through their love "a modest life of usefulness and happiness," a fully appropriate and secure center to their personal lives. And they also discover in their marriage the fulfillment of family relationships that they have wholly lacked as children of prison society. This and the care they give their own and Fanny's children needs no more than a brief mention; it is a gathering of others into their love rather than a widening of the domestic circle. Given the secret wretchedness and open dereliction of *Little Dorrit*'s society, so modest an achievement is nevertheless impressive.

Yet Amy and Arthur have not sustained our interest simply in their own personalities or even, like Pip and Esther, as crucial representatives of a general social and psychological condition. They have suffered a process of loss, disorientation, humiliation, and recovery that is a ritual of the spirit. It has its most significant analogues, as I have been suggesting, in the spiritual journeys of characters like the Red Crosse Knight and Dante and, beyond them, in the life of Christ. (Arthur's phrase of utter resignation to Amy, "it is past," even recalls the last words of Christ in the *Gospel of John*.) Amy and Arthur have been forced by their distinct, separate, and yet complementary experiences to recognize the void in human relationship where they most need love and security.

Both the hero and the heroine awaken to their spiritual conditions as they awaken to their love for each other. The power of active creation of relationships seems still more elusive in this novel than in *Bleak House* and *Great Expectations,* so much so that it is perhaps wholly stilled. Esther conceals her love and resigns the power of decision to Jarndyce, but he at least can act decisively and humanely as a foster father who is benevolent if not entirely clear-sighted. The analogous resolution in *Little Dorrit* depends very directly on the death of William Dorrit; there is no suggestion that Amy would have come to Arthur in the Marshalsea against her father's inevitable prohibitions or that she would resist his plans to arrange a suitably rich marriage for her. The novel, by its own terms, ought to bring her to this test, a choice between the illegitimacy of her father's demands and the truth and worth of Arthur's love. It is the kind of choice Red Crosse and Dante face and make repeatedly.

Yet in ordinary human terms—the terms no Dickens novel can leave for long without impairing its primary strengths—Amy's abandonment of her father might mean his death, just as her absence from Arthur might well leave him in the spiritual wasteland he foresees and might even allow his slow illness to languish into death. In these terms, it seems an impossible choice, and one that, in any case, Arthur would not allow her to make, even without the overwhelming sense of worthlessness, self-inflicted ruin, and need for absolute renunciation with which he greets her return to the Marshalsea. He awaits the changes of the plot as much as she does; and both choose at the novel's end a way of ignorance or, at least, severely limited awareness. Arthur simply, without a thought, resigns all interest in his family's secrets; Amy decides to burn the only record of the Clennam history.

Dickens holds to the mimetic center that Spenser and Dante gradually push to the circumference of the *Faerie Queene,* Book I, and the *Divine Comedy,* as they stress the emerging Christian order; the fantastic nature of these works itself progressively dissociates the heroes from ordinary social reality. Amy and Arthur are not saints or even spiritual questers in a strict sense. They suffer extraordinary spiritual trials with ordinary resources in an ordinary social world; and they must make that complex, imperfect accommodation with a muddled but total reality that Red Crosse and Dante can avoid simply through the relatively "pure" romance medium they inhabit. As Alexander Welsh, the most perceptive commentator on Christian elements in Dickens, has noted: "The principle of grace is wishfully operative in the fiction yet not formally admitted; Christianity apparently contributes more to the complexity of social questions than it does to their solution."[14] Renunciation and retreat from full awareness are too central to *Little Dorrit*'s resolutions for even the modest domestic happiness promised Amy and Arthur to be as perfect as it seems. Renunciation in the traditional Christian myth clears away the illusory and the corrupt so that divine power can transfigure the ordinary world. Renunciation in *Little Dorrit,* where the presence or even the promise of divine power is not a reality for characters or narrator, leaves a near void. It can easily seem a more despairing response to the world than repression—an abandonment or loss of those desires that repression at least keeps alive and often intensifies.

Similarly, it may be true that "the novel distrusts justifications and holds up the non-explaining Amy Dorrit as a reproof to all its other characters";[15] but Amy's acceptance and finally her enforcement of ignorance thwart the struggle for spiritual certainty as much as the less admirable motives of the selfish characters. Again the novel gestures, almost in despair, toward a need that seems frustrated by the very nature of modern existence. The good characters in Dickens sometimes appear, in Welsh's phrase, as sojourners who "dwell in the earthly city without being of it," but Amy and Arthur are sojourners with no final destination.[16]

Esther and Pip finally must confront the knowledge of their origins—more significant even in psychological than in social terms—that they have repressed and fled. This confrontation is the true climax of each career, whichever ending of *Great Expectations* is retained and however dubious the domestic resolution in *Bleak House;* the effects are immediate and profound, enacted in a symbolically patterned plot but also experienced in the evolving, newly resolute consciousness of each character. Through her disfigurement and her awareness of the social implications of her illegitimacy, Esther accepts for the first time the legitimacy of her own individuality. Pip more directly and fully acknowledges his own complicity in the community of aggression, terror, and guilt that is the inescapable social condition in *Great Expectations,* but also acknowledges his loving and generous nature.

Amy and Arthur endure no such encounter and reach no such enlightenment. Their experience is solitary; it acts upon them far more than it is willed or even comprehended. Still, they recognize something of their impotence; their failure to salvage anything from the ruins of their families; their need for each other; and even, uncertainly, their need to avoid the precarious energies of sexuality in order to fulfill more basic desires for security, self-respect, acceptance, understanding, and compassion. After the novel's searching exposure of a spiritual need that is partly cause, partly consequence of the failure of the largest and smallest social pretensions, their marriage seems a necessary and, in many ways, an admirable accommodation. The novel has exposed a spiritual desolation so vast and deep that the very worth of secular existence has been questioned.

The reference in the closing lines to the "Marshalsea and all its blighted fruits" ought to contrast with the happy marriage and the promised "modest life of usefulness and happiness." The landscape and season that close the novel seem to make just this contrast. The loss of spring and summer are tacitly accepted but are redeemed by the harvest of a "healthy autumn".

> On a healthy autumn day, the Marshalsea prisoner, weak but otherwise restored, sat listening to a voice that read to him. On a healthy autumn day; when the golden fields had been reaped and ploughed again, when the summer fruits had ripened and waned, when the green perspectives of hops had been laid low by the busy pickers, when the apples clustering in the orchards were russet, and the berries of the mountain ash were crimson among the yellowing foliage. . . . From the seashore the ocean was no longer to be seen lying asleep in the heat, but its thousand sparkling eyes were open, and its whole breadth was in joyful animation, from the cool sand on the beach to the little sails on the horizon, drifting away like autumn-tinted leaves that had drifted from the trees. (815)

The sea's "joyful animation" expresses the reviving, creative force that could not penetrate the prison of the Marseilles harbor in the opening chapter of the novel, the sea whose promise from the novel's initial perspective could not even be contemplated. Yet the novel has only inched forward in its symbolic time, from August into autumn. Amy and Arthur begin their marriage and in one sense (in the phrase Arthur uses prematurely at the novel's opening) "begin life anew" after summer has past. They leave the blighted fruit of the Marshalsea behind them, but they confront the certainty of winter with no prospect of regeneration, as least none that can touch the larger society that throngs the streets of London. The idyll of a "healthy autumn day," conspicuously barren of even a solitary human figure, conspicuously alien to the streets that environ Arthur and Amy, may thus finally express a consummation in nature unattainable by any human grouping larger than the family—and so rare even there that the novel celebrates its one happy marriage as if it were a precious dying sacrament.

E. Pearlman

INVERSION IN *GREAT EXPECTATIONS*

WHEN DICKENS began work on *Great Expectations* early in 1861 he was aware that the new novel would cover much the same territory that had been traversed a dozen years earlier in *David Copperfield:* "The book will be written in the first person throughout [he wrote to Forster], and during these first three weekly numbers you will find the hero to be a boy-child, like David. . . . To be quite sure I had fallen into no unconscious repetitions, I read *David Cooperfield* again the other day, and was affected by it to a degree you would hardly believe."[1] *Great Expectations* was from its inception rooted in the special circumstances Dickens had celebrated in his earlier autobiographical novel. In *David Copperfield,* Dickens drew directly on personal experience; in *Great Expectations,* he returned to the same source, but those experiences were now screened by advancing time, and also by the fact that they had once before appeared in fictional form. It is not surprising that, though different, the two works are similar in form, plot, character and theme.

Yet Dickens apparently convinced himself that *Great Expectations* would contain no "unconscious repetition" of the earlier novel. Forster, from whose biography this evidence is drawn, agreed with Dickens that the novels were dissimilar. It was mere coincidence, he said, that both works began in graveyards. Neither Dickens nor Forster thought it worth mentioning that the heroes of both novels were abused orphans who came from the provinces to make good in London; that each struggles for emotional and moral maturity, eventually to find true education in the death of a loved one and in foreign travel; that each is placed in a situation where he must choose between two women, one loved with real passion and one admired as a sister. Neither Dickens nor Forster took notice of the coincidental prominence in each novel of the law and lawyers, prisons and prisoners, defective education, Australia, or even of the obvious device of allowing each hero to be attended by a simple, loyal, and undervalued companion (i.e., Traddles and Pocket).

There are in actual fact numerous repetitions of the one novel in the other, and when Dickens asserted the contrary he must have been thinking very narrowly—of specific incidents, or places, or characters' names. But wider definition of the term "unconscious" forces us to a different conclusion. If the unconscious is the layer of experience which lies beneath the skin of rationality, then all Dickens' novels are, for better or worse, unconsciously repetitive. They are recapitulations and transformations of personal experience. The basic stuff may be exploited in many ways—symbolized, condensed, split, reconstituted; what is comic in one novel may surface as tragic in another. But for a writer in whom the autobiographical impulse is so strong and the sources of fiction so personal, all writing is to some extent "unconscious repetition." This is not to minimize Dickens' achievement. It is the reader's great delight to watch the combination and permutation of a limited stock of root notions into a variety that does not wither. Taken in this sense, *Great Expectations,* so closely allied to *David Copperfield,* must in some measure recapitulate it. I take this to be an assumption, not the argument, of this essay. It is not my contention that *Great Expectations* repeats *David Copperfield,* but rather that it repeats it in a very specific way. In the later novel, I feel, the basic material of the earlier work has been inverted; in order to produce *Great Expectations* Dickens has stood the structure of *David Copperfield* on its head.

To demonstrate this we begin with the core of the fable. Both novels center on the class basis of Victorian society. Like many of Dickens' works, these two are stories in which the pain of social distinctions sharpens when a character crosses the line, passes from gentle to proletarian status, or from proletarian to gentle. This transformation, an echo of Dickens' own adolescent wound, is the key to the relationship between the two novels. In *David Copperfield,* the hero is a gentleman's son who through mischance undergoes a period of purgatory in which, as Uriah Heep points out with excessive venom, he becomes "the very scum of society." *Great Expectations* simply inverts this formula. Pip is born a member of the proletariat and is bound to a life at the forge. Utterly by accident he is transformed into a gentleman. Just as *David Copperfield* explores, in its most affecting chapters, the miseries of sudden descent into the working class, so *Great Expectations* explores the exact opposite: the moral perils of a miraculous rise in social status. In this perspective David and Pip are opposed and inverted heroes. The pattern of inversion that governs the relation between the novels proceeds from this engendering circumstance.[2]

It follows, not with rational but with unconscious logic, that one of the many ways Pip and David contrast is in the direction of their moral development. A conventional Romantic child, David moves from innocence to experience; Pip, on the other hand, starts life with a full knowledge of depravity and a conviction of sin, and is obsessed with his own guilt. Because he is alive and his father and his mother and his brothers "Alexander, Bartholomew, Abraham, Tobias and Roger" are dead, he suffers from that well-documented psychological complaint, the guilt of the survivor. And because it has been drummed into him throughout childhood that he has been an insupportable burden to Mrs. Joe, he feels guilt for being alive[3]—" 'Trouble?' echoed my sister, 'trouble?' And then entered on a fearful catalogue of all the illnesses I had been guilty of, and all the acts of sleeplessness I had committed, and all the high places I had tumbled from, and all the low places I had tumbled into, and all the injuries I had done myself, and all the times she had wished me in my grave" (24). Only toward the close of the novel does Pip abandon the conviction of his own guilt and begin to strive for a more balanced mental state. On the other hand David Copperfield, whose earliest days were entirely opposite—he is the pampered only child of a doting mother—seems to be shielded from a knowledge of guilt and sin. Such words do not function in his moral vocabulary. Though he introduces Steerforth into the Peggotty home, David is utterly immune from a feeling of responsibility for Em'ly's fall. David is also the innocent go-between in Murdstone's courtship of his mother, and the initiator of Heep's scheme to procure for himself a share of Mr. Wickfield's law practice. Though these actions, and others, issue disastrously, they fail to touch David's conscience. Only at the end of the novel does he begin to acquire a sense that his actions have moral consequences. For the most part he is, as Littimer calls him, "Young Innocence" (463), while Pip, always battered by his "oppressed conscience" (14), is young guilt.

Setting social and moral questions to one side, there are three principal areas in the construction of the novels where *Great Expectations* inverts the pattern of *David Copperfield*. The first is that Pip's parents—Joe Gargery and Mrs. Joe—are an ingenious transformation of Clara Copperfield and Edward Murdstone; the second, that the character of Miss Havisham is formed by the inversion of a number of the peculiarities of Betsey Trotwood. The third, and most complex, follows from the fact that both Pip and David are faced with similar alternatives in the choice of a spouse. Dora and Agnes, Biddy and Estella, represent equivalent and opposed versions of a single psychological pattern.

The first topic, then, is the inversion of parentage. David Copperfield is a posthumous child; his young, fair, and childishly silly mother takes as a second husband a dark, stern, and sadistic religious fanatic. Clara Copperfield succumbs a year or so after the marriage to the illnesses consequent on childbirth, a martyr (in more ways than one) to

Murdstone's "miscalled firmness" (53). An orphan, David is virtually abandoned by his stepfather to make his own way in the world. Pip, also an orphan, is raised by his sister, the tyrannical and oppressive Mrs. Joe, and gentle, childlike Joe Gargery, the blacksmith. In each family there is one "good" parent—Clara or Joe—who is protective, soft and simple, and one "bad" parent—Murdstone or Mrs. Joe—who is violent, stingy, and brutal. That the sexes are reversed is enough to satisfy Dickens that there has been no unconscious repetition. But Mrs. Joe is uncannily similar to Edward Murdstone, so alike, in fact, that it seems she is thought of, deep in Dickens' imagination, as if she were a man. Is it not possible to conceive of Mrs. Joe, Pip's "mother," as if she were a reincarnation of the psychic image of Edward Murdstone, David's father?

For Mrs. Joe, the "all-powerful sister" (12), is first of all barren of any trace of femininity. As Dickens describes her she is "tall and bony . . . with black hair and eyes" (features which recall Murdstone's "beautiful black hair" [18] and "shallow black eye" [22]): "She . . . almost always wore a coarse apron, fastened over her figure behind with two loops, and having a square impregnable bib in front, that was stuck full of pins and needles" (6). Next to Lady Macbeth's, this is literature's least nurturing bosom. Mrs. Joe (her only slightly less masculine given name is rarely used) is, of course, infertile. The props which define her are distinctly phallic. One is the knife with which she hews slices from the loaf of bread. Another is her weapon, the "tickler," a "wax-ended piece of cane" (7), which is something like the "lithe and limber" (56) cane with which Murdstone beats David. Nor does she allow Joe his implement. When outraged by her husband's meekness, she would "dive at him, take the poker out of his hands, shake him, and put it away" (90). Her tyranny is inexplicable, but is the defining characteristic of the Gargery marriage. Mrs. Joe dominates her husband exactly as Murdstone dominates his wife. She "would be everybody's master" (106), says Orlick, rightly. Her masculinity has its effect on Joe, who finds it best to accede to the fact, as he observes to Pip, that "your sister is given to government . . . of you and myself." This being the case, Joe, like a dependent colonial, decides that it would be injudicious for him to learn how to read and write. Mrs. Joe, says the suffering blacksmith, "would not be over partial to my being a scholar, for fear as I might rise. Like a sort of rebel, don't you see." Here we may wonder whether Dickens was consciously aware of the sexual sense of words like "rise" and "rebel," but certainly he had read enough of Shakespeare and the other dramatists to know how frequently these words referred to tumescence. In any case, Joe pursues equivocation. A number of words—"over," "back-falls," "drop-down," "Ram," "Buster"—suggest that Mrs. Joe has arrogated masculine sexuality to her-

self. " 'Stay a bit. I know what you're a-going to say, Pip; stay a bit! I
don't deny that your sister comes the Mo-gul over us, now and again. I
don't deny that she do throw us back-falls, and that she do drop down
upon us heavy. At such times as when your sister is on the Ram-page,
Pip,' Joe sank his voice to a whisper and glanced at the door, 'candour
compels fur to admit that she is a Buster' " (44). It is almost as if Joe
were afraid of being sexually abused.

Mrs. Joe's masculinity and her predilection toward violence are her
defining characteristics. In some part of Dickens' imagination, she is a
man, even though one who is costumed as a woman. She is an example
of the bad father. It is therefore possible to see her relation with Pip as
still another variation on the obsessive Dickensian theme of the evil father avenged by the son.

This is also a theme of the earlier novel. Though David Copperfield never quite manages to revenge himself upon Murdstone, Dickens
the novelist inflicts death or disaster on a host of father surrogates: Mr.
Spenlow dies suddenly and conveniently after setting himself against
his daughter's marriage to the hero; Mr. Micawber is frequently discovered making motions at his throat with a razor; Wickfield is reduced to
alcoholic impotence, Dr. Strong to impotence per se. David's attack on
Murdstone himself comes when he savagely bites the hand that whips
him. It is an impotent attack, though rich in symbolic content. These
fits and starts of revenge finally come to fruition in *Great Expectations*
when the bad father—Mrs. Joe—is struck down and maimed. Is it only
because Dickens has disguised, even from himself, the basic Oedipal
problem that he can put aside delicacy and allow the "father" to be so
effectively brutalized?

Neither David nor Pip is actually a murderer. But when Orlick
"drops down" on Mrs. Joe with a "heavy weapon," it is Pip who feels
the taint of criminality[4]—"I was at first disposed to believe that *I* must
have had some hand in the attack upon my sister, or at all events that
as her near relation . . . I was a more legitimate object of suspicion
than any one else" (113). This apparently irrational feeling can be
explained by the notion that we feel guilt not only for what we do, but
for what we want to do. Pip wants Mrs. Joe dead because she has made
his life miserable. With her out of the way, moreover, he can expect to
enjoy the complete attention of Joe himself, who is, symbolically at
least, his "real" mother. "You'll drive *me* to the churchyard betwixt you,
one of these days," Mrs. Joe had said proleptically, "and oh, a pr-r-
recious pair you'd be without me!" (8). And a precious pair they come
to be, enjoying an idyllic relationship after the intrusive sister is ren-
dered dumb. It has been a fierce struggle between Mrs. Joe and Pip for
possession of the "mother"—just the sort, though with inverted outcome, acted out in the rivalry of Murdstone and David for the attention
of Clara.

If it is at least plausible that in the deeper level of Dickens' imagination, Mrs. Joe exists as a man—phallic, aggressive, and dominating
then it follows that Joe himself can be thought of, as I suggested above,
as a woman.[5] The description of him, setting aside denotative words
like "man" and "fellow," suggests a Victorian feminine ideal. Joe is a
"mild, good-natured, sweet-tempered, easy-going foolish, dear fellow,
. . . a fair man, with curls of flaxen hair on each side of his smooth
face" (6). He echoes David's manner not only in passivity and dependence but in physical form. He is loving, tolerant, childish. David's
mother is "a very Baby" (5); Joe a "larger species of child."

The parallel relationship causes Dickens to pluck similar rhetorical
strings. When David returns to Blunderstone from Creakle's school, he
enjoys a last private moment with his mother: "I crept close to my
mother's side, according to my old custom, broken now a long time,
and sat . . . with my little red cheek on her shoulder, and once more
felt her beautiful hair drooping over me—*like an angel's wing* as I used
to think, I recollect—and was very happy indeed" (112, emphasis
mine). To this we can compare an intimate moment between Pip and
Joe, just as the bond between them will be broken by Magwitch's reap-
pearance: "Joe laid his hand upon my shoulder with *the touch of a
woman.* . . . O dear good faithful tender Joe, I feel the loving tremble
of your hand upon my arm, as solemnly this day as if it had been the
rustle of *an angel's wing!*" (133, emphasis mine). Is there no "unconscious repetition" here? Does not Joe evoke the memory of the young,
fair, and blonde mother? And isn't the failure of Dickens' prose—the
sentimentality, the heaping of colorless adjectives ("dear good faithful
tender")—a consequence of this, for the apotheosis of womanhood is
one of the subjects which regularly causes Dickens' pen to grow limp.

Moreoever, Joe's femininity does not stand without psychological
justification. For here Dickens is faced with a problem in the construction of the novel: how can he make genuine and credible Joe's failure
to protect Pip from Mrs. Joe's onslaughts and at the same time continue to promote him as the novel's most emulable character? Failure
here would make Joe either unbelievable or unsympathetic. Dickens'
solution is to provide the blacksmith with a coherent psychological
background. This he does brilliantly; and in doing so gives us an explanation which is consistent with the essential femininity of Joe's nature.

Joe's father was a violent drunkard who regularly abused and beat
his wife. Because he has seen one woman suffer, Joe cannot bear to
allow another to be mistreated. Rather than try to assert himself against
Mrs. Joe, he says, "I'm dead afeerd of going wrong in the way of not
doing what's right by a woman, and I'd fur rather of the two go wrong
the t'other way, and be a little ill-conwenienced myself" (45). This
makes a great deal of sense, but is not thoroughly satisfying. What Joe
fails to say, but leaves us to infer for ourselves, is that the only way he

has learned to deal with a mate is on the model of tyrant and victim. And since he identifies not with his father, but with his mother (or, stated more accurately, Dickens has chosen to identify him as a woman, not as a man), Joe enacts the role of the long-suffering wife to Mrs. Joe's brutal husband. The inverted relationship has something in it to satisfy both partners.[6]

Concomitant with this is Joe's desire to "mother" Pip. Dickens makes it clear that Joe was not overwhelmed with passion when he pursued the former Georgiana Pirrip, but was always attracted to the orphaned younger brother. Joe's mother, we are told, barely outlived her husband, who was carried off in a "purple leptic fit." Joe, newly on his own, heard tell of another orphan: "When I got acquainted with your sister, it were the talk how she was bringing you up by hand. Very kind of her too, all the folks said, and I said, along with all the folks. . . . When I offered to your sister to keep company . . . I said to her, "And bring the poor little child. God bless the poor little child. . . . There's room for *him* at the forge!" (43–44). By marrying Mrs. Joe, he was able to adopt Pip, to whom he then could stand as a mother. The psychological utility of this relationship becomes clear after Magwitch (another "father") dies in prison. Pip falls ill, and it is Joe who appears, a ministering angel, to nurse him back to health. Pip is born again to his symbolic and therefore real mother. "I was like a child in his hands . . . Joe wrapped me up, took me in his arms, carried me down to [the coach], and put me in, as if I were still the small helpless creature to whom he had so abundantly given of the wealth of his great nature" (442). At last Pip enjoys what he has missed: a happy childhood, a loving mother. This event dramatically completes the pattern of inversion in *Great Expectations*. In *David Copperfield,* David has a good mother, who dies, and a bad father, from whom he fails to free himself; in the later novel, Pip has a bad father (Mrs. Joe), who dies, and a good mother, whom only in later life is he able to embrace.

There is one further complication. The figure of Murdstone is echoed in *Great Expectations* not only in Mrs. Joe, but also in Magwitch, who announces, unequivocally, "Look'ee here Pip. I'm your second father. You're my son" (304). Like Murdstone, Magwitch is a father by adoption. Is it mere coincidence that both are introduced to their stepchildren as if they have arisen from the dead? In *David Copperfield,* when David first meets Murdstone, "something . . . connected with the grave in the churchyard, and the raising of the dead, seemed to strike me like an unwholesome wind" (42). In *Great Expectations,* the motif is made even more explicit, for when Pip first encounters the convict it is as though "a man [had] started up from among the graves" (1–2). Later, "it is as if he were [a hanged] pirate come to life, and come down" (5) from the gibbet. It is difficult to be sure why Dickens touched on this topic, but it does seem unconsciously repetitive. This is merely a curious detail, but it leads to the larger pattern of inversion. Magwitch's role is to provide the wealth that enables Pip to transform himself into Mr. Pip, while Murdstone delivers David over to the lower class. We have two substitute fathers who arise from the dead and who perform mirrored but reversed actions in terms of the central myth of the story.

We can now see that in composing Pip's family Dickens drew on the experience of *David Copperfield,* and inverted it, decomposing Murdstone into Magwitch and Mrs. Joe, and transforming Clara Copperfield into Joe Gargery. The pattern of inversion that controls this relationship also explains other aspects of the novel including the transformation of Betsey Trotwood into Miss Havisham, to which we now turn our attention.

Though very different, the two women play quite similar roles. Betsey Trotwood rescues David when he has fallen into the proletariat; she is the "good fairy" who magically transforms the toad into a prince. Miss Havisham, on the other hand, pretends to rescue Pip, but deceives him. She is not the good fairy, but, as Pip himself puts it, "the Witch of the place": " 'This is a gay figure, Pip,' said she, making her crutch stick play round me, as if she, the fairy godmother who had changed me, were bestowing the finishing gift" (149). Both women are composed with an eye on the world of the fairy, but one is a black magician, and the other a white. The two women are also opposite in the details with which Dickens marks the reality of his characters. Aunt Betsey is "uncommonly neat" (536) and tidy; no donkeys are allowed to litter her "small square gravelled court" (190). Miss Havisham is compulsively dirty; her garden is a "rank ruin of cabbage stalks" (74), her filth, spiders, and beetles the emblems of her decay. Similarly, Betsey is extremely orderly in her behavior. Her meals are rituals; her toast is cut into uniform strips. Miss Havisham, perfectly disordered, "wanders around at night, eating such foods as she lays her hands on." Betsey is surrounded by dependents (Mr. Dick, David) to whom she is generous and supportive; Miss Havisham is cruel and stingy to the various empty Pockets who solicit her attention and money. Betsey suppresses all emotion and will not admit she has been wronged; Miss Havisham wallows in self-pity. Betsey is fearful of fire; when she comes to stay in London, "she made a great point of being so near the river, in case of conflagration" (501); one night she wakes up, having "inferred from a particular light in the sky that Westminster Abbey was on fire" (505–6). Her pyrophobia is repeated in *Great Expectations* when (unconscious repetition?) Miss Havisham burns to death. Fear of fire introduced as mere eccentricity in one novel is resolved in the other.

Beyond these similarities lie even deeper resemblances. Both Betsey Trotwood and Miss Havisham have been betrayed by their lovers. Betsey's husband is the most shadowy figure in the novel. He was younger than Betsey, he was violent and unfaithful, and he abandoned her to go to India. He has since returned to England, and, impoverished and alcoholic, lived off Betsey's charity. Toward the end of the novel we discover that he has died; David accompanies his aunt to the funeral. Love's wound, we are led to infer, justifies all Betsey's eccentricities. But the words that Betsey Trotwood speaks to her husband could just as appropriately be uttered by Miss Havisham to the unfaithful Compeyson. " 'You stripped me of the greater part of all I ever had. . . . You closed my heart against the whole world, years and years. You treated me falsely, ungratefully, and cruelly' " (688).

Betsey's affectation of indifference to the world masks a kindly heart; in *Great Expectations* a similar situation leads to acute psychotic withdrawal. Abandoned by her perjured lover, Miss Havisham takes to her room, freezes her emotions, and retires from engagement with life. The comedy of *David Copperfield* takes a terrible form in *Great Expectations*.

We also remember that Betsey Trotwood's maid, Janet, is "one of a series of protegées. . . . taken into her service expressly to educate in renouncement of mankind, and who had generally completed their abjuration by marrying the baker" (194). No one expects Janet to remain celibate (she in fact marries a tavernkeeper.) But here is the germ of the story that is treated with overtones of tragedy and madness in *Great Expectations,* where Estella is trained from childhood to wreak revenge on mankind. Misandry is now taken seriously; Estella, emotionally crippled, marries the lumpish Drummle only to infuriate more likely suitors (including Pip). And in *David Copperfield,* Betsey had come to Blunderstone to preside over the birth of Betsey Trotwood Copperfield, the girl with whose emotions there would be no trifling. This unborn Betsey, for whom David substitutes, was "forever in the land of dreams and shadows" (12). But she also remained in the dream and shadow of Dickens' imagination to reappear a dozen years later as Estella. The Betsey Trotwood Copperfield who was not born in one book is born again in the other. In a variety of ways, as witch, villain, purveyor of false hopes, manipulator of hatred and revenge, Miss Havisham is the inverted dark side of Betsey Trotwood.

In addition to basic family structure and the theme of the fairy godmother, there is still a third area in which the pattern of inversion manifests itself, and that is in the relation of the hero to the women whom he courts. This is of special interest in *Great Expectations,* because Dickens faltered when he had to decide whether or not to let Pip marry Estella. There are, as everyone knows, two separate endings for the novel. In the one, Pip and Estella do not marry; in the other, though the resolution is oblique, the suggestion is made that there will be "no further parting." The resolution poses a complicated moral problem, for Pip's relation with Estella is an index of the development of the sensitivity that he so conspicuously lacks in the early part of the novel. It is also a complicated psychological problem, for Pip's continued interest in a woman who humiliates him and in whose presence he "never had one hour's happiness" (287) suggests either irrational devotion or a patent masochism (perhaps rooted in his identification with the mistreated Joe). But in the present context, the ending is important because it serves as a successor and alternative to the vary same problems as they are resolved simply and naively in *David Copperfield*.

In each novel the hero must choose between sex and home, that is, between a woman whom he loves with overpowering passion, and another woman, a surrogate sister, who represents good sense, duty, obligation, motherhood, religion. That these two aspects of womanhood are separate and exclusive is an assumption of *David Copperfield* that is modified only slightly in *Great Expectations*. In *David Copperfield*, the alternative choices are Dora Spenlow, attractive but useless, and Agnes Wickfield, admirable and useful. This is a bit simplified, for the incubus of sexual attraction is itself split into two figures (who stand for the two classes around which the novel is structured). Dora is gentle, but little Em'ly, to whom David is also attracted, is proletarian. The situation (with David at the crossroads) can be schematized thus:

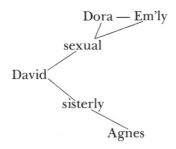

Dickens accepts these alternative stereotypes, but he does not value them equally. It is always made clear that the way of sexuality leads either to gross irresponsibility and disaster (as in the case of Dora, whose postparturient death is an echo of Clara's) or to seduction and abandonment, as in the case of Em'ly (and potentially to prostitution as modeled by Martha Endell). When David falls madly in love with Em'ly, he is alert enough to class differences to know that a gentleman's son cannot pursue a fisherman's niece without disgrace. Later he turns his attention to Dora, and the marriage, though awash in sex, is a perfect failure. After Dora dies David is sufficiently mature to explore the alternative stereotype, and therefore marries Agnes Wickfield, the "sister of [his] boyhood" (519), who is all stained-glass window and upraised finger, an ideal protector and icon. But the ending of the novel is unsatisfactory; Agnes is perfect and spiritual, but semidivine and therefore disembodied. David loves her without passion and marries her to be saved from despair. Agnes is much too obviously his sister; the incest taboo anesthetizes sensuality. The moral, laid out with great but inexplicit power, is that David has wrongly indulged his passion with Dora, and now, chastened, must learn to accept propriety. Dickens, ostensibly the propagandist for feeling and emotion, comes down at last on the side of duty, obligation, and constraint.

The clarity of these opposed stereotypes in *David Copperfield* is muddied in *Great Expectations*. If we were to compare Pip's choices with David's, the new diagram would look like this:

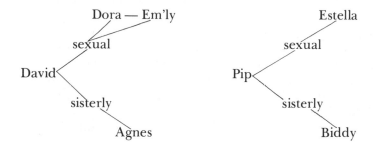

Filling the slot allowed for Agnes is Biddy. Both Agnes and Biddy are women of competence, intelligence, and domestic virtue; both are surrogate sisters; both love the hero so devotedly that they are able to maintain their affection in the teeth of obtuse indifference to their attractions. But the pattern of inversion is again made clear when Biddy does not marry Pip as Agnes marries David. Such a marriage is flirted with, of course. When Pip recovers from his illness, he intends to return to his marsh village and do penance for mistreating his friends by marrying Biddy, only to discover that she has already married Joe. Why is Agnes suitable for marriage to the hero and Biddy so unsuitable? Like Agnes in so many respects, Biddy is unlike her in that she is uncompromisingly proletarian. Agnes is ideal and gentle; Biddy, equally ideal, springs from the class out of which Pip has been translated. So that while there is a good deal of obvious snobbery in Pip's willingness to marry Biddy as an act of contrition, the more palpable snobbery is Dickens' unwillingness to allow his hero to sacrifice himself on that particular altar. And here again, there is a disparity between ideology and implicit moral. Dickens masquerades as the enemy of class bias and social snobbery, but the novel itself speaks counter to that profession. By transforming the gentle Agnes into the proletarian Biddy, and by forestalling the marriage, Dickens has called his own bluff; moreover, he has prevented the novel from coming to any simple conclusion.

Dickens' reasons for keeping Pip and Biddy separate are clear; nothing is clear about Estella. Though Pip is certainly attracted to her sexually, the legitimacy of that attraction is always in doubt. Why is this so? As the diagram shows, Estella combines in her own aspect the two women David desires: Dora and Em'ly. It is Dora for whom David labors through the Forest of Difficulty after the collapse of Aunt Betsey's affairs. He must by his own efforts make himself worthy of Dora's social position. Estella is the star for Pip's bark, the inspirer of his desire to rise. She is Pip's motive exactly as Dora is David's. Little Em'ly, of course, is of no social position whatsoever, and instead of returning David's admiration, runs off with Steerforth. Estella also ignores the hero and prefers a rival, but though she is raised and educated by Miss Havisham, sent to France to be polished and to Richmond to fascinate the Bentley Drummles of the world, she is not really of the class in which she moves. Like Pip and like Em'ly, her origins are lowly, very lowly in fact: she is the daughter of a convict and a gypsy murderess. So that when Dickens came to the end of the story and had to decide the ultimate fate of Pip and Estella, he boggled. Faced with the proletarian Biddy the choice was easy. But would Pip really be free of the class he has forsaken if he married Estella? Would he rise or fall by marrying her? If Estella were one class or the other, she could be either shunned, or embraced. But she is neither, and the ending of the novel is consequently left unresolved.

We must take note of a further difficulty in sorting out questions of sex and love. Pip loves Estella, who is a successor to Dora and Em'ly, with more than brotherly passion, yet he knows her from childhood and, in the person of Miss Havisham, shares with her a surrogate mother. Pip and Estella are tangentially brother and sister. Less remotely, they share a father, for Estella is the natural daughter of Magwitch, Pip's "second father." This is a remarkable concidence, and it is remarkable how little is made of it. The relationship between Pip and Estella is one of the most elaborately disguised of Dickens' many instances of bother-sister incest. But the more disguised, the more erotic. Just as Estella is neither of Pip's class, nor not of it, so she is neither of Pip's "family," nor not of it. It is no wonder that Dickens was unable to bring a novel with such perplexing ambiguity of class and sex to a conclusion. Would marriage to Estella affirm or deny the legitimacy of the class system, the purity of mother and sister, the sanctity of marriage based on a traditional social order? It is impossible to say, since Estella cuts across psychological, social, and sexual stereotypes. Nevertheless, it is clear that either ending of *Great Expectations* is superior to the conventional moralizing that ends *David Copperfield*. For when Dickens inverted *David Copperfield* to produce his new novel he did not borrow from it as from a source; he invaded as a monarch and transformed a rich tale into one still richer and more abundant.

Melanie Young

DISTORTED EXPECTATIONS

Pip and The Problems of Language

> Whether I shall turn out to be the hero of my own life, or whether that station will be held by anybody else, these pages must show. —*David Copperfield*, i, 1 [1]

> My father's family name being Pirrip, and my christian name Philip, my infant tongue could make of both names nothing longer or more explicit than Pip. So, I called myself Pip, and came to be called Pip.— *Great Expectations*, i, 169 [2]

TEN YEARS after he wrote *David Copperfield,* Dickens reread that work in order to avoid unconscious repetition in his next Bildungsroman, *Great Expectations.* [3] *Great Expectations* differs from *David Copperfield* not only in the narrator's ironic tone and sharper characterization, but also in his attitude towards language. A comparison of the beginnings of both novels reveals attitudes that are almost antithetical. The opening of *David Copperfield* implies the positive value of language: it will reveal the truth (whether or not he is the hero of his life) and thus will lead to self-knowledge. But in the first two sentences of *Great Expectations* the relation of language to objective truth is more questionable, for the narrator shows his younger self altering words according to his subjective demands. By changing "Philip Pirrip" to "Pip," the protagonist exhibits a tendency in language to oversimplify or distort the truth. Such differences in perspective are thematically borne out in the two novels. The narrator of *David Copperfield* establishes a positive relation among language, survival, and growth: words function as a "caul" that prevents his drowning in experience, words provide him with a vocation and identity as writer, and the refinement of language parallels the education of his sensibilities. *Great Expectations,* however, exhibits an ironic narrator's distrust of language in its effect upon personal growth: words frequently operate as a deception or misconstruction which prevents the balanced perception of self and external reality. Pip's acquisi-

tion and refinement of language does not reflect a corresponding refinement of sensibility but a fall from grace; as he masters the alphabet,
ambition for wealth and status masters him, and his innocent rapport
with Joe is gradually replaced with casual condescension.[4] Rather than
promoting communication and sympathy, language in *Great Expectations* often creates distances and barriers between men by sorting them
into artificial classes and categories. And while language is not the
primary cause of Pip's moral decline, it contributes to his downfall, particularly as it lends itself to his snobbery and self-deception. Before his
perceptions adequately reflect reality, Pip must overcome three linguistic difficulties: the dissociation of sensibility, linguistic patterns of distortion, and problems in semantics.

The first problem Pip faces is what T. S. Eliot called the "dissociation of sensibility." This separation of feeling and thought operates in
the novel as a dichotomy whose poles center in Joe and Jaggers. Joe,
who serves the moral touchstone of the novel, speaks what I shall call
the "language of the heart or feeling," which is predominantly awkward, vague, ungrammatical, full of mispronunciations, and quite
frequently nonverbal—communicated through touch, look, or gesture.
Jaggers, at the center of a dehumanizing system, uses the "language of
thought": his words reflect the processes of empirical analysis and thus
are precise, impersonal, and morally neutral. Symbolically Joe and Jaggers present the dilemma of whether feeling can ever be adequately
and accurately expressed through language. As Pip passes literally and
psychologically from Joe to his new guardian Jaggers, the problem he
inherits with this transfer is the dissociation of sensibility.

Two modes of language and vision correspond to Pip's second
problem, the misinterpretation of himself and his surroundings
through inadequate and deceptive linguistic patterns. The two patterns
or modes, which function as ironic indices to Pip's distortions, are "the
language of fairy tale and romance" (associated with Miss Havisham
and Estella), and "the language of law" (associated with Jaggers). And
while Pip must learn to experience reality without the intervention of
such misleading systems of language and vision, each mode contains
some truth or helps correct an imbalance in Pip's perceptions.

Pip's third difficulty is semantic: he must learn the meanings of
certain key words, such as "common," "gentleman," "love," and "nature." He also must learn to discriminate objective meaning from the
private significance assigned to words by various individuals. His initiation into semantics becomes an initiation into the complexities of language and reality.

— 2 —

But poetry costs money, cut it how you will.—Joe, vii, 243

The first eleven chapters establish a parallel between ambition and language, linking Pip's acquisition of language with his fall from innocence and grace represented by his rapport with Joe. His first deep feelings of guilt and separation from Joe stem from a misuse of language: Pip's lie about meeting with the convict (he said he went to the Carols) becomes a thorn in his conscience because he cannot bring himself to tell Joe the truth. "The fear of losing Joe's confidence" (vi, 241) silences him, but ironically his *not* telling Joe creates the first breach of confidence and fellowship. As further irony the event motivating his lie (stealing for the convict) leads to the inheritance of wealth and expectations which truly separates him from Joe and the forge.

Another early incident relates the "fall" into language to the fall from grace: Pip's first letter to Joe. This letter has a double significance: it points backward to their bond of fellowship and forward to their coming separation. "woT LARX" (vii, 242) epitomizes their old rapport, while Pip's discovery that Joe cannot read or write looks forward to his later wish that "Joe had been rather more genteelly brought up" so that he would not have taught him "to call those picture-cards, Jacks, which ought to be called knaves" (viii, 268).[5] Later Pip also tries to educate Joe to make him "less ignorant and common, that he might be worthier of my society and less open to Estella's reproach" (xv, 362). Thus the letter ironically symbolizes the ambitions that lead to Pip's condescension toward Joe because of his lack of refined language and genteel manners. Compounding the irony is the fact that Pip writes the letter on the eve of his first visit to Miss Havisham. On that evening his admiration for Joe reaches a new height—"I dated a new admiration of Joe from that night" (vii, 244); yet by the end of the next day his respect has changed to shame at Joe's "commonness." Satis House stimulates Pip's equation of fine language and wealth with the marks of a gentleman and thus ironically confirms Joe's comment that "poetry costs money." Pip's return from Satis House is marked by an image that confirms his fall from grace (and Joe) by suggesting his exclusion from "Eden": "Joe's furnace was flinging a path of fire across the road" (xi, 318).

— 3 —

They must not be confounded together. My Walworth sentiments must be taken at Walworth; none but my official sentiments can be taken in this office.—Wemmick, xxxvi, 99

When Pip leaves the forge to go to the city, he encounters the dissociation of sensibility so aptly symbolized by the "twin Wemmicks" (xlviii, 268) of this quotation. The Wemmick of Walworth is a man of feeling: warm, humorous, delightfully eccentric, he cares for his "Aged Parent" at his home in Walworth with a tenderness that would seem sentimental if it were not for the gentle humor with which he is presented. But the Wemmick of London, of the law office of Jaggers, is another man altogether: dry, pragmatic, and mechanical, with a mouth like a "post-office" he talks of various clients' deaths in relation to his "portable property" with a matter-of-fact complacency that would make him thoroughly repulsive if it were not for his other "twin" at Walworth. His schizophrenic existence which assigns feeling to his private life and dry, analytic thought to his public one ominously suggests that the languages of feeling and thought can never be brought together.[6] But the split between the languages of "heart" and "head" is represented in even greater detail by Joe and Jaggers.

As noted earlier, Joe's language is usually clumsy, imprecise, full of mispronunciations, and frequently nonverbal. For instance, when a stranger in the Three Jolly Bargemen (the village pub) asks him about his relation to Pip, he cannot explain:

> "Son of yours?"
> "Well," said Joe, meditatively . . . "well—no. No, he ain't."
> "Nevvy?" said the strange man.
> "Well," said Joe . . . "he is not—no, not to deceive you he is *not*—my nevvy."
> "What the Blue Blazes is he?" asked the stranger. (x, 293)

At this point Wopsle rescues him and clarifies the relationship, which Joe cannot explain because the relation between himself and Pip is a bond of feeling that cannot be expressed in terms of legal kinship, but in phrases like "woT LARX" (vii, 242) and "Ever the best of friends" (lvii, 412). Joe has similar problems of expression when he and Pip visit Miss Havisham, for Joe refuses to directly address or answer her: "It was quite in vain for me to endeavour to make him sensible that he ought to speak to Miss Havisham. The more I made faces and gestures to him to do it, the more confidential, argumentative, and polite, he persisted in being to Me" (xiii, 340). Just as Joe cannot define their relation in terms of legal kinship, he refuses to speak to Miss Havisham because she not only tries to pay him for Pip's services, but she also implies a binding patron-protégé relation by "returning" Pip to Joe for his apprenticeship. Intuitively Joe perceives that a cash nexus between men breaks down the bonds of feeling.[7]

The language of feeling is also spoken nonverbally through touch, look, or gesture.[8] For example, Joe and Pip express their rapport as they sit together at the hearth, or through their symbolic ritual of eating bread: "In our already-mentioned freemasonry as fellow-sufferers, and in his good-natured companionship with me, it was our evening habit to compare the way we bit through our slices, by silently holding them up to each other's admiration now and then—which stimulated us to new exertions" (ii, 172). Similar to such moments between Joe and Pip is the Walworth Wemmick's communication with his "Aged Parent," which usually consists of a series of nods indicating agreement or positive feeling. The old man is thoroughly delighted when Pip nods at him: "I tipped him several more, and he was in great spirits" (xxv, 531). Some of the most crucial moments of feeling, recognition, and self-knowledge in the novel are expressed through gesture, such as Pip's standing by Magwitch's side in court as the judge sentences him (lvi, 389).

In contrast to the awkward or nonverbal language of feeling, Jagger's speech is the precise and careful language of the most skillful rhetorician in the novel. The beginning of Pip's own dissociation of sensibility occurs symbolically when he is psychologically transferred from Joe to Jaggers on the evening the latter comes to communicate Pip's "great expectations." The confrontation between the two men confirms their antithetical values: Jaggers looks at Joe as if he were "the village idiot" because he will not accept any remuneration for the loss of his apprentice, while Joe reacts angrily, "working round [Jaggers] with every demonstration of a fell pugilistic purpose" (xviii, 412). Yet Jaggers' implication—that Pip's relation to Joe can be translated into "cash"—*is* an insult to Joe's feeling and integrity.

That these two men are speaking different languages is apparent throughout the interview. Jaggers explains Pip's expectations as if he is reading a legal contract, and he particularly stresses that he is paid for his services as legal guardian, or else he "shouldn't render them" (xviii, 411). Nor will he be responsible for anything even vaguely personal, such as Pip's "choice" of a tutor. Joe's language, on the other hand, combines gesture and a few simple words. For instance, when Jaggers again suggests a "compensation" for the loss of Pip's services, Joe lays his hand on Pip's shoulder and replies, "Pip is that hearty welcome . . . to go free with his services to honour and fortun', as no words can tell him" (xviii, 412).[9] The narrator's comment reveals how that gesture expresses Joe's nature much more than any words: "O dear good faithful tender Joe, I feel the loving tremble of your hand upon my arm, as solemnly this day as if it had been the rustle of an angel's wing!" (xviii, 412).

Through several details the interview marks Pip's psychological journey from Joe to Jaggers: Pip "could not retrace the by-paths [he and Joe] had trodden together" (xviii, 412); he runs after Jaggers when he leaves (xviii, 412); after Jaggers is gone he feels estranged from Joe:

"The more I looked into the glowing coals, the more incapable I became of looking at Joe; the longer the silence lasted, the more unable I felt to speak" (xviii, 413). Their old rapport is broken. One other detail underlines the change to Jaggers' world: Pip's "lesson" in language. When Pip tries to thank him for "recommending" Mr. Pocket as a tutor, Jaggers corrects him until he says that he "was much obliged to him for his *mention* of Mr. Matthew Pocket" (xviii, 412, emphasis mine). At that moment Pip has just seen how to use language to evade personal involvement or responsibility for his fellow man.

The premises behind Jaggers' careful rhetoric derive from empirical analysis. "Take everything on evidence," he tells Pip in another such "lesson." "There's no better rule" (xl, 172). But by emphasizing "evidence" he places all value on appearance, although what *seems* true may not be what *is* true. Relying on evidence or data also focuses value on the quantitative rather than the qualitative aspects of life, which leads to a materialistic, "mathematical" view of reality: that of accumulating "portable property." The corollary that follows from this materialistic attitude is that a man's moral worth is equivalent to his material wealth. Perhaps Pumblechook best exemplifies this equation, for he treats Pip like a guilty felon when he is a poor apprentice but like a moral superior when he is a wealthy gentleman; even his conversation, as Pip notes, "consisted of nothing but arithmetic" (viii, 265).

Jaggers' language of thought is language dehumanized, purged of moral responsibility (as his lessons to Pip show) as well as emotional content: he tells a "snivelling" client, for example, "Get out of this office. I'll have no feelings here" (li, 316). By separating words from human sympathies, Jaggers makes language into a mathematical and arbitrary system which can be used to manipulate, deceive, or entrap the unwary.[10]

Pip's own dissociation of sensibility can best be seen in his concept of the word "gentleman" as a person of wealth, cultural refinement, and high social status. This concept leads him to dissociate himself from Joe and feeling, for he does not associate Joe's Christian values of love, tolerance, charity, and humility with the marks of a true gentleman, whereas Joe's values are the basis of sensibility. Instead, Pip chooses Estella as the locus of his feeling, a choice which ironically shows just how dissociated from sensibility he becomes, for to Estella "love" is merely "a form of words; but nothing more" (xliv, 220).

With Jaggers on one hand and Joe on the other as guides, Pip must find a language that synthesizes thought and feeling, head and heart. Like his hollow concept of "gentleman," his language and sensibilities must pass through a process of "rehumanization" before he arrives at a balanced synthesis. The "balance" is important, for a third group of characters in *Great Expectations* have combined thought and feeling, word and gesture, to create a perverse synthesis reflecting their distorted perspectives.

Magwitch, Miss Havisham, and old Bill Barley comprise this third group. In the first chapter Magwitch, for instance, combines terrifying words, such as "your heart and your liver shall be tore out, roasted, and ate" (i, 170), with the equally frightening gesture of turning Pip upside-down upon a tombstone, as if he is forcing upon the child his own inverted perspective: that money can buy social and moral status. And as if prophesied by Pip's upside-down posture, Magwitch's money helps accomplish the inversion of moral and material values in Pip's mind, so that he slights Joe and Biddy for his "better" friends at Satis House.[11]

Miss Havisham's diseased perspective is apparent in her characteristic gesture of putting her hand over her heart and in the private meaning she assigns to "love," which amounts to blind, masochistic self-sacrifice followed by righteous despair and revenge. Her gesture and language represent the indulgence of feeling as an end in itself, isolated from the external world and normal human sympathies. Her romantic expectations and their subsequent failure have led to her grotesque synthesis, which is also objectified by the stopped clocks and decayed surroundings.

Old Bill Barley, however, is finally the most frightening example of language and gesture grotesquely combined. As he thumps on the floor and emits periodic growls, he repeats a circular "Refrain" (in which the narrator substitutes "good wishes for something quite the reverse"): "'Ahoy! Bless your eyes, here's old Bill Barley. Here's old Bill Barley, bless your eyes. Here's old Bill Barley on the flat of his back, by the Lord. Lying on the flat of his back, like a drifting old dead flounder, here's your old Bill Barley, bless your eyes. Ahoy! Bless you!" (xlvi, 245). Bill Barley exemplifies thought and feeling so turned in upon themselves that they are no longer recognizable as such. His language exhibits the circular, self-indulgent nature of obsession, as do his actions: his indulgence in rum and rich food have led to gout, which creates pain, which he tries to dull with more rum and food, which only aggravates the gout, and so on. His refrain also reflects the isolating, solipsistic result of obsession, which creates a paralysis preventing all growth. Furthermore, his words recall young Pip's vision of the graves of his five little brothers, who he believed had "been *born on their backs* with their hands in their trousers-pockets, and had never taken them out in this state of existence" (i, 169, emphasis mine). This image of his brothers born as miniature adults is an intuitional crystallization of the paralysis possible in adult life as a result of some failure to grow or develop. "Lying on the flat of his back," Old Barley is the terrible fulfillment of Pip's intuition. Even his name "Old Barley" suggests a seed that never grew and recalls Pip's wondering, about the seeds and bulbs in Pumblechook's shop, whether they "ever wanted of a fine day to break out of those jails, and bloom" (viii, 265).[12] Old Barley brings together and epitomizes the imagery of perverse synthesis. His degeneration and the decayed circularity of his language and indulgence parallel Miss Havisham's decayed house and her mental fixation, represented by her going round and round the wedding table. The same paralysis, entrapment, and failure of growth are apparent in her stopped clocks and in Magwitch's connection with prisons and chains.

Yet Magwitch and Miss Havisham, as the novel shows, still possess the potential for, if not full transformation, at least change and redemption through recognition of their acts and distortions. For although it is too late to alter the consequences of their past actions, it is still possible to alter the psychological state that originally motivated them. But Old Barley represents man forever imprisoned in his distortions, isolated in a synthesis of language and gesture nearly purged of any referent beyond himself. He fulfills a possibility that is no less real because of its extremity: without a balanced synthesis of thought and feeling, for instance, Pip's expectations and their failure could lead to a similar psychological paralysis.[13] At the very least, a failure to resolve the dissociation of sensibility could result in a schizophrenic existence like that of Wemmick.

— *4* —

I saw in everything the construction that my mind had come to, repeated and thrown back to me.—Pip, xxxviii, 122

Besides integrating the worlds of logic and sensibility, Pip must learn to see through his own distortions. The quotation, referring to Pip's notion that Estella has been reserved for him in marriage, is one of the narrator's most ironic and telling comments on Pip's delusions. Pip's seeing his "construction" in everything is not a recognition of that construction as subjective, but his assumption that everything objectifies his notion as true. By using the word "construction" the narrator ironically undercuts Pip's perceptions and reveals their wishful distortions. In *Great Expectations* there are two modes of language and vision which function as ironic indices to Pip's misinterpretations: the language of fairy tale and romance and the language of law. And although each mode or system primarily points out the negative and erroneous aspects of his vision, each contains some truth about the reality he must learn to see, so that each mode contributes something to the final appropriate balance of perception.

When Pip returns from his initial visit to Satis House, his first act is to lie about what he saw there, in response to Mrs. Joe's and Pumblechook's questions. He describes Miss Havisham "sitting in a black velvet coach" while Estella handed her cake and wine on a gold plate through the window, then he mentions four "immense" dogs which "fought for veal cutlets out of a silver basket" (ix, 290). While the fantastic details reveal a very gifted and fertile imagination, they also suggest the world of fairy tale/romance which becomes Pip's mode of seeing Estella. It is a world in which Miss Havisham herself lives: the perverse fairy tale divorced from rational judgment and moral complexity, where indulgence of feeling is the primary reality.[14] As Pip uses the mode to structure his language and perceptions, he, too, oversimplifies and overlooks some of the complexities of reality. It contributes to his misjudgment of Joe in contrast to Estella: after Satis House his apprenticeship seems like a "thick curtain [that] had fallen on all [life's] interest and romance" (xiv, 361).

Through an ironic juxtaposition of passages, the narrator shows that Pip's romantic fantasies are even echoed in the newspapers. At the end of Chapter xxviii the village newspaper describes "the romantic rise in fortune of a young artificer" and further on calls Pip "our young Telemachus" (558). Chapter xxix begins with Pip's assumption that Estella has been reserved for him, which leads him to envision himself as "the young Knight of romance" who will marry the "Princess," and as the "hero" of a "rich attractive mystery" (1). The thematic and symbolic interaction between the two passages is revealing: while both passages refer to him as a questing hero of romantic adventure, the term "young artificer" suggests that the quest may be false or artificial, with the implication not only of a false *telos* in Estella but of the wrong accouterments for the quest—his limited and artificial concept of a gentleman. Yet the fact that his own constructions are reflected in the newspaper implies that his distortions may have some basis in external reality, and indeed, Miss Havisham implements his delusion of her as his benefactress and of Estella as his prize by bringing them together from time to time. But the newspaper's seeming endorsement of his self-conception points to a central irony: that Pip's quest to be a gentleman through wealth and refinement is not entirely misconceived in a world which values material over spiritual good.[15]

Pip's romantic fantasies also entrap him in deceptive conventions, such as the association of beauty with feeling. When Estella warns him that she has no heart, he thinks, "That I knew better. That there could be no such beauty without it" (xxix, 3). Throughout the novel he perceives his relationship with Estella through the conventions of courtly love poetry. For example, he notes that her pride and willfulness cannot be "separated" from her beauty (xxix, 2), and he mistakes such haughtiness and her warnings not to love her as a conventional pose to further enthrall him. Pip also falls into romantic clichés: of the horrible room where he and Estella have tea, he thinks, "Yet the room was all in all to me, Estella being in it" (xxxiii, 51). Although such conventions in language and thought are not unusual in literature that portrays a young man's first love, they form part of the distortions that lead Pip to more serious sins of omission toward Joe, associated with the Christian concepts of grace, innocence, and love. When Pip tells Estella, "You have been the embodiment of every graceful fancy that my mind has ever become acquainted with" (xliv, 221), he utters not only a romantic cliché but a deeper irony, for Estella is the "embodiment" of every "fancy" that has led Pip away from grace.

One other ironic instance of the language of fairy tale and romance appears near the end of the novel, as Pip is walking back to the forge after his illness. The language is more subtle than in previous examples, yet it nevertheless reveals Pip's romanticization of his imagined future: "Many pleasant pictures of the life that I would lead there, and of the change for the better that would come over my character when I had a guiding spirit at my side whose simple faith and clear home-wisdom I had proved, beguiled my way. They awakened a tender emotion in me; for, my heart was softened by my return, and such a change had come to pass, that I felt like one who was toiling home barefoot from distant travel and whose wanderings had lasted many years" (lviii, 434). That pleasant pictures "beguiled" his way ironically suggests that such pictures are another delusion, while his feeling "like one who was toiling home barefoot from distant travel, and whose wanderings had lasted many years" associates him with a romantic or epic hero, who returns after a life of adventure and suffering has taught him where his "true" home lies. This vision is his last romantic delusion: i.e., that after he has learned from experience and suffered for his errors, he can return to everything as it was before, as unchanged as if time had been stopped in the interim. Furthermore, there are overtones of regression to a childlike, dependent state in his notion of a "guiding spirit," as if he can recapture his lost "Eden." But this fantasy begins to weaken when he finds both Biddy's home and the forge mysteriously "closed" (lviii, 434–35), and its collapse is complete when he discovers that his "guiding spirit" has just married Joe.

Thus Pip learns that he cannot return to his original state of grace and innocence. He realizes that experience and education have made him unsuited to a life at the forge (or anything similar with Biddy), though he has been rehumanized by Joe's values. His education for adult life then complete, he perceives in an instant that his place and métier is at Clarriker's firm with his friend Herbert.

While the language of fairy tale/romance reveals the nature of certain misperceptions in Pip's mind, its mode of vision contains a certain truth. For example, when Pip tells the fantastic lies about Miss Havisham, he unconsciously intuits the fairy-tale quality of the delusions which led to her diseased synthesis of feeling and thought. This mode provides a psychological glimpse into the nature and power of human emotions, for good or for evil.[16] Thus through Miss Havisham's association with the language of fairy tale/romance, Pip learns that feeling as an end in itself is not only self-destructive but blinding, as it blinds Miss Havisham to the effects of her actions on other human beings.

In addition, the convention of the questing hero in fairy tale and romance is not entirely false, though Pip's experiences reinterpret it. For Pip undergoes a psychological journey from innocence to experience and from self-delusion to self-knowledge. His "heroism" would consist not in marrying the "Princess" Estella but in learning from his errors, acting unselfishly, and arriving at self-knowledge.

The fairy-tale/romantic mode centered around Pip's experiences at Satis House; the second system of language and vision focuses on Jaggers. Although his language provides the antithesis to Joe's language of the heart, Jaggers' rhetoric can also be seen as the "language of law." His concept of law focuses upon the "letter" rather than the "spirit" and is indicative of a view of reality which stresses the literal appearance of things, the "evidence" whether valid or not: for example, Jaggers considers using a false witness (xx, 459). By placing all value upon appearances, this literal view leads to false judgments and to the elevation of material good over less tangible realities, such as man's moral, emotional, and spiritual sensibilities. Such inversion of values, in a system that relies upon appearance, creates an equation of material wealth with moral worth—an equation which operates in the trial of Magwitch and Compeyson. Compeyson, who possesses the appearance and refinements of a "gentleman," is awarded a light sentence, while his ragged accomplice Magwitch receives a heavy sentence and the major portion of blame.

Pip himself falls into the same trap of equating material appearances with moral superiority; his condescension toward Joe owes much to this equation, as does his superficial concept of a gentleman. Two early passages foreshadow the process that leads Pip to such misconceptions, a process that also underlies Jaggers' language of law which extrapolates from the "letter": "The shape of the letters on my father's [tombstone] gave me an odd idea that he was a square, stout, dark man with curly black hair. From the character and turn of the inscription, '*Also Georgiana Wife of the Above*,' I drew a childish conclusion that my mother was freckled and sickly" (i, 169). The conclusions Pip draws are not verifiable on the basis of the "evidence," just as the conclusions Jaggers leads to through juggling words in court may not be provable on a closer scrutiny of the validity of the evidence. Furthermore, Pip's extrapolations from the letters foreshadow his later tendency to judge men on their appearance of wealth and refinement, such as his opinion of Biddy as "common" compared to Estella. A similar passage fore-shadows his confusion of material and spiritual values through the same process. Again reading the tombstones, he says, "My construction even of their simple meaning was not very correct, for I read 'wife of the Above' as a complimentary reference to my father's exaltation to a better world; and if any one of my deceased relations had been referred to as 'Below,' I have no doubt I should have formed the worst opinions of that member of the family" (vii, 241–42). Here he completely con-fuses the meanings of "Above" and "Below" by equating their literal, spatial connotations with the moral significance of heaven and hell. This moral interpretation derived from literal meaning resembles Pip's later conception of the word "low," i.e., that material and social "low-ness" indicates moral "lowness."

With their emphasis on the "letter" and the resultant falsifications, both passages exhibit the distortions inherent in Jaggers' language of law. The examples also suggest what Compeyson's trial proves: that rhetoric and appearances can be manipulated to confuse moral judg-ment. Compeyson's language and genteel manner help convince the jury that he is relatively "above" the crimes of Magwitch: he appeals to them "wi' verses in his speech" while the "low" Magwitch can only say, "Gentlemen, this man at my side is a most precious rascal" (xlii, 197). Compeyson's lighter sentence also proves that refined rhetoric and manners can be used to evade moral responsibility by exploiting a lower economic class.[17]

As noted earlier, Jaggers also employs language to evade personal or moral responsibility, though not viciously as does Compeyson. But his "lessons" to Pip clearly reveal his desire to avoid any personal in-volvement or liability. For example, when Pip replies to his question with "I suppose you make it twenty pounds," Jaggers corrects him: "Never mind what *I* make it, my friend. . . . I want to know what *you* make it" (xxiv, 508). Even the slightest implication in someone else's choice repels him. His cautious and skillful rhetoric, in fact, seems designed to avoid moral judgments altogether. While watching him in court, for instance, Pip notes, "Which side he was on, I couldn't make out, for he seemed to me to be grinding the whole place in a mill" (xxiv, 510). Jaggers' refusal to take sides suggests that moral judgments would involve him in the human world more than he would wish.[18]

Yet his attempts to isolate himself from human involvement do not rest, I believe, upon a mere revulsion from his "guilty" clients but upon a profound disillusionment with human nature and the system of which he is a part—a system which all too often finds the poor "guilty" and the wealthy "innocent." His "grinding the whole place in a mill" implies hatred and contempt for such "justice." And although he manipulates language and evidence to entrap the opposition, in at least one case he used such deception against the system itself—to clear a woman who was guilty of a crime of passion. By clearing Molly of murder and saving her child, Jaggers committed a humane and compassionate act which indicts the inequitable system of justice.

This compassionate deception somewhat redeems Jaggers and his rhetoric, though the language of law primarily functions as a negative mode of distortion in relation to Pip. Yet the lawyer's insistence upon "evidence" is advice that in one sense Pip should have heeded to correct his romantic delusions about Estella. He should have paid more attention, for example, to Estella's warnings not to love her, for there was no substantial evidence for assuming that she was assigned to him.

Pip eventually learns to avoid the distortions inherent in the languages of law and fairy tale/romance. At the same time he realizes that empirical analysis and romantic feeling have their value, but in proportion to the more profound Christian values of Joe. Without such values at their center, all patterns of convention—whether law, romance, or language itself—are liable to the extreme distortions of self, environment, and human nature that Miss Havisham, Estella, and Jaggers represent.

— 5 —

If you can't get to be oncommon through going straight, you'll never do it through going crooked.—Joe, ix, 291

Before Pip arrives at self-knowledge and balanced perception, he must also learn the full meaning of certain key words. The first group of words centers around his misconception of the word "gentleman" and his subsequent inversion of human and material values. "Low" and "common," after Pip meets Estella, mean not only social and economic inferiority, but moral inferiority as well, which his remark, "I was in a low-lived bad way" (viii, 269), intimates. He confuses "common" in the sense of "unrefined" with what he considers Magwitch's moral "lowness," thus associating cultural coarseness with a moral meanness of spirit which he later recognizes as his own, in spite of his acquired gentility: "But I never thought there was anything low and small in my keeping away from Joe, because I knew [Estella] would be contemptuous of him" (xxix, 5—6).[19] The moral irony is that Pip's false guilt over being "low" and "common" motivates his denial of Joe, an act which he eventually recognizes as the source of genuine moral guilt. Pip interprets "gentleman" and "uncommon" in the same way, i.e., he assigns a moral elevation to being refined or "uncommon" and a "gentleman." The final irony in the way the four words interact is that Pip's ambitions for wealth and status are truly "common" in the sense of "ordinary," for the majority of characters in *Great Expectations* are concerned with the "common" pursuit of money and/or status (Mrs. Joe, Pumblechook, Wemmick, Jaggers, most of the Pockets, to name a few). Pip's desire to be "uncommon" makes him perform in a morally "low" manner to Joe, whose enduring Christian virtues of love, charity, and forgiveness make him truly the most "uncommon" character in the novel.

While the first group of words illustrates Pip's confusions of value, the word "love" relates more specifically to the dangers of language when it becomes a system of private and arbitrary meanings. Pip comments, on Miss Havisham's use of the word "love," that "if the often repeated word had been hate instead of love—despair—revenge—dire death—it could not have sounded . . . more like a curse" (xxix, 4). The private meaning she has assigned to love—"blind devotion, unquestioning self-humiliation" (xxix, 4)—has led to her use of "love" as "revenge" through Estella's conquests. Thus she teaches Estella to scorn rather than love and to value things rather than human sympathy. Yet she is shocked when her own semantics turn against her: as "love" Estella offers Miss Havisham all her possessions, while presenting her pride and scorn as evidence of how well she has learned her "lessons." "But to be proud and hard to *me!*" responds Miss Havisham (xxxviii, 123). Thus when she expects "love" in the conventional sense of affection and sympathy, she encounters the breakdown of communication as a result of her private system of semantics.[20] Estella's "love" shows Pip the danger of language becoming a mere "form of words" that communicate "nothing more" (xliv, 220) than themselves when divorced from normal human sympathies and referents.

"Nature" and "natural" comprise the third group of key words. Pip begins with a few simple concepts: "natural" means "spontaneous" and "unaffected" (see xii, 338 and xxiii, 505), while human "nature" consists of a "bad" and a "good" side (see xix, 434). But as he encounters different individuals and experiences, "nature" and "natural" assume greater significance and complexity. Pip eventually sees that Estella's unfeeling nature is not "natural"—he says, "Surely it is not in Nature." Estella's reply, "It is in the nature formed within me" (xliv, 220), presents the problem of whether man has any control over his own nature as he develops, or whether he is wholly shaped by external influences.

Similar to Estella's view is Jaggers' bleak, deterministic attitude toward human nature. The two bloated, hideous casts in his office indicate his vision of the darker and weaker side of man's nature as the "true" side, as well as his comment about Bentley "Spider" Drummle as "one of the true sort" (xxvi, 534) and his assumption that Pip will inevitably "go wrong somehow" with his money (xx, 460). Although his vision is distorted, it confronts Pip with the question of what *is* man's "right nature"; he accuses Miss Havisham of "keeping a part of [Estella's] right nature away from her" (xlix, 290) and concludes that it would have been better to "have left her a natural heart" (xlix, 291).

The narrator does not explicitly define man's "right nature" or "natural heart," but the clue, I believe, is in his phrase referring to Joe: "the wealth of his great nature" (lvii, 411). Not only does Joe's "great nature" embody the values and sympathies that rehumanize Pip, but his occupation of blacksmith suggests an attitude towards man's "natural heart" and "right nature." As blacksmith, Joe works with hard natural elements; he forges and tempers stubborn metals into usable shapes. This tempering process is analogous to the effect of Christian love on the harder, darker side of human nature, for it shapes the "natural heart" into a better form (man's "right nature") without making it unrecognizable (as Miss Havisham's twisted heart). Joe's love thus strikes a balance between the rigid repression of positive instincts, which Estella represents, and the complete yielding to negative impulses, which Orlick embodies. Thus only Christian love can guide the precarious journey of man's nature between the extremes of repression and gratification.

Just as Pip learns the meaning of "right nature" through Joe and his Christian love, he also learns that "uncommon" and "gentleman" cannot be defined without this same love. By learning the meaning of certain key words and how they function, Pip not only becomes rehumanized but also more aware of the complex and difficult role of language in conveying subjective and objective reality without serious distortions.

— *6* —

> "And Biddy, her word were, 'Go to him, without loss of time.' That," said Joe, summing up with his judicial air, "were the word of Biddy. 'Go to him,' Biddy say, 'without loss of time.'"—Joe, lvii, 410

Joe's words to Pip as he convalesces are more than just a reiteration of his and Biddy's concern. In their economic simplicity they express the union of profound feeling with language that is precise, realistic, and functional—for it leads to direct positive action. The feeling Biddy's words convey is forgiveness—a forgiveness of the many times Pip deliberately avoided visiting them—while the thought behind the words reveals a direct perception of Pip's needs. Together the thought and feeling lead to an immediate act of love and responsibility. Biddy's seemingly simple command is the human word ideally spoken.[21]

Pip's resolution of the dissociation of sensibility is expressed through a combination of gesture with language as "simple" as Biddy's command. The fusion summarizes Pip's long process of education in moments of self-knowledge. The first such moment also coincides with Miss Havisham's recognition of the effects of her actions. As Pip writes "I forgive her" under Miss Havisham's name, he acknowledges his own errors with "my life has been a blind and thankless one, and I want forgiveness and direction far too much to be bitter with you" (xlix, 290). His sympathies fully awaken in her an emotional awareness of her past actions and she repeats, "What have I done!" (xlix, 290). Later in the same scene, Pip is about to leave Satis House and suddenly has a vision of Miss Havisham hanging from a beam. This feeling-intuition sends him back to check on her, just in time to save her from burning to death. Pip's entire action, from seeing the vision to extinguishing the fire, is nonverbal and unconscious; he "knew nothing" until he saw that the fire was out (xlix, 292). The action reveals the reawakening of Pip's sympathies at a deep, unconscious level and marks the beginning of responsibility in its profoundest sense: the direct feeling-*response* to the sufferings of others. The total scene represents his first crucial synthesis of thought and feeling, through his words of forgiveness and his unconscious action which confirms them.

Magwitch is the focus of his next important recognition. After the river trip, Pip fully realizes that not only was the distance between himself and the convict false but that in an important way Magwitch is morally superior: "I only saw in him a much better man than I had been to Joe" (liv, 366). Pip's feeling of kinship and responsibility is expressed in their joined hands and confirmed through his vow to Magwitch: "I will never stir from your side, . . . when I am suffered to be near you. Please God, I will be as true to you, as you have been to me!" (liv, 366). The crowning gesture which enacts his vow and dramatizes his recognition of responsibility occurs in the courtroom, where Pip holds Magwitch's hand throughout the trial and sentencing, at the end of which "the audience got up . . . and pointed down at this criminal or at that, and most of all at him and me" (lvi, 389).

The third crucial moment is Pip's recognition of Joe and the values he embodies. As Pip goes through a state of delirium, he notices that all the "extraordinary transformations of the human face" had a tendency to "settle down into the likeness of Joe" (lvii, 409), until one day as he is improving, he finally asks "*Is* it Joe?" and discovers him by his side. Pip's words, "O God bless this gentle Christian man!" (lvii, 410) complement his silent recognition of Joe and express his synthesis of Joe's values with the meaning of "gentleman." Through his own experience and Joe's love, Pip has finally synthesized the language of feeling with the language of thought: his phrase "gentle Christian man" expresses clearly and precisely the genuine refinement of thought and sensibility.

A change in Joe also adds a nice touch to the final equilibrium of head and heart: he has learned how to read and write. And the letter he composes to inform Biddy of Pip's recovery establishes a metaphorical symmetry: while Pip's letter foreshadowed the separation from Joe, Joe's letter marks their reunion.

Pip's other important problem is to arrive at a balanced and realistic appraisal of reality, without the intervention of systems of distortion, such as the languages of law and fairy tale/romance. The first sign of more direct perception occurs while Orlick is threatening to kill him. What Orlick says presents "pictures" to his mind so that he sees the past in images rather than "mere words," and he notes, "It is impossible to over-state the vividness of these images" (liii, 339). Pip's comments suggest that by analyzing his life through *images* rather than *words,* he is reinterpreting his experience more clearly and directly—without the intervention or mediation of the language patterns which have often distorted his vision.

The next significant passage occurs on the morning of the river trip. Pip describes his view out the window with crisp, realistic detail which conveys a sense of expectancy without romanticizing the vision: "The river, still dark and mysterious, was spanned by bridges that were turning coldly grey, with here and there at top a warm touch from the burning in the sky" (liii, 341). The words "dark and mysterious," "coldly grey," and "warm touch" reflect a balanced refusal to gloss over contradictions or simplify ambiguities. The description continues, directly stating his feeling of clarified perception: "As I looked along the clustered roofs, with church towers and spires shooting into the unusually clear air, the sun rose up, and a veil seemed to be drawn from the river, and millions of sparkles burst out upon its waters. From me too, a veil seemed to be drawn, and I felt strong and well." Again the details are clear and sharp; "spires shooting," "sun rose up," and "sparkles burst out" convey the rising feeling of hope without distorting the realistic picture. The "veils" that "seemed drawn" from the river and himself explicitly indicate a more direct and realistic appraisal of "the identity of things"—even the qualifying "seemed" suggests a more cautious attention to his perceptions.

The boat trip confirms the increasing clarity of Pip's vision: details about the river, its traffic and currents, and the surrounding areas are presented vividly, precisely, and with an awareness of subjective interpretation, such as "the road that ran with us, *seeming* to sympathise with us" (liv, 361, emphasis mine). One passage in particular records external phenomena so vividly that the objects take on a chaotic life of their own: "Again among the tiers of shipping, in and out, avoiding rusty chain-cables frayed hempen hawsers and bobbing buoys, sinking for the moment floating broken baskets, scattering floating chips of wood and shaving, cleaving floating scum of coal, in and out, under the figure-head of the John of Sunderland making a speech to the winds" (liv, 362). Such direct presentation of details, along with the refusal to force them into a neat subjective pattern, signify Pip's growth toward a vision free of harmful distortions, which he finally attains when he sees that he cannot return to the forge.

Great Expectations illustrates how the complexities and limitations of language are bound up with the difficulties and distortions of perception. Through Pip's progress in understanding language and experience, the narrator shows that although language is intimately connected with his earlier misconstructions and errors, its acquisition and refinement are not an entirely negative achievement but one which is suspicious as an end in itself. Words, like the "natural heart," must be tempered with human sympathies or they become merely an arbitrary system of signs which can be manipulated for private ends rather than communication. And divorced from human referents, words can become hollow, expressive of nothing beyond their own form. As Pip discovers the limitations and misuses of language, his thinking and sensibilities are gradually rehumanized.

Richard J. Dunn

FAR, FAR BETTER THINGS

Dickens' Later Endings

AT THE conclusion of *Pickwick Papers* Dickens grumbles about having to provide a final accounting of his many characters, and at the end of *Oliver Twist* he finds his hand faltering "as it approaches the conclusion of its task, and would weave, for a little longer space, the thread of these adventures" (liii). Readers, well assured that "the brief sunshine of the world is blazing full upon" the Pickwickians and little interested in the further adventures of Mr. Brownlow and the Maylies, may not share the novelist's parting concerns. Here, at the outset of Dickens' career, it is obvious that endings are troublesome for him, that he feels the burden of literary convention and perhaps also something of what George Eliot would later recognize as the "negation" of the final chapter.[1] I do not intend to discuss all of Dickens' endings or even point to everything of interest in those I do examine, but I want to examine the ending of *David Copperfield* and those of the novels following it, for in them Dickens faces repeatedly the matter of finding fit endings for fictions that could not be terminated with totally comic conclusions. For all their concessions to conventionality, these are better conclusions than we may remember. They are presented with artistry, and nearly all of them work with a surprisingly strong awareness of the extent to which much personal experience remains private.

— *I* —

One key to a better understanding of the later novels' endings is to be found in close examination of *Copperfield*'s conclusion. More directly than any earlier conclusion (excepting, perhaps, *Dombey*'s), this ending is conscious of separation and death, and this consciousness extends to (and perhaps from) the pains Dickens felt in parting from his long labor with this novel. As he wrote John Forster on 21 October 1850: "I am within 3 pages of the shore; and am strangely divided, as usual in such cases, between sorrow and joy. Oh my dear Forster, if I were to say half of what "Copperfield" makes me feel tonight, how strangely, even to you, I should be turned inside out! I seem to be sending some part of myself into the Shadowy World."[2] Part of this statement later makes its way into Dickens' preface and gives powerful confirmation that this novel was his favorite child. But the preface does not repeat his sensation of having felt "turned inside out." This statement, together with the sense of sending some part of himself into the shadowy world, comes as a more psychologically intense confession than many that appear in David's narrative. We cannot be sure what Dickens was referring to here, what it was that remained secret even to Forster, who through the autobiographical fragment knew what the novel revealed about Dickens' earlier life. But a look at the book's final number (the closest context in time of composition to this letter) suggests that Dickens may be referring obliquely to the trying period of Mary Hogarth's death, a time during which he had good reason to have felt that he had lost something of himself to death's shadowy world.

Copperfield's last number begins by quickly accounting for a time lag of three years after the end of the eighteenth number. David is on the Continent, enduring what he calls "a long and gloomy night . . . haunted by the ghosts of many hopes, of many dear remembrances, many errors, many unavailing sorrows and regrets (813)." The sixty-third chapter will add yet another ten years' distance to David's memories, but it is the intervening time, described in chapters lix through lxii, that provides the possibility of a happier ending and gives the biographically conscious reader clues about the reasons for Dickens' intense reaction to this part of his novel.

David returns to England and through reacquaintance with old friends finds vicarious pleasures. Activating his memories, he tries to return to the most comforting scenes and events of his past, but ultimately he develops an essentially private vision that will also become characteristic of a number of Dickens' later heroes and heroines. The question of whether David has become the hero of his own life is answered affirmatively by whatever degree that life, like those of Esther Summerson, Louisa Bounderby, and Arthur and Amy Clennam, remains a life apart. As David so directly puts it, "When society is the name for . . . hollow gentlemen and ladies, . . . and when its breeding is professed indifference to everything that can advance or retard mankind, I think we must have lost ourselves in that . . . Desert of Sahara, and had better find the way out" (876).

But the David returning to England seems to find a delightful oasis among Traddles and his family. It is easy for us to dismiss the happy ending of Traddles' procrastinated courtship and legal career as tangential to David's story, but we should, instead, note its obvious connection with Dickens' domestic life at the crucial time of Mary's death. The portrayal of Traddles and his sisters-in-law romping in the cramped upper chambers of Gray's Inn recalls Dickens' own delightful time when he lived with Mary as part of the family in Furnival's Inn. Recalling that time in a diary notation for 6 January 1838, he remarked, "I shall never be so happy again as in those Chambers three Stories high—never if I roll in wealth and fame."[3] Three months earlier he had written his mother-in-law of his connection of the Furnival's Inn life with Mary, who died shortly after Dickens moved to Doughty Street: "I wish you could know how I weary now for the three rooms in Furnival's Inn, and how I miss that pleasant smile and those sweet words which, bestowed upon an evening's work in our merry banterings round the fire, were more precious to me than the applause of a whole world would be." In language more directly anticipatory of the *Copperfield* preface, he went on to hope "we may call up these old memories,—not as shadows of the bitter past, but as lights upon a happier future."[4]

Readers even generally aware of Dickens' relationship with the Hogarths should not be surprised to find Tommy Traddles as much married to his wife's sisters as to her. He delights in his role as "the darling" of these sisters, much in the way Dickens must have wanted to enjoy the continuing presence of a Hogarth sister in his own home. But in *Copperfield* it is particularly significant that Dickens transferred this joy to a minor character and chose to have his hero observing it precisely at the time David was first winning fame as a novelist but was also despairing of his own hopes for such happiness. It may be that the picture of the Traddles home life comes in this fashion to distance pained memories of Mary's death as well as of his increasing impatience with his wife, but the presence of this autobiographical material gives credence to the final number's mixing of fulfilling memories and unfulfilled hopes. In the chapter preceding his reunion with Traddles, David confesses that hitherto he had kept "the most secret current of my mind apart" but now pledges to "enter on it." The specific secret current is his love for Agnes, but his experience of self-examination allows David also to admit more general "perplexities and inconsistencies" in his memories, "shifting currents of the mind" (818–19). His further remark that he was at this time in the midst of his third story, interrupted by his return to England, suggests another link between David and Dickens at the period of Mary's death. When she died in his arms in May 1837, Dickens had started his third story (if we count *Sketches by Boz*), and he was so unsettled by the experience that for the only time in his career he missed his monthly serial commitments.

When he leaves the Traddles chambers, feeling as if he "had beheld a thousand roses blowing," David retires to sit alone before his fire. Like Louisa Bounderby and Lizzie Hexam, he traces his prospects in the live coals, thinking gravely of the past and contemplating "the future in a brave spirit" (830). So positioned as a spectator to fiery change but at the same time immobile in its face, David next turns his thoughts toward restoration of the old order of his life. In the next chapter he returns to his aunt, and meets Agnes again, who reassures him that while he has been away she has delighted "in keeping everything as it used to be when we were children." And, too poignantly, she adds, "For we were happy then, I think" (840). Such greening of memory recurs in Dickens' fiction, and the present novel may be read as his most comprehensive effort to perpetuate pleasant memories while exorcizing unpleasant ones. So regarded, the book is but partially successful. *Copperfield* cherishes its spots of time, especially those establishing the primacy of Clara Copperfield, Peggotty, Em'ly and the curious Yarmouth life, Wickfield's Canterbury, and Steerforth's enchantments. In the adult male memory, David's fixation is with mother-housekeeper-sister loves and with the young man who so delighted and perplexed him. But at this conclusive occasion of adult reunion with Agnes, David determines to "set the seal upon the Past," because he considers his love hopeless. Precisely at this point the burden of predetermined serial length and the conventions of fictional conclusion allow this ending to go astray. Without the set number of pages to fill, *David Copperfield* might have ended with the sudden dispelling of David's misapprehensions, and without the conventional obligation of accounting for a number of other characters the novel might have concluded with stronger focus on David's own state of mind. But the sixty-first chapter moves us to the model prison, ostensibly to dispose of Heep and Littimer and for commentary upon a social issue that had earlier drawn Carlyle's heavier fire. The chapter has little bearing on the novel's conclusion, but its presence does fill a time lapse, permitting David to move in the next chapter on to Christmas when, as "A Light Shines on My Way," he conceives his "new-born hope" that he may call Agnes "something more than sister." The sentimentality intensifies as David declares his bride to be "the centre of my self, the circle of my life, . . . my love of whom was founded on a rock!" (864). If we are inclined toward cynicism we may view David's marriage to Agnes as an emotional shipwreck, but more to the point of the reading I am making, this marriage to the "good angel," former "sister," is precisely the marriage Dickens never had and probably never could have had.[5] The memory of Dora that David and Agnes cherish is not a memory of Mary Hogarth just as David himself is not a fictionalization of Dickens himself. But the *process* of remembering, of remaining most emotionally vulnerable in the face of remembered loss, is a process surely close to what Dickens experienced from the time of that painful spring of 1837.

There remain two chapters of this novel's final number to consider. In them David moves farther in time from the main events of his story and, making an obligatory headcount of old friends, reveals some ambivalences that anticipate those of later Dickens heroes and heroines. Ten years pass after his second marriage, and as David refuses to leave a "ravelled end of one thread" in his fictional web, he tells of Mr. Peggotty's visit and of the report he brings concerning the surprising fortunes of his and the Micawber families. The final chapter, "A Last Retrospect," is the more interesting. It begins with David's noting of faces in the crowd on life's road, mentioning again his childhood favorites, and acknowledging his fame as he hears "the roar of many voices, not indifferent to me as I travel on." But when he sees the face of his son, his thoughts become more perplexing; he finds "it very curious to see my own infant face, looking up at me from the Crocodile stories" (874). There is a similar moment at the end of *Great Expectations* when Pip returns to find his namesake, Joe's son, established in his old place. In both instances more seems at stake imaginatively than nostalgic *déjà vu*. David takes a certain pleasure in viewing the orderly progression of generations—an older Peggotty, Betsey, and Mr. Dick are yet around to treat David's children as they had treated him. But lost, at least for the moment between the older and newer generations is David's present self, a disorientation marked by David's curiosity regarding his "own infant face." At the very least this is a glimpse of his mortality; at the most it is an unsettling moment that pinpricks his novel's *Bildungsroman* quality.

David Copperfield's final paragraphs make the ultimate sentimental declaration of David's two vicarious ideals. Traddles, irrepressible as ever, now has a fine house, where one sister-in-law is "established in perpetuity" much in the way that Georgina Hogarth was established in Dickens' own home from the early 1840s until his death. The more beatific last vision is of Agnes, who David hopes will be with him "when realities are melting from me like the shadows which I now dismiss." These final visions are his security, uncomplicated by any self-scrutiny that might occur in such moments as his curiosity over seeing himself again in his son. Here on the final pages David dismisses shadows, allowing the novelist to evade the shades of his earlier married life and the long shadow cast over it by Mary's death. But, as the following novels indicate, Dickens has not put aside shadows to dwell in sunshine as he had in *Pickwick*. Recurrent in his coming fictions are shadowy worlds of personal frustration as well as images of domestic happiness doomed in social Saharas.

— *2* —

In the novels following *Copperfield* there is a distinct difference between conventional conclusive treatment of minor characters and the less conventional portrayal of central characters and main stories. The Dickens who reunites Rouncewells, gives seriocomic curtain speeches to Sleary, and trots out Mr. F.'s Aunt for a final bow is the writer of ameliorative comic conclusions. But the writer who leaves Esther Summerson and Louisa Bounderby uncertain of their identities, Amy and Arthur Clennam together fronting an indifferent world, and Sydney Carton with prophetic wisdom more felt than expressed is a writer resisting the easy synthesis of comic resolution. Obvious demands of the final double number—the tying of loose ends and the last appearance of many favorite characters—may distract readers from the conclusions' most central statements, and except for Esther and Pip the central characters themselves seldom make strong claims for attention. Often these conclusions seem tensely balanced between the qualified positions of heroes and heroines and the more conventional certainty with which Dickens treats lesser characters. At times the tension is relieved through sentimental fantasy or through more fierce prophetic declarations. Close reading of the best of these conclusions suggests that the tensions are necessary, because when honestly faced they remain humanly irresolvable.

Bleak House ends with the heroine finally capable of raising significant questions about her own life. The novel develops through the counterpointing of Esther's personal history/mystery with the less personal social survey, and the mode of narration sets Esther apart both from the past that bears such a psychic burden and from the present universe, which, in Jarndyce's phrase, is at best "an indifferent parent." That Esther finally is given a husband, a new Bleak House, and even the hope that she may have regained her beauty strikes many readers as dissolution into fantasy. It is reasonable to interpret the ending this way, but to do so we must assume that Esther's story is resolved and resolved unsatisfactorily. Yet the final number maintains a sense of irresolution, and there seems to be a deliberate effort to avoid the sentimental clichés of conventional resolution. The number begins, in a chapter titled "Perspective," with Esther's determination not to allow her narrative to dwell on the sorrow she felt after her mother's death. Her principal concern becomes Richard Carstone, whose health is rapidly declining. The hope of a fit ending to his life, replete with adoring children, becomes one of *Bleak House*'s most abortive hopes. Through Ada and Richard, Esther finds the opposite of the vicarious joy David Copperfield had found among the Traddles, for it is death, not life, that Esther once more experiences. Ada expresses the tender hope that Richard's wasted life will be redeemed through the lives of his children; "a beautiful woman, his daughter, happily married, may be proud of him and a blessing to him" (825). Not until *A Tale of Two Cities* will a Dickens novel even tentatively grant this hope, for as Ada fears, Richard does not live to know his child (which, as fate would have it, is a boy).

Here, as in the sad fact that Caddy Turveydrop bears a handicapped child, the hope for universal happiness is mooted in most *Bleak House* lives. But for Esther, as there had been for David, something of the past is present. In one of her most penetrating personal statements, she realizes that "whatever little lingerings have now and then revived in my mind, associated with my poor old face, had only revived as belonging to a part of my life that was gone—gone like my infancy or my childhood" (831). The immediate occasion is her supposition that Jarndyce will hold her to her engagement and that she must therefore suppress her love for Woodcourt, but as several recent commentators have shown, Esther is a character who frequently expresses great uncertainty about her own being.[6] To deny the past in terms that connect the change in one's face with the suppression of life gone by is to admit tentativity about one's present and future conditions.

When the fairy-tale ending is provided with Jarndyce as godfather, Esther is understandably touched. But she is not swept away, does not begin playing Dame Durden or Mother Shipton to the hilt. Rather, she returns to more intense thoughts about herself and takes up once again the matter of her past, specifically considering her old looks. With a touch of self-torment, she concludes her narrative with the speculation that her dear family and friends "can do very well without much beauty in me—even supposing—." These are not the words of a secure Cinderella. As Lawrence Frank has said, there is not a period at the end of the "novel which is Esther's unfolding self: there is a dash, a hiatus, and no more."[7]

The parts of the conclusion that are more conventional—chapters with such titles as "Perspective" and "Beginning the World"—remain behind the final hiatus. Esther has herself sought perspective throughout; she begins the concluding part of her narrative by turning her attention to other lives, but in the final paragraph she has not yet answered her basic questions about herself. Can she regard herself as physically and morally beautiful? For her, human wholeness and psychological independence seem to depend upon both types of beauty. Earlier, with certain irony, Richard has begun the world by leaving it, and the Chancery case has blown up in court costs. In the more distant, deadened Chesney Wold "passion and pride, even to the stranger's eye, have died away . . . and yielded to dull repose" (876). But at the new Bleak House Esther's pride, if not her passion, yet remains a questionable commodity.

Barbara Hardy has complained that the *Bleak House* conclusion is not sufficiently responsible to the rest of the novel, but surely the last view of the Lincolnshire estate provides much of the "expression of irony, sadness, fatigue" that Hardy calls for.[8] Admittedly there remains an element of escapism in the concept of a new Bleak House, but through the opposing portrayal of the deadened Chesney Wold and more directly through attention to Esther's responses to her good fortune the conclusion does not turn its back entirely upon the novel's persistent concern with the uneasiness of private life and the consumptiveness of public life.

Unlike the monthly serials, *Hard Times* has little room for last-number retrospect, and with fewer characters it contains less final accounting. The number plan is one of Dickens' briefest.

> Weekly Nº 21
> > Conclusion
> > Dispose of Mrs. Sparsit
> > Wind up.
> > The ashes of our fires grown grey and cold.

Only the final line of these notes points to the number's thematic substance, although the penultimate chapter is titled "Philosophical" and presents a last juxtapositioning of Gradgrindian self-interest with the Sleary "Canine philosophy" to the effect that "there is love in the world . . . as hard to give name to, as the ways of dogs is" (292–93).

The last chapter, after having the dauntless Bounderby turn out Mrs. Sparsit, projects Bounderby "into futurity." With more ingenuity than we might expect in a concluding glimpse into the future, Dickens moves easily from Bounderby's characteristically "explosive" self-projection toward a summation of all the major characters' futures as fates largely determined by experiences the novel has already presented. With "balderdash and bluster" Bounderby will endow a Bounderby Hall and a Bounderby Chapel, but he does not foresee that he will die ignominiously and will have his last testament strongly contested. The "futurity" Bounderby sees is, of course, a projection only of what he has been able to see in the past. For Mr. Gradgrind there is hope for more clear-sightedness; he is likely to make his "facts and figures subservient to Faith, Hope, and Charity." Here, as with Louisa, Dickens presents future-awareness with a series of rhetorical questions. "These things she could plainly see. But, how much of the future?" The pattern of the final paragraphs is, "Did Louisa see this? . . . Such a thing was to be." What is to be is inevitable, and future happiness is more mixed than ever it seemed at the end of *Copperfield* or *Bleak House*. Tom, eager for penitence, is to die before he can rejoin his sister. Sissy Jupe will marry and bear children, but her happiness is one that is "never to be" for Louisa. However we may react to the severity with which Dickens regards Louisa as a wronged woman who rightly left her husband but who in doing so foreclosed all possibility of remarriage, the point to note is that the final pages of this novel stress the characters' abilities to see and foreseee. Vision may be the prerequisite for realizing Stephen Blackpool's ideal of "bearing and forbearing"; one must see and foresee before one can easily tolerate other people. Certainly the final character contrasts are between the blindness of Bounderby, Gradgrind's growing ability to know his men, and Louisa's faculty of "watching the fire as in days of yore, though with a gentler and humbler face."

The book's last paragraph pushes the novelist's message to the utmost, making clear-sightedness imperative for his readers as well as for his characters: "Dear reader! It rests with you and me, whether, in our two fields of action, similar things shall be or not. Let them be! We shall sit with lighter bosoms on the hearth, to see the ashes of our fires turn grey and cold" (299). What, exactly, this means is not altogether clear, but notice of "two fields of action" is in keeping with much of the rest of the novel's ending. The novelist whose imaginative fires must cool after long commitment to social questions may someday sit with a lighter bosom on his hearth. Like Louisa, he cannot (perhaps as writer need not) find total satisfaction in his life. In the other field of action, that of the general working public, there must be an awareness of the limited effect visionary or literary efforts will have if not followed by practical actions. Thus there are two fields of action—the artist's and that of the public at large who respond to the artist's call for action. Only for those who have been responsible in their separate fields will there be any possible relief when life's fires grow grey. This reading of the final paragraph is perhaps over-optimistic, but the context hardly justifies a darker interpretation. I agree with Barbara Hardy that *Hard Times'* final passage avoids optimistic flights, but I cannot thereby conclude (nor does she) that they are terribly grim words.[9] The most problematic concern of the ending is its implicit questioning of what can be known and done in this life, where the present is a "muddle" and the future but partly knowable. It is a question not only for the Bounderbys and Gradgrinds but also for the novelist and his public. Can the novel, as novel, stimulate both awareness and action? Or must author and audience ultimately remain separate, one in an imaginative field of action, the other depending in part upon reading to determine how things in life may be changed? Never again in any conclusion will Dickens so admit such inconclusiveness about the ends of art.

On first glance, the conclusion of *Little Dorrit* seems the most deliberately constructed among the later novels. The number begins with "Closing In," moves on with "Closed," "Going," "Going," and "Gone" chapter titles. The first of these contains some of the most complicated plot explanations since *Oliver Twist* or *Martin Chuzzlewit*. (Some foundation should award a prize to the Dickens reader who can recall the most plot details two hours after reading this chapter.) It reveals the nature of Mrs. Clennam's secret and accounts for much of her curious behavior as a consequence of events occurring long before the novel's beginning. This postponed exposition is an encumbrance of plot suspense such as we often find in Dickens' early fiction, and much else in the *Little Dorrit* conclusion is routine. There is some excitement provided by the literal collapse of the Clennam house, some comedy by Pancks' shearing of Casby's patriarchal locks, and there is the mutual reconciliation of the Meagleses with Tattycoram.

Little Dorrit's final chapter, however, once more displays a sense of the division between private and public lives evident in Dickens' other late novels. Arthur, like the central characters of *David Copperfield, Bleak House,* and *Hard Times*, grows more insightful, more sensitive to the present and less obsessed with the past. The chapter opens "on a healthy autumn day" and points up the contrast between the prison, "changeless and barren, looking ignorantly at all the seasons," and the prisoner, now attuned to "all that great Nature was doing" (815). Amy and Arthur will proceed into "the autumn sun's bright rays" on their way to "a modest life of usefulness and happiness." The imagery reinforces the impression that theirs is a uniquely good fortune, though we may wonder just how they will function usefully in "the roaring streets" where "the noisy and the eager, the arrogant and the froward, and the vain, fretted and chafed, and made their usual uproar" (826). Theirs is the happiness of people set apart by their ability to see; in this instance the seeing is defined as sensitivity to nature and to one another. What remains unsaid, and perhaps unseen, is their capacity for turning seeing into being.

Almost as if to distance himself from this issue of vision translated into present action, Dickens turned next to another historical novel, not a private history like *David Copperfield* but a public, popular history of the French Revolution. Such a subject for *A Tale of Two Cities* permitted him another context in which to examine questions of intelligence and action that had been posed in his recent works. As this novel finally centers upon the personal rehabilitation of Sydney Carton, there is a growing uneasiness in accepting the notion that humanity was crushed out of shape by the revolution. Carton is the exception, the Christ-like martyr.

There is but one chapter, "The Footsteps Die Out Forever," to the concluding number of *A Tale of Two Cities,* and it is one of Dickens' most easily misunderstood final chapters. Every reader comes away with some memory of Carton's heroic final speech that takes him, and seemingly the novel, to "a far, far better rest." But the qualification that the text makes of these words is, ironically, often lost in their very force. The chapter starts with impressive descriptions of the tumbrils en route to La Guillotine and of the mobbed streets. It counterpoints these scenes with the calm reassurance of afterlife that Sydney gives the little seamstress who precedes him in death. But at this point there is a break in the text; the following paragraphs come after a gap of several lines, and they come with definite qualification.

We are told what was said of Carton in the city that night; his was the most peaceful face ever beheld at the horrible place of execution. "Many added that he looked sublime and prophetic." We then get the further supposition that "If he had given an utterance to his [thoughts], and they were prophetic, they would have been these": five paragraphs of prophetic vision follow, culminating with the famous "far, far better" passage. The point to note is one that by now should be familiar to the attentive reader of Dickens' conclusions. The character who has developed the ability to see and know may be granted some visionary power, but the substance of the vision remains hypothetical and incommunicable. Thus, for all its Christian overtones and pathos, the *Tale of Two Cities'* conclusion remains one of Dickens' most honest. It does not violate the integrity of characterization to enforce a moral point, and unlike *Hard Times* it does not insert a claim for itself as a fiction designed to make readers see things more clearly here and hereafter. Further, this conclusion artistically settles some of the difficulty of perspective that Dickens admits having had with this novel. The preface to the first edition mentions his "strong desire" to employ the first-person narrative voice, and it also acknowledges his debts to Wilkie Collins' play ("The Frozen Deep," in which Dickens collaborated) and to Carlyle's history. The combination of these sources with a personally verified sense of "what is done and suffered in these pages" produced an obvious strain in the novel's tone that Dickens attempted to overcome by maintaining a more dramatic perspective than usual. By making the prophecy hypothetical, stressing the reaction to Carton's death, the drama ends with the words that might have been heard had anyone been able to hear Sydney's final thoughts. This, not the classic film version where Ronald Coleman mutters the great speech, is the firmly managed ending of Dickens' novel.

Before leaving *A Tale of Two Cities* we should notice several elements of the typical Dickens conclusion that appear in the details of Sydney's prophecy. Sydney sees himself reincarnated in the son of the Darnays and here, more definitively than in David Copperfield's surprise over finding a copy of his earlier self, is the Dickensian vision of reclaimed innocence, this time appearing at the climactic moment of the Darnay Double's life. If this myth of self-perpetuation were pursued very far, it might come into conflict with the traditional hope of other worldly immortality that Sydney holds out to his seamstress friend, and what remains at stake is the question of whether for him, for anyone, death with the capacity for vision is far, far better than life with hope imaged in coming generations of Darnays. Sydney thus both lives and dies by envisioning a future for his friends. As part of that future, the vision once again incorporates the Dickensian desire to keep the memory green, for it shows the survivors blessing Sydney, although they remain necessarily ignorant of what exactly he has realized in his final thoughts.

Great Expectations may seem to be an exception to much that I have been arguing about the artistry of Dickens' endings, for his giving way to Bulwer Lytton's desire for revision of the original conclusion is usually regarded as unfortunate. Butt and Tillotson point out the principal problem with the revision by declaring it "more appropriate that Pip, who had lost Magwitch's money, should also lose his daughter than that he should marry her at the end."[10] It remains inexplicable just why, at a time in his career when he seemed generally confident of his talent and in a novel over which he had exercized tight formal control, Dickens acceded to Bulwer's wishes. The question to deal with critically, however, is not why Dickens made the revision but, rather, what the effect of revision was on the novel. In assessing the relative worth of the two conclusions, critics from Forster on have seldom recognized how well concluded the novel was *before* the critical point of change in the final chapter.[11]

Pip's trials by fire, water, and sickness in the third stage bring him back once more to the formative influences of his earlier life (Miss Havisham, Orlick, Magwitch, and Joe). The novel's third stage thus is one of Dickens' most carefully wrought denouements. I shall not here make detailed analyses of these often discussed sections, but the obvious point is that Pip's moral history completes itself in the events following Magwitch's return at the end of the second stage. The climax of these experiences, the voluntary act which frees his spirit, is his admission to Magwitch of having loved and lost the convict's daughter. "Dear Magwitch, I must tell you, now at last," says Pip, for at last he has found words that at once admit his sense of criminality and banish his social pretensions. Like Esther who suffered an illness immediately after her mother's death, Pip now has a fever and often loses his reason, confounding "impossible existences with my own identity" (438). As is frequent in the personal reconstructions of Dickens' endings, Pip soon is reunited with that part of his past which has proven most persistently beneficial. He awakens to find Joe faithfully nursing him: "I was like a child in his hands. He would sit and talk with me in the old confidence, and with the old simplicity, and in the old unassertive protecting way, so that I would half believe that all my life since the days of the old kitchen was one of the mental troubles of the fever that was gone" (442). All this takes place in the next-to-last number. That part of the final number that was not changed involves a further return to the past, describing Pip's reacquaintance with the Blue Boar and Pumblechook (who sounds like one of *Little Dorrit*'s "froward and vain"). Idealizing the June weather, blue sky, and larks "soaring high over the green corn," Pip constructs "many pleasant pictures" of the life he would lead on the old ground. His dream is shattered by the discovery that he will not have Biddy beside him as "a guiding spirit," blessing him with "simple faith and clear home-wisdom" (453). Pip is not a David come home to an Agnes, for *Great Expectations* here displays a more mature recognition of lost opportunities.

Pip's only recourse is to emigrate (a fate reserved for the fallen or the ne'er-do-wells in *Copperfield*). He remains abroad for eleven years, working with Herbert and doing well. But the conclusive pattern of this novel, like most of Dickens', is toward return, and once again, in the final chapter, Pip tries to come home. This is the chapter affected by the revision. Its unchanged part concerns Pip's discovery of his namesake; "fenced into the corner with Joe's leg, and sitting on my own little stool looking at the fire, was—I again" (457). This incident, combining Dickens' interests in the child as double and in fire gazers, is one of the most remarkable in the final number. Pip is so taken with the child that he asks Biddy to "give Pip to me, one of these days; or lend him, at all events." Martin Meisel has seen this request as part of *Great Expectations'* message that Pip can "neither regain nor remake any stage of the past," but Meisel does not comment upon the fact that Biddy refuses Pip's request.[12] It is evident that the adult Pip, now many years removed from his earlier life, is deliberately ignoring the implications of what he has asked for. To want, however temporarily, to "borrow" young Pip is to express a Magwitch-Havisham desire for shaping a young person's life. That it is an image of his earlier self that he wants to have may make us wonder how secure the adult Pip truly is. The novel does not raise these questions directly, for Biddy puts Pip off with a pleasant, "No, no. . . . You must marry."

The final chapter proceeds to the point of revision, as the original section ends with Pip's declaration to Biddy that he yet loves Estella, but "that poor dream, as I once used to call it, has all gone by." Up to here the novel is running true; its course is one of separating that which can be realized from that which cannot. Morally and psychologically, Pip here is precisely where he had been three chapters (and many years) earlier when he parted with Magwitch. In the confession to Biddy, Pip expresses once more his version of the New Testament argument that to find oneself one must lose oneself.

Although I am more interested in the earlier parts of the third stage and of the final number, I must say that I do not find the terms of the revised ending inappropriate. The final paragraph with Pip and Estella departing from the ruined garden, like the final section of *Little Dorrit,* is autumnal; "as the morning mists had risen long ago when I left the forge, so, the evening mists were rising now, and in all the broad expanse of tranquil light they showed to me, I saw no shadow of another parting from her" (460). Even the "broad expanse of tranquil light," if we recall the earlier appearance of a shaft of sunlight in Magwitch's last days, has an association with death, but the key qualification here concerns Pip's ability to see. He grants change; morning mists have departed. That he can see no shadow of another parting is in itself no guarantee for the future, so at best we may read an appropriate openness in this revised ending. Dickens does not end his novel with a projection into the future, and as the entire third section demonstrates, *Great Expectations* is aware of the limited extent to which one may recapture the past.

Our Mutual Friend's final number begins with John Harmon's continuing effort to efface his personal past. Still masquerading as John Rokesmith, he hears Mr. Inspector declare, "What a game was this to try the sort of stuff a man's opinion of himself was made of" (761). But Harmon's principal object is to test his wife, to "show her . . . better than we ever thought possible" (774). After having given away the secret of Harmon's identity early, this novel has become, in a sense, a protracted conclusion. Like the returned David or Pip, Harmon comes home after many years to find that home greatly changed, himself unrecognized, and his values seemingly ignored. The final number makes an effective recapitulation of these problems, and it presents a final statement of the central division between society's false glitter and the "true golden gold" discovered in the hearts of the central characters. The house of Harmon, once put in order, is, as Boffin terms it, "a pretty and promising picter" (778). But this is not to say that the book ends with a resolution of all the social problems it dramatized. There is the comic clarification that comes with the unmasking of Boffin, the false misanthrope, and there is the joyful establishment of Bella in John's true home. The number's first three chapters follow a broadly comic pattern, culminating in the final disposition of the rascal Wegg in a dustman's cart.

The final three chapters, however, lead toward a final picture that shows the obscurity of the happiness attained by the Harmons, Boffins, and Wrayburns. The fifteenth chapter carries the Headstone-Riderhood rivalry to its disastrous conclusion, the struggle that ends with them both drowned. The sixteenth chapter, stressing the largess of John and Bella, dispenses with "Persons and Things in General," but once more we have a sense of a decidedly private, and thereby limited, resolution. To provide for Rumty Wilfer, one of the few deserving people, is to look out for one's own against a largely indifferent world. The indifference is most evident in the fiercely satirical final chapter, titled "The Last—The Voice of Society." It is ironic that the last completed work of the novelist who from *Copperfield* on paid such frequent attention to enlarging individual perceptions should conclude with this chapter. The last words of *Our Mutual Friend* call attention to its social and moral wastelands, for when the subject of Wrayburn's marriage to the penniless Lizzie Hexam is mentioned in the fashionable world, the verdict is "madness and moonshine. . . . A man may do anything lawful for money. But for no money!—Bosh!" The timid Twemlow here raises a mild plea for the "feelings of a gentleman," to which Podsnap rejoins, "A Gentleman can have no feelings who contracts such a marriage" (819). As another man leaves this party, he rightly wonders which of the people *is* its voice, for only Twemlow seems an exception to collective non-entity and cold authority.

Our Mutual Friend does not really end with its final chapter, because it includes a "Postscript, in Lieu of a Preface." Here, as he had earlier in the final paragraph of *Hard Times,* Dickens turns from the novel to make his own parting remarks. He defends the ingenuity of his plotting, "thinking it worth while, in the interests of art, to hint to an audience that an artist (of whatever denomination) may perhaps be trusted to know what he is about in his vocation." By having so early revealed one basic plot secret, he found himself free "to keep for a long time unsuspected, yet always working itself out, another purpose originating in that leading incident and turning it to a pleasant and useful account at last." He is clearly referring to his effort to turn interest to the matter of the genuineness of Boffin's misanthropy, the scheming that made possible the continuation of Harmon's masquerading. Thus he was able to present Harmon's life as secret and vicarious, a living deception amid many deceptions. The effect is one of fictions within fictions, of a story attending to the lies by which people exist. As I have pointed out elsewhere, even the little dolls' dressmaker, Jenny Wren, plays these games.[13]

Dickens' postscript also makes a claim for the accuracy with which he has presented legal matters and the pauper, Betty Higden, and it concludes with reference to the Staplehurst railway accident in which he and the *Our Mutual Friend* manuscript were involved. The final line of the last novel he completed attests to the "devout thankfulness that I can never be much nearer parting company with my readers for ever than I was then, until there shall be written against my life, the two words with which I have this day closed this book:—THE END." The self-consciousness of this statement that links the end of a work of fiction with the end of life may seem tasteless to modern readers and may cause them to see little advance in the art of Dickens' conclusions from the days of *Pickwick* and *Oliver* when such creaky machinery was most evident. But we must regard this as "post-scriptural," in lieu of a preface. The novel itself has ended, as it must, with the novelist's own voice distanced while division remains between his redeemed and largely quiet good characters and the highly vocal society from which they are estranged. In this last work the novelist wisely removes himself to a postscript, where to his heart's content he is free to express confidence in knowing "what he is about in his vocation." Thus there are not two but three separated voices at the conclusion of *Our Mutual Friend*— those of the central characters, of society, and of the author's afterwords. Here, as in most of the endings after *Copperfield,* the novelist constructs far better conclusions than literary convention might demand or than superficial reading might suggest.

NOTES

INDEX

All page references in the text and in the footnotes of this volume are to The Oxford Illustrated Dickens Edition, various dates from 1948 to 1966, published at the University Press, Oxford.

ANDREW J. KAPPEL and ROBERT L. PATTEN: *Dickens' Second American Tour and His "Utterly Worthless and Profitless" American "Rights"*

[1] Madeline House and Graham Storey, eds., *The Letters of Charles Dickens* (Oxford: Clarendon Press, 1974), III, 275. Cited hereafter as Pilgrim *Letters*.

[2] George Dolby, *Charles Dickens As I Knew Him, The Story of the Reading Tours in Great Britain and America, (1866–1870)* (Philadelphia: J. B. Lippincott and Co., 1885), p. 136.

[3] Ibid., p. 137.

[4] Philip Collins, ed., *Charles Dickens: The Public Readings* (Oxford: Clarendon Press, 1975) incorporates material from several earlier essays by Collins. See also his *Reading Aloud, A Victorian Métier,* Tennyson Society Monograph no. 5 (Lincoln, Lincs., 1972).

[5] John Forster, *The Life of Charles Dickens,* ed:, J. W. T. Ley (New York: Doubleday, Doran and Company [1928]), X, i, 765.

[6] Ibid., ii, 796, n. 485b.

[7] Dolby, p. 155.

[8] Edgar Johnson, *Charles Dickens, His Tragedy and Triumph,* 2 vols. (New York: Simon and Schuster, 1952), p. 1094. Johnson's illustration no. 77 shows Greeley as Mr. Pickwick introducing Dickens at Delmonico's.

[9] Quoted in Philip Collins, ed., *Dickens: The Critical Heritage* (New York: Barnes and Noble, Inc., 1971), p. 567, from Charles Richard Sanders, "Carlyle's Letters," *Bulletin of the John Rylands Library* 38 (1955–56), 223.

[10] "Readings and Lectures—Dickens, Dolby, and the Dollars," p. 4, col. 3.

[11] K. J. Fielding, ed., *The Speeches of Charles Dickens* (Oxford: Clarendon Press, 1960), pp. 378–83; see Forster, X, ii, 795.

[12] Simon Nowell-Smith, *International Copyright Law and the Publisher in the Reign of Queen Victoria* (Oxford: Clarendon Press, 1968), p. 52.

[13] Walter Dexter, ed., *The Letters of Charles Dickens,* 3 vols. (Bloomsbury: The Nonesuch Press, 1938), II, 730. Cited hereafter as Nonesuch *Letters.*

[14] James T. Fields, "Our Whispering Gallery," *Atlantic Monthly* (1871), 27–28, subsequently published in an

expanded version as *Yesterdays with Authors* (Boston: James R. Osgood and Company, 1872). Cited hereafter as *AM;* here, *AM* 28, 222.

15 Forster, VIII, v, 678.

16 *AM* 28, 223.

17 MS Account Books, Chapman and Hall, Victoria and Albert Museum (F.D. 18. 1–3), quoted by permission.

18 *AM* 28, 224.

19 Ibid.

20 Ibid.

21 Ibid.

22 Ibid., 225; Collins, ed., *The Public Readings,* p. xxvi.

23 *AM* 28, 225.

24 Dolby, p. 83.

25 *AM* 28, 225.

26 *American Literary Gazette and Publishers' Circular* 9 (15 May 1867), 37. Cited hereafter as *PC.*

27 Nonesuch *Letters,* III, 527.

28 Ibid.

29 Forster, VIII, vii, 708.

30 Ibid.

31 Johnson, pp. 1087–88.

32 *AM* 28, 225; Dolby, p. 93.

33 Nonesuch *Letters,* III, 530.

34 Advertisement for "Author's American Edition of 'Dickens,'" p. 6, col. 3.

35 Dolby, p. 93.

36 Forster, X, i, 765.

37 21 August 1867, "Dickens Coming Again," p. 4, col. 5. Dolby disembarked on the nineteenth and on the twentieth the purpose of his visit was published in the papers.

38 29 August 1867, "Dickens in America," p. 4, col. 4.

39 6 September 1867, "The Proposed Second Visit of Dickens," p. 4, col. 3. See Peter S. Bracher, "The New York *Herald* and *American Notes,*" *Dickens Studies* 5 (May 1969), 81–85.

40 Dolby, pp. 123–24.

41 "Dickens' 'American Notes' and His Second Visit," p. 6, col. 3.

42 20 November 1867, "Charles Dickens in America," p. 4, col. 2.

43 "Mr. Dickens as a Reader," p. 5, col. 1.

44 Forster, X, i, 765; Dolby, p. 125.

45 *PC* 9 (15 May 1867), 36; the check was deposited in Dickens' Coutts account on 9 May 1867 (MS Coutts, quoted by permission).

46 Pilgrim *Letters,* I, 652.

47 James J. Barnes, *Authors, Publishers, and Politicians: The Quest for an Anglo-American Copyright Agreement, 1815–1854* (Columbus: Ohio State University Press, 1974), p. 53.

48 *PC* 9 (15 May 1867), 36; for textual consequences see Kathleen Tillotson, "*Oliver Twist* in Three Volumes," *Library,* ser. 5, 18 (1963), 113–32, and her introduction to the Clarendon edition of *Oliver Twist* (Oxford: Clarendon Press, 1966), xv–xlvii.

49 Pilgrim *Letters,* I, 417.

50 Barnes, p. 33.

51 *PC* 9 (15 May 1867), 36.

52 Pilgrim *Letters,* III, 291–93; no wonder he was so angry about English piracies of his Christmas books.

53 Pilgrim *Letters,* III, 256–59 (7 July 1842); see also a 28 December 1842 letter to Lea and Blanchard, in which Dickens reiterates his decision, though assuring his present correspondents that there was nothing personal in it (ibid., 404–5).

54 See Peter S. Bracher, "The Lea & Blanchard Edition of Dickens's *American Notes,* 1842," *PBSA* 63 (1969), 296–300, and "The Early American Editions of *American Notes:* Their Priority and Circulation," *PBSA* 69 (1975), 365–76.

55 Peter S. Bracher, "Harper and Brothers: Publishers of Dickens," *Bulletin of the New York Public Library* 79 (1975–76), 320.

56 Harpers reports paying £400 for *Bleak House* (*PC* 9 [1 June 1867], 69 n.), but the *Priority List* and the Bradbury and Evans accounts show only £360 (see Bracher, "Harper and Brothers," p. 327, n. 29; MS Accounts, Bradbury and Evans, Victoria and Albert Museum [F.D. 18. 1–3], cited by permission; and Eugene Exman, *The House of Harper: One Hundred and Fifty Years of Publishing* [New York: Harper and Row, 1967], p. 310).

57 *Nation* 4 (25 April 1867), 328.
58 Henry C. Carey, *Letters on International Copyright* (Philadelphia: A. Hart, late Carey and Hart, 1853), p. 59.
59 Bracher, "Harper and Brothers," p. 328.
60 *PC* 9 (15 May 1867), 36.
61 Kendall B. Taft, "Wiley's Literary Books," in *The First One Hundred and Fifty Years: A History of John Wiley and Sons, Incorporated, 1807–1957* (New York: John Wiley and Sons, Inc., 1957), p. 20. Wiley and Putnam published editions of *Pictures from Italy, The Cricket on the Hearth, The Battle of Life, Dombey and Son, David Copperfield,* and *Christmas Stories.* See *PC* 9 (1 June 1867), 69.
62 *PC* 9 (1 June 1867), 69.
63 Bracher, "Harper and Brothers," p. 325, n. 23, citing the *Harper Catalogue,* p. 109, lists the following payments to Harpers by Petersons for plates and woodcuts:

Dombey and Son	$1,226.25
David Copperfield	1,165.50
Bleak House	1,151.25
Hard Times	306.00
Little Dorrit	2,649.56
"Christmas Tales"	428.25

In addition the Harper *Contract Book,* I, 377, contains an offer to pay Harpers $2,500 for the plates to *Great Expectations.*
64 Bracher, "Harper and Brothers," p. 324, n. 21.
65 See, for instance, *New York Tribune,* 4 May 1867, p. 6, col. 3.
66 *PC* 9 (1 June 1867), 69.
67 *Nation* 4 (25 April 1867), 328, quoted in *PC* 9 (1 May 1867), 5–6 and also, according to *PC* 9 (1 August 1867), 186, in the *London Bookseller.*
68 P. 38.
69 P. 6, col. 3.
70 We are extremely grateful to Ms. Rita L. Paddock, head of the Public Services Department, and Mr. Norman Novack of the Microtext Section of the Harvard College Library, for supplying us with the identification and a copy of this notice.
71 "New Publications," p. 3, col. 6.

See also *PC* 8 (1 April 1867), 325–26, and Bracher, "Harper and Brothers," p. 325.
72 See advertisements in *New York Tribune,* 18 May 1867, p. 6, col. 3, and *PC* 9 (1 June 1867), 84–85.
73 Ibid.
74 Ibid.
75 10 April 1867, p. 6; cf. *Pall Mall Gazette,* 7 May 1867, p. 5.
76 See Nonesuch *Letters,* III, 523, and MS Accounts, Chapman and Hall.
77 *New York Tribune,* 18 May 1867, p. 6, col. 3, and *PC* 9 (1 June 1867), 84–85.
78 *Pall Mall Gazette,* 8 May 1867, p. 4.
79 *PC* 9 (15 May 1867), 36.
80 Ibid. (1 June 1867), 69.
81 25 June 1867, p. 4, col. 1.
82 *AM* 28, 225.
83 Ibid., 225–26.
84 Dolby, p. 107.
85 Nonesuch *Letters,* III, 544.
86 *PC* 9 (1 October 1867), 303.
87 P. 4, col. 3.
88 Dolby, pp. 133–36; cf. Nonesuch *Letters,* III, 553–54.
89 James Parton, "International Copyright," *Atlantic Monthly* 20 (October 1867), 443.
90 Pp. 430–51; it is worth noting that Parton sat at the head table during the Delmonico's farewell dinner for Dickens in May 1868.
91 *PC* 9 (16 September 1867), 265.
92 26 September 1867, "The October Magazines," p. 6, col. 4.
93 Quoted in *PC* 10 (15 February 1868), 216.
94 *Speeches,* p. 21.
95 *PC* 10 (1 November 1867), 7.
96 "International Copyright," p. 443.
97 "Our Weekly Gossip," p. 855.
98 "International Copyright," p. 447; cf. an editorial under "Occasional Notes" in the 7 May 1867 *Pall Mall Gazette,* which after quoting Dicken's praise of Ticknor and Fields' conduct—the letter which roused Sampson Low's ire—concludes: "But is it not a grave anomaly that the American Government should still subject its publishers to the satire implied in

being thanked so warmly for discharging the mere obligation of common honesty?" (p. 5).

99 "International Copyright," p. 442.

100 *Speeches*, p. 21.

101 10 December 1867, "Charles Dickens in New York," p. 7, cols. 1–2.

102 "Dickens, Dolby, the Dollars, and the 'Demnition Public,' " p. 4, col. 3.

103 P. 6, col. 6.

104 P. 4, col. 6.

105 29 October 1867, "Theresa Yelverton and Charles Dickens," p. 6, cols. 5–6.

106 27 October 1867, p. 6, col. 6.

107 29 October 1867, p. 6, cols. 5–6.

108 "The Arrival of Dickens," p. 6, col. 6.

109 P. 1, col. 5.

110 P. 6, col. 5.

111 *PC* 10 (2 December 1867), 81.

112 Dolby, pp. 158–59.

113 9 December 1867, p. 4, col. 6, and p. 5, col. 1.

114 10 December 1867, p. 7, col. 1.

115 Dolby, pp. 187, 159.

116 Franklin P. Rolfe, "Additions to the Nonesuch Edition of Dickens' Letters," *Huntington Library Quarterly* 5 (1941), 137.

117 William Glyde Wilkins, *Dickens in Cartoon and Caricature* (Boston: Boston Bibliophile Society, 1924), Plates XXII, XXVI, XXV. We thank Ms. Marjorie E. Pillers and The Dickens House for supplying us with copies of these rare cartoons.

118 "The Dickens' Ticket Sale," p. 4, col. 5.

119 17 December 1867, "The Dickens Ticket Sale—How to Prevent Further Trouble," p. 4, col. 4.

120 "The Dickens Tickets Counterfeited," p. 5, col. 1.

121 "The Dickens Ticket Business," p. 4, col. 3.

122 "Dickens," p. 6, col. 2.

123 Bracher, "Harper and Brothers," p. 331.

124 See Collins, ed., "Introduction" to *The Public Readings*, esp. pp. lxii–lxv, for more information on the Ticknor and Fields Reading edition.

125 Nonesuch *Letters*, III, 92.

126 Forster, X, i, 765.

127 MS Accounts, Chapman and Hall.

128 Quoted in Forster, X, i, 765.

129 2 (11 September 1858), 578, quoted by Bracher, "Harper and Brothers," p. 332.

130 *The Dickensian* 40 (March 1944), 56.

131 "Dickens, Dolby, the Dollars, and the 'Demnition Public,' " p. 4, col. 3.

132 Quoted in Forster, X, i, 765.

133 Cf. Collins, ed., *Dickens: The Critical Heritage.*

134 William Glyde Wilkins, ed., *Charles Dickens in America* (London: Chapman and Hall, Ltd., 1911), Appendix II, pp. 308–18.

135 See, for example, the *New York World,* 18 November 1867, p. 1, cols. 3–5, and *New York Tribune,* 18 November 1867, p. 1, cols. 1–4.

136 *Speeches*, p. 372.

137 *PC* 9 (1 October 1867), 298.

138 Dolby, p. 271.

139 Forster, X, ii, 795 n.

140 19 May 1868, p. 7, col. 2.

141 "Surely it is time that the pudding-headed Dolby retired into the native gloom from which he has emerged," Dolby, p. 168. This is a misquotation of the *World*'s statement on 14 December 1867 quoted correctly above.

142 "Dickens, Dolby, the Dollars, and the 'Demnition Public,' " p. 4, col. 3.

143 *Speeches*, p. 380.

144 Ibid., p. 381.

145 Collins, ed., *The Public Readings*, lists seventy-five, p. xxvi.

146 Dolby, pp. 331–32.

147 26 November 1867, "Oh, the Dickens!" p. 6, col. 5.

148 *AM* 28, 227.

149 Bracher, "Harper and Brothers," p. 320.

JAMES A. DAVIES: *Striving for Honesty*

1   Respectively: *The Life and Adventures of Oliver Goldsmith* (London: Bradbury and Evans, 1848); *The Life and Times of Oliver Goldsmith*, 2d ed., 2 vols. (London: Bradbury and Evans, 1854); "John Dryden and Jacob Tonson," *The Pic Nic Papers,* ed. Charles Dickens (Philadelphia: Lea and Blanchard, 1841), I, 46–62; "Charles Churchill," *Edinburgh Review* 81 (January–April 1845), 46–88; "Daniel De Foe," *Edinburgh Review* 82 (July–October 1845), 480–532; "Samuel Foote," *Quarterly Review* 95 (June–September 1854), 483–548; "Sir Richard Steele," *Quarterly Review* 96 (December 1854–March 1855), 509–68; *The Life of Jonathan Swift*, vol. I (London: John Murray, 1875). Only the first volume of Swift was published and this not until after *The Life of Charles Dickens,* but the collection of materials and most of the preparatory work was completed by 1860 (see David Woolley, "Forster's *Swift,*" *The Dickensian* 70 (1974), 196); in its approach to literary character, also, it belongs with Forster's earlier work.

2   See my article, "Forster and Dickens: the Making of Podsnap," *The Dickensian* 70 (1974), 145–46.

3   "Charles Churchill," pp. 46–47.

4   G. H. Lewes, *Ranthorpe* (London: Chapman and Hall, 1847), pp. 42–43.

5   *Examiner,* 5 March 1837, pp. 148–49; and 3 November 1839, pp. 691–93.

6   I have consulted R. M. Wardle, *Oliver Goldsmith* (Lawrence Kans.: University of Kansas Press, 1957); C. Churchill, *Poetical Works,* ed. D. Grant (Oxford: Clarendon Press, 1956); J. R. Moore, *Daniel Defoe, Citizen of the Modern World* (Chicago: University of Chicago Press, 1958); C. Winton, *Captain Steele* and *Sir Richard Steele M.P.* (Baltimore: Johns Hopkins Press, 1964 and 1970); S. Trefman, *Sam. Foote, Comedian, 1720–1777* (New York: New York University Press, 1971); S. N. Bogorad, "Samuel Foote: the Prospects for a Life and Works," *Restoration and Eighteenth-Century Theatre Research* 6 (1967), 11–13; I. Ehrenpreis, *Swift: the Man, His Works, and the Age,* vols. 1 and 2 (London: Methuen, 1962, 1967); L. Landa, *Swift and the Church of Ireland* (Oxford: Clarendon Press, 1954); J. Swift, *Journal to Stella,* ed. H. Williams, 2 vols., (Oxford; Clarendon Press, 1948); J. Swift, *Correspondence,* ed. H. Williams, 3 vols. (Oxford: Clarendon Press, 1963–65).

7   "John Forster," *Forster Collection: a Catalogue of the Printed Books* (London: South Kensington Museum, 1888), p. xvii.

8   E. B. de Fonblanque, *The Life and Labours of Albany Fonblanque* (London: Bentley, 1874), p. 58.

9   Macvey Napier, *Selections from the Correspondence,* ed. M. Napier (London: Macmillan, 1879), p. 508. The comment is Francis Jeffrey's.

10   "Daniel De Foe," p. 498.

11   "Charles Churchill," pp. 61–62.

12   "Samuel Foote," p. 500.

13   Respectively: "Charles Churchill," pp. 52, 53; "Daniel De Foe," p. 498; *Goldsmith* (1848), pp. 5, 26.

14   "Sir Richard Steele," p. 529.

15   Lytton Papers: Letters and Papers, vol. xv, 26 April 1862. Quoted by courtesy of the Hertfordshire County Record Office, and by kind permission of Lady Hermione Cobbold.

16   R. W. Armour, *Barry Cornwall: a Biography of Bryan Waller Procter* (Boston: Meador Pub. Co., 1935), p. 266.

17   *Goldsmith* (1848), pp. viii, 540.

18   Ibid., pp. 30–31.

19   "John Dryden and Jacob Tonson," p. 61.

20   *On Heroes, Hero-Worship, and the Heroic in History* (1841; reprint ed., London: World's Classics, O.U.P., 1950), p. 205.

21   Respectively: *Goldsmith* (1848), p. 117; "Samuel Foote," p. 490; *Swift,* p. 131.

22   "Daniel De Foe," p. 528.

23   "John Dryden and Jacob Tonson," p. 46.

24   *Swift,* p. 130.

25   B.M. Add. MS. 34626, f. 148: Forster to Napier, 20 April 1846.

26   *Goldsmith* (1848), pp. 69–70, 71.

27   "John Dryden and Jacob Tonson," pp. 61–62.

28   *Letters,* ed. W. Dexter (London: Nonesuch Press, 1938), II, 83.

29   See R. H. Super, *Walter Savage Landor* (New York: New York University Press, 1954), pp. 455–56.

30   So far as Forster's period is concerned, three points can be made. First, since Fox's Libel Act of 1792 the jury and not the judge decided what was defamatory; thus general middle-class standards prevailed, well understood by Forster the literary adviser with legal training. Second, Campbell's Act of 1843 laid down that "the fact that the matter published was true and for the public benefit was to be a defence to a prosecution" (Sir W. Holdsworth, *A History of English Law,* ed. A. L. Goldhart and H. G. Hanbury [London: Methuen, 1965], xv, 150). But "this is seldom relied on in practice because the defendant must prove the entire statement complained of to be true in substance and in fact, and if he fails, this merely aggravates the damages" (*Halesbury's Statutes of England,* ed. Sir R. Burrows, 2d ed. [London: Butterworth, 1949], xiii, 150). Such aggravation had occurred in 1863 (*Caulfield v. Whitworth*), even as Forster was writing *Landor.* Third, even though "prior to the passing of the Slander of Women Act, 1891, no action lay, without proof of special damage, for words imputing unchastity or adultery to a woman" (Sir H. Fraser, *Principles and Practice of the Law of Libel and Slander,* ed. A. P. Fachiri, 6th ed. [London: Butterworth, 1925), p. 61]), where "special damage" meant any *provable* loss or damage, the rigorous moral climate of the time would have made it comparatively easy to demonstrate such loss and hard to prove the truth of libelous statements. The libel laws must have strongly reinforced the Victorian biographer's tendency toward reticence.

31   See Super, *Landor,* passim, and R. H. Super, "Forster as Landor's Literary Executor," *Modern Language Notes* 52 (1937), 504–6.

32   Respectively: *Walter Savage Landor* (London: Chapman and Hall, 1869), II, 594; II, 593.

33   Respectively: Ibid., II, 595; II, 234; II, 310; I, 181.

34   Respectively: Ibid., I, 3; II, 408.

35   Quoted by C. R. Sanders, "Carlyle's Letters," *Bulletin of the John Rylands Library* 38 (1955–56), 222. The phrase is Forster's.

36   Respectively: Lytton Papers: Letters and Papers, vol. xv, 7 May 1872, 9 December 1862; and Box 61, 4 December 1870. Forster's ill health is vividly recorded in his letters to Bulwer.

37   Respectively: G. A. Sala, *Charles Dickens* (London: Routledge, 1870); [J. C. Hotten], *Charles Dickens: the Story of His Life* (London: J. C. Hotten, n.d.).

38   F. R. Leavis & Q. D. Leavis, *Dickens the Novelist* (London: Chatto & Windus, 1970), pp. ix–x.

39   "Dickens's Obscure Childhood in Pre-Forster Biography," *The Dickensian* 72 (1976), 3.

40   *Dickens and His Readers* (Princeton: Princeton University Press, 1955), p. 160.

41   Respectively: S. Monod, "John Forster's 'Life of Dickens' and Literary Criticism," *English Studies Today— Fourth Series* (1966), pp. 359–60; George H. Ford, Edgar Johnson, J. Hillis Miller, Sylvère Monod, Noel C. Peyrouton, *Dickens Criticism* (Cambridge, Mass.: The Charles Dickens Reference Centre, 1962), p. 32.

42   "1870–1900: Forster and Reaction," *The Dickensian* 70 (1970), 91. See also K. J. Fielding, *Charles Dickens,* rev. ed. (London: Longmans, Green & Co. for The British Council, 1963), p. 9.

43   K. J. Fielding and Gerald G. Grubb, "New Letters from Charles Dickens to John Forster," *Boston University Studies in English* 2 (1956), 153.

44   *The Letters of Charles Dickens,* Pilgrim ed. (Oxford: Clarendon Press, 1965), I, xi. Engel uses this passage to

support his statement that "Madeline House and Graham Storey comment on the amazing objectivity of Forster's volumes" ("Dickens's Obscure Childhood," p. 3). But the reference to "ideal" would seem to indicate Engel's misreading.
45   F. R. Hart, *Lockhart as Romantic Biographer* (Edinburgh: Edinburgh University Press, 1971), p. 43. See Alec W. Brice, "The Compilation of the Critical Commentary in Forster's *Life of Charles Dickens*," *The Dickensian* 70 (1974), 188–89.
46   *Charles Dickens: His Tragedy and Triumph*, 2 vols. (London: Gollancz, 1953), passim.
47   See *Letters of Charles Dickens*, Pilgrim ed., I, xi–xvii. And compare Edgar Johnson, passim.
48   Respectively, *The Life of Charles Dickens* (London: Chapman and Hall, 1872–74, I, 138; III, 441.
49   Pp. 19–20.
50   P. 45.
51   "Dickens's Obscure Childhood," p. 5.
52   *Life*, I, 51–52.
53   Respectively: Ibid., I, 113; I, 139; I, 139.
54   Respectively: Ibid., I, 183; III, 368; I, 264; II, 125.

55   P. 244.
56   Pp. 96–97.
57   *Life*, III, 175.
58   Ibid., 164.
59   P. 330.
60   *Life*, III, 517.
61   *Charles Dickens* (British Council), p. 6.
62   Johnson II, 1110–11) treats Dickens' will as a revealing biographical document. Victorian readers would have reacted similarly, and were meant to do so.
63   P. 243.
64   Pp. 65, 92.
65   *Life*, III, 165.
66   Respectively: ibid., III, 229 (Dickens' italics), III, 224–25, III, 239 (my italics).
67   *Dickens and His Readers*, p. 161.
68   *Life*, I, 99–100.
69   See *Letters of Charles Dickens*, Pilgrim ed., I, xi–xvii.
70   *Dickens and His Readers*, p. 161.
71   *Charles Dickens: a Critical Introduction*, 2d ed. (London: Longmans, 1965), p. 31.
72   Fielding & Grubb, "New Letters," p. 155.
73   *Dickens the Novelist*, p. ix.
74   Forster Collection: MS. 366, f. 47.

EARLE DAVIS: *Dickens and Significant Tradition*

1   George Santayana, "Dickens," *Dial* 71 (November 1921), 542.
2   Charles Gavan Duffy, *Conversations with Carlyle* (London: Macmillan, 1892), pp. 74–76, where Carlyle sneers at Dickens for "wanting to coax and soothe and delude [people] into doing right."
3   Trollope specifically so jibes at Dickens in *The Warden*.
4   This artistic conclusion is explored in detail in Earle Davis, *The Flint and the Flame* (Columbia: University of Missouri Press, 1963), chap. xi.
5   William Searle Holdsworth, a chief justice of England, is still the most reputable authority to quote. He

asserts on p. 81 of his *Charles Dickens as a Legal Historian* (New Haven: Yale University Press, 1928) that Dickens was not exaggerating very much; about *Bleak House* he says that Dickens' analysis was substantially true when he wrote the novel and that apparently the situation had not improved much since then.
6   *Edwin Drood*, chap. xviii.
7   Edgar Johnson, *Charles Dickens: His Tragedy and Triumph* (New York: Simon and Schuster, 1952), II, 762.
8   *Bleak House*, chap. ii.
9   F. R. Leavis, *The Great Tradition* (London: Chatto and Windus, 1948), p. 273.

[10] *Little Dorrit,* Bk. II, chap. xxxiii.

[11] *Little Dorrit,* Bk. II, chap. xxxiv.

[12] See Johnson's biography for a complete description of this change in magazine format with consequent influence on the construction of his novels to be printed in the new magazine.

[13] Johnson, II, 1031, quotes this and more from the MS notes in the Forster Collection.

DAVID PAROISSIEN: *Dickens and the Cinema*

[1] For the impact of Edmund Wilson's seminal essay, "Dickens: The Two Scrooges," *The Wound and the Bow* (Boston: Houghton Mifflin, 1941), on subsequent Dickens criticism, see Ada Nisbet, "Charles Dickens," *Victorian Fiction: A Guide to Research,* ed. Lionel Stevenson (Cambridge, Mass.: Harvard University Press, 1966), p. 74; "'The Dickens Industry,'" quoted by George H. Ford, "Dickens in the 1960's," *The Dickensian* 66 (1970), 172; Earle Davies, *The Flint and the Flame: The Artistry of Charles Dickens* (Columbia: University of Missouri Press, 1963); Edgar and Eleanor Johnson, eds. *The Dickens Theatrical Reader* (Boston: Little, Brown, 1964); Robert Brannan, *Under the Management of Charles Dickens: His Production of "The Frozen Deep"* (Ithaca: Cornell University Press, 1966); William Axton, *Circle of Fire: Dickens' Vision and Style and the Popular Victorian Theatre* (Lexington: University of Kentucky Press, 1966); and Robert Garis, *The Dickens Theatre: A Reassessment of the Novels* (Oxford: Clarendon Press, 1965).

[2] Walter Dexter, "For One Night Only: Dickens's Appearance as an Amateur Actor," *The Dickensian* 37 (1940), 8; Ford, "Dickens in the 1960's," p. 179.

[3] *The Dickens Theatre,* pp. 17-19.

[4] Anna Laura Zambrano, "Feature Motion Pictures Adapted from Dickens: A Checklist—Part I," *Dickens Studies Newsletter* 5 (1974), 106-9; "Part II," 6 (1975), 9-13.

[5] Q. D. Leavis, *Fiction and the Reading Public* (1932; reprint ed., London: Chatto and Windus, 1965), p. 156. Although the adaptations we commonly think of fall after 1932, many silent versions of the novels were made both in Hollywood and Europe. See Zambrano.

[6] Taylor Stoehr, *Dickens: The Dreamer's Stance* (Ithaca: Cornell University Press, 1965), pp. 285-86.

[7] Quoted by Vincent Canby, "Should Movies Have Messages?" *New York Times,* 29 February 1976, sec. 2, p. 15.

[8] In Stoehr's case, there is one exception: see chap. 1, "The Style," where he invokes cinematic concepts while attempting to define the peculiar blend of "photographic realism" and "hallucinated, magic quality" that, for him, characterizes Dickens' literary manner. Using *A Tale of Two Cities* as a representative text, he begins with an analysis of the use of detail in one of the novel's key crowd scenes: the introduction of the revolutionary mob outside the wine shop (I, v). The dropping of the wine barrel, Stoehr suggests, far from confirming Orwell's charge of "unnecessary detail" in Dickens' writing, is a concrete object employed "to set the scene, almost cinematically, by focusing on such particulars. Here the effect is that of a high-angle view, centered on the splintered cask" (p. 3). Later, in the same chapter, he compares the arresting and delimiting effect of Dickens' use in the same passage of the rhetorical device of anaphora ("the repetition of the key word 'Hunger' to introduce and mark off the successive items of the presented scene"), to a filmic "montage-cluster," with its series of detail shots, and likens the overall effect to "a cinematic rendering of continuous space

in continuous time, the narrator functioning as a camera-eye; details make their appearance according to their position in the imagined scene, one thing next to another, and still another next to that" (p. 15). For other critics who have briefly noted similar cinematic qualities of Dickens' style, see E. D. H. Johnson, *Charles Dickens: An Introduction to his Novels* (New York: Random House, 1969), p. 158; Angus Wilson, *The World of Charles Dickens* (New York: The Viking Press, 1970), p. 84; and Martin Fido, *Charles Dickens* (New York: Humanities Press, 1968), p. 51.

9   Johnson, p. 147.

10   Sergei Eisenstein, "Dickens, Griffith, and the Film Today," *Film Form: Essays in Film Theory,* trans. and ed. Jay Leyda (New York: Harcourt, Brace, and World, 1949), p. 208. Future references to the essay will appear in the text.

11   *The Old Curiosity Shop,* Oxford Illustrated Dickens Edition (London: Oxford University Press, 1951), p. 13.

12   Walter Dexter, ed., *The Letters of Charles Dickens* (London: Nonesuch Press, 1938), II, 849–50. Future references to this edition will appear in the text.

13   John Forster, *The Life of Charles Dickens* (London: Dent, 1966), II, 272; Herbert Read, "The Poet and the Film," *A Coat of Many Colours,* rev. ed. (London: Routledge and Kegan Paul, 1956), p. 231.

14   Robert M. Henderson, *D. W. Griffith: His Life and Work* (New York: Oxford University Press, 1972), p. 39.

15   Béla Baláaz, *Theory of the Film: Character and Growth of a New Art,* trans. Edith Bone (London: Dennis Dobson, 1952), p. 31; and Lewis Jacob, ed., *Introduction to the Art of the Movies* (New York: Noonday Press, 1960) pp. 7–8.

16   Robert Richardson, *Literature and Film* (Bloomington, Ind.: Indiana University Press, 1969), p. 37.

17   Quoted in Ivor Montague, *Film World: A Guide to Cinema* (1964; reprint ed., Baltimore: Penguin Books, 1967), p. 100; as Richardson notes, such recent productions as the Fonteyn-Nureyev *Romeo and Juliet* and the standard movie versions of Broadway plays (*The Front Page, Barefoot in the Park,* etc.), "suggest that there is still some demand for the film's simple capacity to copy, for film as theatrical xerography" (p. 20).

18   See A. B. Walkley, "Switching Off: Mr. Griffith and Dickens: A Strange Literary Analogy," the London *Times,* 26 April 1922, p. 12. "He is a pioneer," wrote Walkley, the film correspondent for the London *Times,* "by his own admission, rather than an inventor. That is to say, he has opened up new paths in Film Land, under the guidance of ideas supplied to him from the outside. His best ideas, it appears, have come to him from Dickens, who has always been his favourite author. . . . Dickens inspired Mr. Griffith with an idea, and his employers (mere 'business'men) were horrified at it; but, says Mr. Griffith, 'I went home, re-read one of Dickens's novels, and came back next day to tell them they could either make use of my idea or dismiss me.' " Walkley pointed out that the technique of shifting the story from one group to another "is really common to fiction at large" (examples can be found in Thackeray, Eliot, Meredith, Hardy, Dumas *père,* Tolstoy, Turgenev, and Balzac); this is true, but the importance of Griffith's observation is his stress on Dickens as the authority.

19   Montage is now a generally accepted synonym for both editing and cutting. In its first cinematic usage of assembling or joining pieces of celluloid together to make a "film," the word was taken from the related art of photography, where *montage* (⟨*monter,* to mount) denoted the act or process of providing a composite photograph by combining several different photographs so that they blended together to give the appearance of a single picture (C. W. Ceram, [pseud.], *Archae-*

ology of the Cinema [New York: Harcourt, Brace, and World, n.d.], illus. 120; and Georges Sadoul, *Histoire du cinéma mondial: des origines à nos jours,* 9th ed. [Paris: Flammarion, 1949], pp. 22–23). Later, as narrative film began to evolve as an art form, montage was applied in a more specialized way to signify the creative task of assembling a film not simply from several lengths of celluloid but from a series of shots—fragments of an action—to convey a sense of entirety. Cf. Béla Balázas: "Montage, that is the assembly of 'shots' in a certain order in which not only whole scene follows whole scene (however short) but pictures of smallest details are given, so that the whole scene is composed of a mosaic of frames aligned as it were in chronological sequence" (*Theory of Film,* p. 31).

20   While Eisenstein argued that Griffith picked up a good deal of his narrative sense from Dickens, he was careful not to suggest the novelist as Griffith's sole literary source. On the contrary, film narration owes a debt not only to Dickens but literature in general: "Let Dickens and the whole ancestral array, going back as far as the Greeks and Shakespeare, be superfluous reminders that both Griffith and our cinema prove our origins to be not solely as of Edison and his fellow inventors, but as based on an enormous cultured past; each part of this past in its own moment of world history has moved forward the great art of cinematography. Let this past be a reproach to those thoughtless people who have displayed arrogance in reference to literature, which has contributed so much to this apparently unprecedented art and is, in the first and most important place: the art of viewing—not only the *eye,* but *viewing*—both meanings being embraced in this term" (pp. 232–33). On the extent of Griffith's literary knowledge, see also Richardson, *Literature and Film,* pp. 38–40.

21   William C. Wees in "Dickens, Griffith, and Einenstein: Form and Image in Literature and Film" (a paper presented at the annual meeting of the Association of Canadian University Teachers of English, Kingston, Ontario, 29 May 1973) cites the brief paragraph Dickens devoted to Sydney Carton and the seamstress en route to the guillotine as a good example of Eisenstein's point: "The two stand in the fast-thinning throng of victims, but they speak as if they were alone. Eye to eye, voice to voice, hand to hand, heart to heart, these two children of the Universal Mother, else so wide apart and differing, have come together on the dark highway, to repair home together and to rest in her bosom" (*A Tale of Two Cities,* III, chap. xv). "Griffith held to a similar vision," comments Wees. "The original version of *The Birth of a Nation* concludes with parallel allegorical scenes of War subjecting mankind to misery and death, and Peace—in the person of Jesus—radiating holy light upon worshipful masses" (pp. 9–10). I would like to thank Professor Wees for sending me a copy of his paper and express my indebtedness to his stimulating study.

22   Sergei Eisenstein, "A Personal Statement," and "The Method of Making Workers' Films," *Film Essays and a Lecture,* ed. Jay Leyda (New York: Praeger, 1970), pp. 13–20.

23   Stoehr, p. 19.

24   Forster, II, 279.

25   Montague, p. 104, pp. 102–3.

26   Stanley J. Solomon, *The Film Idea* (New York: Harcourt Brace Jovanovich, 1972), p. 254.

27   Henry James, Preface to *The Spoils of Poynton,* in *The Art of the Novel,* introd. R. P. Blackmur (New York: Charles Scribner's, 1962), p. 120.

28   Nisbet, "Charles Dickens," p. 106.

29   G. K. Chesterton, *Charles Dickens: A Critical Study* (New York: Dodd Mead, 1906), p. 170.

30   [Richard Ford], "Oliver Twist," *Quarterly Review* 64 (June 1839), 90; [George Eliot], "The Natural History of German Life," *Westminster Review* 66 (July 1856), 55; [R. H. Hutton], "The Genius of Dickens," *Spectator* 43 (18

June 1870), [Henry Fothergill Chorley], *"Bleak House," Athenaeum,* 17 September 1853, p. 1087; Ruskin to his Father, 18 January 1863, *The Works of John Ruskin,* ed. E. T. Cook and Alexander Wedderburn (London: George Allen, 1909), XXXVI, 432; see also, Philip Collins, ed., *Dickens: The Critical Heritage* (London: Routledge and Kegan Paul, 1971), pp. 82, 343, 519, 277, and 443.

31 Leon Edel, "Novel and Camera," *The Theory of the Novel: New Essays,* ed. John Halperin (New York: Oxford University Press, 1974), p. 177.

32 In his interview with Walkley (see n. 18), Griffith noted that "much of the work of Dickens was modelled on Fielding." In *Tom Jones,* Bk. V, chap. i, Fielding inserted a "digressive Essay" on the aesthetic advantage of contrast similar to Dickens' montage "treatise" in *Oliver Twist,* chap. xvii. This "Vein of Knowledge," wrote Fielding, "runs through all the Works of the Creation, and may, probably, have a large Share in constituting in us the Idea of all Beauty, as well natural as artificial: For what demonstrates the Beauty and Excellence of any Thing, but its Reverse? Thus the Beauty of Day, and that of Summer, is set off by the Horrors of Night and Winter. . . . Most Artists have this Secret in Practice," he continued, and cited John Rich, the inventor of English pantomime, with its contrast of the serious and the comic, as one who practiced the technique to great advantage. So did Fielding, whose own novel works on the same principle. For Wilson's comment, see "Dickens: The Two Scrooges," p. 36.

33 *Bleak House,* Oxford Illustrated Dickens Edition (London: Oxford University Press, 1948), pp. 627–28.

THOMAS J. RICE: *Barnaby Rudge*

1 Companion studies by Philip Collins, of *Dickens and Crime,* 2d ed. (London: Macmillan, 1965) and *Dickens and Education,* 2d ed. (London: Macmillan, 1965), have contributed to the reassessment of Dickens' essentially conservative attitudes. The second of the studies offers the best available discussion of Dickens' views on education, but one facet of domestic government. Stephen Marcus' excellent essay on *Barnaby Rudge* centers on the symbolic and structural importance of the father-son relationship but omits consideration of the other familial situations in the novel or the governmental theme generally: see "Sons and Fathers," *Dickens: From Pickwick to Dombey* (New York: Basic Books, 1965), pp. 169–212. Additional readings which argue a unifying symbolic or thematic pattern in *Barnaby,* but comment indirectly if at all on Dickens' views of domestic government, are: Harold F. Folland, "The Doer and the Deed: Theme and Pattern in *Barnaby Rudge,*" *PMLA* 74 (1959), 406–17; James K. Gottshall, "Devils Abroad: The Unity and Significance of *Barnaby Rudge,*" *Nineteenth-Century Fiction* 16 (1961), 133–46; and Thomas J. Rice, "The End of Dickens's Apprenticeship: Variable Focus in *Barnaby Rudge,*" *Nineteenth-Century Fiction* 30 (1975), 172–84.

2 The contemporary views of family management which will be discussed in this essay are readily available in the vast literature on domestic government which appeared as home "monitors," or "guardians," or "advisors," as published sermons, and even as appendices to cookbooks. Most of these works (a number of which are noted here) share the same basic concern for defining the roles of individual household members and the relative duties among them.

3 Elsewhere I have demonstrated Dickens' political withdrawal from "sentimental radicalism" in this novel toward a more moderate political

stance. See my *"Oliver Twist* and the Genesis of *Barnaby Rudge,"* *Dickens Studies Newsletter* 4, no. 1 (1973), 10–14.

⁴ Dickens describes his own sense of this prejudice against his early fiction in the 1847 "Preface" to *Pickwick Papers:* see John Butt and Kathleen Tillotson, *Dickens at Work* (London: Methuen, 1957), pp. 76–89, for a description of his intentions for *Barnaby.* For Dickens' attitude toward Scott, see Edgar Johnson, *Charles Dickens: His Tragedy and Triumph* (New York: Simon and Schuster, 1952), passim, and for his attempts to win the esteem of the conservative and the critical audiences, see George Ford, *Dickens and His Readers* (Princeton: Princeton University Press, 1955), pp. 34, 41–42.

⁵ From John Lucas, *The Melancholy Man: A Study of Dickens's Novels* (London: Methuen, 1970), p. 93.

⁶ This opening of the story is but one of several thematic and technical parallels to Shakespeare's *King Lear,* perhaps the most famous exploration of the civil-domestic analogy in our literature. See Marcus, pp. 204–5 and passim.

⁷ Perhaps nowhere is the distance between the reader today and Dickens, and his contemporary audience, so great as at this point in the novel. The modern reader too readily sympathizes with Joe in his absurd plight and, lacking the near-religious veneration for the father-figure (or most authority figures), wonders why he bears with his "old man" as long as he does. In constructing the events preparatory to the revolt, Dickens is carefully guarding against the reader's total alienation from Joe. Ironically, the modern reader, already disposed toward Joe's position, is more likely to be alienated by Willet, a character Dickens clearly sees in a benevolent, comic light. Willet is certainly a fool, but he is no vicious tyrant. Johnson, for example, finds Willet "tiresome" (*Charles Dickens,* pp. 330), while other

readers see in him as threatening a paternal figure as Murdstone (e.g., Marcus, p. 176 and passim.)

⁸ Lucas observes, quite correctly, that the "unnatural horror of Barnaby fighting his own father offers a metaphor of the radical disorders that stem from a refusal to acknowledge the social *status quo"* (*Melancholy Man,* p. 101). The recognition of the spiritual bond between parent and child is a consistent device throughout Dickens' fiction. Also see, for example, Ralph Nickleby's suicide (*Nicholas Nickleby*) and Esther Summerson's responses to Lady Dedlock (*Bleak House*).

⁹ John Angell James writes: "We have considered the father as the *prophet* of his family; we are now to view him as their *king;* and his laws are as important as his instructions": see his *Family Monitor,* 3d ed. (London, 1833), p. 94. For further comment on the sacred kingship of the father in the eighteenth and nineteenth centuries, see Paul Sangster, *Pity My Simplicity* (London: Epworth, 1963), p. 80.

¹⁰ See Willystine Goodsell, *A History of the Family as a Social and Educational Institution* (New York: Macmillan, 1915), p. 441.

¹¹ Quoted by Sangster, p. 30. The authoritarian parent, although a constant in domestic history, flourished in nineteenth-century England as a direct result of the Evangelical revivals, though not necessarily in pietistic homes alone. The Victorian paterfamilias was an entirely different concept of the father's role in home government from that of the eighteenth-century benevolists. See Sangster, passim.

¹² James, p. 94.

¹³ Quoted by Sangster, p. 30.

¹⁴ To counteract this abuse of parental discipline, the Edgeworths emphatically asserted that "if the pain, which we would associate with any action, do not *immediately* follow it, the child does not understand us." See Maria and R. L. Edgeworth, *Practical Education,* 2d ed., I (London, 1801), p. 357.

15 See, for example, one of the best-known commentaries on this subject: William Fleetwood's sermon on "The Case of Parents *Disinheriting* Children," in *The Relative Duties of Parents and Children, Husbands and Wives, Masters and Servants,* 3d ed. (London, 1722), pp. 111–30.

16 See Fleetwood, pp. 117–18.

17 Dickens constructs an interesting parallel between Mrs. Rudge and Hugh's mother and, implicitly, correlates Rudge's villainy with Chester's abandonment of his bastard son. Mrs. Rudge tells Barnaby that "the endeavour of my life has been to keep you two [father and son] asunder" (562). Shortly after, Dickens informs the reader that Hugh's gypsy mother desired as her last wish "that the boy might live and grow, in utter ignorance of his father" (579). Although the strength of the bond frustrates both mothers' wishes and their two sons come to know their fathers, the inference is clear: the crimes of the fathers warrant the attempted severing of the sacred tie.

18 Benjamin Morgan Palmer implicitly defends the right to revolt, in the shadow of the American Civil War, in precisely the same terms as generations of Englishmen had defended civil and domestic disobedience: "If [the parent's] will should, however, deliberately set aside the law of God, which is supreme, and if the child's conscience be sufficiently educated to perceive the issue that is joined, why, then, the case is analogous to what sometimes happens with a people or nation, which is driven by oppression to overturn the despotism; falling back upon rights which antecedently exist by the gift of God, and which no human government can lawfully contravene. In such a collision, the law of obedience to the child is to obey only *in the Lord;* and the responsibility remains with the parent who has perpetrated the outrage." See *The Family in its Civil and Churchly Aspects* (New York, 1876), pp. 113–14. For British commentators who make similar theological and *political* defenses of the conscientious revolt, see James, pp. 127–28, and Samuel Stennett, *Discourses on Domestic Duties* (Edinburgh, 1800), p. 203.

19 Thomas Hood refers to the *Letters* as "a prize book at our academies" in his review of *Barnaby Rudge* in the *Athanaeum,* 22 January 1842, p. 78. Also see Roland W. Nelson, "The Reputation of Lord Chesterfield in Great Britain and America, 1730–1936" (Ph.D. diss., Northwestern University, 1938).

20 The political principles embodied in Chester's domestic policies are more completely developed in Dickens' other historical novel, *A Tale of Two Cities,* where he describes a just revolt against a decadent government. Both Sir John and the Marquis St. Evremond are Dickensian types of the corrupt aristocrat. Chester's home rule is the cognate of the demoralizing government of the rationalistic, degenerate aristocracy in eighteenth-century France.

21 Stennett, pp. 274–75. Also see Fleetwood, pp. 269–310, and James, pp. 193–201. The Augustan Reprint Society has recently republished Samuel Richardson's *The Apprentice's Vade Mecum (1734),* a pamphlet on apprentice behavior which was distributed by the Stationer's Company through the nineteenth century, and which appears to be Dickens' primary source for virtually every vice attributable to Sim Tappertit. See Publication Numbers 169–170 (Los Angeles: William Andrews Clark Memorial Library, 1975).

22 For a contemporary criticism of distinction, see Dr. Johnson's comments in James Boswell, *Life of Johnson* (London: Oxford, 1960), pp. 1054–55. The chief popular lesson of the Gordon Riots seems to have been the disastrous effects of indecisive rule. A lead editorial in the *London Morning Chronicle* for 14 December 1838, reflects that the "moment men in authority hesitate, violence gains ascendancy.

The cowardice of the Lord Mayor of London, in 1780, had nearly converted London to a heap of ruins."

23 See my full analysis of Dickens' systematic analogical method in "The End of Dickens's Apprenticeship: Variable Focus in *Barnaby Rudge*."

24 See Fleetwood's sermon entitled "Ye Wives, be in Subjection to Your Own Husbands [1 Pet. 3:1–2]," pp. 131–50.

ARLENE M. JACKSON: *Reward, Punishment, and the Conclusion of* Dombey and Son

1 "Dickens's Endings," *Studies in the Novel* 6 (1974), 282.

2 A. E. Dyson, "The Case for Dombey Senior," *Novel* 2 (Winter 1969), 131.

3 Ibid., p. 126. Dyson explains: Dombey "is austere in his habits, and by intention a benefactor, with no conscious will to cause suffering or pain. . . . Dombey is neither actively wicked nor in any sense dishonorable; he is merely lacking in all qualities of warmth and love."

4 Julian Moynahan, "Dealings with the Firm of Dombey and Son: Firmness versus Wetness," in *Dickens and the Twentieth Century*, ed. John Gross and Gabriel Pearson (London: Routledge and Kegan Paul, 1962), p. 127.

5 "Dombey and Son," *Novels of the Eighteen Forties* (Oxford: Clarendon Press, 1956), pp. 164–65.

6 There are still discernible, external signs of Dombey's internal struggle. As Kathleen Tillotson points out, Dombey's "thoughtfulness," commented upon by Major Bagstock, suggests "the secret self-doubting of 'stiff-necked sullen arrogance.'" Tillotson, p. 167.

7 Moral conversion in many of Dickens' novels is "the moral change on which action hinges, or appears to hinge." In this respect, Dombey's con-version is not typical of Dickens' work, since it appears at the end of the novel rather than as a turning point closer to the novel's structural center. As indicated, furthermore, his change is not abrupt but has been in the making for much of the story. See Barbara Hardy, "The Change of Heart in Dickens' Novels," *Victorian Studies* 5 (September 1961), 49–67.

8 Moynahan, p. 130.

9 "Dickens and Dombey: A Daughter After All," *Dickens Studies Annual*, 5 (1975), 95–114.

10 Dyson, p. 130.

11 Tillotson, p. 172.

12 *Dickens from Pickwick to Dombey* (New York: Simon and Schuster, 1968), pp. 355–56.

13 A. O. J. Cockshut, *The Imagination of Charles Dickens* (New York: New York University Press, 1962), pp. 105–6.

14 Tillotson, p. 179.

15 "Dombey and Son," *Sewanee Review* 70 (Spring 1962), 194. Dyson, p. 133, also believes that it is hard to make moral sense of Edith: "But Edith, who married him with open eyes, has no reason to be surprised. She provokes him [Dombey], after all, beyond endurance, in her strange plot which destroys Carker as well."

16 Cockshut, p. 106.

STANLEY FRIEDMAN: *Dickens' Mid-Victorian Theodicy*

1 K. J. Fielding, *Charles Dickens: A Critical Introduction*, 2d ed. enl. (London: Longmans, 1965), p. 141.

2 See James R. Kincaid, "The Dark-ness of *David Copperfield*," *Dickens Studies* 1 (May 1965), 70–71; Edward Hurley, "Dickens' Portrait of the Artist," *VN*, no. 38 (Fall 1970), 4; Janet H.

Brown, "The Narrator's Role in *David Copperfield*," in *Dickens Studies Annual*, 2 (1972), 207; Felicity Hughes, "Narrative Complexity in *David Copperfield*," *ELH*, 41 (Spring 1974), 99–100; and Robin Gilmour, "Memory in *David Copperfield*," *The Dickensian* 71 (January 1975), 31.

3   See Miller, *Charles Dickens: The World of His Novels* (Cambridge, Mass.: Harvard University Press, 1958), pp. 155–58; and Welsh, *The City of Dickens* (Oxford: Clarendon Press, 1971), pp. 180–82.

4   See Bert G. Hornback, *"Noah's Arkitecture": A Study of Dickens's Mythology* (Athens, Ohio: Ohio University Press, 1972), pp. 77–79.

5   G. A. Starr, *Defoe & Spiritual Autobiography* (Princeton: Princeton University Press, 1965), p. 33. Hurley notices, p. 3, that Copperfield is not consistent on the supposed privacy of his manuscript: although he states that it "is intended for no eyes but mine" (606), he has previously remarked, "The reader now understands" (56).

6   *The End of the Road*, rev. ed. (Garden City, N.Y.: Doubleday, 1967), p. 83.

7   *Design and Truth in Autobiography* (Cambridge, Mass.: Harvard University Press, 1960), p. 59.

8   Cf. Starr's comment, p. 3, on the Puritan tradition of spiritual autobiography: "To compose any kind of autobiography is to assume one's own importance. In the seventeenth century, only the spiritual autobiographer could avoid the awkwardness of having to justify this assumption." Copperfield's implicit disclaimer seems attributable to the fact that his narrative is not overtly a spiritual autobiography.

9   See Albert Johannesen, *PHIZ: Illustrations from the Novels of Charles Dickens* (Chicago: University of Chicago Press, 1956), pp. 394–95, Plates 39A and 39B.

10   *David Copperfield*, ed. George H. Ford, Riverside Edition (Boston: Houghton Mifflin, 1958), p. 1, and his comment, p. xv. All subsequent references are to this edition and indicate chapter and page.

11   See, e.g., Mark Spilka, *Dickens and Kafka: A Mutual Interpretation* (Bloomington: Indiana University Press, 1963), pp. 47, 179, and Hurley, p. 4.

12   *The Moral Vision of Jacobean Tragedy* (Madison, Wisc.: University of Wisconsin Press, 1960), pp. 237–38.

13   Of course, various scholars have noted that death is a persistent theme in nearly all of Dickens' fiction, but commentators have also stressed that this interest was shared by most other Victorian novelists. See, e.g., David Dale Johnson, "Fear of Death in Victorian Fiction," *West Virginia University Bulletin: Philological Studies* 3 (1939), 3–11; Alan Walbank, "With a Blush Retire," *The Dickensian* 57 (September 1961), 166–73; and William R. Clark, "The Rationale of Dickens' Death Rate," *Boston University Studies in English* 2 (Autumn 1956), 134–35. On the Victorians' obsession with this subject, see John Morley, *Death, Heaven and the Victorians* (Pittsburgh: University of Pittsburgh Press, 1971), and Welsh, esp. pp. 57–72 and 180–228.

14   Although Leo Mason, in *"Jane Eyre* and *David Copperfield*," *The Dickensian* 43 (September 1947), 172–79, and E. D. H. Johnson, in *Charles Dickens: An Introduction to His Novels* (New York: Random House, 1969), pp. 23, 97, consider the possible influence of *Jane Eyre* on *David Copperfield*, neither critic refers to this contrast.

15   Either "ruined" or "ruin" is applied to many characters in the novel: Em'ly (451), Aunt Betsey (499), David (539), Wickfield (578), Martha (681), and Micawber (702).

16   The ways in which Murdstone, Steerforth, and Heep are able to impose their wills on David and others seem to reflect Dickens' intense interest in mesmerism—see Hughes, esp. pp. 100–105. Fred Kaplan, in *Dickens and Mesmerism: The Hidden Springs of Fiction* (Princeton: Princeton University Press, 1975), considers the themes

of will, will power, and lack of will in Dickens' fiction—see esp. pp. 165, 169, 171–72, 184, 186, 201, and 236.

[17] Sylvère Monod, in *Dickens the Novelist* (Norman: University of Oklahoma Press, 1968), pp. 298–99, lists many, though not all, of the coincidences in *David Copperfield;* but his comment, p. 299, that "there are at least a few coincidences in every average human life, and there was no reason why David's should form an exception to the rule," minimizes the enormous emphasis on coincidence. At various times, David himself and other characters directly call attention to coincidences—see, e.g., 34, 68, 256, 311–12, 368, 372, 582, and 795.

[18] *Season of Youth: The Bildungsroman from Dickens to Golding* (Cambridge, Mass.: Harvard University Press, 1974), p. 37.

[19] P. 157. Miller asserts, pp. 155–56, that David provides coherence for his own world through memory and yet is also guided by "the power of divine Providence." See, too, Miller's remarks on pp. 331 and 334.

[20] Eli Marcovitz, "The Meaning of *Déjà Vu,*" *Psychoanalytic Quarterly* 21 (October 1952), 483–84.

[21] Jacob A. Arlow, "The Structure of the *Déjà Vu* Experience," *Journal of the American Psychoanalytic Association* 7 (1959), 625–26.

[22] Jerome M. Schneck, "The Psychodynamics of 'Déjà Vu,' " *Psychoanalysis & The Psychoanalytic Review* 49 (Winter 1962), 48, 50.

[23] E. Pearlman, in "David Copperfield Dreams of Drowning," *American Imago* 28 (Winter 1971), 391–92, 395–99, considers Heep as a sexual figure. Pearlman, p. 392, Spilka, pp. 193–94, and Welsh, pp. 132–33, are among the critics who notice links between David and Uriah.

[24] P. 611.

[25] David's slips seem close to his creator's, who at times gave Mary Hogarth preeminence over her sister, his wife. Edgar Johnson in *Charles Dickens: His Tragedy and Triumph,* 2 vols. (New York: Simon and Schuster,

1952), I, 197, quotes from the June 1837 issue of *Bentley's Miscellany* the notice in which Dickens refers to the recently dead Mary as "the chief solace" of his labors; and in a letter to his mother-in-law, on 26 October 1837, the novelist describes Mary as "the gentlest and purest creature that ever shed a light on earth"—see The Pilgrim Edition of *The Letters of Charles Dickens,* ed. Madeline House and Graham Storey (Oxford: Clarendon Press, 1965), I, 323.

[26] Ernest Jones, in *Hamlet and Oedipus* (Garden City, N.Y.: Doubleday Anchor Books, 1954), pp. 137–43, endorses Otto Rank's view of Brutus and Cassius as "sons" of Caesar. Max Véga-Ritter, in "Structures Imaginaires et Leurs Conflits dans *David Copperfield,*" *Studies in the Later Dickens,* ed. Jean-Claude Amalric (Montpellier: Université Paul Valéry, 1973), does not refer to *Julius Caesar* but does emphasize the theme of rebellious sons, including David, who revolts against Murdstone's "tyranny" (iv, 49), as well as Steerforth, Heep, and Maldon—see pp. 31–32, 35, and 52. Spilka, p. 193, remarks, "Uriah is best described as an economic Steerforth—a commercial villain who triumphs over fathers." Shakespeare's tragedy also includes, of course, Portia, a wife who claims to have qualities resembling the "character and purpose" that David misses in Dora (646).

[27] For all references to Shakespeare, I use *The Complete Works of Shakespeare,* ed. Hardin Craig and David Bevington (Glenview, Ill.: Scott, Foresman, 1973). Brutus' lines are employed in *Martin Chuzzlewit,* when the narrator refers, in chap. x, to "that tide which, taken at the flood, would lead Seth Pecksniff on to fortune."

[28] John Forster, in *The Life of Charles Dickens,* ed. J. W. T. Ley (London: Cecil Palmer, 1928), pp. 523–24, records that Dickens named his eighth child after Fielding "in a kind of homage to the style of work he was now so bent on beginning"—*David Copperfield.* Considering Fielding's influence on

David Copperfield, Earle Davis, in *The Flint and the Flame: The Artistry of Charles Dickens* (Columbia, Mo.: University of Missouri Press, 1963), p. 159, comments that Dickens gave Steerforth "the attractive physical charm and the negative morals of the youthful Tom Jones," but let David "keep Tom's heart of gold and be a more admirable hero." Gwendolyn B. Needham, in "The Undisciplined Heart of David Copperfield," *NCF* 9 (September 1954), 86, compares Tom's need to "learn prudence" with Dickens' "theme of the undisciplined heart." Dickens, of course, also offers a triangle similar to Fielding's: sincere David (who, like Tom, has an "undisciplined heart"), hypocritical Heep (like Blifil, a mean-spirited scoundrel who is the hero's sexual rival), and Agnes (a chaste, angelic paragon like Sophia, "wisdom"). Interestingly, Traddles, who—in contrast to Steerforth—proves a "good" friend, is another *Tom* in love with another virtuous *Sophy*.

29 References in *David Copperfield* to *Hamlet,* as well as to other Shakespearean plays, are examined by Harry Stone, "Dickens's Reading" (Ph.D. diss., UCLA, 1955), pp. 328–35, and by Robert F. Fleissner, *Dickens and Shakespeare* (New York: Haskell House, 1965), pp. 141–84.

30 See pp. 167–84 and 150.

31 Janet Brown, p. 207, observes that Copperfield evades "seeing the causative relation between Spenlow's death and his learning, only just the day before, of David's pursuit of his daughter." See also A. O. J. Cockshut, *The Imagination of Charles Dickens* (New York: New York University Press, 1962), p. 122; Welsh, p. 106; and Christopher Mulvey, "*David Copperfield:* The Folk-Story Structure," in *Dickens Studies Annual,* 5 (1976), 90.

32 John Lucas, in *The Melancholy Man: A Study of Dickens's Novels* (London: Methuen, 1970), p. 197, observes that the deaths of Steerforth and Dora "form part of the novel's total scheme, its study of lives that do not come to

what was planned." Charles Cannon, in "'As in a Theater': *Hamlet* in the Light of Calvin's Doctrine of Predestination," *SEL* 11 (Spring 1971), 211, maintains that "the idea of external control over existence at both the natural and the supernatural levels appears frequently in *Hamlet,"* and adds, "the mind as well as the body is subject to forces beyond its control." Indeed, Cannon, p. 221, sees *Hamlet* as a "vehicle for the theme of the providential ordering of life."

33 See, e.g., Kathleen Tillotson, *Novels of the Eighteen Forties* (Oxford: Clarendon Press, 1954), pp. 131–32, and Buckley, *The Triumph of Time: A Study of the Victorian Concepts of Time, History, Progress, and Decadence* (Cambridge, Mass.: Belknap Press of Harvard University Press, 1966), p. 98.

34 *Version of the Self: Studies in English Autobiography from John Bunyan to John Stuart Mill* (New York: Basic Books, 1966), p. 5.

35 *Yesterday's Woman: Domestic Realism in the English Novel* (Princeton: Princeton University Press, 1974), p. 167.

36 P. 52. Barbara Charlesworth Gelpi, in "The Innocent I: Dickens' Influence on Victorian Autobiography," in *The Worlds of Victorian Fiction,* ed. Jerome H. Buckley (Cambridge, Mass.: Harvard University Press, 1975), p. 59, observes that although autobiography affected the novel, there was also a reverse influence.

37 See J. Paul Hunter, *The Reluctant Pilgrim: Defoe's Emblematic Method and Quest for Form in Robinson Crusoe* (Baltimore: Johns Hopkins University Press, 1972), p. 93, and Welsh, pp. 73–75, 123–24, both of whom stress the persistent theme of providential design.

38 II, 690.

39 *Charles Dickens* (1924; reprint ed., Port Washington, N.Y.: Kennikat Press, 1966), p. 117. Needham, pp. 82–84, considers and responds to criticisms of this kind.

40 Pp. 18, 164, and 176.

41 *Season of Youth,* p. 40.

42 "Dickens and the Past: The Novel-

ist of Memory," in *Experience in the Novel,* Selected Papers from the English Institute, ed. Roy Harvey Pearce (New York: Columbia University Press, 1968), p. 114.
[43] "The Darkness of *David Copperfield*," p. 70.
[44] P. 183.
[45] In F. R. Leavis and Q. D. Leavis, *Dickens the Novelist* (New York: Pantheon Books, 1970), p. 90, Mrs. Leavis refers to "David's vision in Chapter LXII of the miracle his life had been."
[46] Among those who comment on Steerforth's fate are E. D. H. Johnson, p. 99; Harvey Peter Sucksmith, *The Narrative Art of Charles Dickens: The Rhetoric of Sympathy and Irony in his Novels* (Oxford: Clarendon Press, 1970), pp. 309-10; and Mario Praz, *The Hero in Eclipse in Victorian Fiction,* trans. Angus Davidson (New York: Oxford University Press, 1956), p. 162. For discussion of Dickens' overall use of providence, see Harland S. Nelson, "Dickens' Plots: 'The Ways of Providence' or the Influence of Collins?" *VN,* no. 19 (Spring 1961), 11-14, a view endorsed by Archibald C. Coolidge, Jr., "Dickens and Latitudinarian Christianity," *The Dickensian* 59 (January 1963), 60.
[47] *Robinson Crusoe,* ed. Michael Shinagel, Norton Critical Ed. (New York: W. W. Norton, 1975), p. 116.
[48] Forster, p. 35. Mrs. Leavis, p. 92, mentions this passage in her discussion of *David Copperfield.* Angus Wilson, in "Dickens on Children and Childhood," in *Dickens 1970,* ed, Michael Slater (New York: Stein and Day, 1970), p. 207, refers to Dickens' recognition of the fact that, while his parents' neglect endangered his genius, the blacking warehouse experience actually assisted his development as an artist.
[49] For example, Morris, p. 223, notes the "confidence . . . in the utility and ultimate beneficence of pain" expressed by English autobiographers from Bunyan to John Stuart Mill.

[50] See, e.g., Needham, p. 96, and E. Pearlman, "Two Notes on Religion in *David Copperfield,*" *VN,* no. 41 (Spring 1972), 18.
[51] See, respectively, "The Darkness of *David Copperfield,*" p. 70, and "Symbol and Subversion in *David Copperfield,*" *Studies in the Novel* 1 (Summer 1969), 203.
[52] "The Darkness of *David Copperfield,*" p. 51.
[53] Gilmour, p. 38, and Véga-Ritter, pp. 41-44.
[54] See John Butt and Kathleen Tillotson, *Dickens at Work* (1957; reprint ed., London: Methuen, 1963), p. 128.
[55] *Novels of the Eighteen Forties,* p. 145, n. 3.
[56] *The Heart of Charles Dickens, As Revealed in His Letters to Angela Burdett-Coutts, Selected and Edited from the Collection in the Pierpont Morgan Library,* ed. Edgar Johnson (Boston: Little, Brown, 1952), p. 144. Monroe Engel, in *The Maturity of Dickens* (Cambridge, Mass.: Harvard University Press, 1959), p. 29, quotes from this letter and comments, "For his own fiction, Dickens had similar hopes." Harry Stone, in "Dickens's Reading," pp. 222-23, discusses Dickens' great interest in *The Vicar of Wakefield,* and Steven Marcus, in *Dickens: from Pickwick to Dombey* (New York: Basic Books, 1965), pp. 24, 29-30, considers this work's influence on *Pickwick Papers.*
[57] See Forster, p. 523.
[58] See Edgar Johnson, II, 624-25.
[59] Françoise Basch, in *Relative Creatures: Victorian Women in Society and the Novel,* trans. Anthony Rudolf (New York: Schocken Books, 1974), p. 221, after referring to Em'ly, considers the background of the literary motif of seduction and mentions the example in *The Vicar of Wakefield.* But in another eighteenth-century novel of sentiment, Henry Mackenzie's *The Man of Feeling,* ed. Brian Vickers (London: Oxford University Press, 1967), pp. 48-73, appears an incident that has not, I believe, previously been cited as a possible source for features in the

Em'ly-Steerforth strand: Mackenzie's protagonist, Harley, encounters a seduced girl who has become a prostitute—this character, also named Emily, is sought by her grieving father, who, like Mr. Peggotty, visits a parent (in this case, the father) of the seducer. Dickens' general interest in Mackenzie is discussed by Stone, in "Dickens's Reading," pp. 206, n. 35, 345, 395, 529, and also by Monod, pp. 138, 166–67. In *Catalogue of the Library of Charles Dickens,* ed. J. H. Stonehouse (London: Piccadilly Fountain Press, 1935), p. 76, an eight-volume edition of Mackenzie's complete works is listed as among Dickens' possessions at the time of his death. (Needham, p. 85, suggests, "Dickens, had he written in the eighteenth century, might well have called David's story 'The History of a Man of Feeling.' ")

60 Pp. 180–82.

61 The crime for which Uriah has been sentenced, bank fraud, may have been suggested to Dickens by an article which he himself prepared with W. H. Wills for the 21 September 1850 issue of *Household Words,* "Two Chapters on Bank Note Forgeries: Chapter II"—see *Charles Dickens' Uncollected Writings from Household Words 1850–1859,* ed. Harry Stone, 2 vols. (Bloomington: Indiana University Press, 1968), I, 151–62 ("Chapter I" of this article, attributed by Stone, I, 151, to Wills alone, appeared in the *HW* issue for 7 September 1850). The reference to Uriah's crime is found in the final double number of *David Copperfield,* an installment which Dickens apparently began on 22 September and completed on 22 or 23 October 1850—see Butt and Tillotson, p. 173.

62 Pearlman, "Two Notes on Religion in *David Copperfield,*" p. 20.

63 Ham's remark is compared to Hamlet's "If it be now, 'tis not to come; if it be not to come, it will be now; if it be not now, yet it will come" by Joseph Gold, in *Charles Dickens: Radical Moral-*ist (Minneapolis: University of Minnesota Press, 1972), p. 183, and by Garrett Stewart, in *Dickens and the Trials of Imagination* (Cambridge, Mass.: Harvard University Press, 1974), p. 181. Fleissner, p. 162, and Stewart, p. 181, suggest links between the names "Ham" and "Hamlet."

64 Pp. 157–59.

65 See, e.g., Philip Collins, *Dickens and Crime* (1962; reprint ed., Bloomington: Indiana University Press, 1968), p. 82; Richard J. Dunn, "*David Copperfield:* All Dickens Is There," *English Journal* 54 (December 1965), 793; and Hornback, p. 70. Kincaid, in "The Darkness of *David Copperfield,*" p. 74, even suggests, "There are strong hints that the newspaper account of Micawber's success, since it was written by himself, is greatly exaggerated, if not absolutely falsified." But such a view apparently ignores Dan'l Peggotty's testimony concerning Micawber's effort and accomplishment (870).

66 *Charles Dickens' Uncollected Writings from Household Words,* I, 88. Stone, in an editorial note (I, 87), observes a connection between this article and the migration to Australia in *David Copperfield,* a link also suggested by Butt and Tillotson, in n. 1 on pp. 166–67.

67 *The Inimitable Dickens: A Reading of the Novels* (New York: St. Martin's, 1970), p. 131.

68 P. 197.

69 Véga-Ritter, pp. 37–38, considers characters in other Dickens novels who also find that death transfigures memories of the mother.

70 "The Iconography of *David Copperfield,*" *HSL* 2 (1970), 3, 11.

71 P. 177.

72 *The Uses of Enchantment: The Meaning and Importance of Fairy Tales* (New York: Alfred A. Knopf, 1976), pp. 10–11. Harry Stone, in "Fairy Tales and Ogres: Dickens' Imagination and 'David Copperfield,' " *Criticism* 6 (Fall 1964), 324–30, considers the novel's use of elements from fairy tales.

BERT G. HORNBACK: *The Hero Self*

[1] *The Autobiography of William Butler Yeats* (New York: Collier Books, 1965), p. 48.

[2] "Poetry is the spontaneous overflow of powerful feelings; it takes its origin from emotion recollected in tranquility." Wordsworth, *Preface to Lyrical Ballads,* 1800 edition.

[3] A very good teaching fellow who was working with me once asked a class which character they would remember most from *David Copperfield* in five or ten years. The answers came as Mr. Micawber, Miss Betsey, Mr. Dick, and other favorites. Then one student—a fine, bright young man named Dave Gass—said he would remember David. The class laughed. "What will you remember about him?" they asked. Dave thought for a minute and then said, "Well, the novel, I guess."

[4] *The Notebooks for Crime and Punishment* (Chicago: University of Chicago Press, 1967), pp. 9–10.

[5] *Biographic Literaria,* chap. 4 (Modern Library edition), p. 155.

[6] Ibid., chap. 13, p. 263.

[7] Ibid., chap. 12, p. 242.

[8] *The Prelude,* bk. 14, lines 413–14, 446–50.

[9] *Oliver Twist* (Penguin edition), p. 33.

[10] Cf. *Our Mutual Friend,* for Dickens' formulaic representation of this idea: "And oh, there are days in this life, worth life and worth death. And oh, what a bright old song it is, that oh, 'tis love, 'tis love, 'tis love, that makes the world go round!" (Penguin edition, p. 738).

[11] *A Christmas Carol,* in *The Christmas Books,* I (Penguin edition), p. 134.

[12] *A Christmas Carol,* p. 131. Dickens seems originally to have conceived the sentence about Scrooge to read something like "He became as good a master, as good a friend, as good a man, as any old city knew." As he writes it, however, the line expands, building itself upon repetitions of the word "good": "He became as good a master, friend, as good as a [friend] master, and as good a man, as [any] the good old city knew, or any [old] other good old city, town, or borough, in the good old world" (manuscript of *A Christmas Carol* [Pierpont Morgan Library, New York], fol. 65).

[13] *A Christmas Carol,* p. 161.

[14] Though not designated a retrospect in its title, Chapter xxxiii—a chapter full of Dora and David and Julia Mills and the Desert of Sahara—ends: "Of all the times of mine that Time has in his grip, there is none that in one retrospect I can smile at half so much, and think of half so kindly" (490).

RICHARD BARICKMAN: *The Spiritual Journey of Amy Dorrit and Arthur Clennam*

[1] T. S. Eliot, *The Complete Poems and Plays, 1909–1950* (New York, 1952), p. 127. F. R. Leavis in *Dickens the Novelist* (London: Chatto & Windus, 1970), p. 216, and A. E. Dyson in *The Inimitable Dickens* (London: Macmillan, 1970), p. 205, have noticed the relevance of the *Four Quartets* to *Little Dorrit.*

[2] James Kincaid, *Dickens and the Rhetoric of Laughter* (Oxford: Clarendon Press, 1971), p. 198.

[3] G. K. Chesterton, "Introduction" to the Everyman edition of *Little Dorrit* (London: 1908), vii.

[4] Joseph Gold, in his chapter on *Little Dorrit* in *Charles Dickens: Radical Moralist* (Minneapolis: University of Minnesota Press, 1972), gives a de-

tailed account of the novel's religious allusions. They have, of course, been noticed by a number of critics since Trilling's influential essay. Recently, Edward Heatley has discussed the spiritual elements of *Little Dorrit* in the context of Jungian theories in "The Redeemed Feminine of *Little Dorrit*," *Dickens Studies Annual*, 4 (1975), 153–64. He stresses the "psychotherapeutic confrontation of the masculine and feminine in both its sacred and profane modes" (p. 163). The most perceptive and stimulating general discussion of religious elements in Dickens is Alexander Welsh's *The City of Dickens* (London: Oxford, 1971).

5   Kincaid, p. 200. Similar conclusions about the novel's presentation of a powerless society are drawn by J[oseph] Hillis Miller, *Charles Dickens: The World of His Novels* (Cambridge, Mass.: Harvard University Press, 1965), pp. 227–47, and by Trilling in the essay Kincaid refers to: "Little Dorrit," *The Opposing Self: Nine Essays in Criticism* (New York: Viking, 1955).

6   John Lucas, *The Melancholy Man: A Study of Dickens's Novels* (London: Methuen, 1970), p. 247.

7   Gold, pp. 226–27. See also H[erman] M. Daleski, *Dickens and the Art of Analogy* (New York: Schocken Books,

1970), pp. 233–34, and Miller, p. 241.

8   Leavis, p. 236; Miller, pp. 246–47; and Kincaid, pp. 200–201.

9   See Daleski, p. 233, and Gold, p. 226, for example.

10   A[nthony] E. Dyson, *The Inimitable Dickens: A Reading of the Novels*, (London: Macmillan, 1970), p. 210. Janice M. Carlisle describes Amy's deceptions in similar terms in "Little Dorrit: Necessary Fictions," *Studies in the Novel* 7 (Summer 1975), 200–204. But she argues that Amy's "acts of deception do not undercut the moral status of the novel. They are not open to questioning on moral grounds: they are acceptable simply because they are necessary" (p. 204).

11   See, for instance, John Wain, "Little Dorrit," in *Dickens and the Twentieth Century*, ed. John Gross and Gabriel Pearson (London: Routledge and K. Paul, 1962), p. 176, and Welsh, p. 208.

12   Wain, p. 176. See also Welsh, pp. 208–9.

13   Miller, *The Form of Victorian Fiction: Thackeray, Dickens, Trollope, George Eliot, Meredith, and Hardy* (Notre Dame, Ind.: University of Notre Dame Press, 1968), p. 96; Welsh, pp. 170–79, 208–12.

14   Welsh, p. 141.

15   Kincaid, p. 198.

16   Welsh, p. 118.

E. PEARLMAN: *Inversion in* Great Expectations

1   John Forster, *The Life of Charles Dickens*, 2 vols. (London: Palmer, 1927), II, 285.

2   This was first noted, as far as I am aware, by Edmund Wilson, "Dickens: The Two Scrooges," in *The Wound and the Bow* (New York: Doubleday, 1947), p. 53.

3   Pip's native guilt has also been explained this way: "The infant . . . competes for love with uncanny determination, for he believes that his very existence depends on it. Competitors for love he wishes out of his way, his equivalent for death. The death or disappearance of parent or sibling in

early childhood fills the infant with fear and guilt. He believes that his wishes are magical, that they cause death, and that others know this" (L. J. Dessner," *Great Expectations:* The Ghost of a Man's own Father," *PMLA* 91 [1976], 438).

4   The connection between Pip's guilt and Orlick's acts is explored in J. Moynahan, "The Hero's Guilt: The Case of *Great Expectations*," *EIC* 10 (1960), 60–79. Moynahan demonstrates that Orlick can be seen as "a sort of double, *alter ego*, or shadow of Pip" (67). He also thinks that Bentley Drummle functions in much the same

way. In another paper ("David Copperfield Dreams of Drowning" [*AI* 24 (1971), 399–413], reprinted in *The Practice of Psychoanalytic Criticism,* ed. L. Tennenhouse [Detroit: Wayne State University Press. 1976], pp. 105–19) I tried to show that an important structural principle in *David Copperfield* is the tripartite relation between David and two characters who are his doubles: Steerforth and Heep. It would not be difficult to show that there are certain inverted correspondences between Drummle and Steerforth, Orlick and Heep (as well as between two other doubles, Trabb's boy and Ham Peggotty).

5   In "Crime and Fantasy in *Great Expectations,*" in *Psychoanalysis and Literary Process,* ed. F. Crews (Cambridge: Winthrop Publishers, 1970), pp. 25–65, A. D. Hutter asserts that Pip's attitude toward the father is split into two components, symbolized by Magwitch and Joe. Magwitch is "the castrating father"—the "pirate," the "snake," the "terrible beast" come to

cut the organs out of little Pip. The "measure of tenderness" and "admiration for the father are concentrated on Joe" (33–34). Hutter also suggests that Joe is "virtually feminized" in his relations with Pip (34). Dessner ("ghost"), though conceding that Joe Gargery is "the least masculine" of the men in the novel, is not concerned with his feminine qualities, preferring instead to see him as "more like Pip's child than Pip's father" (444).

6   In "Beating and Cringing: *Great Expectations,*" *EIC* 24 (1974), A. L. French traced Joe's acceptance of his marriage to his childhood condition. Joe "relive[s] his parents' marriage in his own; . . . the sexes are reversed but the relationship is the same" (150–51). French also noted the implicit colonial themes in the marriage of unequals. "Joe feels his subservience to his wife is not only inevitable, but right: as though a slave should defend his not rebelling on the ground that his master is wiser" (150).

MELANIE YOUNG: *Distorted Expectations*

1   Charles Dickens, *The Personal History of David Copperfield* (London: Chapman and Hall, 1850). I am particularly indebted to Dr. Robert Patten for his criticism and encouragement.

2   Charles Dickens, *Great Expectations* in *All the Year Round: A Weekly Journal,* IV and V (London: Chapman and Hall, 1861). All notations in the text are from this edition; I have included chapter numbers because the pagination is not continuous from IV (chaps. i–xxviii) to V (chaps. xxix–lix).

3   Jerome Hamilton Buckley, *Season of Youth: The Bildungsroman from Dickens to Golding* (Cambridge: Harvard University Press, 1974), p. 43.

4   George Levine, in "Communication in *Great Expectations,*" *Nineteenth Century Fiction* 18 (September 1963), 175–81, makes a similar point: "Pip's acquisition of literacy is the beginning of his break with everything

Joe stands for. The more Pip 'learns,' as a matter of fact, the less honest and dignified he becomes" (177).

5   A recently published article also discusses the significance of Pip's learning to read and write, in particular his problem of learning how to read texts correctly. See Max Byrd, "'Reading' in *Great Expectations,*" *PMLA* 91 (March 1976), 259–65.

6   Sylvia B. Manning, in *Dickens as Satirist* (New Haven: Yale University Press, 1971), p. 195, says of Pip: "To see things rightly, he must learn the meaning of Wemmick's schizophrenic existence . . . the truth of the values it strives to preserve but also the perils of such disjunction and the necessity of an integrated life."

7   K. J. Fielding notes that *Great Expectations* "is also a searching study of a society in which what Marx called 'the sordid cash nexus is the chief bond be-

tween man and man'" in his book *Charles Dickens: A Critical Introduction* (Boston: Houghton Mifflin, 1965), p. 214. William F. Axton, p. 279, notes the importance of the patron-protégé relationship to the theme of instrumentality and exploitation in *"Great Expectations* Yet Again," *Dickens Studies Annual*, 2 (1972), 278–93.

[8] What I call the "language of feeling" Levine, pp. 179–80, calls "the language of love." He relates this language to Joe and observes that "full communication in *Great Expectations* comes usually through gestures, inarticulate noises, or ungrammatical and irrational speech." See also Ruth M. Vande Kieft, "Patterns of Communication in *Great Expectations," Nineteenth Century Fiction* 15 (March 1961), 325–34, who points out that communication in *Great Expectations* may be irrational or inarticulate, employing "symbolic actions which convey meaning through gesture, ceremony, or ritual" (334).

[9] Jack B. Moore and Charles R. Forker both discuss the importance of hand gestures in *Great Expectations* as a unifying symbol, an index to character, and an eloquent mode of communication. See "Hearts and Hands in *Great Expectations," The Dickensian* 61 (Winter 1965), 52–56 and "The Language of Hands in *Great Expectations," Texas Studies in Literature and Language* 3 (1961), 280–93, respectively.

[10] What I call the "language of thought," in order to clarify the dissociation of thought and feeling, is similar to what Randolph Quirk calls "the language of calculation and materialism" in reference to *Hard Times*. See *Charles Dickens and Appropriate Language* (Durham, England: Folcroft Press, 1959), p. 20.

[11] Harry Stone, in "Fire, Hand, and Gate: Dickens' *Great Expectations," Kenyon Review*, 24 (Autumn 1962), 662–91, makes much of Magwitch's "upending" of Pip, connecting it with Pip's errors of vision and his yielding to "society's upsidedown morality" (678–79).

[12] One might also note, as William H. New does in "The Four Elements in *Great Expectations," Dickens Studies,* 3 (October 1967), 111–21, that a "pip" is a seed (118).

[13] Miss Havisham's words to Pip underline the possibility of such paralysis by drawing an ominous parallel: "I saw in you a looking-glass that showed me what I once felt myself" (xlix, 290).

[14] G. W. Kennedy, in "Naming and Language in *Our Mutual Friend," Nineteenth Century Fiction*, 28 (September 1973), 165–78, associates the vocabulary of fairy tale with escape into Edenic time and protection (173). But Miss Havisham's world of frozen time is hardly Edenic, however protective. Yet Pip's fairy-tale vocabulary and image of Estella do associate her with an anticipated Edenic time.

[15] Shirley Grob, in "Dickens and Some Motifs of the Fairy Tale," *Texas Studies in Literature and Language* 5 (Winter 1964), 569–79, observes that the fairy tale references in *Great Expectations* "are carefully selected to provide highly ironic commentary on the theme of 'expectations'" (572–73).

[16] Michael Kotzin, in *Dickens and the Fairy Tale* (Bowling Green, Ohio: Bowling Green University Press, 1972), p. 31, notes that the fairy tale provided a "symbolically realistic image of the urges of the psyche."

[17] One might also note, in connection with the negative value of "fine language," that Compeyson writes "fifty hands," according to Orlick (liii, 339).

[18] Jaggers' desire to avoid moral judgments is reinforced by his Pontius Pilate-like habit of washing his hands. For an illuminating discussion of his complex role as a figure who "embodies both law and the human cost of law" (111), see Anthony Winner, "Character and Knowledge in Dickens: The Enigma of Jaggers," *Dickens Studies Annual*, 3 (1974), 100–121.

[19] Axton, pp. 281–82, points out Pip's equation of social "lowness" with moral evil.

20 Kennedy, pp. 169–71, makes a similar point about language in *Our Mutual Friend:* he observes that when responsibility for the meaning of words breaks down, language becomes exploitative and characters identify themselves with closed verbal systems at their peril.

21 Kennedy's observation, pp. 174–75, could also be applied to Pip:

"But, before his salvation can be complete, Eugene must be initiated into a new linguistic realm where words are tied to concrete facts and emotions by the magical power of human commitment." Through Jenny's words, as through Biddy's, "language itself is magically restored as an effective means of initiating action."

RICHARD J. DUNN: *Far, Far Better Things*

1 *The George Eliot Letters,* ed. Gordon S. Haight (New Haven: Yale University Press, 1954), I, 316.

2 *The Letters of Charles Dickens,* ed. Walter Dexter (London: Nonesuch, 1938), II, 240.

3 *The Letters of Charles Dickens,* ed. Madeline House and Graham Storey (Oxford: Clarendon Press, 1965), I, 630.

4 Ibid., 323.

5 Philip Collins notes that the phrasing descriptive of Agnes' "pointing upward" had earlier appeared in a letter Dickens had written in 1842 remembering how "the heavy sorrow has pointed upward with unchanging finger for more than 4 years." Collins also mentions that T. N. Talfourd and John Forster may have been prototypes for Traddles. *"David Copperfield:* 'A Very Complicated Interweaving of Truth and Fiction,' " *Essays and Studies by Members of the English Association,* n.s. 23 (1970), 71–86.

6 See especially Alex Zwerdling, "Esther Summerson Rehabilitated," *PMLA* 88 (1973), 429–39; Lawrence Frank, " 'Through a Glass Darkly': Esther Summerson and *Bleak House";* Gordon D. Hirsch, "The Mysteries in *Bleak House," Dickens Studies Annual,* 4 (1975), 91–112, 132–52.

7 Frank, p. 112.

8 *The Moral Art of Dickens: Essays* (New York: Oxford University Press, 1970), p. 13.

9 Ibid., pp. 15–16.

10 *Dickens at Work* (London: Methuen, 1957), p. 33.

11 Martin Meisel, "The Ending of *Great Expectations," Essays in Criticism* 15 (1965), 326–31.

12 Ibid., 329.

13 "Dickens and the Tragi-Comic Grotesque," *Studies in the Novel,* 1 (1969), 147–56.

INDEX

All the Year Round, 7, 8, 12, 13, 31, 62, 71
American Notes, 2, 9–12 passim, 11, 12, 19, 23, 31
American publishing trade: piracies within the, 11, 14
Austen, Jane: significance of, 49
"Authorization": quarrel over, 18–19
Axton, William, 68

*Baker, Russell: on praise for *Seven Beauties*, 70
Bancroft, George: *History of the United States*, 22
Barnaby Rudge: religious intolerance in, 50; analogous relationships in, 81; and the sanctity of the home, 82; a divided novel, 83–85; civil sphere in, 86–95; moral world of, 87; country justice of, 89; parallel domestic argument in, 96–102; ends with rewards and punishments, 104; mentioned, 11
Barth, John, 129
Bennett, James Gordon: stirs up controversy around Dickens, 23; compares Dickens to Mrs. Yelverton, 24; and Dickens' New York welcome, 25; sympathetic to Dolby and Dickens, 27; mentioned, 9, 19, 26
Bentley, Richard: Dickens' relations with, 43
Bentley's Miscellany, 11
Bettelheim, Bruno, 150
Biographical Essays, 39
Bleak House: complete seriousness by Dickens in, 54–62; mysteries in, 166; symbolic coincidences in, 167; social forms in, 170; ending in, 226–27; central characters of, 230; mentioned, 12, 17, 63, 79, 121, 141, 144, 163, 186, 187, 228

Bracher, Peter S., 12
Brannan, Robert, 68
Brice, Alec W.: on "Romantic theory of biography," 41
Brontë, Emily: significance of, 49; mentioned, 141
Brown, Norman O., 183
Browne, Hablot K., 131, 149
Buckley, Jerome Hamilton, 137, 142
Bulwer-Lytton, Edward G. E.: friend of Forster, 34; on Forster's selection of material, 36; Forster corresponds with, 40; Forster valued associate of, 46; mentioned, 29, 38, 232

*Capital punishment: issue in *Barnaby Rudge*, 89
Carey, Henry C.: censure by, 22; mentioned, 12, 21
Carlyle, Thomas: equates Forster's biography to Boswell, 3; mentioned, 84, 224, 231
Cavalcanti, Alberto, 69
Chapman, Frederick: consolidated all volumes published by Bradbury and Evans, 14; on sales of Dickens' books, 28
Chase Copyright Act of 1891, 4
Chesterton, G. K., 78
Childs, George W.: and "The Dickens Controversy," 17–18; mentioned, 16
Chorley, H. F., 78
Christian symbolism: in *Little Dorrit*, 163
Christmas Carol, A: moral fable in, 53; metaphysical state of happiness in, 157–58
Churchill, C., 34, 35, 37, 38
Clarity: search for, 77
Coleridge, S. T., 154, 157